"Candid detailed descriptions of the provinces and their major cities, as well as restaurant and hotel recommendations in every price range."

—Travel & Leisure

"Offers detailed descriptions of each city and province and—perhaps most important—French phrases to know."

—Bloomsbury Review

"Will help you travel, eat, and enjoy your way through eastern Canada."

—Philadelphia Daily News

"An in-depth description of the part of Canada nearest us . . . Extremely practical."

—Erie Times, Pennsylvania

"Gives descriptive details of m   . . .   . and more than 500 restaurants and p

"If you haven't already complete   . . .   of Canada, hurry and pick up a copy. . . . For one who has seen eastern Canada, I recommend it very highly. Aside from the fact it's a year-round, practical guide . . . it features up-to-date information on everything . . . information you can use no matter where you travel."

—Northeast Detroiter, Harper Woods Herald,
St. Clair Shores Herald

Help Us Keep This Guide Up to Date

Every effort has been made by the author and editors to make this guide as accurate and useful as possible. However, many things can change after a guide is published–establishments close, phone numbers change, hiking trails are rerouted, facilities come under new management, etc.

We would love to hear from you concerning your experiences with this guide and how you feel it could be made better and be kept up to date. While we may not be able to respond to all comments and suggestions, we'll take them to heart and we'll also make certain to share them with the author. Please send your comments and suggestions to the following address:

The Globe Pequot Press
Reader Response/Editorial Department
P.O. Box 480
Guilford, CT 06437

Or you may e-mail us at:

editorial@globe-pequot.com

Thanks for your input, and happy travels!

Guide to
Eastern Canada

Seventh Edition

edited by
Barbara Radcliffe Rogers
and
Stillman Rogers

The
Globe
Pequot
Press

Guilford, Connecticut

Cover photo by G. Aherns / H. Armstrong Roberts

Interior photos courtesy of the Information Office of Québec; the Québec Ministry of Leisure/Pierre Pouliot; Industry, Science, and Technology Canada/Fred Cattroll; HRM/P. Franklin; and other Canadian national and provincial tourism offices.

Library of Congress Cataloging-in-Publication Data

Guide to eastern Canada / edited by Barbara Radcliffe Rogers and Stillman Rogers — 7th ed.
    p. cm.
    Rev. ed. of Guide to eastern Canada / by Frederick Pratson. 6th ed. c1998.
    Includes index.
    ISBN 0-7627-0648-1
    1. Canada, Eastern—Guidebooks.   I. Rogers, Barbara Radcliffe. II. Rogers, Stillman, 1939– III. Pratson. Frederick John. Guide to eastern Canada

F1009 .P7 2001
917.1304'4—dc21
                        2001023234

Manufactured in the United States of America
Seventh Edition/First Printing

Although the authors have received and used information and photographs from many different sources, *this guide is not an official publication of any company, association, or government agency mentioned or described herein.* This guide has been independently researched and written by the authors and independently produced and marketed by the publisher. Within this guide, reference is made to a number of attractions, rides, systems, components, entities, products, fictional and animal characters, processes, and the like that are protected by copyrights and trademarks, both registered and pending, used by particular companies, attractions, and entertainments that own them. No attempt has been made by the author and the publisher of this guide to infringe these and other copyrights and trademarks. Every effort has been made to present this trademarked and copyrighted material in those contexts to which they legally and properly belong and to no other.

Contents

Part One—General Information

Part Two—Ontario and Québec

Part Three—Atlantic Canada

Tranquil, beautiful land- and seascapes offer bountiful inspirations to photographers and artists visiting Eastern Canada.

Part One

General Information

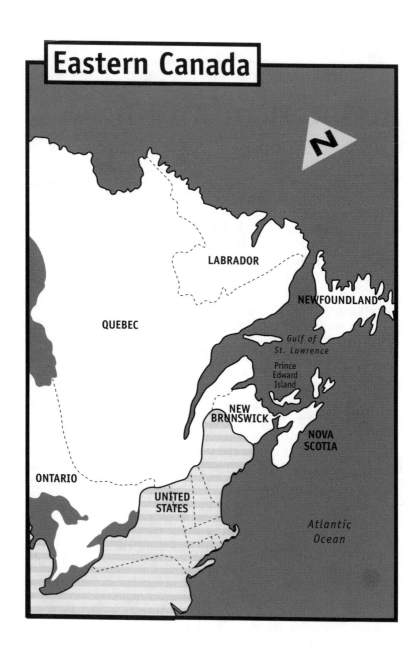

Eastern Canada

LABRADOR

NEWFOUNDLAND

QUEBEC

Gulf of
St. Lawrence

Prince
Edward
Island

NEW
BRUNSWICK

NOVA
SCOTIA

ONTARIO

UNITED
STATES

Atlantic
Ocean

CHAPTER 1

Visiting Canada

For Americans, Eastern Canada combines all the best parts of a foreign vacation without the worst. It is clearly a foreign country, with a different currency, different languages and accents, and a different view of the world and of us. Menus offer dishes we haven't seen before; local ingredients and products differ too. People welcome us as foreign guests, but treat us like family.

What's lacking are the day-to-day annoyances and inconveniences of being in an alien and bewildering culture—and the time it takes to get there. It's close: no long trans-Atlantic or even longer trans-Pacific flights. For many Americans, it's within driving distance, for others just a short flight. The details of travel are straightforward and familiar. Even in the one province where English is not the official language, most people understand it and welcome your attempts at French. Rules of the road are much like our own, as is sign terminology.

Best of all, Canadians are among the most civil and polite people on earth. Common courtesies are common indeed. Hospitality is a way of life, not an overlay in hopes of a tip or of profit. They recognize and appreciate differences and find them interesting; as a result they find us interesting. They are very well informed on our politics, culture, and history, if sometimes puzzled to find that we know very little of theirs.

Canadians, like their American neighbors, are a widely diverse people, and most of those various groups are represented in the eastern half of the country. Although they may not always agree, and may not even want to live in the same country, they usually behave civilly and respect each other's cultural and religious differences. Canadian society values the differences, so you will find colorful local festivals and traditions wherever you go, represent-

> Canada has a population of almost 30 million, rapidly growing primarily through immigration. Close to two thirds of this total reside in Ontario and Québec, and about 75 percent of all Canadians live within a hundred miles of the U.S. border (most of the important urban centers of Canada are near the border).

ing cultures as diverse as Scottish, Algonquin, Danish, Thai, and Japanese.

A 1989 United Nations survey named Toronto the world's most ethnically cosmopolitan city. The people of the First Nations were prophetic when they chose a name for it that meant "meeting place." Asians comprise the largest percentage of Toronto's immigrant peoples, with Chinese the most common. Chinatown, where Chinese, Vietnamese, and others of Asian origin have gathered, is considered the largest in North America. Travelers can immerse themselves in its sounds, sights, and flavors any day, but especially on Sunday, when Dundas Street is alive with market stalls selling everything from lotus flowers and lemongrass to live chickens. A fortune cookie factory there makes more than 10,000 cookies each day.

In Antigonish, Nova Scotia, you can be just as immersed in Scottish culture, with days of bagpipe music, caber tosses, and Highland flings. New Brunswick's Miramichi has the world's largest festival of Irish culture, and in several parts of the same province you can stay in traditional lodgings of the descendants of the men and women who greeted the first French settlers five centuries ago. And, of course, Québec is a piece of transplanted French culture, with a Canadian accent.

We haven't yet touched on the many land- and seascapes of eastern Canada, which range from tundra and bird-filled coastal marshes to the soaring fjords of Newfoundland; from places that are more temperate than New England to places that are frozen in ice and snow all year long. Nor have we described its historic sites, which include many New World "firsts" and a number of sites intimately connected with U.S. history. Nor on its recreational opportunities, which are almost endless.

The warmest ocean beaches north of Virginia for swimming, wilderness lakes and rivers for canoeing, hundreds of miles of trails for hiking, beautiful cycling trails that extend the length of Prince Edward Island and across New Brunswick into Québec, world-class ski resorts in the Laurentians, some of the east's most exciting coastal kayak waters, outstanding golf courses, and a day adventure program that puts New Brunswick on the map as the most "try it" place on the continent—we could go on and on without exhausting eastern Canada's possibilities for active travelers.

For its color, its infinite variety of people and landscapes, its adventure and outdoor opportunities, its wild places and wildlife, its rich history, and the warm welcome its people give travelers, eastern Canada is hard to beat. We add our welcome to those you will hear from the moment you cross the border or land at the airport, and hope this book will help you enjoy it to its fullest.

What This Guide Will Tell You

No one book can possibly be a thorough guide to even half of Canada, which is the second largest country in the world. But as a traveler, you don't want to find everything in a book. You want to explore and discover your own Canada.

What a book can do—and must do—is provide you with the background, the know-how, and the general guidance to plan a trip and decide where you want to go. Once there, the book can steer you to sightseeing, dining, and lodgings to get you started and to make sure you don't miss the highlights. Beyond that it can offer you insights and guidance that enable you to explore on your own and to know the greatest of all a traveler's thrills: discovering something perfectly splendid that no guidebook mentions.

Please do not rely on this book as your only source. Each province publishes excellent guides of its own, and although the places listed in these are often those who have chosen to pay for their space, the information is still golden, and updated each year. Use these, and more importantly, use the provincial road maps that each will send you. Even if you are not traveling by car, a good and current map is essential to getting the most out of your trip. And however reliable maps from the Internet and automobile clubs may be, they do not replace the official highway maps of a province, which are usually keyed to tourism information and show places like information offices and the exact location of attractions.

Package Tours

Although Canada is very easy for independent travelers, package tours do offer some advantages for many people. If you are traveling alone, they provide you with a more sociable atmosphere. If you prefer not to drive, they are more convenient than relying entirely on public transportation. They offer you the advantage of group buying power, and are often less expensive than the sum of their parts would be.

Along with the guided tours that companies such as Collette Tours offer, there are specialty tours that take you cycling through Nova Scotia or birding in New Brunswick or kayaking in Newfoundland. Ski packages are especially attractive; they can include transportation from the nearest airport to a resort with lodging and dining right at the slopes, so you don't need to have a car at all. Similar summer vacations reach islands such as Grand Manan or the Magdalenes, where cars are superfluous. Cruise packages can take you along the Saint Lawrence River or along the coasts of the Atlantic provinces.

Collette Tours, (888) 344–5578 or www.collettetours.com, offers both escorted and Discovery Tours, which are independent packages that let travelers take advantage of low group rates and the convenience of pre-arranged lodging and even meals, without traveling with a group. Tours cover single provinces or combinations.

Fountain Tours, (987) 921–5510, (800) 946–8301 or www.fountaintours.com, specializes in eastern Canada, offering deluxe tours with historic, cultural, garden, architecture and seasonal themes. Travelers can choose pre-planned packages or a-la-carte custom trips.

Free Information for U.S. Visitors

Provincial tourism organizations are your best resources for free information and advice on almost every aspect of travel to their communities and countryside. They will provide you with free brochures and maps and will answer your questions. The best way to reach these tourism organizations is by making a telephone call, in most cases toll-free, from your home.

The following provincial tourism organizations await your call:

Ontario Travel
Queen's Park
Toronto, Ontario M7A 2E5
(800) ONTARIO
From Canada, continental
U.S.A., and Hawaii (800)
668-2746
From Toronto calling area:
English (416) 314-0944
French (416) 314-0956
Telecommunication Device
for the Deaf (416)
314-6557
Summer Campground Vacancies and Winter Cross-Country Skiing (416)
314-2000
www.ontariotravel.net

Tourisme Québec
CP 979
Montréal, Québec H3C 2WB
From United States and
Canada (800) 363-7777
From Montréal calling area
(514) 873-2015
www.Bonjourquebec.com

Department of Economic
Development and Tourism
P.O. Box 12345
Woodstock, New Brunswick
E0J 2B0
From United States and

Canada, including New
Brunswick (800) 561-0123

Nova Scotia Tourism
Information
Box 130
Halifax, Nova Scotia B3J 2M7
From United States and
Canada (800) 565-0000
From Halifax (902)
453-5781
explore.gov.ns.ca/virtual.ns

Tourism P.E.I.
P.O. Box 940
Charlottetown, Prince Edward
Island C1A 7M5
From United States and
Canada (800) 463-4734

Department of Tourism
Box 8730
St. John's, Newfoundland
A1B K2
From St. John's (709)
576-8106, from U.S. and
Canada (800) 729-2830

Some Facts about Canada

Before going to Canada, it might be helpful to know a little about how it is governed and how it came to be a country. These two aspects of Canada—its history and government—are intertwined, and explain some of its current policies, attitudes, and even problems.

It is important to remember two things about Canada's government; first that it is a confederation of provinces, not a union of states, and second that it has a parliamentary form of government. These are perhaps the great distinctions between the two countries of Canada and the United States.

Unlike the United States, Canada's modern government did not begin with a revolution. Instead, Canadian people pressured the English king and parliament to allow them to control more of their own affairs, and England gradually gave up its power, a process that has continued right up into recent times.

In April 1982 Canadians witnessed a historic event when Elizabeth II, Queen of Canada, before a crowded assembly of the House of Commons and Senate of the Parliament of Canada in Ottawa, presided over the proclamation of the Constitution Act of 1982. This new act made important changes in Canada's Constitution and is a milestone in the nation's political history. With the proclamation of the Constitution Act, Canada patriated its Constitution and shed the last antiquated vestige of its colonial past. Patriation means the end of the role of the United Kingdom Parliament in the amendment process of the Canadian Constitution. Canada is finally fully independent in the legal sense.

Today, although the queen still appoints the governor-general, the prime minister tells her who to appoint, and the job is only ceremonial. The prime minister, Canada's chief executive officer, is chosen by the majority of the members of parliament instead of in a separate election. This makes the executive completely in the control of the legislative branch, unlike the U.S. system of dividing power equally among three different branches. All cabinet members must also be elected members of the House of Commons (or sometimes the Senate) and each one is head of a government department. This is also different from the U.S. system, where cabinet members are completely independent from Congress.

A Brief History

To understand the history of Canada, you must begin with a sense of its geography. Containing more than two fifths of all of the land in North America, Canada is the second largest country in the world. At its center, covering nearly all of Ontario and Québec, is an

A Quick Look at Canada's Eastern Provinces

New Brunswick
Population: 762,000
Capital: Fredericton
Largest City: Saint John
Fact: New Brunswick has two official languages, French and English, both of which are taught in public schools.

Newfoundland and Labrador
Population: 563,600
Capital: St. John's
Largest City: St. John's
Fact: With its own time zone, Newfoundland is a half hour ahead of the rest of the Atlantic provinces.

Nova Scotia
Population: 947,900
Capital: Halifax
Largest City: Halifax
Fact: Halifax has one of the world's finest natural harbors.

Ontario
Population: 11,407,700
Capital: Toronto
Largest City: Toronto
Fact: Toronto has the most ethnically diverse population of any city in Canada.

Prince Edward Island
Population: 137,200
Capital: Charlottetown
Largest City: Charlottetown
Fact: Prince Edward Island is the smallest province in both land area and population.

Québec
Population: 7,419,900
Capital: Québec
Largest City: Montréal
Fact: Québec's only official language is French; it is the only province where English is not one of the official languages.

exposed part of the earth's crust, called the Canadian Shield, made up of some of the oldest rock on the face of the earth.

The earliest human inhabitants were peoples who came across a narrow piece of land that once connected Alaska to Asia at the end of the Pleistocene Epoch, about 10,000 years ago although some new evidence suggests a date as early as 22,000 B.C. Small groups of these peoples fanned out over the continent, following herds of wild game. In the frozen north the pre-Dorset peoples lived by hunting seals and small game. They occupied the eastern parts of Canada from about 4,000 to 2,100 years before the present. You can see relics of their presence in northern Newfoundland and Labrador.

After about 2,000 years ago, a new group, called the Dorset after Cape Dorset on Baffin Island had established itself in the eastern Arctic and in Newfoundland. Hunters and fishermen, the Dorset people used bone and stone tools and implements and made ornaments of walrus ivory. Their winter houses were of sod, built partly underground; in summer they lived in tents made of hides. By about A.D. 1200 they disappeared. In Newfoundland they were followed by the Beothuk, a hunting and fishing people who continued to live on the island until after the arrival of Europeans. The last Beothuk died in 1829. You can see some of their artifacts in Newfoundland.

While the Dorset and the Beothuk settled the northern part of the country, along the Atlantic coast other peoples moved into the more temperate areas, establishing the Algonquin tribe and its subgroups, such as the Huron who lived in the area around Montréal. South of the Saint Lawrence River in what is now Quebec, New England, and northern New York, the Iroquois established their own culture.

Norse sagas written in the thirteenth and fourteenth centuries and based on older oral traditions told of the adventures of Vikings Eric the Red and his son, Leif Eriksson. These intrepid Norsemen sailed west from Greenland between A.D. 965 and 1000 and, according to the sagas, came upon new lands that they called Markland and Vineland. Although the exact locations of these places are unknown, scientists at L'Anse aux Meadows at the northwest tip of Newfoundland have found the remains of a short-lived Viking settlement from that era.

Fishermen from several European nations had very early discovered cod on the shallow continental shelf off the eastern shore. Their summer settlements on Newfoundland, where they dried and prepared their catch, were the first European communities, and fishing remained a primary reason for settlements on the east coast of Canada.

The next wave came when Europeans raced one another to find new routes to the spices and riches of Asia. John Cabot, an Italian navigator hired by England's King Henry VII, sailed west, exploring Newfoundland in the *Matthew* in 1497. Cabot claimed it for England, making Newfoundland the first colony in the British Empire.

French explorer Jacques Cartier, looking for a route to Asia, sailed into the Saint Lawrence River in 1535. He found an encampment of First Nations People, named Stadacona, at a place they called Québec. Establishing a fort there, he sailed 165 miles farther upstream to another First Nations village, Hochelaga. The rapids there stopped him, but he named the hill behind the village Mont Réal. Samuel de Champlain came to Mont Réal in 1603.

Champlain explored the area south of the Saint Lawrence, well into Vermont, returning in 1608 to found Québec. Lightly populated by traders, it struggled before becoming a center for fur trading. To control the fur trade, in 1627 France created a private company called the Company of One Hundred Associates, which ruled the lives of settlers and traders. In 1642 Paul de Chomedey, Sieur de Maisonneuve, led a settlement at Mont Réal, naming it Ville Marie de Montréal. It soon became a center of fur trade and commerce.

Samuel de Champlain was aware that the Algonquin, Huron, and Iroquois were often at war with one another. He made a treaty with the Algonquin and Huron, joining them in war against the Iroquois from the 1640s until 1701. The British were also interested in the fur trade; they sent trappers and fur traders into Hudson Bay and established trading posts on rivers that emptied into the bay. In 1670 the British created the Hudson's Bay Company to operate the fur trade, giving the company a tract of land that forms the bulk of Canada.

Champlain's first colony for France was at Port Royal in Acadia, now Annapolis Royal, Nova Scotia. French there and in other parts of Nova Scotia and Prince Edward Island struggled to farm and fish. European wars in the early 1700s spread to North America, and Port Royal was captured by the English in 1710. The European peace treaty also gave the British Hudson Bay, Newfoundland, and Acadia, but the French retained Cape Breton and its massive fortress at Louisbourg.

France again made war on New England—the French and Indian Wars—sending raiding parties through Lake Champlain and down the Connecticut River. Britain and New England reacted by mounting an invasion that captured the French Fortress Louisbourg in 1758, Québec in 1759, and Montréal in 1760, ending French rule in North America.

Under the British, French settlers were allowed to keep their government and legal forms and to practice the Roman Catholic religion (even though that religion could not be practiced in England at the time).

During the revolution, Americans under General Richard Montgomery captured Montréal in 1775, and Britain used Canada as a base for attacking the American colonies. War with the United States threatened again in 1812 and at other times up to the 1840s before tapering off with the final establishment of the international borders.

Discontent with British rule led to several small rebellions in Canada in the late 1830s, and although they were easily put down, discontent led to the passage of the Act of Union by the British parliament in 1840. This act joined several colonies in formerly separate Québec and western Canada. Québec was renamed Lower Canada and the lands to its west became Upper Canada. The capital of the new Province of Canada was in Kingston, now in Ontario. Disputes with the United States over Oregon and other borders led to the removal of the capital to Ottawa.

Following discussions between leaders of the provinces of Upper and Lower Canada and the colonies of Prince Edward Island, New Brunswick, and Nova Scotia in 1864, the British North America Act was passed by Parliament in 1867. It joined Ontario, Québec (now given its old name back), Nova Scotia, and New Brunswick into a confederation called the Dominion of Canada. Prince Edward Island and the western colonies joined the confederation in the 1870s. Newfoundland did not join Canada until after World War II.

A railroad joining the country from sea to sea was finished in 1885, and it became the means for distributing later waves of immigrants. In the late 1800s the Canadian government recruited immigrants, many from eastern Europe. These new prairie settlers produced huge quantities of wheat and grains, which were shipped by boat and train to the grain elevators of Montréal. The new railroad had opened up the western lands and drew the country together as a nation, in the process making Montréal a major commercial and transportation center.

During World War I more than 600,000 Canadians fought for the Allies; 10 percent died and 20 percent were wounded. These sacrifices led to the Statute of Westminster in 1931, which created equality between Britain and the other Dominions nations. More than a million served during World War II, when Canada played a critical role in providing the ships, equipment, and food needed to win the war. In 1982 the Constitution Act, passed by Britain's Parliament, ended England's control of Canadian government.

Since World War II, a dominant theme of life in Canada has been the repeated quest of Francophone separatists to make Québec an independent French-speaking nation. Feeling that their French culture was threatened by the predominantly English-speaking majority of the rest of the country, an extremist group, Le Front de Liberation du Québec, began a series of violent kidnappings and murders in 1963. While these violent acts were stopped, a separatist political party, Le Parti Québécois, was formed in 1968 to promote political independence. A series of referenda seeking independence through the 1990s failed to pass, but a vote in 1995 came very close to carrying. The threat of the disruption of Canadian commerce that separation would bring has been costly to Québec, as major businesses have moved their headquarters to other provinces. The Atlantic Provinces, which would be cut off from the rest of Canada by Québec secession, watch uneasily too.

Canada is still very much a country in political transition. The encouraging note in this great national debate is that Canadians as a whole are among the most reasonable people on earth, they are not likely to let their political destiny be forged in violence, as is the case in so many nations; it will evolve out of the innate good sense of the Canadian people themselves.

Entering Canada

Citizens or permanent residents of the United States do not require passports or visas and may usually cross the U.S.–Canadian border without difficulty or dealy. Proof of such citizenship or residency is required, however; a birth certificate or similar document will do. Natualized U.S. citizens should carry a naturalization certificate or other evidence of citizenship. Permanent residents who are not citizens must carry their alien registration receipt card. Persons under age eighteen who travel to Canada without an adult must have a letter of permission from a parent or guardian. U.S, citizens may also enter Canada from any other country without a passport or visa.

All other persons, except U.S. citizens or legal residents, citizens of France residing in Saint-Pierre and Miquelon, and resdents of Greenland, require a valid passport, visa or other acceptable travel document to gain entry into Canada. If you are entering Canada from the United States, make sure that your travel documents are acceptable to the U.S. Immigration Service before you leave, so that you won't have trouble getting back into the country.

If you want to work or study in Canada, you must obtain a student or employment authorization before coming to Canada. Employment authorizations are not issued if there are qualified Canadians or permanent residents available for the kind of work that you are seeking. Persons wishing to work or study in Canada should contact the nearest Canadian Consulate for general information.

By Car

The entry of vehicles and trailers into Canada for touring purposes, for periods of up to twelve months, is generally a quick, routine matter that does not require the payment of duty. Motor vehicle registration forms must be carried, as well as a copy of the contract if you are driving a rented vehicle. If you are driving a vehicle registered to someone else, you must carry that person's authorization to use the vehicle.

All national driver's licenses are valid in Canada, including the International Driver's Permit.

By Private Aircraft

Visiting pilots should plan to land at an airport that can provide customs clearance. You must report to Canada Customs immediately and complete all documentation. In emergencies, you may land at other fields, but you must then immediately report your arrival to the nearest regional customs office or the Royal Canadian Mounted Police. For more details on flying your own plane to Canada, contact your nearest Canadian consulate general.

By Private Boat

If you're planning to come to Canada on your own boat, contact your nearest Canadian customs office for a list of ports of entry that provide customs facilities and their hours of operation. You should immediately report to customs and complete all documentation when you arrive. If you have an emergency and have to pull into a nonofficial port, immediately report your arrival to the nearest regional customs office or the Royal Canadian Mounted Police.

Metropolitan Montréal

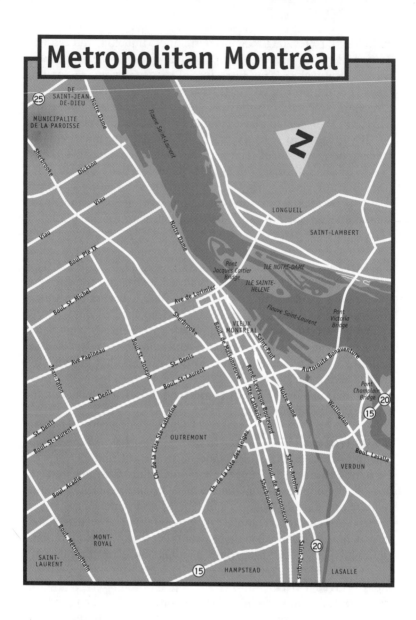

Personal Exemptions

Everything that you bring into Canada in excess of allowances must be declared and may be inspected by customs on your arrival in the country.

Tobacco. Persons sixteen years of age and older may bring in duty-free 50 cigars, 200 cigarettes, and 2 pounds of manufactured tobacco.

Alcoholic beverages. You may bring into Canada duty-free 40 ounces of liquor or wine or 288 fluid ounces of beer or ale.

Gifts. You may bring in duty-free bona fide gifts for friends and relatives provided that the value of each gift does not exceed $60 (Canadian dollars) and that the item is not tobacco, liquor, or advertising material.

Regular duty fees and taxes must be paid on tobacco, alcoholic beverages, and gifts that exceed the above limitations.

Pets. You may bring your dogs and cats into Canada, provided that each animal has a certificate from a licensed veterinarian that confirms vaccination against rabies within the preceding thirty-six months. Puppies and kittens under age three months and Seeing Eye dogs accompanied by their owners can enter Canada without certification or restriction. An exception is Newfoundland, where dogs and cats, whether or not accompanied by their owners, require entry permits in advance from the Provincial Veterinary Service (Government of Newfoundland, P.O. Box 7400, St. John's, Newfoundland A1E 3Y5; 709–729–6897).

Firearms. Firearms that have no legitimate sporting or recreational use (e.g., handguns) are not permitted entry into Canada. Canada has extremely strong handgun laws, and they are strictly enforced. Failure to report your weapons at customs may result in their seizure and forfeiture. If you are bringing in a handgun for competition shooting, you must obtain a permit in advance from a Canadian local registrar of firearms.

Long guns, those used for hunting and competition shooting, may be brought into Canada and used without a permit by visitors age sixteen years or older. Nonresident hunters may bring in 200 rounds of ammunition per person duty-free.

Reentry into the United States

To reenter the United States, you must satisfy U.S. Immigration authorities of your right to do so. This is usually accomplished by some form of identification and/or proof of citizenship (passport, birth certificate, or other document). You would do well to list all the purchases that you are taking home before you confront the

U.S. officials. Keep sales receipts and invoices handy, and pack purchases separately for an easier inspection.

You may take out of and bring into the United States up to $10,000 (U.S. funds). Any amount over this limit requires reporting with U.S. Customs.

Items of cultural, historical, or scientific value to the heritage of Canada that are more than fifty years old (for example, certain antiques) may not be taken out of the country without special permission. For more information, call Canada Customs (613–523–8120).

If you have stayed in Canada for at least forty-eight hours, you may leave the country with up to $400 (U.S. dollars) of personal purchases duty-free. Members of the same family may combine their exemptions into a larger duty-free total. For example, if five of you are traveling together and Mother finds a terrific mink stole for $2,000 in Montréal, she may bring it back into the States duty-free (five family members times a $400 exemption per member equals $2,000). Duty-free purchases must accompany you back across the border.

Included in the duty-free exemptions are up to 100 cigars, so long as they are not Cuban, which are absolutely prohibited. You may also return with 200 duty-free cigarettes and 1 liter of liquor (the minimum age is twenty-one).

Gifts may be sent to friends and relatives in the United States duty-free if the value of each gift does not exceed $50. The package should be marked "Unsolicited Gift."

Emergencies

In an emergency, simply dial 911 or 0 and ask the telephone operator for the police, who have been specially trained to handle and coordinate all types of emergencies. The larger towns and cities and the provinces of Ontario and Québec have their own separate police forces. The Royal Canadian Mounted Police (RCMP) provides security and traffic services in the other provinces, particularly on main roads, in small towns, and in rural areas. The famous Mounties are one of the best police forces in the world, even giving you a traffic ticket with a smile and courtesy.

If someone has an urgent need to get in touch with you but does not know where or how, this person should contact the RCMP in the area where you are traveling (leave your itinerary with a friend or relative back home). Several times each day many of the

Important

All provinces in Canada require visiting motorists to produce evidence of financial responsibility in case of an accident. U.S. motorists are advised to obtain from their insurance agents a Canadian nonresident interprovincial motor vehicle liability insurance card, which is issued free of charge. If you have an accident in Canada and don't have this card, your vehicle may be impounded and other serious legal action may be taken against you. (Don't leave home without it!)

You are inviolation of the law if you don't use seat belts throughout Canada. You may be subject to fines and other penalities if you violate Canada's seat belt laws.

The Canadian Automobile Association provides full member services to members of the American Automobile Association. Similar reciprocal services are provided by other auto clubs. Check with yours before traveling in Canada.

Gas and oil are sold in Canada by the liter: 1 U.S. gallon equals 3.78 liters; 1 Canadian imperial gallon, however, equals 4.5 liters. Canadian petroleum products tend to be costlier than in the United States but cheaper than in most other countries.

Canadian Broadcasting Corporation (CBC) radio outlets broadcast the names of individuals traveling throughout Canada, asking them to contact the nearest RCMP office for emergency messages.

You Need Health Insurance

No one wants to land in the hospital while on a trip, but sometimes the unexpected does happen. *Important:* Make sure that your health insurance plan covers you and your family members while traveling in Canada and that you have adequate coverage to pay all or most costs for treatment. Although Canadians enjoy the benefits of an excellent, low-cost health care system, travelers from the United States must pay the going rate, which is as high as back home. Consult your insurance company or agent, your travel agent, or your nearest Canadian consulate general on how best to handle your particular situation.

Sporting Regulations

Hunting

Hunting is governed by provincial, federal, and territorial laws. Nonresidents are required to obtain a hunting license from each province in which they plan to hunt. Weapons are forbidden in many of Canada's provincial parks, reserves, and adjacent areas.

Fishing

Fishing, like hunting, is governed by provincial, federal, and territorial laws. For freshwater fishing, you must have a nonresident license for the province in which you wish to fish. No license is required for saltwater fishing. No permit is required to bring in your own gear.

A special fishing permit is required to fish in all national parks. These permits may be obtained at any national park site for a nominal fee and are valid in all the national parks across Canada.

National Parks

Any person entering a national park must seal firearms or any devices for capturing or killing game. The seals are provided at the entrance of the park. An exception is made in the case of persons traveling by motor vehicle through Fundy, Prince Edward Island, Cape Breton Island, or Terra Nova national parks during the hunting season of the province in which the park is located. In these cases only, all firearms and devices are to be dismantled and kept within the vehicle.

Important Numbers and Dates

Time Zones

All of Atlantic Canada, except for the island of Newfoundland, is on Atlantic Standard Time. Newfoundland is on Newfoundland Standard Time (6:00 A.M. Atlantic Time is 6:30 A.M. Newfoundland Time). Labrador, however, is on Atlantic Time. The easternmost portion of the Northwest Territories, east of Frobisher Bay, is also on Atlantic Standard Time.

Most of Québec and Ontario are on eastern time (6:00 A.M. Atlantic time is 5:00 A.M. Eastern time), but easternmost Québec along the north coast of the Gulf of Saint Lawrence is on Atlantic time. The westernmost portion of Ontario, west of Thunder Bay, is on central time. Most of the eastern portion of the Northwest Territories, between Frobisher Bay and Repulse Bay, is on eastern time.

Telephone Area Codes

Laurentians and most of the Eastern Townships:	819 and 450
London and west to Windsor area:	519
Montréal (metropolitan area and south):	514
New Brunswick:	506
Newfoundland:	709
Nova Scotia and Prince Edward Island:	902
Ottawa to the Saint Lawrence River region:	613
Québec City and eastern Québec:	418
Toronto (metropolitan area):	416, 647, and 905
Southwestern Lake Ontario region:	905

National Holidays

New Year's Day (January 1)
Good Friday
Easter Monday
Victoria Day (third Monday in May)
Canada Day (July 1)
Labour Day
Thanksgiving Day (second Monday in October)
Remembrance Day (November 11)
Christmas (December 25)
Boxing Day (December 26)

Banks, government offices, factories, commercial offices, and many stores are closed on these holidays. Most hotels and motels and many restaurants, however, are open for business.

The Metric System

All measurements in Canada now follow the metric system. Temperature is given in degrees Celsius; gas is sold by the liter, groceries by grams and kilograms; clothing comes in centimeter sizes; and road speeds are posted in kilometers per hour.

In Newfoundland, however, you may find these rules bent or broken. Like Americans, Newfoundlanders retain a degree of personal independence in their relationship with the federal government, and many have simply chosen not to convert to metric. So you will find a mixed bag, and even young people are more likely to tell you how far the next town is in miles instead of kilometers.

The Canadian government has prepared the following helpful conversion table:

Speed
15 miles per hour (mph) = approximately 25 kilometers (km) per hour (or kph)
30 miles per hour = approximately 50 kilometers per hour
50 miles per hour = approximately 80 kilometers per hour
60 miles per hour = approximately 100 kilometers per hour

Length
1 inch = 2.54 centimeters (cm)
1 foot = 0.3 meters (m) or 30 centimeters
1 yard = 0.9 meters or 90 centimeters
1 mile = 1.6 kilometers or 1600 meters

Mass
1 ounce = 28 grams (g)
1 pound = 0.45 kilograms (kg) or 450 grams

Volume
1 fluid ounce = 28 milliliters (ml)
1 imperial pint* = 0.57 liters (l) or 570 milliliters
1 imperial quart* = 1.14 liters or 1140 milliliters
1 imperial gallon* = 4.5 liters or 4500 milliliters
1 U.S. gallon = 3.78 liters or 3780 milliliters

Temperature
86° Fahrenheit (F) = approximately 30° Celsius (C) (hot summer day)
68°F = approximately 20°C (room temperature)
32°F = 0° C (water freezes)
–6°F = approximately –20°C (very cold winter day)

* Imperial size is larger than American measurement.

CHAPTER 2

Money Matters

The monetary system of Canada, like that of the United States, is based on dollars and cents. There is, however, a difference in value between the two currencies, which works out to the benefit of U.S. residents and for travelers from other countries.

The value of the Canadian dollar has fluctuated in recent years, but is always *below* the U.S. dollar, depending on the current market rate. This means that Americans and others traveling in Canada have been getting more in Canadian money for each $1.00 U.S. This advantageous difference between Canadian and U.S. money is a strong incentive to travel in Canada and splurge a bit more than you would in other parts of the world.

Some of this saving, however, is negated by sales taxes on both the federal and provincial level, which can add up to as much as 18 percent in some provinces.

Canadian coins are 1, 5, 10, and 25 cents, $1.00 (called a Loonie because a loon is pictured on one side of it) and $2.00 (called a Tooney because it is worth two Loonies). Bills are $5, $10, $20, $50, and $100.

Although U.S. money is sometimes accepted, especially by businesses close to the border, you cannot depend on this, nor on getting the most favorable exchange rate. Some stores, gas stations, hotels, and restaurants keep a fairly current table of rates and are able to approximate the official rate, but more often, especially at hotels, you will get a lower rate. It is always best to exchange money and deal in Canadian dollars. Besides, it's good manners. Except at border businesses, we expect Canadians to use our money when they visit us, so the reverse is fair.

It's a good idea to begin your trip with a small amount of Canadian money in your pocket, especially if you plan to arrive on a weekend or at other than business hours.

By far the best way to exchange money is on your credit card or by direct bankcard transaction. You will always get the best rate of exchange—the commercial rather than street rate—and the banking fees are usually much lower than the exchange fee for cash.

The worst way to exchange is in small amounts of cash. Fees for cash exchange, especially on small amounts, can sometimes eat up much of the money exchanged (this is true nearly everywhere). If you exchange cash, do it less often and in larger amounts.

The same is true of traveler's checks, which are treated like cash in terms of exchange fees. Although they are still used by some travelers, these checks are becoming less common as more inexpensive and convenient means of ATM exchange are available. ATMs are located nearly everywhere, even in most small towns, and the per-transaction fee varies from free to a few dollars, depending on the bank.

Normal banking hours in Canada are shorter than in the United States; banks often close at 3:00 P.M. But more and more banks, especially in cities, are extending their hours and opening Saturday mornings.

Taxes

Canada now has a nationwide Goods and Services Tax. The GST, as it is known, is similar to the Value Added Tax found in many European countries. As with the VAT, U.S. visitors to Canada may claim a full rebate on the tax they pay on goods that they take out of Canada. Refund forms are available in many locations, and refunds may be obtained in airports and at many border crossing points.

Most provinces also have a Provincial Sales Tax (PST), which varies and is usually combined into one unified tax. Refund policies for visitors also vary. In Ontario, for example, the PST on both merchandise and accommodations can be refunded. In Québec the tax is refundable only on merchandise costing $500 Canadian or more. If you are applying by mail for refunds on both taxes, apply for the GST first. Both taxes require receipts for proof of purchase and export; receipts submitted for the GST will be returned, but the provinces do not return receipts.

Special Fares in Canada

If you are sixty-five or older, you may be eligible to receive reductions on air, rail, and bus fares within Canada, provided that proof of age is supplied when you purchase your tickets. Young people between ages thirteen and twenty-one may also travel in Canada at reduced rates; other rate reductions may be available for children twelve and younger. Proof of age (birth certificate, driver's license, or passport) is necessary when you purchase your tickets. Ask your travel agent for details.

Credit Cards

Most major credit cards are widely accepted throughout Canada, with Visa and MasterCard (and their international variations) being the most popular. You should ask your hotel, restaurant, or store before purchasing goods or services whether it accepts yours. Most places display signs and decals, at or near entrances, cash registers, and so on, showing the cards that they accept.

Major credit cards are necessary for renting automobiles. They are also necessary for registration at most hotels that allow you to charge additional services to your room bill.

Calculating Costs

Because of fluctuating prices, this guide uses a scale of relative prices—*expensive, moderate,* and *inexpensive*—to indicate costs for accommodations and restaurants. Here is how it works (*note*—all figures here represent Canadian dollars):

Accommodations
An *expensive* double room at a top hotel in Toronto, Ottawa, Québec City, or Montréal costs more than $150 a night. A *moderate* double would be more than $90, a decent *inexpensive* double $75 and up. There are variations in each of these categories, depending on the quality of the accommodations and when you want them. Toronto, Ottawa, Québec City, and Montréal are among the most expensive places to stay in Eastern Canada. Prices in other cities and towns of Eastern Canada are somewhat lower, depending on the location, season, quality of accommodation, and consumer demand. To cut some of the cost, ask about weekend or seasonal packages and special policies concerning children, senior citizens, groups, and commercial travelers.

Within each of the above cost categories, hotels and motels have a range of rates for doubles and singles. If you can make your booking well in advance, you should be able to get a more favorable rate. Also, if it's a slow week or season, you might be able to get some terrific bargains. The converse is also true: If you book at the last minute and if the city is filled with convention delegates and package tours, you may have to be content with whatever you can get at the price they want you to pay.

Dining

Again we use the relative categories of *expensive, moderate,* and *inexpensive* to indicate the price of dining in restaurants listed in this guide. The cost of meals throughout Eastern Canada is fairly consistent. The cost of meals in the countryside should be somewhat less, except at fine resorts and inns. While touring in rural areas and smaller cities and towns, you will often find the best dining in motels, inns, and hotels. Fast-food places can be found everywhere in Eastern Canada.

An *expensive* evening meal is one at which the main course is priced at $30 and up. The total cost of an expensive meal for two could go well over $125, when you figure in drinks and tips.

A *moderate* meal for two averages about $90, while an inexpensive meal for two would cost below $50. Remember that these figures are in Canadian currency.

Attractions

Many of the attractions mentioned in this guide are *free*. Others are marked *admission charge*. The amount charged can range from a voluntary donation to several dollars. Major attractions usually have several prices—for adults, children, senior citizens, groups, and tours. During the peak summer vacation season, from the end of June to Canada's Labour Day, most attractions are open every day from 10:00 A.M. to 5:30 P.M. Some major attractions (amusement parks and historical villages) offer evening hours during the peak season.

Each attraction has its own method of operation. Sometimes when a historic home or local museum, for example, is closed on a Sunday or Monday, the curator just might open it for you. Don't be too shy to inquire if you have a particular interest.

Communications

Toll-free Calls

Most major transportation companies, hotel and motel chains, and rental car companies have toll-free reservation and information telephone numbers. In fact, many accommodations and services listed in this guide have toll-free numbers. Before making a toll call, dial toll-free information—(800) 555–1212 for both the United States and Canada—to find out if the place you want to contact has a toll-free number that can be accessed from your location.

Airport Services

International airports in Eastern Canada are located in Gander, Halifax, Montréal, Ottawa, and Toronto. American travelers returning to the United States from Toronto and Montréal clear U.S. Customs in the airports of these cities.

Although this may sound like a good idea, it may not seem so when you miss your connecting flight home due to long lines at Customs in Montréal. But you have no choice when flying out of these airports, so arrive early to allow for it or make sure the airline gives you plenty of time in between flights if you are connecting.

Special services offered at the larger international airports include foreign exchange, lockers, telephones, duty-free shops, bars, restaurants, newsstands, book and gift shops, and drugstores. Most of these terminals have accommodations nearby.

All major airports have bus, taxi, and limousine services to and from the city centers. Most of the major rental car companies also have desks at these terminals.

Most terminals have facilities for persons with special needs. Such facilities include ramps, specially equipped washrooms, automatic doors, baby changing rooms, and other conveniences.

Free Culture

A treat while touring in Eastern Canada by auto is tuning into a Canadian Broadcasting Corporation radio station. A government-operated network, CBC provides some of the finest news, discussion, cultural, and entertainment programming in North America. Its broadcasting of classical music is outstanding in variety and amount.

Part Two

Ontario and Québec

Eastern Canada's lighthouses are beacons of welcome for travelers to this diverse and fascinating region.

CHAPTER 3

Toronto

The first thing visitors see, no matter how they approach Toronto, is the tall needle of the CN Tower rising on the shore. It dwarfs First Canadian Place and Scotia Plaza buildings, Toronto's first skyscrapers, which are each about half its height. They in turn dwarf the building that once dominated the skyline, the still imposing twenty-six-story Royal York Hotel, built in 1929 to serve upscale passengers arriving on the railroad. Three generations of the British Royal family, including Queen Elizabeth II and her father, King George VI, have stayed at the Royal York, along with a list of other kings, presidents, prime ministers, and premiers.

More stunning new skyscrapers concentrate in the downtown Financial District, the most elegant of them Toronto's City Hall, whose curved glass towers hug a park. Nearby Royal Bank gleams with windows that are colored by 15,500 pounds of real gold.

Old Toronto, where commerce thrived in the glory days of the late 1800s, begins in their shadow. The monumental Bank of Canada Building is a fine representation of the era's grandiose architecture. Colburne Street's buildings are decorated in stonework of contrasting colors.

Yet once beyond the striking contrasts of downtown architecture, Toronto seems more like a group of smaller towns pasted together into a collage, so distinct are the different neighborhoods. Some are ethnic enclaves, others seem to reflect a commonality of lifestyle more than of heritage. Kensington is the half-hippie, half-immigrant heart of downtown, lively and colorful, its narrow

Toronto's modern and historic buildings give substantial evidence of the ongoing vitality of the city. To the left is the SkyDome; beside it looms the CN Tower, the world's tallest freestanding structure.

Finding Your Way

Toronto's street signs are in different colors, indicating direction. All signs for east–west streets are yellow (remember the path of the sun). North–South streets are marked in blue, leading to the waters of Lake Ontario.

streets lined with Victorian houses-turned-shops. The streets are alive with market stalls, reflecting an entire world of nationalities.

Bohemian Queen West is a mix of restaurants, outdoor cafes, and funky boutiques; it is one of the most popular shopping districts for young Torontonians and a center for pop music. The City-TV building is a television studio with many outdoor events.

Elegant Yorkville is a neighborhood of stylish boutiques, designer clothing stores, art galleries, and restaurants, many tucked into little courtyards connected by narrow alleys.

Little Italy housed newly arrived Italian families who have since moved northward, with Portuguese immigrants moving into their old houses. But many of the Italian families who used to live here still call it home, and its streets are lined with trattorias, cafes, and Italian groceries. Toronto's Italian population is the largest of any city outside of Italy.

Two Chinatowns in the city itself and three more in the suburbs grew suddenly as well-to-do people left Hong Kong. In the Indian Bazaar neighborhood, women wear bright saris, sold in more than twenty boutiques there.

For the visitor, Toronto's colorful neighborhoods vie for attention with its world-class museums and its lively cultural life. It's hard to know where to begin.

A Brief History

Until 1793 Toronto was a sparsely populated area on the north shore of Lake Ontario. It was visited in 1615 by the French explorer Étienne Brûlé, and by 1720 a trading post was established here, called Fort Rouillé—later Fort Toronto ("meeting place" in Algonquian). After the defeat of the French forces on the Plains of Abraham in 1759, the fort was destroyed so that the victorious English could not use it.

Metropolitan Toronto

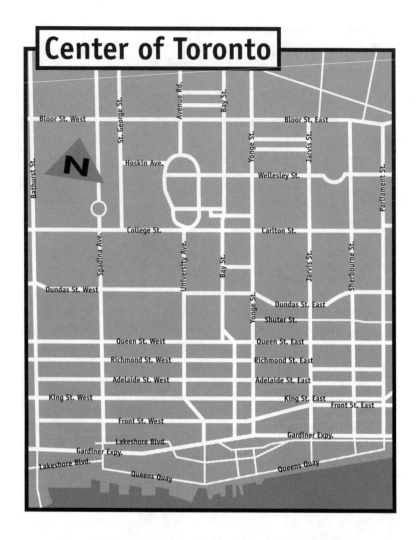

Center of Toronto

The American Revolution divided the continent into the United States and British North America. In 1793 Lieutenant Governor John Graves Simcoe, a British army officer, selected the former site of Fort Toronto for the new settlement of York, which was to provide a defensive position for the British against their main enemy, the Americans. York became the capital of Upper Canada (Ontario) and a refuge for loyalists from the United States who wanted to continue to live under the British monarchy rather than in the new republic. British military families and Loyalists formed the first permanent population of York and became the social, political, and economic elite of the community. Their position was strengthened through "family compacts" both in Toronto and in Great Britain and was maintained until well into the twentieth century.

During the War of 1812, York was captured, looted, and burned by American troops. In retaliation, the British burned Washington, D.C., in 1814.

York was incorporated as a city in 1834, at which time it also took on the name of Toronto. In 1837 Toronto's first mayor, William Lyon Mackenzie, a passionate nationalist who favored a republican system of government for the country, attempted a coup by armed force. Mackenzie's short-lived rebellion failed to rouse many citizens to his cause.

In 1841 Toronto ceased to be the capital of Upper Canada when that province was united with Lower Canada (Québec) into the Province of Canada. In 1849 the city became the capital of Canada, which did not then include the Maritime Provinces. With Canada's confederation in 1867, Toronto became the capital of Ontario.

Between the confederation and the end of World War II, Toronto occupied itself primarily with economic growth, as a burgeoning center for finance, manufacturing, and transportation. With continual expansion of population and economic activity, in 1954 the thirteen independent municipalities of the Toronto area, including the city itself, formed themselves into a federated metropolitan government to consolidate many of their public services and to plan more effectively for future growth. Metropolitan government has worked exceedingly well in Toronto, where it has earned the reputation of being uncommonly well managed and honest as well.

With the influx of immigrants after World War II, the population of the city ballooned and diversified. Magnificent new buildings changed Toronto's skyline from dowdy to splendid. With these cultural and physical changes, Toronto entered a new period in its history in considerably better shape than most other big cities on the continent. The transformation continues today.

How to Get to Toronto

Toronto is located on the northwest shore of Lake Ontario, 98 miles (157 km) from Buffalo, New York, and 323 miles (517 km) from Montréal.

By Car

From New England, New York State, and Ohio, take I–90 to Buffalo, then take the Queen Elizabeth Way (Q.E.W.) to Toronto. From the Detroit area, cross the bridge to Windsor, Ontario, and then take Highway 401 to Toronto.

From Western Canada, travel the Trans-Canada Highway to Orillia, Ontario, then take Highway 11, which becomes Highway 400 and goes into Toronto.

From Eastern Canada, travel the Trans-Canada Highway to Montréal, where you pick up Highway 20, which becomes Highway 401 at the Ontario border and goes into Toronto.

Driving distances to Toronto from:

Boston	545 mi (872 km)
Chicago	498 mi (797 km)
Detroit	221 mi (354 km)
Halifax	1,073 mi (1,717 km)
Montréal	323 mi (517 km)
New York City	531 mi (850 km)
Ottawa	239 mi (382 km)
Philadelphia	528 mi (845 km)
Rochester	160 mi (256 km)
Washington, D.C.	540 mi (864 km)

By Air

Many domestic and international airlines serve Toronto from other areas of Canada, from the United States, and from other countries. Lester B. Pearson International Airport is located at Highways 427 and 401, 19 miles (30 km) northwest of the city center. Air Canada and Canadian Airlines International provide frequent, daily service from numerous domestic and international cities. The airport's general information number is (905) 676–3506. Contact your local travel agent for information on airlines flying to Toronto from your area.

Lester B. Pearson International Airport has both Canadian and U.S. Customs clearances, a duty-free shop, restaurants, lounges, book and magazine shops, and many other conveniences. There is frequent (every twenty minutes), low-cost express bus service to and from several leading downtown Toronto hotels, such as the Sheraton Centre, and to and from the York Mills, Yorkdale, and Islington subway stations. Call (416) 393–7911 for bus schedules. The Toronto Transit Commission (TTC) also runs a bus service to and from the airport. Call (416) 363–4636. In addition, there are taxi and limousine services to and from the airport. Near the airport are hotels, motels, restaurants, and shopping centers, plus several attractions and conference facilities.

By Rail

VIA Rail provides passenger rail service to Toronto from major cities in Canada. Union Station, an architectural masterpiece from the peak days of railroading, is the main terminal for all passenger services. Located at Front and Bay Streets and across from the Royal York Hotel, the station is also on the subway line and has its own stop. For more information on VIA Rail service, call (416) 366–8411.

Amtrak provides service from New York City to Toronto, through Niagara Falls (one train a day). Amtrak also has frequent service to Buffalo, where you can make easy bus connections to Toronto. Call Amtrak at (800) 872–7245 for details.

By Bus

Greyhound provides bus service to Toronto from throughout Canada and the United States. Travelways and Voyageur Colonial provide service to many Ontario and other Canada destinations. All out-of-town buses arrive and depart from the Bus Terminal, 610 Bay Street, at Dundas West (downtown). Call (416) 393–7911 for information.

Rental Cars, Limousine Services, and Taxis

Rental cars—Avis, Hertz, Tilden, Thrifty, and so on—are available at Toronto International Airport and at other city locations. You are advised to reserve a car ahead through your local travel agent or by calling the company's toll-free number. Some companies, such as Thrifty, will deliver a car to your hotel and complete the paperwork there.

Limousines and taxis are available at the airport. While staying in Toronto, make limo and taxi arrangements through your hotel concierge.

General Information

Time zone: Eastern
Telephone area codes: 416 and 905
Police: dial 911
Medical emergencies: dial 911 or call Community Information

Centre of Metro Toronto for information on health and social services available in the city—(416) 392–0505 (access available twenty-four hours a day).

Weather information: dial (416) 739–4994 for more detail

Tourist Information

The Province of Ontario has a visitor information office, which dispenses free information, literature, and maps, in the Eaton Centre Galleria on Level One, 220 Yonge Street. This office is open weekdays from 10:00 A.M. to 9:00 P.M., Saturdays from 10:00 A.M. to 6:00 P.M., and Sundays from noon to 6:00 P.M.

Also contact the Metropolitan Toronto Convention and Visitors Association office located at Queen's Quay Terminal at Harbourfront, 207 Queen's Quay West, Suite 590, (416) 203–2500 or (800) 363–1990.

Toll-free Travel Information

Call (800) ONTARIO (688–2746) for information on Toronto and all other areas of Ontario. Free literature can be ordered through this toll-free number, or you can visit their Web-site at www.ontariotravel.net.

Also call Tourism Toronto at (416) 203–2500 or (800) 363–1990.

Climate and Clothing

Toronto has a more moderate climate than most Eastern Canada cities. It is comparable with that of southern New England. The average low temperature in February is 17°F (–8°C), the average high 31°F (0°C). The average high temperature in August is 78°F (25°C), the average low 60°F (16°C). Rainfall is similar to that of New England: 26 inches (66 cm) annually.

If you're visiting Toronto for pleasure, fashionable casual clothes for the season can be worn during the day and the evening. Ties and jackets are recommended for men and elegant garb for women for an evening on the town, where style, elegance, and a certain degree of formality are expected in the better restaurants, lounges, and places of entertainment. Toronto is very style conscious and the men and women here spend a lot of money to be à la mode.

Sweaters, raincoats, walking or jogging shoes, and knockaround clothes should also be packed. Warm topcoats are essential in the winter.

Convention/Business Meeting Information

The Metro Toronto Convention Centre, located downtown at 255 Front Street, West, is a comprehensive, modern facility. Recently expanded to the tune of $180 million, it is situated at the foot of the CN Tower and adjacent to the SkyDome Stadium. The Convention Centre covers 180,000 square meters and contains seventy meeting rooms and 41,000 square meters of exhibit space. It is within walking distance of more than 15,000 hotel rooms. Airport bus service is available at the front door. The deluxe Crowne Plaza–Toronto Centre is connected to this complex.

Some of the best convention/executive hotels are Four Seasons Toronto, Metropolitan Hotel, Radisson Plaza Hotel, King Edward Hotel, Crowne Plaza, Park Hyatt, Royal York, the Sheraton Centre, Sutton Place, Westin Harbour Castle, and Inn on the Park.

How to Get Around Toronto

The Central Area

Toronto is a sprawling urban area. The terrain is essentially flat, though creased with ravines, rivers, and streams. Toronto lies on the north shore of Lake Ontario, which has several offshore islands that are popular recreational areas for the city's residents and visitors. Although Toronto is Canada's largest city, most of its attractions are concentrated in a central area, which can be easily covered by foot, subway, or taxi.

Nathan Phillips Square, on Queen Street, West, marks the center of the city. Inside this square are the unusual modern buildings of City Hall, and across from City Hall stands the Sheraton Centre complex. Nearby is the Eaton Centre.

Running south from this center is Bay Street, the financial district of the city, as well as Union Station, Harbourfront, and the ferry to the harbor islands.

East of the center, running north and south, is Yonge Street, famous throughout Canada for its many stores, restaurants, and places of amusement. Yonge, Toronto's most lively street, serves as a "paseo" for the young, for drifters and unusual characters, and for visitors. Yonge is also the world's longest street, running from the waterfront to Rainy River.

West of the city center, University Avenue leads north to the buildings of Parliament and Queen's Park. To the west of Queen's Park are the University of Toronto and many government buildings. To the north of Queen's Park, running from east to west, is Bloor Street, which is Toronto's version of New York's Fifth Avenue, graced with many fine stores, hotels, and restaurants. In the Bloor Street area are also the Royal Ontario Museum, the Yorkville section, and the handsome library building.

Most of Toronto's attractions, hotels, and restaurants are within or near this grid of streets. Remember to keep Nathan Phillips Square, with the New City Hall, as your central landmark. South is toward Lake Ontario, and north is toward Queen's Park and Bloor Street. The main east–west streets are Front, King, Queen, Dundas, College, and Bloor. The main north–south streets are Yonge, Bay, University, Queen's Park, and Spadina Avenue.

The Subway System

Toronto's subway system (operated by the Toronto Transit Commission) is fast, frequent, safe, clean, and convenient. A single fare will take you anywhere in the system by rail, bus, or streetcar. The subway runs north and south under Yonge Street, makes a loop at Union Station, and runs north and south under University Avenue. It also runs east and west under Bloor Street, north and south under Spadina Avenue. A Light Rail Transit provides rapid public transportation between downtown and Harbourfront. For information about Toronto's subway system and fares, call (416) 393–INFO.

Subway stations provide access to many of Toronto's important sites:

Stations	Destinations
Bay	Bloor Street
Bloor-Yonge and St. George	Library, Bloor Street shopping area, connections on the Bloor-Danforth line to the Metropolitan Toronto Zoo and Lester B. Pearson International Airport
College	University of Toronto, Parliament buildings, provincial government offices, Kensington Market
King	Financial district
Museum	Royal Ontario Museum, Bloor Street, Yorkville shopping area

Toronto Subway System

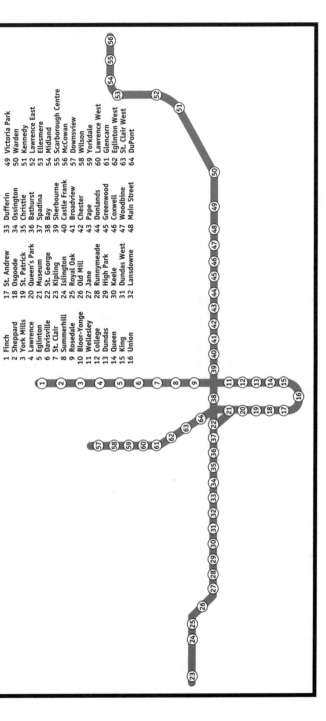

1 Finch	17 St. Andrew	33 Dufferin	49 Victoria Park
2 Sheppard	18 Osgoode	34 Ossington	50 Warden
3 York Mills	19 St. Patrick	35 Christie	51 Kennedy
4 Lawrence	20 Queen's Park	36 Bathurst	52 Lawrence East
5 Eglinton	21 Museum	37 Spadina	53 Ellesmere
6 Davisville	22 St. George	38 Bay	54 Midland
7 St. Clair	23 Kipling	39 Sherbourne	55 Scarborough Centre
8 Summerhill	24 Islington	40 Castle Frank	56 McCowan
9 Rosedale	25 Royal Oak	41 Broadview	57 Downsview
10 Bloor-Yonge	26 Old Mill	42 Chester	58 Wilson
11 Wellesley	27 Jane	43 Pape	59 Yorkdale
12 College	28 Runnymeade	44 Donlands	60 Lawrence West
13 Dundas	29 High Park	45 Greenwood	61 Glencarn
14 Queen	30 Keele	46 Coxwell	62 Eglinton West
15 King	31 Dundas West	47 Woodbine	63 St. Clair West
16 Union	32 Lansdowne	48 Main Street	64 DuPont

Osgoode	Nathan Phillips Square, City Hall, Chinatown, Sheraton Centre, Eaton Centre
Queen	Nathan Phillips Square, City Hall, Chinatown, Sheraton Centre, Eaton Centre
Queen's Park	University of Toronto, Parliament buildings, provincial government offices, Kensington Market
Saint Andrew	Financial district
Union	VIA Rail terminal, Royal York Hotel, and Harbourfront

The Toronto subway system operates from 6:00 A.M. to 1:30 A.M. Monday through Saturday, and from 9:00 A.M. to 1:30 A.M. Sunday.

Guided Tours and Cruises

Guided tours of Toronto are available through Gray Line Sightseeing, (416) 594–0343, which picks up passengers at major hotels and also has tours to Niagara Falls and other major attractions outside the city. Olde Town Toronto Tours, (416) 798–2424, shows you the city from inside a charming 1920s Peter Witt trolley.

ATR provides aerial tours of Toronto and Niagara Falls, (416) 203–1199. Niagara Helicopters, (905) 357–5672, also offers flights over Niagara Falls.

See Toronto by bike: A Taste of the World, (416) 923-6813 or www.interlog.com/~ataste, has an organized tour and supplies bikes and helmets.

The following companies provide boat tours on Toronto Harbour and its islands: Toronto Harbour Tours, (416) 869–1372; Mariposa Cruise Line, (416) 203–0178. All sailings depart from Harbourfront.

Niagara Falls tours are provided by Gray Line, (416) 594–3310, and Niagara Tours, (416) 869–1372.

Major Events

For more information on these major events, call Tourism Toronto at (416) 203–2500 or, from the United States, (800) 363–1990.

Metro International Caravan, the best multicultural festival anywhere, involves the entire Toronto area for nine days in mid-June, when each ethnic group shows the best of its culture through art, music, dance, drama, food, and costumes. Pavilions to house the events are set up in the various neighborhoods, and visitors purchase passports admitting them to the different worlds of Caravan. One can sample the best of several foreign countries without leaving the city. Caravan has become one of Toronto's most popular annual events. If you're lucky enough to be in town when Caravan is taking place, buy a passport and just plunge in.

The Queen's Plate, the oldest continuously run horse race in North America, is held in June at Woodbine Race Track.

Caribana (Caribbean Festival), held in July, celebrates the presence of Toronto's black population, who came from the islands of the British West Indies. Caribana features steel bands, calypso music, fruit and straw markets, a nightclub, parades, limbo dancing, art exhibitions, fashion shows, and the marvelous cuisine of the islands. The festival lasts about a week and is held in downtown Toronto.

Canadian National Exhibition, which runs from mid-August to Labor Day, is the oldest and largest annual country fair in the world. It features many displays of agricultural, industrial, and cultural products, Canada's largest midway, an international air show, an aquatics show of swimmers and water-skiers, and topstar entertainment. Located at Lakeshore Boulevard, it offers great fun for the entire family. Admission is charged.

Toronto International Film Festival, ten days and nights in September is the second largest film festival in the world. It's an international extravaganza of film showings, parties, and appearances by high-profile Hollywood stars.

The Royal Agricultural Winter Fair, held for ten days in November at the National Trade Centre, features the Royal Horse Show, with international teams competing in various jumping and dressage events.

Attractions

Toronto's Parks

Toronto's lovely parks and recreational lands are open to the public for year-round enjoyment. These parks are generally clean and safe.

The Leslie Street Spit is a man-made peninsula jutting out into the lake. It doesn't look like much from a distance, but during the past few years, the city's wildlife has claimed it for its own. It's a wonderful spot for bird-watching, and nature lovers come here to find "the country in the city" while enjoying stunning views of the skyline.

High Park, off the Queensway, Bloor Street, West, is available for hiking, touring, cross-country skiing, jogging, boat launching.

James Gardens, accessible via Edenbridge Drive, East, and Royal York Road, contains twenty-seven acres of lawns, flower gardens, pools, and streams. It is especially noted for its wildflowers and tulip garden.

Toronto Islands park is accessible by ferries that leave from the foot of Bay Street every twenty minutes. The park has areas for picnics, swimming, fishing, boating, jogging, and bicycling; for children, a farm with barnyard animals, swings, pony rides, and an amusement area; hiking walks, trails, and gardens; restaurants; and a magnificent view of the Toronto skyline. This splendid, low-cost recreational area should not be missed.

Central Don Park, via Eglinton Avenue, East, offers hiking, nature study, horseback riding, picnic spots, and playing fields.

Edwards Gardens, via Lawrence Avenue, East, and Leslie Street, is a beautiful area of rolling lawns, stately trees, rock gardens, floral displays, and streams, with a rustic bridge—an exquisite park for walking and relaxing.

Morningside Park, via Morningside Avenue south of Ellesmere Road, is fine for hiking, picnics, jogging, cross-country skiing, and nature walks.

Historic and Cultural Attractions

Art Gallery of Ontario, 317 Dundas Street, West, has a permanent collection of more than 7,000 works of art. About half of these works are by Canadian artists, from both modern and early periods. The gallery has the world's largest public collection of works by the English sculptor Henry Moore, housed in a stunning wing of the museum, as well as the Klamer family collection of Inuit art, one of the most extensive in the world. The Art Gallery of Ontario is one of Canada's finest museums for painting and sculpture. Open throughout the year. Admission charge.

The Grange, built in 1817, is the oldest brick house in the city. Reached through the Art Gallery of Ontario, the Grange is an elegant Georgian-style mansion of beautiful rooms filled with antiques. Poet Matthew Arnold was most pleased with his stay here.

CN Tower, 301 Front Street, West, at 1,815 feet (553 m) high, is the world's tallest freestanding structure. The CN (Canadian National) Tower has become Toronto's most familiar landmark and symbol. It's the best place in town, day and night, for breathtaking views of the Toronto area, Lake Ontario, and the surrounding countryside. On especially clear days, you can see as far as Niagara Falls and the New York State shore of the lake. In the evening the lights of the city far below create an enchanting panorama. For a dramatic experience, ride up the glass-enclosed outside elevators. You'll feel like Superman zooming up into the heavens. There is an observation deck on the 1,100-foot (335 m) level, another one at 1,500 ft (457 m). On top of the tower is a revolving gourmet restaurant. Open throughout the year. Admission charge.

The Hockey Hall of Fame is housed in a renovated historic building (it was once a bank) at the corner of Yonge and Front Streets. This museum houses all kinds of hockey memorabilia, from Jacques Plante's mask to Bobby Hull's hockey stick. A series of themed "zones"—a mock-up of a dressing room, a rink where you can "play" against a computer, a broadcast area and a film theater showing some of the best moments in hockey—lets visitors absorb the excitement of Canada's most popular sport. Open daily. Admission charge.

Ontario Place is a cultural and entertainment complex built on three man-made islands on Lake Ontario, at 955 Lakeshore Boulevard. A kind of mini-Expo, it supplies enough attractions to keep you and your family busy and interested throughout the day. It features IMAX films shown on a giant screen, big-star entertainment at the 16,000-seat Molson Amphitheatre, the Atlantis Entertainment complex, and parklands, restaurants and pubs, and a variety of boutiques. The annual Benson & Hedges fireworks competition is held here. Open from mid-May to mid-September. Admission charge.

Casa Loma, 1 Austin Terrace, is Toronto's famous medieval-style castle, built in 1914 for $3 million. With its ninety-eight rooms, crenellated towers and turrets, secret passages, elaborate halls, and sumptuous bedrooms, Casa Loma is a freak on the North American landscape but immense fun to visit. Open throughout the year. Admission charge.

Fort York, Garrison Road (entrance off Fleet Street), is a complex of blockhouses and ramparts dating from the War of 1812. The restored officers' quarters contain bedrooms, game rooms, and a sitting room. The Centre Blockhouse features an audiovisual presentation on the history of Fort York and battles in the area. During the summer months, the Eighth King's Regiment, dressed in nineteenth-century uniforms, performs infantry drills and artillery salutes. Open throughout the year. Admission charge.

Black Creek Pioneer Village, on Murray Ross Parkway in the Downsview area of Toronto, thirty minutes north of downtown, is the re-creation of a nineteenth-century rural Ontario settlement. You can visit authentically restored and furnished buildings: log farm buildings; a church, firehouse, and schoolhouse; a museum housing the largest collection of nineteenth-century toys in Canada; and shops demonstrating such crafts as broom making, flour milling, weaving, gunsmithing, and blacksmithing. The staff, dressed in period costumes, performs household tasks and village trades. There are all kinds of barnyard animals, including oxen, geese, and chickens. An 1850s inn and stagecoach stop offers delicious full-course meals and afternoon tea. The 78th Fraser Highlanders show aspects of nineteenth-century military life. Open mid-March to the end of the year. Admission charge. Call (416) 736–1733.

Canadian Broadcasting Centre. This spiffy new high-rise at 250 Front Street, West (opposite the equally modern glass-fronted Metro Toronto Convention Centre), houses state-of-the-art radio and television studios and a concert hall with excellent acoustics, named after Glenn Gould, Canada's famous pianist. There are regularly scheduled concerts, tours of the building by appointment, a gift store, and a fascinating broadcasting museum with interactive displays. Open weekdays. Call (416) 205–8605.

Playdium Toronto is at 126 John Street in the Festival Hall Complex. Here you will find plenty of interactive games, entertainment, and attractions, plus a 40-foot climbing wall and food vendors. Call (416) 260–1400, or visit www.playdium.com.

Playdium. Situated in Mississauga (99 Rathburn Road West), this high-tech kingdom of interactive attractions, motion simulators, and video games gives visitors a glimpse into the world of tomorrow. There are more conventional attractions as well, like a mini-golf course, rock-climbing wall, and a go-cart raceway. More than 180 electronic games. Call (905) 273–9000.

Colborne Lodge, at the south end of High Park, a fine nineteenth-century residence in a beautiful setting, was the home of John G. Howard, an architect and city surveyor. Its picture gallery has more than a hundred of Howard's original drawings and paintings. Demonstrations of nineteenth-century crafts are also held at Colborne Lodge. Open throughout the year. Admission charge.

George R. Gardiner Museum of Ceramic Art, 111 Queen's

Park, features an excellent collection of porcelain and pottery: pre-Columbian pottery (2000 B.C. to fifteenth century), Italian majolica (fifteenth and sixteenth centuries), seventeenth-century English delftware, and Continental and English porcelain of the eighteenth century. Part of the Royal Ontario Museum; one admission covers both.

New City Hall is a complex of two curved office towers of different heights surrounding the saucer-shaped Council Chamber building. Until the opening of the CN Tower, New City Hall, designed by the Finnish architect Viljo Revell, was the main symbol for contemporary Toronto. While New City Hall is striking, it seems somehow incomplete, as the towers lack windows on the far side and thus appear to be turning their backs against parts of the city. New City Hall is located on Nathan Phillips Square, which has a fine Henry Moore sculpture and a reflecting pool that becomes a public ice-skating rink in the winter. Guided tours of New City Hall are provided every half hour daily. Free.

St. Lawrence Hall, located on the southwest corner of King and Jarvis Streets, was established in 1850 as a hall for public gatherings. Jenny Lind, the "Swedish Nightingale," sang here in 1851. It is one of the more attractive historical buildings in Toronto and can be hired for meetings.

Royal Ontario Museum (ROM), Avenue Road at Bloor Street, is Canada's foremost public museum. The ROM's wide-ranging collection includes some of the finest pieces of ancient Chinese art in the world, as well as ancient Egyptian, medieval, Renaissance, and American Indian art. The museum also offers extensive displays of minerals, fossils, mammals, birds, fish, and other natural history areas. Special theme exhibitions are held all year. Open throughout the year. Admission charge.

Children's Own Museum is in the McLaughlin Planetarium Building at 90 Queen's Park. Children ages one to eight will enjoy exploring their own little town, which includes kiddie-size stores, businesses, and even a theater and an animal hospital. Call (416) 542–1495. Admission charge.

The Bata Shoe Museum is at 327 Bloor Street, West, on the edge of ultra-chic Yorkville. As you enter, note the shape of this Raymond Moriyama building. Its resemblance to a shoebox is no mistake. The impressive collection documents the history of shoes, from the sandals that decorate the walls of 4,000-year-old Egyptian tombs to the latest aerobic runners. There are all kinds of footwear on display, including Queen Victoria's ballroom slippers, Elton John's platforms, and the tiny lotus shoes used by Chinese women with bound feet. Although shoes may not seem the most arresting subject, displays are lively, creative, and intelligently presented. This is a must-see museum in Toronto. Closed Mondays. Admission charge.

The Parliament buildings, located on Queen's Park, form the seat of government for the Province of Ontario. The huge Romanesque sandstone buildings, designed by Boston architect H. H. Richardson, look down University Avenue and are a focus for many parades and ceremonies, such as a "royal progress" when the queen or members of the royal family visit. A fine statue of Queen Victoria graces the front of the buildings. The historic Legislative Chamber and precious mineral displays in the corridors are of interest, as are the interior decorations and portraits. Open throughout the year. Free guided tours are provided. Call (416) 326–1234.

Canada Sports Hall of Fame, Exhibition Place, off Lakeshore Boulevard, depicts the history of sports in Canada and features exhibitions about the nation's great athletes. Open throughout the year. Free.

Mackenzie House, 82 Bond Street, was home for William Lyon Mackenzie, Toronto's first mayor and leader of the rebellion of 1837. This restored home is furnished with mid-nineteenth-century antiques. Open throughout the year. Admission charge.

Marine Museum of Upper Canada, Exhibition Place, housed in the officers' quarters of an 1841 Stanley army barracks, shows Toronto's maritime history: ship models, relics of sunken ships, and Saint Lawrence Seaway lore. An old steam tug rests outside. Open throughout the year. Admission charge.

Metropolitan Toronto Library, 789 Yonge Street, designed by Raymond Moriyama, is one of the most unusual and appealing public reference libraries on the continent. Around a large atrium hung with plants are the floors for books and magazines. A stream flows through the main floor, and there are splashes of bright color everywhere. You may not have come to Toronto to visit a library, but this one is a must. Open throughout the year. Free. Call (416) 393–7196.

University of Toronto, across from Queen's Park, is where scientists discovered insulin and developed the first heart pacemaker and pabulum. The University of Toronto is composed of several colleges, among them King's (the oldest) and Trinity (the most prestigious). The campus has a diverse collection of architectural styles: For example, Hart House is neo-Gothic, and University College is Romanesque. Feel free to stroll the campus. Many concerts, exhibitions, and special events are open to the public.

Free guided walking tours of the historic midtown campus are available during the summer. Call (416) 978–6397.

Allan Gardens, at Sherbourne and Jarvis Streets, is an extensive downtown greenhouse complex displaying tropical and semitropical trees, flowering creepers, and plants. This is a wonderful place in the winter. Open throughout the year. Free.

Montgomery's Inn, 4709 Dundas Street, West, built in 1832 and a fine example of Loyalist or late Georgian architecture, has been restored and furnished in its period. A costumed staff works at the crafts of the mid–nineteenth century. Open throughout the year. Admission charge.

Osgoode Hall, Queen Street, West, next to the New City Hall, is a large neoclassical mansion, built in the early nineteenth century. The Law Society of Upper Canada has been housed here since 1830. Osgoode Hall is the finest example of historical architecture in Toronto. It is enclosed by a wrought-iron fence with special gates designed to keep cows from entering the grounds. There are no official visiting hours, but you may be permitted to see some of the interior. The Great Library on the second floor is the prize jewel of the building.

Campbell House, 160 Queen Street, West, a fine brick mansion, was the home of William Campbell, chief justice of Upper Canada from 1825 to 1829. It has period furnishings and features a model of the town of York as it was in 1825. Open throughout the year. Admission charge.

The SkyDome, located adjacent to the CN Tower, is Toronto's spectacular venue for sports and entertainment. The SkyDome is the home for the Toronto Bluejays baseball team (American League), the Argonauts football team (Canadian Football League), and a variety of other sporting and entertainment events. The SkyDome features a retractable roof that can open or close in just twenty minutes, providing ideal climate conditions for players and spectators. It also has a gourmet restaurant, the "world's longest cocktail bar," and many other amenities.

Harbourfront Centre, a unique indoor-outdoor recreational and entertainment complex, is located on the shore of Lake Ontario. It includes Queen's Quay Terminal (an extensive shopping complex), an antiques market, a railway museum, a Sunday flea market, art galleries, craft shops, hotels, restaurants, playgrounds for children, cinema, and plenty of beautiful space for walking, enjoying the waterfront, dancing, and listening to concerts—all in downtown Toronto. Ferries for the Toronto Islands leave from near here.

Toronto Stock Exchange, 2 First Canadian Place, is the largest stock exchange in Canada. The TSE offers free tours and an audiovisual presentation of how it operates. Free.

Spadina House, 285 Spadina Road, is the fine estate of James Austin, a leading Toronto "money man." Tours through this impressive mansion and its beautiful grounds are available. Call (416) 392–6910, or visit www.torontohistory.on.ca. Admission charge.

Museum of the History of Medicine, 277 Bloor Street, has exhibits describing centuries of medical research and health care. Free.

Redpath Sugar Museum, 95 Queen's Quay, shows how sugar is refined and tells about the industry in Canada. Redpath family history is also shown. Free.

Air Canada Centre, 40 Bay Street, is the home of the Toronto Maple Leafs (hockey) and the Toronto Raptors (basketball), as well as host to major concerts, shows, and other events. Call (416) 815–5500 for schedule of events.

The Towers of Mammon

The Royal Bank Plaza, corner of Front and Bay Streets, is probably one of the most beautiful and extravagant modern buildings in North America. Its serrated glass walls are embedded with hundreds of thousands of dollars' worth of gold dust, and its atrium contains a waterfall, trees, plants, flowers, and an unusual hanging sculpture consisting of nearly 9,000 aluminum tubes.

The Toronto Dominion Centre, with handsome black shafts designed by Ludwig Mies van der Rohe, is nearby. The Toronto Dominion Bank Tower features art exhibitions and a gourmet restaurant on the fifty-fourth floor.

First Canadian Place, also nearby, has seventy-two stories and is the tallest office structure in the city.

All these complexes are part of the underground city and financial district of enclosed walkways replete with shops and restaurants.

Just Outside Toronto

Metro Toronto Zoo, 25 miles (40 km) northeast of downtown, via Highway 401 (and accessible by subway and bus), is an exceptional zoo and ranks with the best in the world. It is unique in that it re-creates in six zoogeographic regions the natural environment, including plants, soil, and climate, of the animals on display. Here you can see Siberian tigers, orangutans, gorillas, polar bears, and more. The Metro Zoo occupies a 710-acre site, displaying some 5,000 mammals, birds, reptiles, amphibians, and fish. The attractive pavilions that house the various zoogeographic regions are also equipped with audiovisual aids to enhance your visit. An elevated monorail train takes you through natural areas where magnificent wolves and other large North American animals make their homes. During the winter visitors are encouraged to tour the zoo on crosscountry skis (rentals are available). Open throughout the year. Admission charge. Call (416) 392–5900.

Ontario Science Centre, Don Mills Road at Eglinton Avenue, East (accessible by subway and bus), is considered one of the foremost museums of science and technology in the world. Designed by Raymond Moriyama, the facility is built on the top, side, and bottom of a steep ravine, and you take special escalators up and down the different levels. This unique museum features nearly 600 exhibits, many of which can be operated by visitors (touch 500,000 volts of electricity and have your hair stand on end). Museum displays explore space, earth, biology, communications, transportation, industry, and chemistry. Everyone in the family will enjoy the Ontario Science Centre and will learn a great deal as well. There are a restaurant and gift shop. Open throughout the year. Admission charge. Call (416) 696–3127.

McMichael Collection of Canadian Art, located in Kleinburg, 25 miles (40 km) north of downtown, is a beautiful museum, built from hand-hewn timbers and native stone, set in a 600-acre park overlooking a lovely river valley. Some of the gallery rooms focus on the works of Canada's immortal "Group of Seven" painters: Tom Thomson (the founder of the group and its most famous member), A. Y. Jackson, J. E. H. MacDonald, Lawren Harris, Arthur Lismer, Frederick Varley, Franklin Carmichael, A. J. Casson, Frank H. Johnston, Edwin Holate, and Lionel Lemoine Fitzgerald. The museum also has Clarence Gagnon's paintings for the famous book *Maria Chapdelaine*, depicting early Québec rural life, and a large collection of original Inuit prints and carvings and Canadian Indian paintings. Tom Thomson's painting shack and the graves of several Group of Seven painters are on the premises. Special exhibitions are held throughout the year. This museum has a restaurant and a shop offering works of Canadian artisans for sale. Open throughout the year. Admission charge. Call (905) 893–2588.

Paramount Canada's Wonderland, located between Rutherford Road and Major MacKenzie Drive on Highway 400, 20 miles (32 km) north of downtown, is a 320-acre theme park. It features the Hanna-Barbera cartoon characters (Yogi Bear and his pals), a storybook mountain whose cascading waterfall is the central point in the park, the Crystal Palace, a medieval fair, an international street of shops and bazaars, and many exciting rides, including eight roller coasters. There are all kinds of restaurants, including several selling ethnic foods, and much, much more. Paramount Canada's Wonderland is similar in quality to the large and very popular theme parks (such as Disneyland) in the United States. Open late May to early September. Admission charge. Call (905) 832–7000.

Parkwood, 270 Simcoe Street in Oshawa, is the fifty-five-room grand mansion of the late Colonel R. S. McLaughlin, founder of General Motors of Canada. This beautiful estate has an art gallery, tea house, gardens, and a main house filled with many beautiful antiques. Admission charge. Call (905) 433–4311.

Hamilton

When you are traveling between Niagara Falls and Toronto via the Queen Elizabeth Way, consider stopping midway in the large industrial city of Hamilton to visit these major attractions:

African Lion Safari and Game Farm, Highways 8 and 52, 11 miles (18 km) northwest of Hamilton, allows you to drive your car through the domains of lions, cheetahs, and other African and North American animals that roam freely. A monkey jungle is home to a hundred African baboons. Open May through October. Admission charge.

Canadian Football Hall of Fame, City Hall Plaza, depicts the history of Canadian professional football over the past century. Open throughout the year. Admission charge.

Dundurn Castle, Dundurn Park, York Boulevard, is a splendid nineteenth-century mansion built by Sir Allan Napier MacNab, prime minister of the Province of Canada (1854–56). This thirty-six-room mansion, one of the finest in all of Canada, is furnished with period antiques, and the gardens and grounds are especially lovely. Open throughout the year. Admission charge.

Royal Botanical Gardens, via Highways 2 and 6, located at the westernmost tip of Lake Ontario, consists of some 2,000 acres of gardens and nature walks and a 400-acre arboretum. Visitors are encouraged to relax at the Tea House, overlooking beautiful scenery, and to hike the shoreline of Coote's Paradise Marsh and the trails along the wooded ravine lands. Open throughout the year. Free.

Recreational Sports

Toronto is well supplied with opportunities for sports at any time of the year. In the winter you can rent skates to circle the 75,000 square feet of ice at **RINX** on Orfus Road, (416) 783–6492. You can go ice fishing on Lake Simcoe with **Canadian Trophy Fishing,** (416) 663–3994 or www.cdntrophyfishing.com, or in the summer, take a half-day, full-day, or evening fishing trip.

Golfers can head in almost any direction and find greens. **Deer Creek Golf,** only thirty-five minutes away in Ajax, has forty-five premium holes of public golf, (905) 427–7737 or www. golfdeercreek.com. **Glen Abbey Golf Club** in Oakville is a Jack Nicklaus– designed course with an excellent clubhouse dining room, (905) 844–1800 or www.clublink.ca.

Toronto's parks and waterfront have miles of paths for walking, running, and cycling. The park at **Toronto Islands** has a swimming beach and plenty of other outdoor fun facilities. **Kawartha Kayaking** will take you on one-day trips among the islands of Stony Lake, (877) 877–2735, or www.web-xpress.net/kawarthakayaking.

Professional Sports

The Toronto Blue Jays play baseball at the SkyDome, adjacent to CN Tower in downtown. The sensational Blue Jays, two-time winners of the World Series, offer baseball fans the chance to see them as well as the Yankees, the Red Sox, and other American League teams play in Toronto. Call (416) 341–1111 for ticket and schedule information.

The Argonauts are fierce competitors in the Canadian Football League. They also play their home games at the SkyDome. Call (416) 870–8000 for ticket information.

The Toronto Maple Leafs, of the National Hockey League, have won the coveted Stanley Cup eleven times, which makes them one of the best teams in professional hockey history, though their record in recent years has not been up to their previous excellence. At any rate, tickets for home games sell out fast. The

Maple Leafs play at the Air Canada Centre, 40 Bay Street. Call (416) 815–5500 for information.

Horse races take place at the Woodbine Race Track, Rexdale Boulevard, at Highway 427. The Queen's Plate, Canada's most prestigious Thoroughbred race, is held here in June. Call (416) 675–3993 for the schedule.

Accommodations

Toronto has a wide assortment of hotels and motels, both in the central city and in outlying areas. The Royal York has been a top Toronto hotel for decades, and sumptuous, full-service new hotels, such as the Sheraton Centre, Four Seasons Toronto, Harbour Castle Westin, Crowne Plaza, and King Edward Hotel offer the sophisticated traveler deluxe comfort and first-rate conveniences. There are also plenty of moderately priced accommodations for those with more limited budgets. And U.S. and other foreign visitors can get good value because of the favorable exchange rate. In addition, many of the better hotels offer special weekend packages that give you splendid accommodations at about half the cost of the weekday rate, city tours, and other goodies. If you're traveling with children, ask whether they can stay in your room for free. Commercial travelers and senior citizens should also inquire about special rates. Most major credit cards are accepted in hotels and motels, but inquire about yours ahead of time. Save yourself a lot of time and trouble by having your travel agent do the bookings for you. Because Toronto is busy throughout the year, advance reservations are highly recommended.

Four Seasons Toronto, 21 Avenue Road, (416) 964–0411, offers excellent accommodations and services. The Four Seasons is Toronto's best hotel and has been consistently so through the years. Located in the chic Bloor-Yorkville area, with its vast array of smart shops and restaurants, and within walking distance of the Royal Ontario Museum and the stunning Metropolitan Toronto Library, the hotel features a swimming pool, health facilities, restaurants, and lounges. Truffles is its elegant, gourmet dining room, and La Serre is a relaxing place for cocktails and entertainment. Expensive.

The Sheraton Centre, 123 Queen Street, West, (416) 361–1000, has one of the best downtown locations: It's across the street from New City Hall, on top of the extensive underground city of shops and restaurants, and within a few steps of the fabulous Eaton Centre. It features its own inner park with a waterfall that flows into the lobby; a swimming pool with a South Seas motif; a health club; several restaurants; and an authentic English pub, Good Queen Bess, that was shipped over, lock, stock, and Watney's from the mother country. The Sheraton Centre, a favorite hotel for conventions, has adequate space for even the largest meetings. Expensive.

King Edward Hotel, 37 King Street, East, (416) 863–9700, fully restored to its former glittering magnificence, specializes in European-style service, the finest cuisine, and opulent decor. Among its features are twenty-four-hour room service, secretarial services, a whirlpool, and a sauna. Expensive.

Renaissance Toronto Hotel at SkyDome, 1 Blue Jays Way, (416) 360–7100, is located in the spectacular SkyDome complex and includes seventy stadium-view rooms. Expensive.

Marriott Eaton Centre, 525 Bay Street, (416) 597–9200, has luxurious accommodations, with an indoor pool and health club, concierge floor, and family-style restaurant. This seventeen-story hotel overlooks the seventeenth-century Trinity Church and is adjacent to Eaton Centre, a galleria with 340 shops and seventeen movie theaters. Moderate to expensive.

Westin Harbour Castle, 1 Harbour Square, (416) 869–1600, set right on the edge of the waterfront and overlooking Lake Ontario and the harbor islands, offers first-class accommodations and service for the sophisticated traveler. It also is a favorite with businesspeople and conventions. An elegant restaurant, The Lighthouse, sits atop the building, slowly revolving and providing magnificent vistas of the city skyline and of the lake; the restaurant's Sunday brunch offers a wide assortment of foods at a reasonable price. The hotel also features a swimming pool, health club, boutiques, and many other conveniences. Expensive.

The Royal York, 100 Front Street, West, (416) 368–2511, the "grande dame" of Toronto's hotels, has been an integral part of the city since 1929. Across the street from Union Station and in the heart of the financial district, the recently renovated Royal York is popular with travelers and businesspeople. Among its outstanding restaurants is the Acadian Room, which features fine cuisine. The Royal York is connected to the shops and attractions of the underground city. Expensive.

Sutton Place, 955 Bay Street, (416) 924–9221, offers large rooms and outstanding personal service. Fine restaurants, swimming pool, health club, and sauna are some of its conveniences. Expensive.

Hyatt Toronto, 4 Avenue Road, (416) 924–5471, is a favorite hotel with top entertainers and executives, stressing personal service and high quality. Recently renovated, the hotel has a spa and swimming pool. Expensive.

Bradgate Arms, 54 Foxbar Road, in the St. Clair area, (416) 968–1331, is a small, elegant hotel. It's favored by those who want a pleasant urban refuge that's a bit removed from the frenetic pace of the city center. The hotel's restaurant is superior for its continental cuisine and fine service. The Bradgate has a lovely atrium, a library with comfortable leather chairs, and a lounge. There's a nice little park in front. Moderate.

Crowne Plaza, Front Street (next to the Convention Centre), (416) 597–1400, is a deluxe hotel offering all the amenities, plus a convenient downtown location to all attractions and shops. Expensive.

Other Fine Accommodations

Delta Chelsea Inn, 33 Gerrard Street, West, (416) 595–1975, located in downtown Toronto, offers good value for your money in accommodations and conveniences, such as a swimming pool, restaurants, lounges, a health club, and game rooms. Some rooms have balconies. Ideal for families. Moderate.

Marriott Bloor-Yorkville, 90 Bloor Street, East, (416) 961–8000, is built around a courtyard planted with trees, grass, and flowers—a delightful place, especially in the winter. A swimming pool, health club, and sauna are available to guests at the Bloor Park Club, which is in the building. Moderate.

Toronto Colony Hotel, 89 Chestnut Street, (416) 977–0707, provides several restaurants and lounges, as well as swimming pools, sauna, game rooms, sun terrace. Moderate.

Best Western Primrose, 111 Carlton Street, (416) 977–8000, has a swimming pool and saunas. Moderate to expensive.

Venture Inn/Toronto Yorkville, 89 Avenue Road, (416) 964–1220, a hotel from an up-and-coming Canadian chain, is located in the middle of chic Toronto. Moderate.

Couryard by Marriott–Downtown Toronto, 475 Yonge Street, (416) 924–0611, provides newly renovated accommodations in a centrally located hotel. Coffee shop. Moderate.

Comfort Hotel Downtown, 15 Charles Street, East, (416) 924–1222. This European-style hotel in a strategic downtown location near Eaton Centre and Bloor Street provides many guest amenities, including free shoeshine service and morning paper. It has a good restaurant and cocktail lounge. Moderate.

Day's Inn Downtown Toronto, 30 Carlton Street, (416) 977–6655, has comfortable rooms with small refrigerators, a swimming pool, a sauna, and a sports bar. Moderate.

Clarion Essex Park Hotel, 300 Jarvis Street, (416) 977–4823, offers nicely refurbished rooms in an older hotel, near downtown attractions and shopping. It has a restaurant and lounge. Moderate.

Airport Area Accommodations

Wyndham Bristol Place, 950 Dixon Road, (416) 675–9444, is a super luxurious hotel, well regarded for its high level of personal service. It features gourmet restaurants and lounges, swimming pools, a health club, and saunas. Moderate to expensive.

Regal Constellation Hotel, 900 Dixon Road, (416) 675–1500, features comfortable accommodations and fine dining, with a swimming pool, indoor tennis, health club, and game room. Moderate to expensive.

Days Inn, 6257 Airport Road, (905) 678–1400, has comfortable rooms and a good restaurant, with a swimming pool in the garden area. Moderate to expensive.

International Plaza Hotel, 655 Dixon Road, (416) 244–1711, offers modern accommodations and full hotel services at reasonable prices. Moderate.

Dining

In the not-too-distant past, Torontonians with a craving for truly fine haute cuisine had to travel all the way to Montréal. Although Montréal still cannot be topped for French-inspired haute cuisine, its reputation for gastronomic superiority is being challenged by Toronto. And for variety of restaurants (more than 5,000), no city in Canada can top Toronto, not even Montréal.

Toronto offers you elegant and expensive restaurants, ethnic restaurants representing the national cuisines of almost every country on earth, novelty restaurants, and every kind of low-cost, fastfood place ever invented. Toronto, a voracious consumer of all kinds of goods and services, attracts the best products from all of Canada's regions. Canadian western beef, for example, is considered by connoisseurs to be the finest in North America.

Dining habits in Toronto are similar to those in major cities throughout the continent. There is no essential difference between the business luncheon in Toronto and the one in New York City. The evening meal at a restaurant usually begins any time after 7:00 P.M., and while leisurely, it is not necessarily the lengthy ritual that it can become in Montréal (Torontonians usually want to get on with other activities). Both men and women should dress well for dining in the better restaurants; Toronto is a highly fashion-conscious city. On the other hand, there are many excellent eateries that welcome you as you are—sometimes the more outrageous and eclectic, the better.

Toronto is a very active restaurant town throughout the year. Advance reservations are recommended for the better and more popular spots. Most restaurants accept major credit cards.

Liquor is served in lounges and most restaurants from noon to 1:00 A.M. The legal drinking age in Ontario is nineteen years old.

The following is a listing of recommended restaurants in Toronto:

Barberian's, 7 Elm Street, near Eaton Centre, (416) 597–0335. The steak is so tender that it just about melts in your mouth, and all the fixings are delicious and generous. First-time visitors are made to feel like regulars, and the service is good. Expensive.

Csarda, 45 Elm, (416) 971–8843. Hearty traditional Hungarian fare eaten to the sound of Gypsy violins. Live music can be heard on Friday and Saturday nights. Moderate.

Barmalay, 505 Mount Pleasant, (416) 480–0048, specializes in Russian food, songs, and a warm and welcoming atmosphere. Tea is served from a samovar, in a restaurant that looks like an old Russian country inn. Dinner is served nightly, and there is always live music. Moderate.

Scaramouche, 1 Benvenuto Place, at Avenue and St. Clair, (416) 961–8011, is a popular gourmet restaurant hidden away in the basement of an apartment building. Amusing eclectic decor and a menu of unusual dishes, the creations of chefs who combine flair with taste. Expensive.

Lobster Trap, 1962 Avenue Road, (416) 787–3211. Here you pick the live lobster you want, and the chef will cook it the way you want. Considering the price of lobster, the tab for what you get is fair and a better buy than at most top restaurants. Celebrities frequent the Lobster Trap, and you may get to snap open lobster claws near one. Moderate to expensive.

Sassafraz, 100 Cumberland Street, (416) 964–2222. During the summer there is an outdoor cafe. Pretty setting, movie-star sightings. Moderate.

Le Select Bistro, 328 Queen Street, West, (416) 596–6405. French bistro fare, very cozy, excellent food. Moderate.

Mövenpick of Switzerland, 165 York Street, (416) 366–5234; and 133 Yorkville near Avenue Road, (416) 926–9545. The European food served at these restaurants is as fresh as the air of the Alpine mountains. Each location has several eateries under one roof, with different price levels. Two new eateries, marketed under the name Marché (market) have been added to the chain in recent years. Mövenpick also has several bistros throughout the city. Inexpensive to expensive.

Le Trou Normand, 90 Yorkville Avenue, (416) 967–5956. The fashionable Yorkville section of Toronto is where you can dine on Normandy-style cooking, such as *lapin* (rabbit). It's a nice change from the usual *cuisine de Française*. Expensive.

Club Windows at the SkyDome, 1 Blue Jays Way, (416) 341–2424. Baseball buffs love this place because they can see right over the entire field. Even those who are not particularly into sports will enjoy this giant eatery's unique ambience and the modestly priced but tasty international cuisine. Moderate.

Canoe Restaurant & Bar, situated on the fifty-fourth floor of the TD Bank Tower (66 Wellington Street West, 416–364–0054), in the heart of the financial district, this has become one of *the* places to eat in Toronto. It attracts wheeler-dealers of all stripes and those who want to be seen in high places (literally). Spectacular views over the city. As its name suggests, it specializes in regional Canadian cuisine, such as roast caribou from the Yukon and flavorful Ontario pheasant. Expensive.

Ginsberg and Wong, 71 McCaul Street, is within the Village by the Grange, (416) 979–3436. Here you can order a pastrami on rye with an egg roll on the side; or matzoh balls with lobster sauce. Ginsberg and Wong serves up the best of two worlds exceedingly well for not much money. Inexpensive.

Pearl Harbourfront Restaurant, 207 Queen's Quay, (416) 203–1233, is a cut above the usual Chinese restaurant; the word *elegant* is not inappropriate here. There is a much more interesting (exotic) selection of culinary concoctions. An ideal choice if you want an "upscale" Asian dining treat. Moderate to expensive.

Florentine Court, 97 Church Street, (416) 364–3687. When the folks at Florentine Court say, *"Mangia!"* (Eat!), they mean dig into a magnificent seven-course Italian feast—everything from salami to sweets. If you leave hungry, it's your fault. Moderate.

Blue Bay, 2243 Dundas Street, West, (416) 533–8838. Like its home country, this casual Mauritian restaurant blends Asian, African, and French flavors and ingredients. Seafood and vegetarian dishes top the menu and you'll have trouble spending $50 here on a dinner for two. Inexpensive.

Bombay Palace, 71 Jarvis, (416) 368–8048. Tandoori, curry, and kebab are specialties of this attractive Indian restaurant, one of three in the city and the best of its kind. Moderate.

Chiado, 864 College Street, (416) 538–1910. As you might have guessed by the name, this place is Portuguese through and through, and as in Portugal, you'll find the freshest of fish that is never overcooked. Look also for baccalau, smoked sausages, and sardines as good as any you'll find in the Alfama. The wine list is splendid, and you can finish off with a rare Madeira. Moderate.

Shopsy's Delicatessen Restaurant, 33 Yonge Street, (416) 365–3333. It's old and well known for its breakfasts and deli. Inexpensive.

Bistro 990, 990 Bay Street, (416) 921–9990, comes by its name honestly. The restaurant is remarkably like a French Provençal eatery. The ambience is warm, cozy, and intimate. A favorite hangout with Toronto's glitterati, this trendy spot serves marvelous seafood and, of course, the best French cuisine. A wide selection of good wines by the bottle or by the glass. Expensive.

Fred's Not Here/The Red Tomato, 321 King Street West, (416) 971–9155. Fred's Not Here is an upstairs dining room. The Red Tomato is a downstairs bar and restaurant heavy on appetizers. Great food. Moderate.

Happy Palace, 436 Dundas Street, West, (416) 598–2222. Walk upstairs to this no-nonsense old-fashioned Canton dining room. Enjoy your soup (no charge), then continue with stir-fried beef or sweet-and-sour pork chops. Inexpensive.

Jacques' Bistro du Parc, 126A Cumberland Street, (416) 961–1893. Jacques', a pretty place in colorful Yorkville, can give you a choice from close to twenty different omelettes, and there are also quiches, sandwiches, salads, and many other good things to eat. Inexpensive to moderate.

Sai Woo, 130 Dundas, West, (416) 977–4988. Situated in the heart of what used to be Toronto's biggest Chinatown (the city now has several), this large, no-frills restaurant has been serving banquet-size Cantonese meals for more than forty years. Inexpensive.

The Keg, 515 Jarvis Street (at Wellesley Street), (416) 964–6609, offers good roast beef, steak, and seafood and a salad bar. The restaurant is in the former home of Vincent and

Raymond Massey (King George V and Queen Mary stayed here). Inexpensive to moderate.

Ouzeri, 500A Danforth Avenue, (416) 778–0500, is a trendy Greek restaurant with a generous and varied wine selection. Lively atmosphere. Moderate.

The Sultan's Tent, 1280 Bay Street, (416) 961–0601, offers Moroccan cuisine and ambience. Inexpensive to moderate.

Entertainment

Toronto has evolved into the entertainment capital of Canada. Today Toronto is second only to New York City in the performing arts: live theater, ballet, symphony, and opera. Toronto was the home of such great stars as Mary Pickford, Raymond Massey, and Lorne Greene. Many of today's top entertainers with Canadian roots, such as Donald Sutherland and Christopher Plummer, began their careers in Toronto.

There is some live theatrical or musical event being performed in Toronto almost every night of the week throughout the year; most often there are several excellent choices for an evening's entertainment. The larger hotels have services that provide information on current entertainment and assist you in getting tickets.

The following is a listing of performing arts centers, theaters, dinner theaters, cabarets, and discotheques in downtown Toronto:

The Hummingbird Centre for the Performing Arts, Front Street East at Yonge Street, (416) 872–2262, is home for the outstanding National Ballet of Canada and the Canadian Opera Company. It also presents a wide variety of popular dramatic and musical performances. Concerts by the National Ballet are especially recommended, as this troupe ranks among the top ballet companies in the world.

Royal Alexandra Theatre, 260 King Street West (416) 872–1212, is the grande dame of live theater houses in Canada. Here you can see the most popular Broadway and London dramas and musicals with the world's leading entertainers.

St. Lawrence Centre, 27 Front Street East (416) 366–7723, presents performances by a resident repertory company and by visiting theater, opera, and dance companies.

The Roy Thomson Hall, 60 Simcoe Street, (416) 593–4255, is home for the Toronto Symphony Orchestra and the Mendelssohn Choir, also a venue for concerts by other groups and individuals.

The magnificent 100,000-square-foot (9,293 sq m) hall, designed by Arthur Erickson, features a sunken courtyard and an auditorium that can seat 2,800 people. Its unusual curvilinear shape is covered with reflective glass, which shimmers in daylight and becomes transparent in the evening as the interior lights shine through. The Roy Thomson Hall gives Toronto one of the foremost concert facilities in the world.

Princess of Wales Theatre, 300 King Street, West, (416) 593–4142 or (800) 724–6420, www.onstagenow.com, hosts musicals and other live theater.

Leah Posluns Theatre, 4588 Bathurst Street, (416) 630–1880, shows innovative, avant-garde works in a modern facility.

Factory Theatre, 125 Bathurst Street, (416) 864–9971, stages contemporary Canadian plays.

Pantages Theatre, 244 Victoria Street, (416) 324–5800 or (800) 249–6999, www.livent.com, presents live performances. This theater made its name with *Phantom of the Opera,* which played here for years.

Theatre Passe Muraille, 16 Ryerson Avenue, (416) 504–PLAY, has been staging avant-garde Canadian works since 1968.

The Bluma Appel Theatre and the Jane Mallett Theatre, in the St. Lawrence Centre for the Performing Arts, 27 Front Street East, (416) 368–3110, are the sites for exciting plays, concerts, dance performances, and film screenings.

Toronto Truck Theatre, 94 Belmont Street, (416) 922–0084, puts on Agatha Christie's *The Mousetrap.*

Ukrainian Caravan Restaurant Cabaret, 5245 Dundas Street, West, (416) 231–7447, features Cossack dances, songs, comedy, and food.

Second City Comedy Theatre, 56 Blue Jays Way, (416) 343–0011, is highly recommended for zany humor. Dan Aykroyd and the late John Candy got started here.

Limelight Dinner Theatre, 2026 Yonge Street, (416) 482–5200, presents food and Broadway musicals.

Yuk Yuk's, 1280 Bay Street, (416) 967–6425, features stand-up comics. See new talent before they become hot.

Bamboo, 312 Queen Street, West, (416) 593–5771, is the place for Latin, reggae, and world beat music.

El Mocambo, 464 Spadina Avenue, (416) 928–3566, is one of Canada's top spots for rock music.

Shopping

Toronto is a shopper's mecca. There are enough attractive stores here to loosen your grip on your purse or wallet. The best way to deal with the temptations of Toronto's stores is to bring a few extra dollars and splurge on something unusual and extravagant. It's better to do this than to fill your bags with a lot of souvenir junk.

One of the best treats of being in Toronto, however, is vicarious shopping, poking in and out of the splendid stores and retailing areas. Here are some of the best:

Eaton Centre, 220 Yonge Street, has to be one of the most spectacular enclosed central-city shopping complexes in North America. It features a multilevel glass-ceiling Galleria containing fountains, trees, gardens, benches, and even live birds. The Galleria's southern end connects with the Bay, a large department store. The Eaton Centre is another way in which Toronto shows us how uplifting a modern city can be.

Kensington Market, Dundas Street West to College Street, Spadina Avenue to Augusta Street, is a fascinating area of stores selling every imaginable ethnic food. Poles, Greeks, Italians, Jews, Portuguese, Jamaicans, Germans, and others come here to purchase those essential ingredients to make their national foods. Kensington Market is colorful, fragrant, and raucous; it's the crossroads of the world in Toronto. The best time to visit Kensington Market is Friday afternoon and evening and Saturday morning. There are several good restaurants and delicatessens in the area.

Village of Yorkville, between Yonge Street and Avenue Road north of Bloor Street West, was once a run-down albeit architecturally interesting section of private residences. During the 1960s it became Canada's version of Greenwich Village. Architects, designers, and builders who saw the potential in Yorkville restored the beauty of the buildings and gave them new life as fine boutiques, art and craft galleries, and restaurants.

Also in the Yorkville area is Hazelton Lanes, 55 Avenue Road, a large and attractive shopping complex of fifty-five stores

and restaurants. At 2 Bloor Street is the Hudson Bay Centre, another huge complex consisting of the Hudson Bay Company, sixty shops, ten restaurants, and the Hotel Plaza II.

Chinatown, on Dundas Street West, at Elizabeth Street, behind New City Hall, and Spadina Avenue, is packed with Chinese restaurants, grocery stores, and curio shops. It's right in the center of the city and an exotic place in which to stroll anytime. Chinatown continues to grow and now extends west beyond Spadina.

Toronto Underground is a system of walkways and shopping complexes in the heart of Toronto. This underground system, attractive and safe, interconnects the Sheraton Centre, Eaton Centre, Richmond Adelaide Centre, First Canadian Place, Toronto Dominion Centre, Commerce Court, Royal Bank Plaza, Royal York Hotel, and Union Station. Within these walkways are countless shops, restaurants, and other conveniences. The subway system, with stations at Queen Street, King Street, Union, Saint Andrew's, and Osgoode, provides access to the shopping complexes in the Bloor Street area, Parliament buildings, the University of Toronto, and the Royal Ontario Museum. The beauty of this underground network is that it separates people from traffic and weather and gives them easy access to important places in the city in the most pleasant possible environment.

Village by the Grange, McCaul Street at Dundas West, is an old-world-style shopping and dining complex. Some one hundred stores and restaurants line cobblestone streets, and the atmosphere is human-scale and very comfortable.

Saint Lawrence Market, 95 Front Street East, established in 1844, has many food stalls selling meat, fish, cheese, fruits, vegetables, and many other goodies in a noisy atmosphere where loud yelling and hard bargaining go together. Open Tuesday to Saturday. On Saturday farmers sell their goods at the Farmers' Market across the street.

CHAPTER 4

Ottawa

Ottawa, Canada's national capital, spreads out along the south bank of the historic Ottawa River. The majestic neo-Gothic buildings of Parliament seem more European than North American. Their towers and spires dominate the city and give it a romantic feel.

The city is part of a capital region that also includes the city of Hull, Québec, across the Ottawa River, and a number of surrounding towns in both Ontario and Québec. Hull is an integral part of the federal district, having a number of major federal government offices, the extraordinary Canadian Museum of Civilization, and nearby Gatineau Park. When you take into account all the towns and cities in this quasi-independent area, the population is just over one million.

The main businesses of Ottawa are government and high technology; tourism ranks third. The offices of most federal agencies and departments are here. The embassies of most foreign countries and their resident nationals help to make Ottawa a cosmopolitan city. Ottawa has become one of Canada's centers for high-technology research and development, a fast-growing one at that, earning it the nickname Silicon Valley North. Many high-tech laboratories and companies are situated within the metropolitan area, with new enterprises sprouting up like tulips in spring.

A Brief History

Samuel de Champlain paddled by the bluffs of Ottawa in 1613, and his log described Chaudière Falls and the surrounding countryside for future explorers. During the old French regime, the

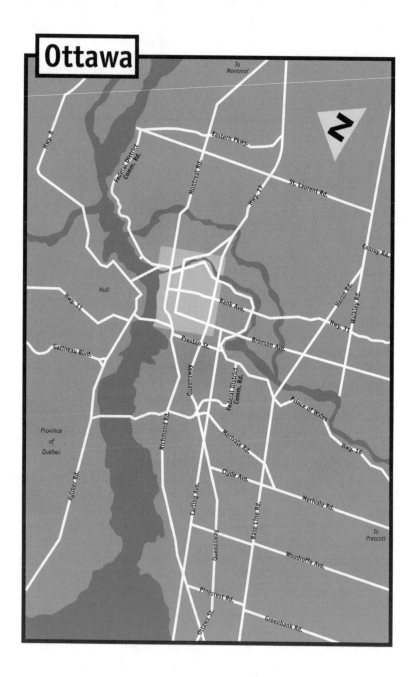

Ottawa River was part of the main fur-trading route that extended beyond the Great Lakes and across Canada. However, not until after the American War of Independence was any permanent settlement attempted here by whites. Philemon Wright, a Loyalist from Massachusetts, established a lumber mill on the Hull side of the river in 1800, and not much later Nicholas Sparks settled himself on the Ottawa side in lieu of pay from Wright.

From Wright's settlement to 1826 Ottawa was primarily a backwoods lumbering operation, populated by rugged woodchoppers. In 1826, fearing American attack from the New York side of the Saint Lawrence River and needing a safe alternative water route between Montréal and Toronto, the British began construction of the Rideau Canal system, 124 miles (198 km) from Kingston to Ottawa. Colonel By, of the Royal Engineers, completed the project on schedule. Never used in war, it became a major transportation route for lumber, agricultural products, and other supplies. Today it is a popular recreational boating area and, in winter, the "world's longest skating rink."

Ottawa was plucked from obscurity by Queen Victoria in 1857, when she selected it as the permanent capital of the United Provinces of Upper and Lower Canada. Earlier the capital had shifted between Kingston, Toronto, Montréal, and Québec City, and there was constant bickering over just where the capital should be set. Ottawa was an entirely new site—that is, nonpolitical in contrast to the others—and it was located on the edge between Upper Canada (Ontario) and Lower Canada (Québec).

In 1860 the Prince of Wales (later Edward VII) laid the cornerstone of the Parliament buildings, holding the first meeting in 1865. In 1867 Ottawa became the capital of the new Dominion of Canada, with the confederation of the provinces, a role that it has played since that time.

How to Get to Ottawa

By Car
The fast track from Montréal to Ottawa is the Trans-Canada Highway, Highway 40 to Highway 417, a distance of 127 miles (203 km). If you're traveling in the Laurentians, you can dip down to Ottawa via Highway 105, off Highway 117. From Toronto, take Highway 401 northeast to Highway 16, then go north, a distance of 249 miles (399 km). You can also go along Lake Ontario and the Saint Lawrence River via Highway 401 to Highway 416 or 31.

By Air

Air Canada has daily flights to and from Ottawa direct from New York, Washington, Boston, and Chicago.

There are taxis, limousines, and bus service from the airport to downtown locations. The terminal, expanded and modernized, is about a fifteen-minute drive from city center.

Rental cars are available from Tilden, Avis, Budget, and Hertz.

By Rail

VIA Rail provides frequent daily service from Montréal and Toronto. The trains stop at a modern station at the southeastern end of Ottawa, at 2000 Tremblay Road. Call (613) 244–8289 for rail-travel information. Taxis are available for the trip downtown.

By Bus

Bus service, provided by Voyageur Lines, (613) 238–5900, offers hourly service from Montréal and frequent service from Toronto, including express.

General Information

Time zone: Eastern
Telephone area codes: 613 in Ontario; 819 in Québec
Police and medical emergencies: dial 911
Weather information: (613) 998–3439

Tourist Information

Brochures and maps are available free at Capital Infocentre, 90 Wellington Street (across from Parliament Hill), (613) 239–5000. You can also call Province of Ontario information toll-free at (800) 668–2746 from the United States or Ottawa information in Canada at (800) 465–1867. For convention and travel-trade information, contact the Ottawa Tourism and Convention Authority, 130 Albert Street, Suite 1800, Ottawa, Ontario K1P 5G4 (613) 237–5150 or (800) 363–4465.

For information on Hull, Québec, call the Association Touristique l'Outaouais at (819) 778–2222 or (800) 265–7822.

How to Get Around Ottawa

Tour buses offer tours and shuttle bus services, making stops at attractions, and taking visitors around Ottawa's core area on Confederation Boulevard and around Sussex Drive to the National Aviation Museum. Shuttle buses have information officers on board to assist visitors. They operate from June to Labour Day and on a limited schedule until November 15.

The Central Area

Downtown Ottawa, containing most of the major attractions, is a relatively small area and compact enough so you can see almost everything on foot.

The buildings of Parliament are your central landmark. The tall Peace Tower can be seen easily from most parts of the city. Behind Parliament are the Ottawa River, Hull, Québec, and the Gatineau Hills. Wellington Street runs in front of the Parliament. The Rideau Canal bisects the city between the Parliament area and the Chateau Laurier. Elgin Street runs nearly parallel with the Rideau Canal and is perpendicular to Wellington Street. These streets converge at the National War Memorial. Sparks Street is parallel with Wellington and joins Elgin in the vicinity of the National War Memorial and the National Arts Centre.

To the northeast is Sussex Drive, which leads to Hull via the Alexandria and Macdonald Bridges. Sussex also takes you to the Canadian War Museum, Royal Canadian Mint, Ottawa City Hall, Rideau Hall, Rideau Falls, and the exclusive Rockcliffe area.

Guided Tours and Cruises

Guided tours of attractions in the city and outlying areas are provided by Gray Line, (613) 725–1441, which picks up passengers at major hotels, and by Capital Double Decker & Trolley Tours, (613) 749–3666, which uses London-style double-deckers. Paul's Boats Lines, (613) 225–6781, and Ottawa Riverboat, (613) 562–4888, offer sightseeing cruises along both the Ottawa River and the Rideau Canal. There are also many taxis and limousines in the city that can be hired for touring.

To find the unique pleasures of this often overlooked city, we suggest you get a copy of "Secret Ottawa" by Laura Byrne Paquet. It is fun to read and will take you to places you'd never find without it, such as ethnic restaurants, a haunted walk, rooftop terraces, and virtually unknown museums and specialty shops.

Center of Ottawa

Wellington St.
Sparks St.
Queen St.
Albert St.
Slater St.
Laurier St.
Hwy. 17
Lisgar St.
Somerset St.
Rideau St.
Hwy. 17B
Cambridge St.
Bronson Ave.
Percy St.
Bay St.
Lyon St.
Kent St.
Bank St.
O'Connor St.
Metcalf St.
Elgin St.
Nicholas St.
Hwy. 17
Gladstone Ave.
Frank
Greenfield
Hwy. 17
Catherine St.
Queensway
Chamberlain Ave.
Isabella St.
Pretoria Ave.

Major Events

For detailed information on the following events, call toll-free
(800)ONTARIO (668–2746) in the United States or (800)
465–1867 in Canada, or call (613) 239–5000 locally. Also contact
the Ottawa Tourism and Convention Authority (the address and
telephone number are listed under "Tourist Information").

Canadian Tulip Festival, mid-May, is the world's largest tulip
festival. Millions of tulips herald the spring season and dazzle the
eye with colorful floral displays all over the city. (The original
bulbs were given to the people of Canada by the government of
the Netherlands, grateful for the protection afforded the Dutch
royal family during World War II.) During the festivities there are
all kinds of events—outdoor concerts, crafts markets, exhibitions,
and parades.

Canada Day Celebrations, beginning on July 1, honor Canadian confederation, featuring patriotic, cultural, sporting, and entertainment events.

Ottawa International Jazz Festival, a ten-day music fest, fills the city's clubs, parks, and streets with the hot summer sound of jazz. World-famous performers as well as top local talents stage concerts (there are more than a hundred) and drop in on informal jam sessions, accessible with a modestly priced "passport" button.

Festival of Lights runs from December 4 to January 4. Decorative lights illuminate Parliament Hill and many other sites throughout the city for the holiday season. There are special musical concerts on Parliament Hill throughout December.

Winterlude, held in February, is three weekends of fun to celebrate winter. This outstanding festival features harness races on ice, an ice sculpture competition, parades, skating races, dancing, singing, fireworks, hot air ballooning, canoe races, great food and cheer, and all sorts of other activities to warm the spirit.

Attractions

Confederation Boulevard—the Mile of History is a ceremonial route that extends from Parliament Hill along Wellington Street and Sussex Drive and goes as far as Rideau Hall, the governor-general's residence. Attractions along this route include renovated nineteenth-century homes, shops, galleries, and restaurants.

Parliament Buildings, off Wellington Street, is the seat of the Canadian government. The complex consists of three neo-Gothic buildings set on Parliament Hill. The Centre Block, holding the House of Commons, the Senate, and the Parliamentary Library, is graced by the 291-foot (89 m) Peace Tower, with its carillon of fifty-three bells. The tower, which commemorates Canadians who gave their lives in the world wars, houses the Memorial Chamber with the Book of Remembrance. The Parliamentary Library is one of the most exquisite pieces of architecture in the city. It is all that remains of the original buildings, which were largely destroyed in a fire. The interior of the Centre Block is richly ornamented, and the House of Commons and the Senate chamber are especially worth seeing. (You can attend a session of Commons through advance arrangement with a member of the House.) The Centennial Flame in front of the buildings burns perpetually as a symbol of Canada's nationhood. The buildings on either side of the Centre Block are used as offices for the legislators, the prime minister, and members of the cabinet. Free tours of the buildings of Parliament are conducted throughout the year. During June, July, and August, you can make same-day reservations for a tour at the Infotent, located west of the Centre Block.

There are guided walking tours of Parliament Hill, from late June to early September. Call Parliamentary Guide Service at (613) 996–0896 for more information. Also attend the spectacle of the Sound and Light Show on Parliament Hill. It runs from May to September.

Changing of the Guard, on the broad, lovely grounds in front of the Parliament Buildings, is one of the most splendid free shows in Canada. Patterned after the changing of the guard ceremonies in Great Britain, the Ottawa version features the spiffy Governor-General's Foot Guards and the Canadian Grenadier Guards. They perform a ceremony of precise maneuvers to stirring martial music. This ceremony takes place daily, weather permitting, at 10:00 A.M., from the end of June to the end of August. Don't miss it!

Supreme Court of Canada, Wellington Street at Kent, allows visitors to see the building's beautiful lobby and court chambers, one for the Supreme Court and two for the Federal Court of Canada. You can attend proceedings. Free. Call (613) 995–5361.

National Arts Centre, Elgin Street near Confederation Square, is a contemporary complex consisting of a 2,300-seat main auditorium, an 850-seat theater, a 350-seat studio, a 150-seat salon, and a gourmet cafe. The paintings, sculpture, and other artworks decorating the interior are interesting. Here is Ottawa's main venue for symphony concerts, opera, classical and experimental theater, and popular entertainment by top performers. The grounds around the arts center are graced with sculptures and flower gardens. This complex overlooks the Rideau Canal, where there are boat tours in summer and ice skating in winter. Free tours of the National Arts Centre are offered. Call (613) 947–7000.

National Gallery of Canada stands on Nepean Point overlooking the Ottawa River, Sussex Drive, and St. Patrick Street. The National Gallery of Canada is housed in one of the most beautiful buildings in North America, designed by Moshe Safdie. This modern "crystal cathedral" houses the largest collection of Canadian art in the country, including works by the famous Group of Seven painters. It has a significant collection of art from the Middle Ages to the present, including works of Rembrandt, van Gogh, and Picasso. Guest amenities include underground parking, a gallery shop, cafe and restaurant, guided tours, and wheelchair access. Open all year. Admission charged for special exhibits only. Call (613) 990–1985.

National Archives, 395 Wellington Street, has an extensive collection of original documents relating to Canada's history. Open throughout the year. Free. The National Library, a repository for Canadian publications, is also at this location. Open throughout the year. Free. Call (613) 995–5138.

Canadian Museum of Civilization is located on Laurier Street in Hull, Québec, overlooking the Ottawa River, across from the Parliament buildings. The museum, reached from Ottawa via the Alexandra Bridge, is near the National Gallery of Art. This spectacular museum, designed by Douglas Cardinal, perhaps the finest of its genre in the world, tells epic stories of the Canadians: where they came from, how they survived in a hostile wilderness, how they lived and worked, how they created their various cultures, and how their nation will move into the future. Visitors come into the Grand Hall, which houses a dramatic reconstruction of a Pacific Coast Indian village as it might have looked a hundred years ago. Other guest services include a children's museum, festivals and performances, an IMAX/OMNIMAX theater showing exciting films, educational programs, a resource center, a museum shop, two restaurants, and wheelchair access. Open throughout the year. Admission charge. Call (819) 776–7000.

Canada Science and Technology Museum, 1867 Saint Laurent Boulevard, has a large number of participatory exhibits where you can test your skills and learn more about various aspects of science. This complex also has excellent displays of locomotives, vintage cars, aircraft, and unique products of technology. A new astronomical observatory is open to the public by appointment. Open throughout the year. Admission charge. Call (613) 991–3044.

Canada Aviation Museum, Rockcliffe Airport, housed in a new delta-shaped building, displays nearly a hundred historic aircraft, from the *Silver Dart,* one of the first Canadian-developed airplanes, to modern planes. Its exhibits include the history of the Royal Canadian Air Force, the heritage of wilderness bush flying, the age of transport, Canada's tradition of innovation in flight, and the opening of the nation's frontiers. Open throughout the year. Admission charge. Call (613) 993–2010.

National Postal Museum, 100 Laurier Street in Hull, is part of the Canadian Museum of Civilization. Staff members are happy to help with inquiries, and stamps can be purchased at the museum boutique. Admission charge. Call (819) 776–8200. (Serious stamp collectors should get in touch with the Government Postal Archives at 995–8085.)

Canadian War Museum, 330 Sussex Drive, has many dramatic and interesting displays of weapons, uniforms, and medals relating to Canada's military heritage, from wars during colonial periods to its United Nations peacekeeping efforts. Open throughout the year. Admission charge. Call (819) 776–8600 or (800) 555-5621, or visit www.warmuseum.ca.

Royal Canadian Mint, 320 Sussex Drive, allows visitors to see the making of Canadian money. There is also a good collection of coins and medals from around the world. Open throughout the year. Admission charge. Tours by appointment only. Call (613) 993–8990 or (800) 276-7714, or visit www.rcmint.ca.

National War Memorial, at Elgin and Wellington, is Canada's official memorial, a heroic sculpture of twenty-two bronze figures commemorating the nation's sacrifice and contribution to victory in World War I. King George VI unveiled this impressive monument in 1939, the year when World War II began. For a memorable account of Canada's effort in World War I, read Pierre Berton's *Vimy,* an absorbing account of one of the world's greatest land battles.

Government House (Rideau Hall), on Sussex Drive, is the official residence of the governor-general of Canada, the head of state and the queen's representative. Built in 1838 by Thomas MacKay, a stonemason from Perth, Scotland, Government House is the ceremonial heart of Canada. Here the Order of Canada is awarded, and here visiting royalty and heads of state are received. Free tours of its grounds are offered to visitors throughout the year. Be sure to see the Changing of the Guard ceremony, which takes place on the hour from the end of June to the end of August, in front of this splendid building.

Laurier House National Historic Site, 335 Laurier Avenue, East, was the home of Sir Wilfred Laurier and William Lyon Mackenzie King, both prime ministers of Canada. This Victorian mansion houses many personal items belonging to Laurier and King as well as the contents of the study belonging to Lester B. Pearson, a more recent and much beloved prime minister who also

won the Nobel Peace Prize. Open throughout the year; closed Mondays. Admission charge.

Nepean Point, Mackenzie Avenue, overlooking the Ottawa River behind the National Gallery of Canada, is site of the Astrolabe Theatre and a statue of Samuel de Champlain, who explored the river in 1613. The theater hosts several activities and festivals in the summer. Call (613) 239–5000.

Nicholas Gaol, 75 Nicholas Street, was a grim prison in the 1800s. In 1869 the last public hanging in Canada took place here, when Patrick Whelan was executed for the assassination of Thomas D'Arcy McGee, a Father of Confederation. The Gaol now serves as an international youth hostel. Tours are offered on Sundays by appointment; (613) 235–2595.

Museum of Canadian Scouting, 1345 Baseline Road, has a fine collection of the history of scouting in Canada and of Lord Baden-Powell, its founder. Open throughout the year. Free. Call (613) 224–5131.

Major's Hill Park on Mackenzie Avenue is a small park offering views of Rideau Canal locks. It is located between the Château Laurier hotel and the National Gallery of Art. Colonel By's home was in the area; its foundations still exist.Also in this area is the National Artillery Memorial.

Bytown Museum, on the west side of Rideau Canal, was the commissariat store, office, and treasury of Colonel By, the builder of the Rideau Canal. It contains more than 3,500 items relating to the history of the city. Open early May to mid-November and thereafter by appointment. Admission charge. The quay for Ottawa River cruises is at the far end of this park, just below Parliament Hill. Call (613) 234–4570.

Bank of Canada Currency Museum, 245 Sparks Street, presents exhibits on the history and development of money, from prehistoric currency to the present. Open throughout the year, Tuesday through Saturday. Free. Call (613) 782–8914 or visit bank-banque-canada.ca/museum.

St. Andrew's Church, 82 Kent Street, is the oldest church in Ottawa. The current building dates back to 1873, although a kirk was on this site from 1828. Information is available at (613) 232–9042 or visit www.standrews.ottawa.on.ca

Christ Church Cathedral, 439 Queen Street, is Ottawa's center for Anglican worship. This building also dates back to 1873. Call (613) 236–9149.

St. Bartholomew's Church, 125 MacKay Street, the parish church for twenty governors-general of Canada. It is also the chapel for the Governor-General's Foot Guards and is Queen Elizabeth's place of worship when she visits Ottawa.

Cathedral-Basilica of Notre Dame, Sussex Drive, was consecrated around 1840. In 1932 Colonel By gave the land on which it stands to Catholics so that they could have their own place of worship. An Ottawa landmark, the Notre Dame interior is lavishly decorated. Open daily. Call (613) 241–7496.

Rideau Canal and Locks, built under orders from the Duke of Wellington of Waterloo fame, were completed in 1832. Pleasure craft can cruise the Rideau Canal system from Kingston to Ottawa. The locks in Ottawa will bring boaters to the Ottawa River for a pleasant downstream sail to Montréal. Along the banks of the canal, in central Ottawa, you can stroll or jog. In the winter the canal becomes one of the world's longest skating rinks, particularly charming with the spires of Parliament and the Château Laurier as background. Open various hours from mid-May through mid-October; call (613) 283-5170 or (800) 230-0016 for information, or visit www.parkscanada.pch.gc.ca/rideau.

Central Experimental Farm, on Prince of Wales Drive, is a 1,200-acre farm not far from downtown. Here you can see a blue-ribbon herd of dairy and beef cattle, take a horse-drawn wagon ride, and visit greenhouses, an arboretum, and a botanical garden. Open throughout the year. Free. Canada's National Agricultural Museum is also located here. Open all year. Admission charge. Call (613) 991–3044.

Gatineau Park, access through Hull, Québec, is a magnificent 75,000-acre wilderness area with a system of touring roads, picnic sites, hiking trails, and many other recreational features. There are some excellent views of Ottawa's skyline from here. Open throughout the year. Call (613) 827–2020.

Moorside, located in Gatineau Park, was the summer home of the late William Lyon Mackenzie King, prime minister of Canada during World War II. There is a museum here containing his memorabilia, a nice public tearoom, and lovely gardens. There are also stone relics on the grounds from the first Parliament buildings, which were destroyed by fire. King, an outstanding politician and national leader, had many strange aspects to his personal life, such as conversing with the spirit of his dead mother. Moorside and Gatineau Park are nice respites from urban Ottawa. Open afternoons from late May to mid-October.

Rockcliffe Park Village, via Sussex Drive, is Ottawa's elite residential area. Here are the homes of the governor-general, prime minister, and leader of the opposition, and those of many foreign

ambassadors and leading business executives. Also within Rock-cliffe are the home barracks and stables of "N" Company of the Royal Canadian Mounted Police, who are famous for their exciting "Musical Ride."

Sports

Baseball and Hockey

The triple-A baseball Ottawa Lynx of the International League, who play at Ottawa Stadium, are very popular. Tickets can be hard to come by on sunny weekend afternoons. Call (613) 747–5969 for information.

Between October and April the National Hockey League's Ottawa Senators pack 'em in at the Corel Centre in Kanata, a state-of-the-art entertainment complex. Call (613) 599–0100.

Biking and Hiking

There are many miles of special biking trails in the Ottawa area maintained by the National Capital Commission. In the summer both the Colonel By and the Ottawa River parkways are closed to auto traffic on Sundays for the enjoyment of bike riders. Rent-a-Bike is located on Mackenzie Avenue behind the Château Laurier; (613) 241–4140.

There are a number of hiking and nature trails in the Ottawa area, with the best ones in Gatineau Park. Ottawa has many active joggers, and the various trails are also widely used by runners. There is also excellent running in Gatineau Park and along the Rideau Canal.

Swimming and Boating

Most of the hotels and motels have heated outdoor swimming pools and/or indoor pools. There are public beaches at Mooney's Bay, on the Rideau River near Hog's Back, off Riverside Drive, and at lakes in Gatineau Park. Canoes can be rented at the Dows Lake Pavilion, on the Rideau Canal, 1001 Queen Elizabeth Drive, and in Gatineau Park.

White-water Rafting

Several companies offer white-water rafting expeditions down the thrilling Rocher Fendu Rapids on the Ottawa River. Wilderness Tours, (613) 646–2241; River Run, (613) 646–2252 or (800) 267–8504; and Owl Rafting, (613) 238–7238 or (800) 461–7238, are well-established operators.

Tennis and Golf

There are more than forty public tennis courts throughout the city. Call the recreation departments of various municipalities under the heading of "Tennis" in the phone directories. The National Capital Commission operates the Canadian Golf and Country Club in Ashton, Ontario, (613) 780–3565, and the Champlain Golf Course in Aylmer, Québec, (819) 777–0449.

Horseback Riding

Horseback riding is available at the National Capital Equestrian Park, 401 Corkstown Road, in the Greenbelt; (613) 829–6925.

Skiing

The best skiing in the area is found in Québec at these Gatineau Park area locations: Mont-Cascades, in Cantley, (819) 827–0301; Edelweiss Valley, in Wakefield, (819) 459–2328; Vorlage, in Wakefield, (819) 459–2301; Camp Fortune, in Old Chelsea, (819) 827–1717.

Accommodations

Ottawa has a number of good hotels and motels. As the national capital, Ottawa now attracts a great many conventions, and there are conferences on every conceivable topic almost every week of the year. In addition, salespeople continually stream in and out of town in quest of orders from federal agencies. All this means that advance reservations are absolutely necessary. A smart time to visit the city is on weekends, when there is a decreased demand for hotel space and a greater chance to take advantage of lower-cost packages. Many tour operators offer complete packages that include Ottawa. Check with your travel agent for details.

    Marriott Ottawa, 150 Albert Street, (613) 238–1500, is one of Ottawa's better hotels, located near government offices and a short walk from Parliament Hill. It features gourmet dining in the

Carleton Restaurant. The hotel has a swimming pool and exercise facilities. Expensive.

Radisson Hotel Ottawa Centre, 100 Kent Street, (613) 238–1122, offers high-quality rooms, a central location, many facilities, and a high level of personal service. The hotel is connected to an underground shopping area of boutiques and restaurants. La Ronde is Ottawa's revolving rooftop restaurant. The food is excellent here, and so are the views of the city and surrounding landscape. Expensive.

Château Laurier, Confederation Square, (613) 241–1414, is an impressive structure with the look of a Loire Valley château and is Ottawa's most famous hotel, a bastion for politicians and wheeler-dealers. It has a gourmet restaurant and an indoor swimming pool. The Château Laurier is in a very good location, across the street from Parliament Hill, the Rideau Canal, and the National Arts Centre. Expensive.

Crowne Plaza, 101 Lyon Street, (613) 237–3600, is a downtown hotel with fine accommodations, services, and restaurants, one of which is located on the top of this high-rise and offers marvelous views of the city. The hotel is connected to the underground system of shops and restaurants and has an indoor pool. Moderate.

The Carmichael Inn & Spa, 46 Cartier Street, (613) 236–4667, is housed in a handsome, century-old brick building ten minutes from Parliament Hill. It is one of few hotels in the city to offer spa treatments—facials, massages, mud and seaweed wraps, and the like—making it a favorite with business travelers. The rooms, furnished with antiques, are elegant but cozy. The public lounge, which has a fireplace, is always filled with newspapers. Moderate to expensive. Packages are available.

Lord Elgin, 100 Elgin Street, (613) 235–3333, is a fine old hotel that has a great location and comfortable, recently renovated rooms. Expensive.

Westin Hotel, 11 Colonel By Drive, (613) 560–7000, is one of the top accommodations in the city. It's close to everything and is connected to the convention and shopping center. The Westin offers all deluxe hotel amenities and many elegant touches. Expensive.

Delta Ottawa, 361 Queen Street, (613) 238–6000, is an excellent choice in a central location. Delta is one of Canada's better hotel chains, providing good value for a fair price. Expensive.

Best Western Victoria Park Suites, 377 O'Connor Street, (613) 567–7275, has self-catering studios and one-bedroom units with kitchenettes. Exercise facilities. Within walking distance of downtown. Moderate to expensive.

Chimo Inn, 1199 Joseph Cyr Street, (613) 744–1060, although away from downtown, offers many guest amenities. Moderate to expensive.

Les Suites, 130 Besserer Street, (613) 232–2000, is within walking distance of the bustling Byward Market and the Rideau Centre with its dozens of stores. One- and two-bedroom suites are particularly suitable for families. (Children under eighteen stay free in parents' room.) Indoor pool and fitness center. Moderate.

University of Ottawa, 100 University Avenue, (613) 562–5885, May to late August, provides adequate accommodations in dormitories and is in a central location. Inexpensive.

Carleton University, 261 Stormont House, (613) 520–5611, May to late August, offers good accommodations in student residences. It also has a cafeteria, swimming pool, squash and tennis courts, jogging track, and sauna. The location is several blocks from the center of town. Inexpensive.

Ottawa International Hostel, 75 Nicholas Street, (613) 235–2595, is a former jail—gray and forbidding—and you sleep on cots in what were cells. The experience is unique and also about as cheap as you'll find in Ottawa. Inexpensive.

Ottawa Bed and Breakfast Association, 488 Cooper Street, Ottawa, Ontario K1R 5H9; (613) 563–0161. Inexpensive to moderately priced accommodations in Ottawa-area private homes.

Hull, Québec, Area Accommodations

Château Cartier Sheraton, 1170 Aylmer Road, Aylmer, Québec, (819) 777–1088, is an upscale golf resort situated ten minutes from the center of Ottawa. Large, elegant rooms and suites. Exercise facilities include tennis, squash, racquetball, and an eighteen-hole golf course. Expensive.

Le Château Montebello is at 392, rue Notre Dame, in Montebello, Québec; (819) 423–6341. Le Montebello is one of Canada's premier resorts, once the exclusive bastion of the rich and powerful, offering superb accommodations and dining. Amenities include an eighteen-hole golf course, swimming, tennis, marina, acres of woodland, frontage on the Ottawa River, cross-country skiing, and many other recreations. Highly recommended. Expensive.

Hotel des Gouverneurs Gatineau is at 111, rue Bellehumeur in Gatineau; (819) 568–5252. Moderate to expensive.

L'Hotel Centreville is located at 35, rue Laurier in Hull; (819) 778–6111. Moderate to expensive.

Dining

Ottawa offers a diverse selection of restaurants, representing the traditional cuisines of many countries. There is something to satisfy almost every taste, from basic North American fare to exotic dishes.

Mexicali Rosa's at Dow's Lake Pavilion, 1001 Queen Elizabeth Drive, (613) 234–8156, serves Mexican food in a contemporary dining and recreational facility. A terrace overlooks the lake, a gift shop, and other amenities. Moderate.

Bravo, Bravo, 292 Elgin Street, (613) 233–7525, is on a lively street lined with trendy eateries. Flavorful Italian and Mediterranean fare is served amid Tuscan decor. Enjoy an after-dinner game of pool or stay for drinks at the granite bar. Moderate.

Mamma Teresa's, 300 Somerset Street, (613) 236–3023, fills you with great veal, homemade pasta, and antipasto. A lot of good Italian "soul" food for a reasonable price. Moderate.

Japanese Village, 170 Laurier Avenue, West, (613) 236–9519, serves tempura, sushi, teriyaki, and other exotic Japanese dishes. Moderate to expensive.

Nate's Deli, 316 Rideau Street, (613) 789–9191, has by now become a venerable Ottawa institution for its smoked meat sandwiches, blintzes, pierogies, kishke, and kreplach. You don't even have to be Jewish to adore Nate's offerings. Inexpensive.

Friday's Roast Beef House, 150 Elgin Street, (613) 237–5353, is a nicely appointed restaurant in a Victorian-era house. The roast beef here is excellent, as expected. Moderate to expensive.

Courtyard Restaurant, 21 George Street, (613) 241–1516, is located in an ancient stone building within the Byward Market district. Rack of lamb and beef Wellington are specialties. Expensive.

The Old Fish Market, 54 York Street, (613) 241–3474, offers fresh fish cooked without gimmicks. It's a good place for seafood purists. Moderate.

Le Metro, 315 Somerset Street, West, (613) 230–8123, serves French cuisine in a romantic, candlelit Parisian setting. Sophisticated wine list. Expensive.

Bay Street Bistro, 160 Bay Street, (613) 234–1111, features California Italian cuisine—unique pasta, seafood, meat dishes, and "designer" pizzas. Moderate.

The Cafe Colonnade, 280 Metcalfe Street, (613) 237–3179, offers some of the best pizza in town. The decor is plain, but the place is usually packed. Inexpensive to moderate.

Siam Bistro, 1268 Wellington Street, (613) 728–3111, serves up Thai foods with a mild taste. Moderate to expensive.

The New Mill, Ottawa River Parkway, (613) 237–1311, offers North American cooking in a historic mill overlooking Chaudière Falls and the Ottawa River. Roast beef with Yorkshire pudding is the specialty. Moderate to expensive.

Hull, Québec, Area Restaurants

Café Henry Burger, 69, rue Laurier in Hull, (819) 777–5646, offers fine French food and ambience. Expensive.

L'Orée du Bois, chemin Kingsmere in Old Chelsea, (819) 827–0332, has excellent French cuisine and the setting to go along with it. Moderate to expensive.

Oncle Tom, 138, rue Wellington in Hull, (819) 771–1689. Situated in a historic house, the menu features a good range of French cuisine. This restaurant's wine cellar rates among the best in the Ottawa/Hull region. Moderate to expensive.

Entertainment

Thanks to the National Arts Centre, (613) 996–5051, Ottawa cultural life is very much alive throughout the year and open to the general public. Here you can see the great ballet companies of Canada and other countries, grand opera performances, and both classical and experimental live theater. The National Symphony Orchestra plays at the Arts Centre, as do leading theatrical companies, musical groups, and entertainers from around the world.

Other theatrical venues in the Ottawa area are the Ottawa Little Theatre, Rideau and King Edward Streets, (613) 233–8948; the Great Canadian Theatre Company, 910 Gladstone Avenue, (613) 236–5196; Centrepointe Theatre, 101 Centrepointe Drive, Nepean, (613) 727–6650; and Théâtre de l'Ile, 1, rue Wellington in Hull, (819) 595–7455.

There are also comedy, cabaret, and dinner theaters: Yuk Yuk's Komedy Kabaret, at 88 Albert Street, (613) 236–5233; and Eddie May Murder Mystery at The Marble Works, (613) 850–9700.

Ottawa has many bars and lounges featuring live entertainment and music—rock and roll, jazz, country and western, blues. The bars and clubs in Hull, Québec, stay open until 3:00 A.M., longer than those in Ottawa. Ask the concierge at your hotel for recommendations on which places are currently hot. Also ask for copies of the *Ottawa Citizen,* *X-Press,* and the magazine *Where Ottawa-Hull,* which provide listings of current entertainment offerings in the Ottawa area as well as dining and shopping suggestions.

Shopping

Sparks Street Mall, off Confederation Square, is a car-free shopping street lined with boutiques, bookshops, and cafes. The mall features open-air art exhibitions, fountains, and floral displays.

Ottawa Congress Centre and Rideau Centre is a convention and shopping complex, conveniently located along the bank of the Rideau Canal, across from the National Arts Centre and facing Rideau Street. The Congress Centre provides facilities for conventions and association meetings of all kinds. The Westin Hotel is connected by passageways to this modern complex. Rideau Centre is downtown Ottawa's top enclosed shopping mall. It has more than 230 shops, a cinema, and several restaurants.

ByWard Market, a block north of Rideau Street, is where area farmers have been selling their fresh fruits, vegetables, meat, cheese, breads, and other products since 1846. ByWard Market is one of the most lively and entertaining places in the city. There are many fine restaurants and shops here. It is a great place for people-watching and carefree strolling.

Upper Canada Village

About fifty miles (80 km) southeast of Ottawa via Highway 31 is Upper Canada Village, the re-creation of an early-nineteenth-century Ontario settlement. Upper Canada Village, located in Morrisburg, features an inn, a lovely Anglican church, a woolen mill, pioneer homes, a blacksmith shop, and a sawmill. There are forty buildings, corduroy roads, canals, and a fort, all of which can be seen on foot. Or you can ride through the village on an ox cart and sail through the canals on a bateau. In this working historic community, the staff dresses in pioneer costumes and performs the various household and community tasks typical of bygone days. Upper Canada Village is one of the outstanding living museums of Canada, and a visit here is highly recommended. Open mid-May to mid-October. Admission charge.

Other Morrisburg attractions include Crysler Farm Battlefield Park, right next to Upper Canada Village, which commemorates a British and Canadian victory during the War of 1812, and the Upper Canada Migratory Bird Sanctuary, both open throughout the year.

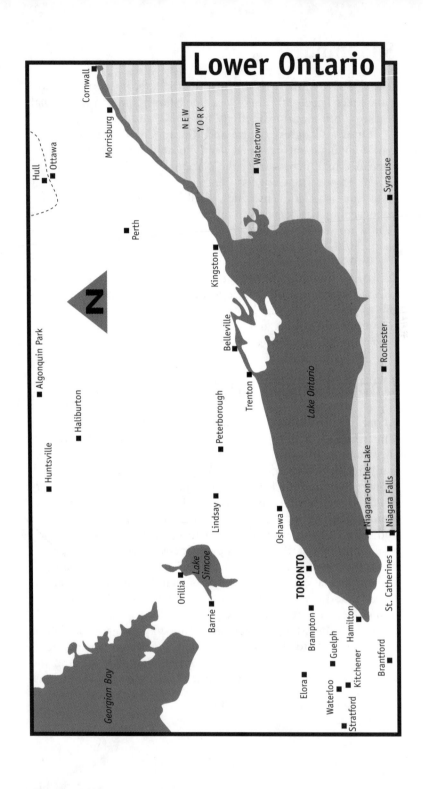

Lower Ontario

CHAPTER 5

Southeastern Ontario Vacation Regions

Southern Ontario has some of Canada's best resorts, where you can enjoy all sorts of recreation and be pampered with fine accommodations and services. These resorts are located within magnificent scenery of lakes, hills, and forests. Many are open all four seasons of the year. Any time is perfect for an Ontario resort vacation.

Niagara Falls is one of the natural wonders of the world. Not only can you see the falls, but you can also ride a boat that takes you right to where the waters explode at the bottom of the gorge. There is so much more to do and see in the Niagara area: family attractions and entertainments of all kinds, the Shaw Festival Theatre in historic Niagara-on-the-Lake, fortifications from the War of 1812, and charming inns reflecting the region's grace and traditions.

To the west of Toronto are Stratford, with its famous theater festival featuring the plays of Shakespeare and others, and the interesting cities of Guelph, Kitchener-Waterloo, and Brantford. In Kitchener-Waterloo, you can attend one of the best German Oktoberfest celebrations in North America and purchase fresh fruits and vegetables grown by Mennonite and Amish farmers.

About midway between Toronto and Ottawa is the old city of Kingston, once the capital of Upper Canada, with its many historic attractions, such as Upper Canada's military academy and hockey hall of fame. From Kingston you can cruise the beginning of the Saint Lawrence River and see the famous Thousand Islands with their castles.

For more information on the following vacation areas and other regions of Ontario, call toll-free (800) ONTARIO.

The Great Resorts of Ontario

Fine resorts cluster along the lakeshore of Ontario with most located an easy drive from Toronto, Niagara Falls, Windsor, Kingston, and Ottawa. They offer swimming (in lakes and heated pools), boating, canoeing, kayaking, windsurfing, and fishing. Many have their own golf courses, tennis courts, and exercise facilities with recreation programs designed for adults and for children. Some offer sports programs: fly-in fishing expeditions to remote lakes, rivers, and streams; equestrian sports; winter ice fishing, Alpine skiing, cross-country skiing, horse-drawn sleigh rides, snowshoeing treks, snowmobile touring, ice skating. For more information, contact Resorts Ontario, 10 Peter Street North, Orillia, Ontario; (800) 363–7227 toll-free from Canada and the United States.

All of the following resorts are in the moderate to expensive price range.

The Lakelands Region

The Lakelands is one of Ontario's premier vacation areas, located directly north and northeast of Toronto. The area is reached via Highways 400 and 11 from Toronto, about a four- to six-hour drive.

Blue Mountain Resorts, in Collingwood, (705) 445–0231, is Ontario's largest Alpine skiing complex. Blue Mountain also offers cross-country skiing. It has a giant summer water slide, indoor pool, sandy beach, squash, racquetball, tennis, exercise facilities, and other recreations. The accommodations are excellent, as are the food and entertainment.

Clevelands House, in Minett, (705) 567–1177.

Deerhurst Resort, on Peninsula Lake in Huntsville, (705) 789–6411.

Delawana Inn, in Honey Harbour, (800) 627–3387.

Fern Resort, in Orillia, (705) 325–2256.

Pinelands Resort, on Lake Muskoka in Port Carling, (705) 765–3226.

Rocky Crest Resort, on Lake Joseph in MacTier, (705) 375–2240.

Severn Lodge, on the Trent-Severn Waterway in Port Severn, (800) 461–5817.

Windermere House, on Lake Rousseau in Windermere, (705) 769–3611. Open May to October.

Central Ontario

This region is between Toronto and Ottawa and is easily accessible from either city.

Domain of Killien Resort, in Haliburton, (705) 457–1100, is a sophisticated, upmarket hotel with superb food.

PineStone Resort and Conference Centre, in Haliburton, (705) 457–1800.

Closer to Toronto, The Briars, on Lake Simcoe in Jackson's Point, (905) 722–3271, is a 200-acre family-run resort with an eighteen-hole golf course.

Eastern Ontario

Eastern Ontario is the tourism region southwest of Ottawa and northeast of Toronto. Algonquin Provincial Park, located here, is the preserved wilderness area closest to the major population centers of eastern Ontario. Inside the park is Arowhon Pines, at Algonquin Provincial Park near Huntsville; (705) 633–5661, summer; (416) 483–4393, winter.

Niagara Falls

No matter how many times you have seen Niagara Falls, they still take your breath away by their sheer size—both height and breadth—and by the volume of water that plummets over them.

No doubt Niagara Falls, reached via Queen Elizabeth Way (about a ninety-minute drive from Toronto), became a prime tourist attraction as soon as the first humans set eyes on them. They are still one of North America's most famous landmarks.

Niagara Falls form part of the border between Canada and the United States. The crescent-shaped Horseshoe Falls, 176 feet (54 m) high and 2,100 feet (641 m) wide, are in Ontario, while the American Falls, 182 feet (56 m) high and 1,076 feet (328 m) wide, are in New York State. The waters of nearby Lake Erie and the other upper Great Lakes flow through the Niagara River (of which the falls are a part) down into Lake Ontario, then through the Saint Lawrence River, which empties into the Gulf of Saint

Lawrence and ultimately into the Atlantic Ocean. To the east of the Niagara River is the Welland Canal, part of the Saint Lawrence Seaway, which allows passage of oceangoing ships between Lakes Erie and Ontario.

The roar from Niagara Falls is so thunderous that it can be heard day and night for many miles into Ontario and New York State. On occasion the waters freeze to a trickle during a particularly cold winter, the roar seems to stop, and local residents get an eerie feeling that nature has gone askew. The cascading waters create a perpetual boil at the bottom and send up thick mists, which catch sunlight and produce beautiful rainbows.

Niagara Falls has been a favorite attraction for honeymooners ever since Napoleon III's newlywed brother and his wife came up from New Orleans by stagecoach for a visit. It is unclear why a huge, noisy cataract enhances marital ardor, but somehow it seems to work.

Niagara Falls has also attracted an unusually large number of daredevils, who have gone over them in barrels or walked across on tightrope wires. But most tourists come to Niagara Falls to be impressed by the power of nature, and they leave astounded.

Niagara Falls are a beautiful sight at any time of year. In the evening they are illuminated by colored lights, making quite a spectacle, especially in winter, when the falls become a giant freeform ice sculpture. A 25-mile (40 km) park system stretches from the falls down to the town of Niagara-on-the-Lake. This park offers many fine views of the falls.

The Niagara Parks People Movers is a bus system that will transport you to the main attractions all day for one low price, allowing you to get on and off as many times as you want. This shuttle operates from mid-May to mid-October.

For more information, contact the Niagara Falls, Canada, Visitor and Convention Bureau, 5433 Victoria Avenue, Niagara Falls, Ontario L2G 3L1; (905) 356–6061.

Attractions

Where there are tourists and a natural attraction of this magnitude, you can be sure that there will be plenty of ways to see and experience it.

Maid of the Mist, located in the Maid of the Mist Plaza at the foot of Clifton Hill, is now easily accessible via four elevators (all wheelchair accessible). These tough boats push upriver against the strong current and take you right into the Horseshoe and the main falls. The noise is deafening, and the spray comes down on you like a rainstorm (you are supplied with hooded raincoats to protect your clothing). The experience is a lifetime memory. The *Maid of the Mist* boats operate daily from mid-May to mid-October. Admission charge.

Table Rock Scenic Tunnels, Niagara Parkway, takes you into the falls through a system of tunnels so that you view the downpour of water from the inside looking out. You are issued raincoats to protect your clothing, as some of the viewing areas are splashed with spray. Open throughout the year. Admission charge.

Great Gorge Adventure, 4330 River Road, has an elevator that takes you down in the Niagara River gorge below the falls. From here you go on a walkway to the famous Whirlpool Rapids. Open May to October. Admission charge.

Minolta Tower Centre, 6732 Oakes Drive, features a 665-foot (203 m) observation tower above Niagara gorge, in which there are restaurants and lounges. It also has a Family Entertainment Centre with video games, a simulator space ride, and a "waltzing waters" show. Open throughout the year. Admission charge.

Skylon Tower, 5200 Robinson Street, takes you up 520 feet (159 m) to an observation area above the falls. There is a revolving restaurant at the top, and shops, restaurants, and amusement stands are at the bottom. Open throughout the year. Admission charge.

Niagara Falls IMAX Theatre & Daredevil Adventure, adjacent to the Skylon Tower, shows the majesty, thrills, and history of the falls on a movie screen six stories high, with a six-track sound system. Admission charge. Call (905) 358–3611.

Ride Niagara, 5755 River Road under the Rainbow Bridge, offers a high-tech simulated ride aboard the Hydro Shuttle, which takes you under the falls, then up to the top of the falls, followed by a plunge into the raging waters of the Niagara River, all in total safety and without getting a drop of water on you. Open all year. Admission charge. Call (905) 374–7433.

Niagara Helicopters, 3731 Victoria Avenue, provides flights over the falls and surrounding area, throughout the year, weather permitting. Admission charge. Call (905) 357–5672.

Rainbow Tower Carillon, Rainbow Bridge, has fifty-five bells and gives concerts during the summer. Free.

Parks Commission Greenhouse & Fragrance Garden, Niagara Parkway, has year-round floral displays with special seasonal exhibitions. Open throughout the year. Free.

Maple Leaf Village, Rainbow Bridge, is a shopping and amusement complex featuring a giant Ferris wheel from which you get great views of the falls. Open throughout the year. Free admission into the village; admission charge for amusements.

Marineland, 7567 Portage Road South, (905) 356–9565, features trained killer whales, dolphins, and seals. There are also a wildlife park and Dragon Mountain, a roller coaster. Open throughout the year. Admission charge.

W. Kurelek Art Collection, Queen Elizabeth Way, is housed in the Niagara Falls Art Gallery, which also features the works of other Canadian, American, and European artists. The late William Kurelek was a world-famous Ukrainian-Canadian artist who painted religious and allegorical themes. His *Passion of Christ,* consisting of 160 panels, is the highlight of this museum. Open throughout the year. Admission charge.

Casino Niagara, 5705 Falls Avenue, (905) 374–5964. This elegant gaming hall, which is open twenty-four hours per day year-round, has 3,000 slot machines and 123 gaming tables. Be prepared for waiting lines.

Accommodations

Best Western Cairn Croft Hotel, 6400 Lundy's Lane, (905) 356–1161, has a dining room and swimming pool. Moderate to expensive.

Roadway Inn, 7720 Lundy's Lane, (905) 358–9833, features a swimming pool. Moderate.

Holiday Inn by the Falls, Murray and Buchanan Street, (905) 356–1333, offers fine accommodations and dining and has heart-shaped tubs and waterbeds for honeymooners. Moderate to expensive.

Renaissance Fallsview Hotel, 6455 Buchanan Avenue, (905) 357–5200, features excellent accommodations, dining, and recreational facilities. Moderate to expensive.

The Old Stone Inn, 5425 Robinson Street, (905) 357–1234, has a warm, charming ambience and gracious hospitality in what was a rustic flour mill at the turn of the twentieth century. Beautifully restored into a unique place of accommodation, it has a restaurant, lounge, swimming pool, health club, and many guest amenities. Moderate to expensive.

The Niagara Region Bed and Breakfast Service, Butterfly Manor, 4917 River Road in Niagara Falls, (905) 358–8988.

Sheraton Fallsview Hotel and Conference Center, 6755 Oakes

Drive, (905) 374–1077, features luxurious accommodations, fine dining, great views of the falls, and a health club. Within walking distance of Marineland. Moderate to expensive.

Niagara-on-the-Lake

Niagara-on-the-Lake is one of the loveliest small towns in Canada. Just 8 miles (13 km) north of Niagara Falls, via the Niagara Parkway, Niagara-on-the-Lake is a favorite place for artists and writers.

Attractions

The Shaw Festival Theatre houses an outstanding professional acting company that presents the plays of George Bernard Shaw and others. The internationally famous Shaw Festival runs from early May to late September. Call (905) 468–2172 for ticket information.

Fort George defended British Canada from the Americans during the War of 1812. Its interesting Navy Hall Museum is housed in a structure built during the American Revolution. Open mid-May to the end of October. Admission charge.

Laura Secord Homestead, off River Road in Queenston Heights, was the home of a brave woman who warned the British of a forthcoming American attack in 1813. Laura Secord's heroism helped to win a victory in the Battle of Beaver Dam. Her home has been restored and furnished with priceless Upper Canada antiques. Open mid-May to mid-October. Admission charge.

McFarland House, Niagara Parkway, is a fine early-nineteenth-century Georgian-style brick house. During the War of 1812, it was used by both the Americans and the British as a hospital. Open mid-May to mid-September. Admission charge.

Niagara Apothecary, 5 Queen Street, is an authentic restoration of a late-nineteenth-century drugstore, complete with walnut and butternut fixtures, crystal gasoliers, and a rare collection of apothecary glassware. Open mid-May to Labour Day. Free.

Niagara Historical Society Museum, 43 Castlereagh Street, features items belonging to John Graves Simcoe, founder of Toronto; uniforms and weapons of the War of 1812; and personal possessions of Laura Secord. Open throughout the year. Admission charge.

if you love live theater, you should top off your visit to Ontario with a performance at Stratford. Here the works of Shakespeare and other great dramatists come to life in one of the most renowned theaters in North America.

Accommodations

Oban Inn, 160 Front Street, (905) 468–2165, expensive.

Prince of Wales Hotel, 9 Picton Street, (905) 468–3246, expensive.

Queens Landing, Byron Street, (905) 468–2195, expensive.

Pillar and Post, King and John Streets, (905) 468–2123, expensive.

Bed-and-breakfast accommodations are also available in town.

Stratford

Like Stratford in England, this pretty town sits on a River Avon and has a connection to William Shakespeare. The banks of the tree-lined waterway, which winds through the town center, are scattered with picnic tables; and here, as at Stratford-upon-Avon in England, visitors can feed a flock of graceful white swans. The town comes alive for the Stratford Festival, a celebration of the works of Shakespeare and easily among the best live theater in North America. Leading actors and directors from around the English-speaking world come here to recite the immortal words of the great bard. Modern plays and musicals are also presented at the festival, which runs from May to mid-November. For information, call (519) 273–1600.

Other places worth visiting in Stratford include the downtown crafts stores, antiques shops, a farmers' market, restaurants and pubs, The Gallery Stratford, and Brickman's Botanical Gardens, an English-style herb garden with a small bird sanctuary.

Accommodations in Stratford include Queen's Inn at Stratford, 161 Ontario Street, (519) 271–1400, moderate to expensive; Victorian Inn, 10 Romeo Street, (519) 271–4650, moderate to expensive; and Bentleys, 99 Ontario Street, (519) 271–1121, moderate to expensive.

Stratford also has many other motels, inns, and bed-and-breakfast places. For help in planning where to stay, call the Stratford Festival Accommodations Bureau at (519) 273–1600.

The Guelph-Kitchener-Brantford Area

It is appropriate that Guelph, which was founded by a novelist, should continue to have such a tradition of the arts. From the beginning it was planned with an eye to its beauty, with wide streets and plenty of open space for leafy parks and gardens. While that may not seem unusual today, in 1827 it was a revolutionary idea.

The **MacDonald Stewart Arts Centre**, (519) 836–1482, on the campus of the University of Guelph, shows an excellent collection of Inuit and other Canadian artworks, interpreted by informative signs. You can take a tour of the entire campus of this university, which includes Canada's largest agricultural college. The campus has a number of buildings of outstanding architecture.

The **Colonel John McCrae Home**, 102 Water Street, is the birthplace of the author of the poem *In Flanders Fields*, written during the Battle of Ypres in 1915. Open mid-May to mid-October. Admission charge.

Guelph Civic Museum, 6 Dublin Street, houses collections relating to the history of the city. Open throughout the year. Free. The phone number for both the home and the museum is (519) 836–1221.

The **Church of Our Lady** is modeled after the great cathedral of Cologne, Germany, and dominates the city from its site on the highest hill.

Fine dining is another art that Guelph takes seriously, with more than a hundred restaurants, several of them very good indeed. Georgian Creed's, on Douglas Street, (519) 837-2692, is among the best for dinner. Moderate. Try Bookshelf Cafe on Quebec Street, (519) 821–3333, for lunch. Inexpensive.

For more than twenty years, Elora, north of Guelph, has been a summer mecca for music lovers. In July, and usually running into August, every Friday, Saturday, and Sunday and a few weekdays in between bring a major concert. Music styles range from hymns, sacred dance, and gospel singers to Brahms, Vivaldi, choral masses, and a chamber series. There are programs by the Elora Festival Singers, well-known soloists, and bands such as Spirit of the West. Expect Broadway, pops, jazz and cabaret, flamenco, and Japanese drums along with the classics. For a complete schedule and tickets, contact the Elora Festival at (519) 846-0331 or www.elora.org.

One of the concert venues is a floating stage in the former quarry, now a park for hiking and picnicking. Elora Gorge, where the Grand River drops over cascades between 70-foot sheer walls, is part of another park, with camping and lake swimming.

Overlooking the gorge is Elora Mill Country Inn, Mill Street, (519) 846-5356, www.eloramill.com. La Cachette, also on Mill Street, serves French Provençal dishes, using locally grown produce, (519) 846-8346, and Desert Rose Cafe, Metcalf Street, (519) 846-0433, serves an international menu of vegetarian dishes. All are moderately priced.

Kitchener and Waterloo are twin cities that have a common heritage. Many of the early settlers were German farmers and Amish and Mennonite people who came from the United States. Oktoberfest in this area is famous throughout Canada—nine days of beer drinking, sausage and kraut eating, oompah music, parades, amusements, and sporting events. Oktoberfest, one of the biggest festivals in North America, is held in mid-October.

Doon Pioneer Village, off Homer Watson Boulevard, has sixteen restored historic buildings depicting early rural life in this area of Ontario. It has a Conestoga wagon, an 1823 Eby Bible, and the first mass-produced car built in Canada. Open May to late October. Admission charge. The area's farmers' market is one of the best in Canada. Mennonite and Amish farmers sell homemade bread, preserves, cheese, sausage, and a vast array of fresh vegetables. Open Saturday throughout the year, early morning to early afternoon.

Brantford is named for the famous Mohawk Chief Joseph Brant, an important ally of the British in the early development of Canada.

Brant County Museum, 57 Charlotte Street, has a fine collection of items related to the Six (Iroquois) Nations and important figures in Brantford's history, such as Joseph Brant, Alexander Graham Bell, and E. Pauline Johnson, one of Canada's best-loved poets. Open throughout the year. Admission charge.

Chiefswood, via Highway 54, was built in 1853 by Chief Johnson, leader of the Six Nations, for his English bride, E. Pauline Johnson, to whose memory it is now dedicated. Open mid-May to Labour Day. Admission charge.

Her Majesty's Royal Chapel of the Mohawks, Mohawk Street, was built in 1785, the oldest Protestant church in Ontario. Open April to November.

Woodland Cultural Centre, 184 Mohawk Street, has some excellent displays of First Nations artifacts telling the story of the culture and history of native people in North America. Open throughout the year. Admission charge.

Bell Homestead, 94 Tutela Heights Road, is where Alexander Graham Bell lived as a young man and where he worked on his most famous invention—the telephone. Open throughout the year. Admission charge.

Glenhyrst Art Gallery of Brant, 20 Ava Road, is a sixteen-acre estate overlooking the Grand River. Here is a fine old house with gallery shows of paintings, prints, sculpture, and photography, set on beautiful grounds with a nature trail. Open throughout the year. Admission charge.

Kingston

Located on Lake Ontario at the beginning of the Saint Lawrence River, Kingston can be reached via Highway 15 from Ottawa, via Highway 401 from Toronto and Montréal, and via I–81 through upstate New York over the International Bridge.

Settlement of the Kingston area dates back to the seventeenth century. Kingston was once the site of Fort Frontenac, a major French fur-trading post. Because of its strategic location, Kingston was a key military stronghold in protecting British North America from the enemy to the south. It also served as the capital of Upper Canada and of the United Provinces of Canada. For more information on Kingston, contact the Tourist Information Office at (888) 855–4555, visit www.kingstoncanada.com, or e-mail tourism@kingstoncanada.com.

Bellevue House National Historic Park, 35 Centre Street, an 1840 Tuscan-style villa, was the home of Sir John A. Macdonald, the first prime minister of Canada. This fine mansion contains furnishings and personal possessions belonging to one of Canada's most illustrious political leaders. Open daily except holidays, April through October. Admission charge.

Fort Henry, a massive fortification, was once the principal stronghold of Upper Canada, as it guarded the entrance to both Lake Ontario and the Saint Lawrence River. Its museum houses an extensive collection of military uniforms, weapons, and equipment. The highlight of a visit is to watch the Fort Henry Guard, dressed in nineteenth-century uniforms, performing intricate drills, with fifes and drums, and artillery salutes. Highly recommended. Open mid-May to October. At 7:30 P.M. on Wednesday in July and August, weather permitting, a special "Sunset Ceremony" is performed. Admission charge.

Military Communications and Electronics Museum, Vimy

Barracks, 1 mile (1.6 km) east on Highway 2, has displays relating to the history of the Royal Canadian Corps of Signals. Open Monday through Friday all year, daily from mid-May through October. Free.

Kingston City Hall, Ontario Street, built in the mid-nineteenth century, was once the capitol of the United Provinces of Canada. A domed structure built from limestone, it is considered one of the finest historical buildings in Canada. Open throughout the year, with daily tours mid-June to Labour Day. Free.

Fort Frederick Museum (Royal Military College Museum), at La Salle Causeway, east of the city off Highway 2, has a fine collection of historic items relating to Fort Frederick and the Royal Military College (Canada's West Point) housed in a large Martello tower. It also contains the small arms collection of Porfirio Diaz, president of Mexico at the turn of the twentieth century. Open mid-June to Labour Day. Free.

Brock Street, in the center of Kingston, features nineteenth-century–style shops. It's a great place to stroll, sample the goodies, and buy souvenirs.

Confederation Tour Trolley is owned and operated by the Kingston Chamber of Commerce, and offers tourists a fifty-minute narrated ride around the city to see many interesting sights. Call (613) 548–4743, or visit www.kingstonchamber.on.ca.

The Haunted Walk of Kingston departs from the Tir nan Og pub at the Prince George Hotel, 200 Ontario Street. The ninety-minute tour will bring you through the evening streets of Kingston by lantern, as the guides take you past Kingston's hidden graveyards, the Organist's Ghost, and the haunted old courthouse that might still echo the moans of those hanged there. For tickets, call (613) 549–6366, or visit their Web site at www.hauntedwalk.com.

Correctional Service of Canada Museum, 555 King Street West, (613) 530–3122, gives a thorough history of Canada's penitentiary system from its start to the present. Open daily May through September, the rest of the year on weekdays by chance or appointment. Admission is free.

Pump House Steam Museum, 23 Ontario Street, is a restored 1849 steam-driven pumping station with a unique steam engine collection. Open mid-June to Labour Day. Admission charge.

International Ice Hockey Museum, York and Alfred Streets, memorializes the top players of the National Hockey League and other professional and amateur leagues in Canada and the United States. Open daily mid-June to mid-September (on weekends the rest of the year). Admission charge.

Murney Tower Museum, McDonald Park, corner of Barrie and King Streets, is a Martello tower built in 1846, that was once part of the harbor defenses and the entrance to the Rideau Canal system. The museum houses a collection of early military and pioneer artifacts. Open late May to Labour Day. Admission charge.

Marine Museum of the Great Lakes, Ontario and Union Streets. Recently restored, this interesting museum houses a collection depicting the history of Great Lakes shipping from the seventeenth century to the present, including artifacts from old vessels sunk in the lakes. Open daily June through October, weekdays January through May, closed November and December. Admission charge.

Agnes Etherington Art Centre, University and Queen's Crescent, on the Campus of Queen's University, is a newly renovated art gallery with Ontario's largest collection of more than 3,000 works. It has exhibitions of local, national, and international art. Open throughout the year. Free. (613) 545–2190.

Rideau Canal system goes for 124 miles (198 km) from Kingston to Ottawa and includes forty-nine locks. If you're traveling by or hauling a pleasure boat, a trip through the lakes, locks, and channels of the Rideau system is one of the great experiences of this area. The Duke of Wellington ordered Colonel By to construct the system, which he completed in 1832. It passes through the beautiful interior of Ontario, and there are many historic and cultural features along the way. For more information on taking your boat through the Rideau Canal from Kingston to Ottawa, call (613) 283–5170.

Boat buffs can cruise the Rideau Canal in all kinds of vessels—from canoes to fully equipped houseboats. Boat-rental companies include Ayling & Associates, (613) 269–4969, and Houseboat Holidays, (613) 382–2842.

Those who prefer to let somebody else do the driving can take a four- to six-day cruise on the *Kawartha Voyageur,* an attractive little boat that accommodates only thirty-eight passengers. Ontario Waterway Cruises, which operates the cruise ship, offers passengers hearty, home-cooked meals in a relaxed ambience. Call (800) 561–5767.

Accommodations

Ambassador Resort Hotel and Convention Centre, 1550 Princess Street, (613) 548–3605. Moderate.

Best Western Fireside Inn, 1217 Princess Street, (613) 549–2211. Moderate.

Conway's Inn, 1155 Princess Street, (613) 546–4285. Inexpensive.

Days Inn Kingston, 33 Benson Street. (613) 546–3661. Moderate.

Holiday Inn, 1 Princess Street, (613) 549–8400. Moderate to expensive.

Howard Johnson's Confederation Place Hotel, 237 Ontario Street, (613) 549–6300. Moderate to expensive.

Hotel Belvedere, 141 King Street East, (613) 548–1565 or www.hotelbelvedere.com. Moderate to expensive.

Prince George Hotel, 200 Ontario Street, (613) 547–9037. Moderate to expensive.

Seven Oaks Motor Inn, 2331 Princess Street, (613) 546–3655. Moderate.

Econolodge, 2327 Princess Street, (613) 531–8929. Inexpensive.

Ramada Plaza Hotel, 1 Johnson Street, (613) 549–8100. Moderate to expensive.

Hochelaga Inn, 24 Sydenham Street, (613) 549–5534. Moderate to expensive.

Thousand Islands Cruises

The best way to see the Thousand Islands is to take a boat cruise. Several operators offer cruises through these beautiful islands with their magnificent baronial mansions. Kingjston 1000 Islands, Brock Street Dock, Kingston, (613) 549–5544 or ww.1000island-cruises.on.ca has cruises of Kingston Harbour and the Thousand Islands on board the paddle-wheeler *Island Queen* as well as a romantic sunset cruise. Operates mid-May to mid-October. Gananoque Boat Line, Customs Dock, Gananoque, Ontario, (613) 382–2144, offers a three-hour tour on a double-deck vessel, covering the Thousand Islands area. Operates mid-May to mid-September.

CHAPTER 6

The Province Of Québec

For Americans, visiting the province of Québec is like traveling abroad. It's a real foreign country in looks, sounds, tastes, and the electricity in the air, and yet it has a familiar ring too.

Québec is European and French, but with a distinctly New World flavor. For one thing, although it fiercely protects its language, it is not as disdainful of things American as its European parent. (Nor, in fact as critical of American influence as its neighbors just west in Ontario.) It embraces all sorts of Americanisms, from fast food to shopping malls, but insists that they be renamed in French. You'll find the familiar face of Colonel Sanders over a sign that reads POULET FRIT À LA KENTUCKY.

While we may (and often do) laugh at the absurdities of Québec's Language Police (which even many local Francophones call "Tongue Troopers"), this very Gallic crankiness accounts for many of Québec's appealing quirks. And with it comes a passion, a verve, a sparkle of pure joie de vivre. And it's infectious.

As you might expect of a place populated mainly by people of French heritage—however many centuries removed from their homeland—Québécois are passionate about food and wine. They demand quality and they usually get it, so much so that it is not unusual for people to travel there just for a weekend of fine dining in Montréal or at one of the numerous country inns. Many of

Ile d'Orléans' rural beauty and simplicity remind Québécois of their past as seen through romantic perpectives.

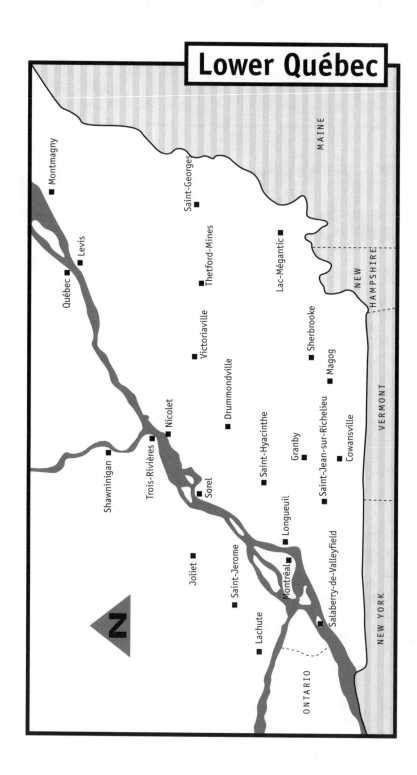

these auberges are known as much for the accolades of their chefs as for the stylish warmth of their ambience.

If you have visited only the smart cosmopolitan cities of Montréal and Québec, you may have a surprise coming when you venture into the hinterlands of the province. The French charm and joie de vivre are still there, but once you stray from the resort areas and tourist paths, you will find yourself in a different world.

Small communities cluster both literally and metaphorically around their parish church, which often looms as a large physical presence in their midst. Community social, political, and spiritual life is centered there, and the parish priest has a great deal more influence over the lives and opinions of his parishioners than his colleagues do in the city parishes.

One result of this influence is that it is these rural towns that provide the strongest push for Québec separatism. On the reccurring referendum votes, the *oui* votes come heavily from these areas, which have less involvement in the economic and political realities of modern culture in the province as a whole.

But these differences make travel among them all the more interesting. For a real linguistic and cultural immersion, as well as a rollicking good time, join them at a church supper or in a *cabine de sucre* for a spirited evening of good, hearty habitant food. Here you are likely to hear the unforgettable sound that personifies the indomitable spirit of these regions: fiddle music. We promise you that your feet will be tapping in tune within five minutes.

For those who long for facts, here are a few about Québec. Its population exceeds seven million, of which 80 percent speak French The other 20 percent represents a shrinking number of Anglophones, more of whom move away with each referendum on separatism. Their numbers are replaced by immigrants who arrive in Montréal in a regular stream. These immigrants, on becoming voting citizens, also represent a firm voting bloc against separatism.

The Landscape

The massive province of Quebec—963,000 square miles of it—begins east of the easternmost part of the United States and extends as far as the western end of New York State. It reaches from the United States border on the south to (and along the eastern shore of) Hudson Bay and James Bay in the north. Much of the western section of the province is part of the Canadian Shield, a huge piece of the inner part of the earth exposed by geological movements and scraped down by several glacial periods.

Along Québec's southern border, which touches the states of Maine, New Hampshire, Vermont, and New York, as well as the province of New Brunswick, most of the land is a fairly level plain along the Saint Lawrence River. This is some of the most agriculturally productive land in the province. North of the Saint Lawrence the terrain rapidly becomes more rugged, with steeper hills leading off to mountains. These regions, particularly the area north of Montréal and the Charlevoix region, are famed for their ski resorts. Beyond this fringe are few roads and fewer settlements. Heavy forests yield to tundra and eventually to the ice and snow of the Arctic.

The Saint Lawrence River itself is the great heart of the province. From the beginning it was the primary highway for trade and commerce and it still serves that function. The importance of the river was enhanced significantly by the completion of the Saint Lawrence Seaway canal system in the 1950s. Ships passing through and stopping in the province carry grains, minerals, and goods from the middle-western United States and western Canada through the Great Lakes to the rest of the world.

On the east end of the province, the Saint Lawrence River empties into the broad Gulf of Saint Lawrence. On the south shore of the gulf is the rocky, mountainous peninsula of Gaspé. Its granite shore cliffs are home to many Francophone fishing communities. On the north shore of the gulf, population quickly dwindles as one travels east of Québec City.

Québec's History

The story of Québec Province is the story of its two greatest cities, Québec and Montréal. More than anywhere else in Canada, the history of the province of Québec contains within it the roots of the collision of two great cultures, a collision that continues to this day.

Well before the English settled New England, the French had established themselves in the dark inland woods of North America. They first came seeking a passage through North America to Asia, the mythic Northwest Passage. Jacques Cartier was the first, sailing into the huge Gulf of Saint Lawrence in 1534. In 1535 he reached a native settlement called Stadacona on a narrow shelf of land at the foot of a towering headland. He named the cliffs Cap

Diamant (Cape Diamond). The First Nations name for the place was *Quebec,* "place where the river narrows." Cartier set up a small fort and set out to explore upriver, hoping it would be the Northwest Passage to Asia. Only 165 miles upstream, however, he met strong and dangerous rapids that stopped him. Beside the rapids was a native village of about fifty houses, called Hochelaga. Wishing to see what lay beyond, Cartier visited the village, then climbed the mountain behind it, naming the mountain Mont Réal. He then returned to his fort at Québec, and it was not until 1603 that the second French explorer, Samuel de Champlain, saw the site. Returning to Québec, Champlain built a stronger fort there and began a settlement, naming it Place Royale.

In its infancy Place Royale (Québec City) struggled along as a trading post, swapping European goods for furs with the native people. Fur was a popular item in European fashion; beaver, which was used in the manufacture of men's hats, was particularly popular. At first natives brought furs to the settlement, but soon French settlers fanned out into the woods, becoming trappers and traders. Unlike what was to happen in British New England, in French North America the settlements were primarily trading posts, not colonies.

It wasn't until 1642 that Europeans returned to Hochelega to settle. Paul de Chomedey de Maisonneuve, a French soldier, led a group of fifty soldiers and Catholic missionaries who named their new settlement Ville Marie de Mont Réal. Their goal was to convert and "save" the Huron, Algonquin, and Iroquois who inhabited this territory. In 1655 there were 719 men in the community but only 65 women. To right the imbalance, the King of France paid the dowry of more than 700 orphaned women who agreed to go to Ville Marie to marry. They were very popular women in New France.

Subjected to frequent attacks by the First Nations, Ville Marie wasn't able to relax its defenses until 1701, when a treaty was reached. About this time it became known simply as Montréal.

England and France had already clashed in Nova Scotia and Newfoundland, and Britain was highly aware of the importance of the inland areas of New France. The first major inland conflict came in 1690 when Governor William Phips of Massachusetts attempted to conquer Québec. The British fleet tried to take the city again in 1711, only to be destroyed in the Gulf of Saint Lawrence.

In 1758 the final phase of the contest between the two countries for control of North America began with the fall of the

French fortress at Louisbourg. At Québec the following year, the 2,900 soldiers and 13,000 civilians under the command of General Louis Montcalm fought the 27,000 trained soldiers of the English General James Wolfe from June until September, when the French were defeated on the Plains of Abraham. Both generals were killed in the battle and the place where each fell is marked; the plains are now a park.

In 1760 Montréal also became British territory and France ceased to be a part of North America. With French defeat, almost all of the leaders of New France returned to France, leaving behind the mass of settlers, called habitants.

From the beginning, the Roman Catholic church was central to the life of New France. Missionary zeal was, in part, as important as trade. When French leadership withdrew, Royal Governor James Murray allowed the French to keep their civil law and their land laws but, more importantly, the habitants were allowed to practice their religion, which was outlawed in England at the time.

Only a few years later, England found itself defending the former French lands from the upstart United States. In 1775 Americans under General Richard Montgomery captured Montréal. General Benedict Arnold then tried to capture Québec but, contrary to American expectations, French citizens did not help the invaders. After a bitter winter, American troops withdrew from Québec and Montréal in 1776.

The British then used the old French and Indian War trails to try to split the American colonies in half. Montréal was their headquarters and the area between the Saint Lawrence and Lake Champlain became a battleground. After the war, border tensions were high, and in 1812 Americans and the British were at war again. There was another attempt to take Montréal and more talk of invading Canada.

During the early years of the nineteenth century, border negotiations between Britain and the United States dragged on. British sympathy for the Confederacy during the American Civil War only served to heighten the tension. At one point Montréal served as the base for a Confederate raid on St. Albans, Vermont, yielding $200,000 for the Rebel coffers.

If religion and the French language are two of the factors that tie Montréal and Québec together, the Saint Lawrence River is the third. Québec was the original primary city, but growing fur trade shifted the focus west, to Montréal. In the 1820s a canal bypassed the Lachine Rapids that had stopped Cartier and Champlain, and the western lands were opened. A transcontinental railroad opened in 1885. As western Canada developed and the new wheat and corn fields sent their grain for shipment, the ports of both cities prospered. But Montréal's prospered more than Québec's.

Although the city of Québec retained much of its political power, Montréal grew into the commercial, industrial, and economic powerhouse of Canada. The city's economy no longer leads the nation, but it still has a strong economic base.

French is the official language of the province of Québec and strict laws govern the public use of other languages on signs. While Québec does have a small Anglophone population, French is definitely dominant and you are unlikely to hear any other language spoken on the street, except in its ethnic enclaves.

The age-old conflict between the French and British heritages of the province of Québec came to the fore in the mid-1960s, when a radical separatist group began a series of kidnappings and killings. Even though Québec has contributed several Canadian prime ministers and the government of the province is dominated by French speakers, the fear of English domination over French heritage and culture led to the formation of Le Parti Québécois, which seeks the creation of a separate French-speaking Québec nation.

Speak the Language

While you can get by in Québec without speaking a word of French, it is good manners and a source of pleasure to your hosts to acknowledge graciously, so far as you are able, their native tongue. Below are some basic words and phrases to help get you started speaking one of the world's most beautiful languages.

General Expressions

Bonjour.	Good morning or good day.
Bonsoir.	Good evening.
Bonne nuit.	Good night.
Bienvenue.	Welcome.
Merci (beaucoup).	Thank you (very much).

S'il vous plaît.	Please.
De rien.	You're welcome.
Pardonnez-moi.	Pardon me.
Comment allez-vous?	How are you?
Très bien.	Very well.
Je vais mal.	I am not well.
J'ai faim.	I am hungry.
J'ai soif.	I am thirsty.
J'ai froid.	I am cold.
J'ai sommeil.	I am sleepy.
J'ai mal à la tête.	I have a headache.
J'ai mal aux pieds.	I have sore feet.
Ici, nous parlons anglais.	English is spoken here.
Combien est-ce?	How much is it?
A quel prix?	What is the price?
La voiture est en panne.	The car broke down.
Bonne chance.	Good luck.

People

Monsieur	Mister
Madame	Mrs. (married or older woman)
Mademoiselle	Miss (young unmarried woman or girl)
Le garçon	The waiter or boy
La serveuse	The waitress
La dame	The woman
L'homme	The man
La jeune fille	The girl
Les enfants	The children
Le fonctionnaire	The civil servant
L'ouvrier	The workman
Le fermier	The farmer
L'homme d'affaires	The businessman

Places

La chambre d'hôtel	The hotel room
La salle de bain	The bathroom (for bathing)
La toilette	The bathroom (toilet)
La gare	The railroad station
La boîte de nuit	The night club
La centre ville	The city or town center
Le magasin	The store
La maison	The house
L'école	The school

L'église	The church
L'ascenseur	The elevator
Ouvert	Open
Fermé	Closed
Entrée libre	Free entrance
Sortie	Exit
Poussez	Push
Tirez	Pull

Food

Je voudrais un menu	I would like a menu
Le petit déjeuner	Breakfast
Le déjeuner	Lunch
Le dîner	Dinner
L'addition	The check
Le potage	The soup
Le fromage	The cheese
Le poulet	The chicken
Le poisson	The fish
Le bifteck	The beefsteak
Le porc	The pork
L'agneau	The lamb
Le veau	The veal
Le pain	The bread
Le beurre	The butter
Le vin	The wine
Le café	The coffee
Le lait	The milk
L'eau	The water
Le sucre	The sugar
La crème	The cream
La glace	The ice or ice cream
Le gâteau	The cake
Une fourchette	A fork
Un couteau	A knife
Une cuiller	A spoon
Une serviette	A napkin
Un pourboire	A tip

Days of the Week

Dimanche	Sunday
Lundi	Monday

Mardi	Tuesday
Mercredi	Wednesday
Jeudi	Thursday
Vendredi	Friday
Samedi	Saturday

Numbers

Un	One
Deux	Two
Trois	Three
Quatre	Four
Cinq	Five
Six	Six
Sept	Seven
Huit	Eight
Neuf	Nine
Dix	Ten

Weather

Le soleil	The sun
Le vent	The wind
La neige	The snow
La pluie	The rain

Traffic Signs

Arrêt	Stop
Gauche	Left
Droite	Right
Tout droit	Straight ahead
Nord	North
Sud	South
Est	East
Ouest	West
Autoroute	Expressway
Défense d'entrer	No entry
Défense de passer	No passing
Défense de stationner	No parking
Stationnement	Parking
Zone de remorquage	Tow-away zone

The Québécois have learned to make winter a joyous time. Every kind of winter sport is played throughout the province. Just bring a good spirit and you won't be disappointed.

General Information

Time zone: Eastern (most of Québec) and Atlantic (easternmost Québec)
Telephone area codes: Montréal and south to Granby and the New York State and Vermont borders: 450
The Island of Montréal: 514
The Laurentians, the Hull area, and most of the Eastern Townships, including Sherbrooke: 819
Québec City and all the rest of the province north, south, and east of the metropolitan area: 418

Climate and Clothing

Southern Québec summers are warm and pleasant. Generally, there is very little humidity in Montréal and Québec City, making these cities refreshing refuges for people coming up from sweltering Boston, New York, Washington, D.C., or Philadelphia. The average high temperature in August is 77°F (25°C) in Montréal and 74°F (23°C) in Québec City. The evenings are mostly cool.

You get a taste of autumn around the end of August. The Laurentians and the Eastern townships come ablaze with color in September.

The first snows come in November and can last into late April. Québec winters are long, cold, and snowy. In February Montréal averages 18 inches (58 cm) of snow and a high of 26°F (–3°C), while Québec expects 23 inches (46 cm) and 24°F (–5°C). Montréal's underground city and Québec City's Winter Carnivals take some of the bite out of the cold season. The province is well known as a center for winter sports.

A very lovely but all-too-brief spring comes around mid-May.

Casual clothing is appropriate for vacationers in the cities, at resorts, and while touring; however, both men and women should be careful about what they wear into churches, shrines, and cultural institutions. Most Québécois dress up for evenings in fine restaurants and at cultural events. Keep in mind that Montréal is one of the most fashionable cities in North America; bring cloth-

ing that will show your respect for your hosts and that will gain you respect in return. Jackets, sweaters, and light windbreakers are necessary for all seasons in Québec.

The best recommendation for business travelers is to dress as you would at your office or while visiting New York, London, Paris, or Tokyo on business. The Québécois businessperson is very aware of fashion and the status that it conveys, perhaps more so than people in other parts of Canada. Women on business trips would do well to bring some chic cocktail dresses. Flair and good taste are much appreciated in Montréal.

Tourist Information

For brochures and maps on the eighteen tourist regions of Québec, contact Tourisme Québec, P.O. Box 797, Montréal, Québec H3C 2W3.

Call toll-free (800) 363–7777 from Québec, Canada, and the United States, or visit www.bonjourquébec.com; in the Montréal area call (514) 873–2015.

For special-interest sports vacations in the province of Québec, ask for these brochures:

Québec Snowmobiling Guide
Québec Boating Guide
Québec Camping Guide
Québec Skiing Guide
Québec Golf Guide
Québec Provincial Parks Guide
Québec Hunting and Fishing Packages

The government of Québec requires that hunters and anglers use the services and facilities of licensed outfitters who control some of the better territories under lease arrangements with the province. In addition to guiding you to some of the best hunting and fishing, many outfitters also provide food, transportation, accommodations, and equipment. Many of the guides also draw on their own experiences, sharing tall tales of adventure in the wilds and of legendary characters.

The north coast of the Gulf of Saint Lawrence offers the big-game hunter and especially the Atlantic salmon fisher some superb opportunities. In many instances you will need the assistance of bush pilots to get you into remote areas, a service that outfitters can provide.

Nonresidents of Québec are required to obtain permits for all freshwater fishing and special permits for salmon. You may obtain permits from game wardens, fish and game outfitters, and most sports shops. Certain parks and reserves require their own special permits.

Game in Québec includes deer, black bear, moose, caribou, hare, duck, goose, partridge, fox, and wolf. Fish species include bass, pike, walleye, trout, landlocked salmon, Atlantic salmon, and Arctic char.

Accommodations

Québec's hotels and inns reflect the dual charms of the province: the contrast of glistening new state-of-the-art architecture and design with the continental charm of old traditions. It's irresistible. The eloquently old and lavish detail of hotels like Château Frontenac in Québec or Montréal's Ritz and Queen Elizabeth and the provincial coziness and charm of the auberges of the Laurentians remind us of all that was good about yesterday, while the spanking new resorts and chrome-and-glass city hotels like Québec's Hilton and Château Tremblant make us appreciate the best of modern style. Boutique lodgings such as Auberge du Vieux-Port, in a revitalized old stone warehouse in Vieux Montréal, offer a charming mix of both old and new.

Lodgings are in all price ranges and styles, with plain motel rooms and simple country B&Bs at one end of the scale and bastions of city or resort luxury at the other. Most lie somewhere in the middle, at rates pretty close to their U.S. counterparts. As in U.S. cities, you will often find lower weekend rates at city hotels, and lower weekday packages in the countryside and at resorts. Thrifty travelers take advantage of this, and at the same time can enjoy the increased cultural offerings of weekends in the city.

Dining

Like lodging, dining is a blend of many influences and styles. But as in language, the French clearly predominates. That does not necessarily mean the very richly sauced dishes of classical French cooking, however. You will find these, but more likely you will find the underlying traditions of fine French provincial cuisine: impeccably fresh ingredients, innovative combinations, and a total respect for the integrity of each flavor and ingredient.

On the whole (although this is changing) there is less of what Americans know as fusion cooking. Dishes and the restaurants themselves tend to reflect one influence at a time. You will find close attention to how a dish is presented. Although presentations may be less architectural and three-dimensional than the extremes to which some American chefs have gone, the plate will be artistic in upscale restaurants. Chefs are artists, after all.

Dining tends to be leisurely, and your waiter will not hurry you through a fine meal. This is not considered sloppy service, but a respect for your right to linger and savor the evening. Your plate will not be whisked away and replaced with the next course as soon as you lay down your fork. This is especially true in the country auberges, where guests treat dinner as their evening's entertainment.

In the countryside and small towns, you will often find good, reliable restaurants attached to modest motels. These will usually serve more mainstream foods, and in some you may have a chance to sample some of the traditional old Québec dishes. You can also find these at sugar cabins.

Here are some of the best known habitant dishes. Fricot is a rich chicken stew, usually with whole chicken parts and chunks of seasonal vegetables in a broth. Pea soup is made with yellow or green peas, usually with a base of meat stock with finely chopped onions and sometimes carrots and other vegetables blended into its thick, hearty puree. Tourtiere is a meat pie, which your editors think to be one of the greatest contributions of Québec culture. Made right (and it usually is), it's a well-seasoned blend of ground meats cooked to form a textured pâtés, then baked in a piecrust. Sugar pie is very sweet, with a smooth texture like the center of a southern pecan pie, but made with maple instead of molasses.

Of the native foods, try Matane shrimps, cod from the Gulf of Saint Lawrence, Québec cider, anything made from maple syrup, cheeses from the monasteries at Oka and Saint-Benoît du Lac, salmon, and venison. When you are touring the countryside (the Laurentians, the Eastern Townships, the Gaspé), be sure to ask for the specialty of the area (for example, the bouillabaisse is far more splendid on the Gaspé than in the big cities).

Travelers on the road will find fast foods for lunch, although not in great abundance. More likely you will want to stop at a cafe in a small town or at one of the motel restaurants, where they will serve you a light meal or a sandwich promptly.

CHAPTER 7

Montréal

There is a tendency to describe Montréal (*Mohn-ray-ahl*) as the Paris of North America, but except for its French heritage, Montréal is no more like Paris than Boston is like London. Montréal is a distinctly North American city, an important point to remember because so many visitors compare the city with Paris, in its language, cultural traditions, and ambience. For travelers who know Paris, Montréal will be a welcome surprise: The people here are very friendly to visitors and pride themselves on their warm hospitality. This is quite a contrast to Paris!

Montréal is the financial, manufacturing, and transportation capital of Québec and is second only to Toronto as a Canadian economic center. The current population of greater Montréal is more than three million, nearly half the population of the entire province.

Most Montréalers are French-speaking Québécois, and many are bilingual. An Anglophone population lives mainly in the western section of the city (Westmount) and in the western suburbs. Montréal has always had one of the largest Jewish populations in Canada. In addition, there are large communities of Chinese, Portuguese, Italian, and other ethnic groups. Their distinctive neighborhoods enliven the city's rich cultural mix.

Montréal is a well-run city of stunning high-rise buildings, featuring one of the best public transportation systems on the continent and a dynamic urban environment.The city itself is on a boomerang-shaped island, 32 miles (51 km) long and more than 10 miles (16 km) wide at its center. It is surrounded by the Saint Lawrence, the Rivière des Prairies, and two lakes.

Montréal's impressive skyline of high-rises is set against beautiful Mont-Royal and along the Saint Lawrence River, which, before the days of aviation, used to be Canada's lifeline. Although a thousand miles from the Atlantic Ocean, Montréal has always been one of Canada's major ports. Its harbor can accommodate scores of ocean-going vessels, including the largest luxury liners. Montréal has two international airports. Dorval International Airport is fifteen minutes from downtown. Mirabel International Airport also offers charter flights. The city is served by VIA Rail, Canada's passenger rail system, and Amtrak from the United States. Excellent highways and roads give easy access to the city.

Montréal has some of the finest hotels and restaurants in Canada. In particular, its French cuisine is considered exceptional. The city is also the French Canadian center of fashion, movie production, book publishing, and architectural and interior design. The second largest French-speaking city in the world, Montréal is the capital of French (distinctly Québécois) culture in the Western Hemisphere.

So much happens in the city that Montréal never seems to sleep. Montréal accepts a wide range of lifestyles, from the most conservative to radical chic. Yet religion, particularly the Roman Catholic faith, is evident everywhere—in an abundance of churches and shrines.

Montréal is a four-seasons city. In the winter, you can enjoy the weather-protected and attractive "underground city," in more than 18 mi (30 km) of passageways, and the excellent skiing and plush resorts of the Laurentians are only a short drive away. Spring, though brief, is a time of sultry breezes and colorful flowers—most pleasant days for a visit. Summer offers fun at La Ronde, one of the largest amusement parks in Canada. You can enjoy a special treat in the autumn through foliage tours of the Eastern Townships and the Laurentians.

Most visitors come away raving about their stay in Montréal, and you surely will too.

Tourist Information

For additional information, visit the Greater Montréal Convention and Visitors Bureau, 1001 du Square-Dorchester Street, or telephone Infotouriste at (514) 873–2015 or (877) BONJOUR; www.tourism-montreal.org. The bureau invites you to visit its Infotouriste Centre, located downtown at 1001, rue du Square-Dorchester (between Peel and Metcalfe), or the branch office in Old Montréal at 174 Notre Dame Street East, or log onto www.bonjourquebec.com.

How to Get to Montréal

By Air

Many domestic and international airlines, including Air Canada, Delta, American Airlines, and Canadian International, provide daily service to Montréal.

Dorval-International Airport in a suburb west of Montréal, is 14 miles (22 km) from downtown. Dorval airport is used for domestic flights and flights to the United States. The recently renovated terminal has a high-end restaurant, cafes, gift and duty-free shops, and bookstores. Returning American travelers clear U.S. Customs at Dorval rather than back in the United States. Taxis and limousines are plentiful. Frequent service is available to and from the city (the Queen Elizabeth Hotel is a major pickup point). There are several excellent hotels nearby.

Montréal Mirabel International Airport, located 34 miles (54 km) to the north of downtown, is primarily used for flights by charter and cargo carriers to and from the European continent and other international destinations. Mirabel has a number of conveniences for the traveler, including accommodations, restaurants, lounges, and boutiques. Frequent bus service operates between downtown Montréal and Mirabel and between both airports. Taxis and limousines are also available.

By Car

From New York City take I–87 to Autoroute 15. From western New York State, take I–90 to I–81 as far as Highway 401 in Ontario, which goes east to Montréal. Visitors from central and western New England can go from I–91 to I–89 and then to Autoroute 10, or from Vermont they can take I–91 directly to Autoroutes 55 and 10 (Sherbrooke, Québec). Eastern New Englanders (from eastern Massachusetts, Rhode Island, and New Hampshire) can take I–93 to I–89, Route 133, and then pick up Autoroute 10.

From Western and Eastern Canada, travel the Trans-Canada Highway, or from Toronto, Highway 401. An alternative for travelers from the Maritimes is to cut across Maine, New Hampshire, and Vermont using I–95, I–89, or I–91.

For current road condition information, call (877) 393-2363.

Driving distances to Montréal from major cities

Boston	307 mi (512 km)
Chicago	850 mi (1,417 km)
Detroit	585 mi (975 km)
New York City	365 mi (608 km)
Philadelphia	458 mi (763 km)
Québec City	162 mi (270 km)
Toronto	324 mi (539 km)
Vancouver	2,881 mi (4,801 km)
Ottawa	114 mi (190 km)
Winnipeg	1,445 mi (2,408 km)
Calgary	2,246 mi (3,743 km)
Halifax	750 mi (1,249 km)
Washington, D.C.	586 mi (977 km)
Seattle	2,848 mi (4,747 km)
Los Angeles	3,015 mi (5,025 km)

Driving in Montréal

Drivers should have no problem driving in and around Montréal. The highways are well marked, maintained, and illuminated, as are the city streets. Obey all signs and speed limits. The Montréal police are not tolerant of traffic violations. For the most part, however, you will not need your car in the city and will probably want to leave it parked while you ride public transportation.

Rental Cars

Rental cars are available at Dorval and Mirabel airports and at other city locations from Avis, Hertz, and Tilden. Because of the demand for rental cars during busy tourist and convention periods, we advise making reservations before you leave home.

By Rail

VIA Rail, the Canadian passenger rail system, provides service to Montréal from points west in Canada and from the Maritimes, with frequent daily service from Québec City, Ottawa, and Toronto. VIA Rail trains arrive and depart Gare Centrale (Central Station), located next to the Queen Elizabeth Hotel and across the street from Place Bonaventure. From Montréal, call (514) 989–2626 for VIA Rail information and reservations; from elsewhere in Canada, call toll-free (800) 361–1234, or visit www. viarail.ca.

The Bonaventure Metro station, located in Place Bonaventure, is a short walk from Central Station.

By Bus

Greyhound provides frequent daily service to Montréal from the United States and from other cities in Canada. Check with your local Greyhound agent for details. Montreal Bus Central Station (514) 843–4231, the city's main bus terminal, is located next to the Berri-Uqam Metro station, where subway trains radiate to almost every section of the city. Bus service is available from here to many destinations in Canada.

General Information

Time zone: Eastern
Telephone area code: 514 (suburbs 450)
Fire, police, and medical emergencies: dial 911
Weather information: (514) 283–4006

English-Language Newspapers and Television

Most major English newspapers and magazines published elsewhere are available throughout the city. In addition to French-language television stations, Montréal receives a large number of English-language American and Canadian stations.

Sales Tax and Tips

There is a tax on hotel rooms, clothing, textiles, meals, and furniture. There is a 7.5 percent sales tax on most goods and a 7 percent GST tax. This tax can be reimbursed to tourists either at customs or by filling out a form. There is also a $2 room tax in the city of Montréal. This cannot be reclaimed. The customary tip is 15 to 20 percent of the food and drink bill. For details on tax reimbursment, visit www.ccraadrc.gc.ca/ tax/nonresidents/visitors/ tax-e.html.

Convention Centre

Montréal's modern Convention Centre is located at 201, avenue Viger, and occupies the block between avenue Viger and rue Saint-Antoine, just below the Vieux (Old) Montréal section. It is already one of the largest convention facilities in North America and is being renovated and enlarged as we write. Its main exhibition hall has 100,000 square feet (9,293 sq m) of space; there are an additional 50,000 square feet (4,646 sq m) on the Convention Level, a large number of meeting rooms, a cafeteria, and a first-class restaurant. The Convention Centre is situated in the heart of

Chinatown, with its many fine restaurants and colorful shops. This section is becoming one of the more appealing areas of the city and a wonderful place in which to roam about after the stress of a convention or association meeting. Call (800) 268-8122.

Other convention and business-meeting facilities in Montréal include Queen Elizabeth Hotel, the Montréal Bonaventure Hilton, Marriott Château Champlain, Hotel Wyndham Montréal, Montréal Airport Hilton, Olympic Stadium, Place des Arts, McGill University, Concordia University, and the University of Montréal.

Montréal's top downtown hotels for convention-goers are the Queen Elizabeth, Le Centre Sheraton, Montréal Bonaventure Hilton, Marriott Château Champlain, Holiday Inn Crowne Plaza Downtown, Omni Mont-Royal, the Ritz-Carlton Montréal, Delta Centre-ville, Radisson Gouverneurs, Loews Hotel Vogue, and Inter-Continental.

How to Get Around Montréal

The Central Area

Although Montréal is a large metropolis, the visitor will find it easy to get around. Much of what you'll want to do and see is in a rather compact area, which can be covered on foot and via the Metro subway system.

From a visitor's point of view, the center of the city is Place Ville-Marie, a complex of high-rise buildings on boulevard René-Lévesque. Other landmarks in this area are the Queen Elizabeth Hotel, Cathedral Marie-Reine-du-Monde, Gare Centrale, Place du Canada–Château Champlain Hotel, McGill College Avenue, and Dorchester Square. To the north is Mont-Royal; to the south, the Saint Lawrence River.

The street just north of René-Lévesque and running parallel to it is rue Sainte-Catherine, which is lined with big department stores: the Bay, Ogilvy, and the trendy new Simons, which is favored by young Montréalers. Small shops and inexpensive places to eat, including familiar fast-food places, abound near them.

Two or three streets north of Sainte-Catherine is rue Sherbrooke. Sherbrooke has high-fashion shops, art galleries, the McCord Museum, business offices, the campus of McGill University, the Museum of Fine Arts, and the venerable Ritz-Carlton Hotel.

North of Sherbrooke are Avenue du Mont-Royal and beautiful Parc Mont-Royal. On the other side of Mont-Royal are the campus of the Université de Montréal and Saint Joseph's Oratory, one of Québec's important religious shrines.

Center of Montréal

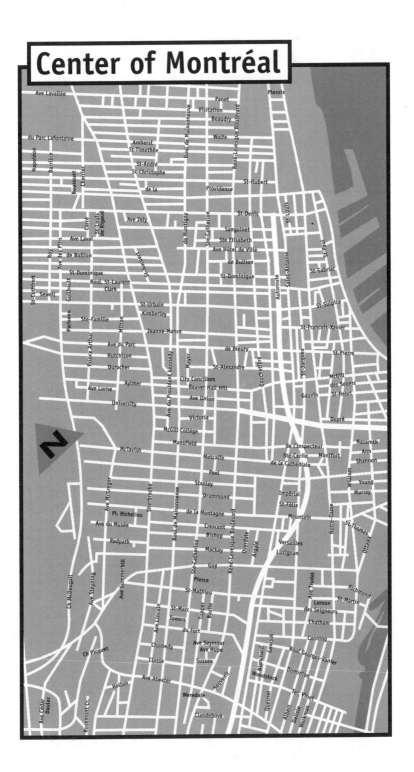

Ave Lavallée · Panet · Plessis · Visitation · Beaudry · du Parc Lafontaine · Amherst · St-Timothée · Wolfe · René-Lévesque Boulevard · Boul de Maisonneuve · Napoléon · Barrière · Cherrier · Bousquet · St-André · St-Christophe · St-Hubert · de la · Providence · de Montigny · St-Catherine · St-Dominique · St-Louis · St-Denis · Ave Joly · Sanguinet · Ste Elisabeth · Ave Hôtel de Ville · de Bullion · St-Paul · St-Gabriel · Autoroute · Saint-Antoine · Ave Laval · Ave Laval · de Bullion · Roy · Ave des Pins · Corré · St-Louis de Higaud · St-Dominique · St-Cuthbert · Sewell · Guilbault · St-Dominique · Boul. St-Laurent · Clark · St-Sulpice · St-Urbain · Kimberley · St-François-Xavier · Parizeau · Ste-Famille · Milton · Jeanne-Mance · Prince Arthur · Ave du Parc · de Bleury · St-Pierre · Hutchison · Mayor · St-Alexandre · Gauchetière · St-Jacques · Durocher · City Concillors · McGill · Aylmer · Beaver Hall Hill · des Souers · Ave Lorne · Ave Union · Gauvin · St-Henri · University · Ave du President Kennedy · Dupré · Victoria · McGill Collège · Nazareth · Mansfield · de l'Inspecteur · Ann · McTavish · Metcalfe · Ste-Cecile · Montfort · Shannon · de la Cathédrale · Peel · William · Young · Stanley · Murray · Ave McGregor · Drummond · Impérial · Sherbrooke · Boul de Maisonneuve · de la Montagne · St-Félix · Pl. Richelieu · Crescent · Mountain · Ave du Musée · Bishop · St-Thomas · Redpath · Mackay · Versailles · Ottawa · St-Catherine · René-Levesque Boulevard · Lusignan · Overdale · Argyle · Guy · Ave Summerhill · Pierce · Ch. McDougall · Ave Steyning · St-Mathieu · Ave Trudel · Richmond · Ave Lincoln · St-Marc · Leroux · St-Martin · Tupper · Basile · des Seigneurs · Towers · du Fort · Chatham · Ch Picquet · Chomedy · Ave Seymour · Canning · Ave Hupe · Blanchard · Couzsol · Boul Georges-Vanier · Closse · Sussex · Holton · Ave Atwater · Southam · Dominton · Quesnel · Ter Vihot · Woodstock · Albert · Ave Cédar · Daulac · Weredale · Dalisle · Workman · Rosemont Cr · Clandebove

N

Old Montréal

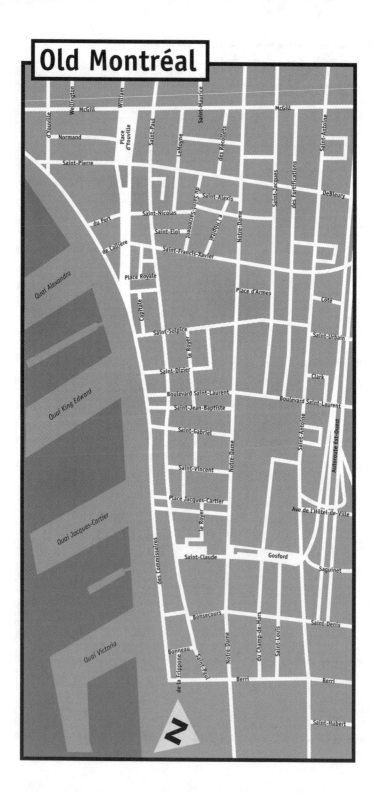

To the south of Place Ville-Marie flows the Saint Lawrence River. The lovely Île Sainte-Hélène, site of La Ronde amusement park and the David M. Stewart Museum at the Old Fort, can be reached by the metro.

To the southeast of Place Ville-Marie is Old (Vieux) Montréal, the city's preserved historic section; to the east is Place des Arts (the performing arts center), the Convention Centre, Complexes Desjardins and Guy Favreau, Maison de Radio-Canada (CBC production and broadcasting facility), and Chinatown. Further east are Olympic Park and the Botanical Gardens, both easily reached by metro.

To the west of Place Ville-Marie are rue Crescent, rue Mackay, and rue Bishop, with their trendy restaurants, boutiques, lounges, and discos. Westmount is a cozy area of mansions, residences of Montréal's power elite.

Montréal's Subway System

Montréal's Metro can take you to most downtown attractions quickly, inexpensively, and efficiently. Each station is a work of

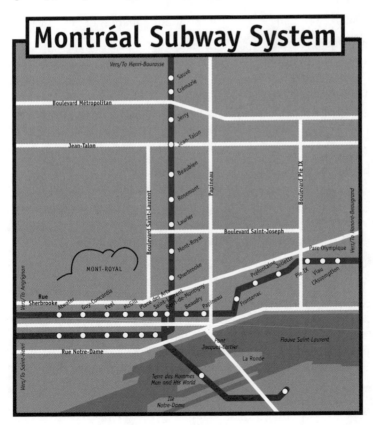

art, beautifully decorated, clean, and safe. Easy-to-read maps of the system are posted on the station walls and inside the trains. You'll see that the Metro interconnects everything in the "underground city."

Adult fare for the Metro is $2.00, or you can buy a strip of six tickets for $8.25. Those who will be doing a lot of traveling about the city might want to take advantage of the STCUM Tourist Card, allowing unlimited rides for one day or three days, $7 and $14 respectively. Visit www.stcum.gc.ca for more information.

Although the Metro serves a large metropolitan area, most visitors will find these stops most convenient:

Station	Destinations
Atwater Le Forum	Westmount Square shopping area
Berri-Uqam (central station, where three of the four converge, and the bus terminal)	Latin Quarter/rue Saint-Denis area, train to Île Sainte-Hélène, Longueuil
Bonaventure	downtown Montréal, Place Ville-Marie, Place du Canada, Place Bonaventure, Central Station (rail)
Champs de Mars	Old Montréal (Place Jacques-Cartier), City Hall, and attractions
Guy Concordia	rue Sherbrooke, Ritz-Carlton, Museum of Fine Arts, rue Crescent boutiques and restaurants
McGill	rue Sherbrooke, McGill University, rue Sainte-Catherine department stores, central Montréal, Place Ville-Marie
Peel	rue Sherbrooke, Ritz-Carlton, Museum of Fine Arts, rue Crescent boutiques and restaurants

Station	Destinations
Pie-IX	Botanical Gardens
Viau	Biodome
Place d'Armes	Convention Centre, Complexe Guy Favreau, Complexe Desjardins, Old Montréal, Chinatown, Palais de Justice, Saint-Jacques Street
Place des Arts	Place des Arts performing arts center
Square Victoria	Place Desjardins, Place Victoria, Montréal Stock Exchange, rue Saint-Jacques to Vieux (Old) Montréal

Guided Tours and Cruises

Guided tours of Montréal are available from Autocar Royal (514) 871–4733 or www.autocarroyal.com and Gray Line (514) 934–1222 or www.graylinemontreal.com—both pick up guests at major hotels; Guidatour (514) 844–4021; Step On Guide Inc. (514) 935–5131; and Visites de Montréal (514) 933–6674. Royal Gray Line tours start at Infotouriste (Square Dorchester).

Another way to see Montréal, perhaps the most romantic way, is to hire a calèche (a horse-drawn carriage and driver), which can be found around Dorchester Square, Place Jacques Cartier, Parc Mont-Royal, and Place d'Armes. If you want to take a more active part in your tour of the city, there are also walking and cycling tours available. Guidatour offers guided walks through old Montréal, and private group tours can be arranged; call (800) 363–4021. You can also hop on a rented bike with your own guide and tour the city with Le Maison des Cyclistes from May through September. Call (514) 521–8356 or visit www. velo.qc.ca.

Cruises on the Saint Lawrence River are offered by Montréal Harbor Cruises, (514) 842–3871, and Montréal AML Cruises, (800) 667–3131. Lachine Rapid Tours, (514) 284–9607, provides thrilling jet-boat and rafting trips down through the churning, historic Lachine rapids. This is an excellent wilderness adventure right next to the city. The boarding area for Saint Lawrence River trips and cruises is at the Victoria Pier on the waterfront, near Place Jacques Cartier.

Major Events

Montréal thrives on shows, galas, spectacles, and grand events that capture the attention of the world. The following is a brief listing of significant annual events in Montréal. (For more information on these and upcoming special events, contact the Greater Montréal Convention and Tourism Bureau at 514–844–5400.)

Fête des Neiges, February, Parc des Îles, on the island of Sainte-Hélène. A sliding and tubing hill, horse-drawn sleigh rides, dogsled rides, ice sculptures, a huge ice fortress, cross-country skiing and snowshoeing (both with rental equipment), skating rinks, and a chance to learn the sport of curling.

Montréal Canadiens hockey at the new Molson Centre, built to replace the venerable Forum, from autumn through spring

Montréal Highlights Festival is held in February. Call (888) 477–9955 or visit www.montrealenlumiere.com for information.

Montréal Symphony Orchestra, performances at various times throughout the year, at Place des Arts and Notre-Dame Basilica

Les Grands Ballets Canadiens, performances at various times of the year, at Place des Arts

Montréal International Jazz Festival, late June to early July.

Concours Internationale d'Art Pyrotechnique, the International Fireworks Competition, June and July. Viewing stands are in La Ronde Amusement Park, but you can watch the fireworks free from the Jacques Cartier Bridge, which is closed to traffic while fireworks makers from all over the world show off their best displays.

Players of Canada Formula 1 racing, in June, at Île Notre-Dame

Tour de l'Île Cycling Competition, in June (departure from Olympic Park)

Festival Bell Just for Laughs (comedy), late July

The Montréal World Film Festival, late August to September

Attractions

The Underground City

Montréal's biggest year-round attraction is its so-called underground city (Montréal souterrain), a vast complex consisting of clusters of modern buildings located in various parts of the city and connected by the Metro subway system, shopping promenades, and passageways. The underground city incorporates many conveniences: residences, offices, stores, restaurants, theaters, hotels, recreation, and public transportation. It is quite possible to live, work, and enjoy life here without ever setting foot outdoors, especially important during Montréal's long, cold winters. This concept has been copied in a number of other cities.

Montréal's underground city began in the 1960s with the opening of Place Ville-Marie, a complex of office high-rises built over a labyrinth of boutiques, restaurants, and service establishments. Place Ville-Marie was connected by attractive, often glittering passageways to the Queen Elizabeth Hotel, Central Station, the métro, and Place Bonaventure, another massive complex of offices, eateries, boutiques, hotel, and exhibition areas. As the city continued to modernize through the 1970s, more complexes were connected: Place des Arts, Westmount Square, Place Victoria, Complexe Desjardins, Complexe Guy Favreau, the Convention Centre, Place du Canada, and several others. The Metro links all these complexes plus many other stores and office buildings together into an attractive, enclosed, climate-controlled, urban living network more than 18 miles (30 km) long.

Touring the underground city is a pleasure. There seems to be an infinite number of shops and boutiques, selling everything from high fashion to the bizarre (and some bizarre high fashion!). The window displays and interiors of many of the shops are nearly works of art—most are at least entertaining. You can spend many delightful hours just window-shopping and poking in here and there. In the Place des Arts you can attend symphony, opera, ballet, a contemporary art museum, and dramatic performances. And you can experience another unique pleasure—riding an attractive, clean, safe subway to almost anywhere in the underground city.

Old Montréal (Vieux Montréal)

Although Montréal is one of North America's most modern cities in appearance and spirit, it has not turned its back on a distinguished heritage. Much of Montréal's past has been lovingly preserved and restored in a section known as Old Montréal. The architecture in Old Montréal is predominantly eighteenth and nineteenth century, and the section is dotted with superb French restaurants, cafes, bistros, boutiques, and handicraft shops. To learn more about this old part of the city, visit Web site www.vieux.montreal.qc.ca.

Place Jacques Cartier, a sloping cobblestone square ringed by cafes, shops, and restaurants, is where young people and lovers of all ages come to sip wine and espresso and listen to songs, poetry, and political ideas. Many of the buildings around the Place have been recently renovated. Place Jacques Cartier, the most intimate public place in the city, has long been and continues to be a central meeting place for Québécois intellectuals, artists, and literati. At the top of Place Jacques Cartier, on rue Notre-Dame, is the Nelson statue (1809), and across from it is the Second Empire–style edifice of Montréal's City Hall, which has frequent cultural exhibits for the public.

Any visitor interested in history or in architecture will want to get a copy of the excellent booklet *Discover Old Montréal*. In a series of well-illustrated walking tours, it leads through this quarter's nearly four centuries of history as it brings you through the streets. With this guide in hand, you will see details you would never spot otherwise.

Château Ramezay, 280, rue Notre-Dame, built in 1705, is one of the city's oldest buildings. The Norman-style structure has housed French and English governors, offices of the West India Company, General Benedict Arnold during his retreat from Québec City, and Benjamin Franklin and his party during their mission to convert the Québécois to the American revolutionary cause. Today it houses one of Québec's best collections of historical artifacts and documents. Open throughout the year, closed Monday in the off-season. Admission charge.

Archaeology Museum, Pointe-à-Calliére, 350, place Royale, (514) 872–9150. This museum has been built around the old foundations of buildings dating back several centuries. Visitors are taken back to Montréal's past by means of a sound and light show, holograms of "personalities" who explain the history of the city and, of course, the old stone walls themselves. Open daily except Monday. Admission charge.

Basilique Notre-Dame, 116, Place d'Armes, was designed by New York architect James O'Donnell and features twin towers, a neo-Gothic style, and a lavish, ornate interior. The elaborate carvings, paintings, and dramatic lighting make for an impressive liturgical show. Opened in 1829, Notre-Dame has been the spiritual focus for Roman Catholics in the city ever since, though it no longer serves as the ecclesiastical seat of the diocese. Notre Dame is where the Luciano Pavarotti Christmas music special, broadcast annually on television, was filmed. There is an interesting little museum of local and church history here. Admission charge for the museum and to tour the Basilica.

Place d'Armes itself is a square marked by a fine heroic statue

Immortalized in Glass

Stained glass windows in the Basilica of Notre Dame pay tribute to two women who were among the first settlers that came with Paul de Chomedey de Maisonneuve. Jeanne Mance and Marguerite de Bourgeoys began Montréal's longstanding tradition of civic responsibility as they worked to help both settlers and native peoples. In 1645 Jeanne Mance founded the first hospital in Canada to treat the sick and injured from wars with the Iroquois.

Marguerite de Bourgeoys founded the teaching order of Sisters of the Congregation de Notre Dame. In 1658 she opened the first school for women in New France. Much of what historians know of the daily life and hardships of those early years is from her diaries.

of Paul de Chomedey de Maisonneuve, founder of Ville-Marie (as Montréal was first called). Next to the church is a 1685 stone wall protecting the Sulpician Seminary (the Sulpicians predate the Jesuits in Québec), which is the oldest building in the city. And across Place d'Armes is the nineteenth-century edifice of the Bank of Montréal, which has a museum on early banking practices that is open to the public. (A substantial sum of money was deposited here by the Confederates during the American Civil War.) Free.

Marché Bonsecours, on rue Saint-Paul, whose handsome dome and colonnade are reminiscent of the Palladian style, is one of the most outstanding pieces of historic architecture in the city. At one time closed, it is again open to the general public.

Notre-Dame-de-Bonsecours, the sailor's church, is next to Marché Bonsecours at 400, rue Saint-Paul. Montréal's oldest church (circa 1657), it was founded by Sister Marguerite Bourgeoys, an immortal in Québec history and a saint since 1982. Visit the church museum honoring this great educator and religious leader and climb up into the spire to see the city and the harbor.

Parc Historique National Sir George-Étienne Cartier, 458, rue Notre-Dame, is the home of one of the fathers of Canadian Confederation. The Cartier family lived here from 1848 to 1871. Open April through December. Admission charge.

Montréal History Centre, 355, rue Saint-Pierre, at Place d'Youville, has exhibits on the development of the city from its early beginnings. Open throughout the year. Admission charge.

Old Montréal is a compact area, and everything is within walking distance. Automobiles here are a nuisance, and parking is difficult. Take a taxi from your hotel or the Metro to either Champs de Mars or Place d'Armes station. Another nice and romantic way of experiencing Old Montréal is by calèche (horse-drawn carriage), which can be hired in Place Jacques Cartier.

The Islands and the River

Île Sainte-Helene and Île Notre Dame, in the middle of the Saint-Lawrence River, form the grassy and tree-covered Parc des Îles, with beaches for swimming, paths for bicycling, and acres of gardens. The twin islands are connected to the city by the Metro, bridges, and ferries.

Both Expo 67 and the Floralies Internationales in 1980 left the islands with even more attractions. Acres of beautiful formal gardens from the Floralies form a stunning show and botanical garden and include a rare collection of flowers from the far north.

The French Pavilion from Expo 67 is now Montreal's casino and Buckminster Fuller's giant geodesic dome, built as the U. S. Pavilion, is the Biosphere (easy to confuse with the Biodome). It is a museum of water, and explores the ecosystems of the St. Lawrence River.

La Ronde, on Île Sainte-Hélène, is Montréal's spectacular amusement park. There are more than thirty exciting rides of all kinds, games, entertainment, and restaurants. A visit to La Ronde is a must if you are bringing children. La Ronde has a roller coaster with loops that turn cars (and passengers) upside down. Kids love it. Adults endure it. Open mid-May to Labour Day. Admission charge.

David M. Stewart Museum, at the Old Fort on Île Sainte-Hélène, is an old British arsenal, containing artifacts from the early seventeenth century to the mid-1800s. Inside the museum is a model of the entire old quarter of Montréal, showing with lights and voice description how it has changed over the centuries. During the summer the Compagnie Franche de la Marine and the 78th Fraser Highlanders, dressed in period costume, perform eighteenth-century military drills. Open throughout the year except Monday. Admission charge.

Le Casino de Montréal, 1, avenue du Casino, (514) 392–2746 or (800) 665–2274, www.casinos-quebec.com. Since it opened in 1993, this hugely popular gaming hall has been raking in money for its owners, the government-controlled Loto-Québec. The ritzy casino, which is housed in the revamped French pavilion from

Expo 67 on Parc des Îles, has 112 games tables and more than 2,700 slot machines. Dress code. Open twenty-four hours a day.

Saint Lawrence Seaway, via the Victoria Bridge and Highway 15 to Saint Lambert Lock, gives visitors a close look at large ships making their way through the complicated but efficient locks that allow them to pass to and from the major ports on the Great Lakes. There is a splendid view of the Montréal skyline from here. Observation deck open from May to October.

The Lachine Canal, formerly a commercial waterway, has been turned into an off-road bike trail running from Old Montréal to the nearby city of Lachine. Two museums give an overview of the area's past: the Lachine National Historic Site, 1255, boulevard Saint-Joseph, Lachine, (514) 637–7433, which documents the fur trade; and the Lachine Canal Interpretation Centre, Seventh Avenue and boulevard Saint-Joseph, (514) 637–7433, where exhibits explain the construction of the canal.

Downtown and Mont-Royal

Parc Mont-Royal, on the top and slopes of Mont-Royal, is the city's favorite and most beautiful green space. Designed by Frederick Law Olmsted, the great American landscape architect, the park offers magnificent vistas of the city and the Saint Lawrence River. This is a perfect place to bring a picnic, to stroll along Beaver Lake, to ride in a calèche under majestic trees, to see an art exhibition, or to enjoy music from itinerant players. There is a nature center here. At the summit of Mont-Royal, a huge cross, illuminated at night, marks the spot where in 1535 Jacques Cartier planted the cross in honor of his king. In the winter there are cross-country skiing, ice skating on Beaver Lake (an old tradition in Montréal), and sledding and skiing on the slopes. Open throughout the year.

At Maison Smith is a new reception center that is open year-round. Here you can find out about the many programs and activities sponsored by Amis de la Montagne. For more details on these, call (514) 843-8240.

Saint Joseph's Oratory, 3800, chemin Queen Mary, built through the inspiration of Brother André, is one of the world's largest basilicas and Montréal's most important religious shrine, drawing thousands of pilgrims annually. Religious services are held every day. Even if you are not a Roman Catholic, the oratory is worth seeing for its huge dome set on the northern slope of Mont-Royal. It is one of the great landmarks of Montréal. Organ concerts regularly.

Montréal Museum of Fine Arts, 1379-80, rue Sherbrooke, ouest, is Québec's leading fine arts museum. It is Canada's oldest and now also houses the Decorative Art Museum. It has a superb permanent collection of Canadian and European paintings, sculpture, furnishings, and other rare and exotic objects. It is also the gallery for important traveling international exhibitions. One should not leave the city without spending some time visiting this outstanding collection. Open throughout the year, Tuesday to Sunday. Telephone (514) 285–2000. Admission charge.

Place des Arts, 175, rue Sainte-Catherine, ouest, is, like New York City's Lincoln Center, a complex of theaters and other facilities that accommodate performances by symphony orchestras, dance and opera companies, drama troupes, and individual entertainers. For information, call (514) 842–2112 or visit www.pdarts.com

Museum of Contemporary Art, also at Place des Arts, features recent works by Canadian and international artists. Open throughout the year, Tuesday to Sunday. Admission charge.

Canadian Guild of Crafts, 2025, rue Peel, is a main showplace for artisans. The gallery displays pottery, weaving, carving, furniture, jewelry, and the work of native Indian and Inuit artisans. All these wares are for sale at attractive prices. Open throughout the year, Tuesday to Saturday. Free.

Montréal Planetarium, 1000, rue Saint-Jacques, ouest, presents the entire universe to the general public. This is a must place to visit if you are interested in science or if you have never seen a first-rate planetarium before. Open throughout the year. Admission charge. Call (514) 872–4530.

McCord Museum, 690, rue Sherbrooke, ouest, across the street from McGill University, is the best anthropological museum in the province, specializing in North American Indian and Inuit cultures. Open throughout the year except Monday. Admission charge. Call (514) 398–7100.

McGill University, rue Sherbrooke, ouest, is a venerable institution of higher learning, with its campus right in the middle of the city, just below Mont-Royal. You are welcome to stroll the campus and to visit the Redpath Museum of Natural History.

Bibliothèque Nationale du Québec, 1700, rue Saint-Denis, has manuscripts originating from 1643 to the present, including notarial deeds, family papers, maps, original drawings, and photographs. If you are doing some genealogical research, it can be an important resource. Open throughout the year. Free.

Christ Church Cathedral (Anglican), on rue Sainte-Catherine in the heart of the downtown shopping district, is a fine neo-Gothic structure with a lovely interior. Open daily for worship.

Cathedral of Marie-Reine-du-Monde (Mary Queen of the World), on boulevard René-Lévesque, ouest, across from the Queen Elizabeth Hotel and in front of Place du Canada, is inspired by Saint Peter's in Rome. Built in 1870, this elegant house of worship has an interior less frenetic than Notre-Dame's in Old Montréal. Visitors of all faiths are welcome.

Olympic Park

In 1976, Montréal hosted the Summer Olympic Games, and built the Olympic Village on a hill overlooking the city. After the Olympics, these buildings and grounds were put to other uses. The modern pyramid-shaped dormitory that housed athletes is now an apartment building. Today the main stadium is used for baseball home games of the Expos and the Montréal Alouettes Football Club and for entertainment events requiring seating for thousands. Open throughout the year. Admission charge for tours. Tickets for sports events can be ordered through Ticketmaster, (514) 790–1245.

Olympic Stadium, avenue Pierre de Coubertin, is easy to spot by the huge slanted tower that supports the roof. The roof, shaped like a circus tent, was designed to be lifted off by big cables. This is the world's largest inclined tower, and you can ride to its top in a cable car for a spectacular view over the top of the city. Admission charge. The public can swim in the stadium pool used by Olympians.

The Biodome, avenue Pierre de Coubertin, is a brilliant recycling (no pun intended) of another Olympic stadium, the round Velodrome where bicycle races were held. It is now a mini-world filled with a variety of different ecosystems. You can explore a jungle or a northern forest, walk underwater with huge fish, and watch penguins here. The Tropical Forest is the most exotic, with real trees, bright-colored birds, rare monkeys, capybaras, and caimans. Bats fly and hang upside down from the ceiling of a cave and piranhas swim in the stream. In the Laurentian Forest you can watch a beaver in his house via a spy camera. A tunnel leads under a replica of the Saint Lawrence River, where you are eye-to-eye with sturgeon. Open year-round. Admission charged.

Botanical Garden and Insectarium, 4101, rue Sherbrooke, est, near Olympic Park, is a beautifully landscaped, extensive open space, with thirty gardens containing some 26,000 species of plants and flowers. Ten greenhouses display flowers and plants from all the world's climatic regions. Open throughout the year. Admission charge. Call (514) 872–1400 or visit www.ville.montreal.qc.ca/jardin.

Recreational Sports

Montréal has been praised by *Bicycling* magazine as the most bicycle-friendly city on the continent. To that we would add that it is probably the most skater-friendly too. In the summer you'll find in-line skaters of all ages on the paths along the Lachine Canal and in parks throughout the city. In the winter, the city is filled with skating rinks. Parks are everywhere, from the middle of the river to the top of Mont-Royal, and every few blocks in between. Not just parks, but well-kept, well-equipped parks that people use. Most have gardens, many have state-of-the-art playground equipment, all have plenty of benches.

Professional Sports

You can see the Montréal Expos play at Olympic Stadium from April through October. Call (514) 790–1245 for ticket information.

Harness races are run at Blue Bonnets Raceway, 7440, boulevard Décarie, throughout the year except on Tuesday. Call (514) 739–2741 for information.

Les Montréal Canadiens of the National Hockey League are a blue-chip team of professional hockey and one of the best sports teams of any kind in Canada. Les Canadiens are a sporting legend, and they play their home games at the downtown Molson Centre at 1260 LaGauchetiére Street. Tickets for home games go fast. Call (514) 932–2582 for information. The regular season runs from October through April.

Tickets for major sports events may be purchased at the Montréal Reservation Centre, (514) 284–2277, or Voyage Astral, (514) 866–1001.

Les Alouettes (football) are gaining a reputation and their games are popular. They play at McGill Stadium. Visit www.canoe.ca/alouettes.

Accommodations

Montréal has accommodations for every budget, from deluxe hotels to intimate bed-and-breakfasts. Most major hotels offer less expensive weekend and holiday packages and lower rates for senior citizens and commercial travelers. Some allow children to stay in the same room with their parents free of charge. Ask about packages, special rates, and discounts when booking your rooms. These often include tickets to museums, festivals, or attractions. The Montréal Convention and Visitors Bureau publishes a summer and winter package guide. For a copy, telephone Infotouriste at (877) 266–5687. To access the Web sites of individual hotels, visit www.tourismmontreal.org.

Omni Mont-Royal, 1050, rue Sherbrooke, ouest, (514) 284–1110 or (800) 228–3000, is a very elegant accommodation, located on Montréal's most fashionable street, right across from the campus of McGill University. The rooms are spacious and well appointed and the service is first-rate and friendly. The hotel has a fitness facility, swimming pools, and massage and suntan rooms. Queen II is a favorite spot for power lunches among the business community. L'Apéro is its popular piano bar for after-hours relaxation and for grand buffets on weekends. Expensive.

Hotel Le Reine Elizabeth (The Queen Elizabeth), 900, boulevard René-Lévesque, ouest, (514) 861–3511 or (800) 441–1414, offers the best location in town. It is linked to Place Ville-Marie and the underground city and convenient to the Gare Centrale. The Queen Elizabeth has a long-standing reputation for excellent service. Its revamped Beaver Club is considered one of the best traditional dining rooms in North America. Expensive.

Delta Centre-Ville, 777, rue Université, (514) 879–1370 or (800) 333–3333, is a beautiful hotel with a revolving rooftop restaurant. This hotel features an indoor pool and a health club. Expensive.

Le Centre Sheraton, 1201, boulevard René-Lévesque, ouest, (514) 878–2000 or (800) 325–3535, offers luxury guest rooms and suites. It features an indoor swimming pool that opens onto a broad outdoor terrace, a health club and sauna, a game room, a concourse of boutiques, and several restaurants and bars. The Boulevard Restaurant on the third floor is popular with business people. Expensive.

Marriott Château Champlain, 1, Place du Canada, (514) 878–9000, is the most architecturally interesting hotel in Montréal: a slender high-rise with half-circle windows, offering good views of the city and a central location close to the Molson Centre and the underground city complex. For all its eye-catching architecture, it has been nicknamed the "cheese grater."

Le Gauchetière, its midrange restaurant, serves international cuisine. Expensive.

Hotel Wyndham, 1255 rue Jean-Mance, (514) 285–1450 or (800) 361–8234, is part of Place Desjardins, a massive but extremely attractive complex of boutiques, restaurants, and offices. The hotel is across the street from Place des Arts and linked to the rest of the underground city by the Metro. The rooms here are spacious and attractive. There is an indoor pool in a greenhouse setting. Moderate.

Hilton Montréal Aeroport, Dorval Airport, (514) 631–2411 or (800) HILTONS, offers deluxe accommodations, a swimming pool, a private flower garden, restaurants, a disco, and a health club. Bus service, via the airport, to downtown Montréal. Expensive.

Renaissance Hotel du Parc, 3625, avenue du Parc, (514) 288–6666 or (800) 363–0735, next to Parc Mont-Royal, has a health club with access to nearby McGill University's swimming pools, squash and tennis courts. The hotel is connected to a shopping arcade that contains many boutiques, restaurants, and cinemas. Moderate.

Montréal Bonaventure Hilton, 1, Place Bonaventure, (514) 878–2332, is one of Montréal's most unusual hotels. It is located on top of Place Bonaventure, a titanic building of stores and exhibition space. The rooms look out either on the city or on beautiful gardens. The heated outdoor pool can be used even on the coldest winter's day or during a snowstorm. Le Castillon is the hotel's award-winning gourmet restaurant. Expensive.

Ritz-Carlton Montréal, 1228, rue Sherbrooke, ouest, (514) 842–4212, is Montréal's most famous hotel. Here the rich, famous, and powerful have stayed in its elegantly decorated rooms. Even if you don't stay here, you should stop in to see its grand lobby. Le Café-de-Paris is famous for its gourmet cuisine. When the weather is good, Jardin-du-Ritz, an outdoor restaurant in a lovely garden, offers elegant alfresco dining. Expensive.

Auberge du Vieux-Port, 97, de la Commune, est, (514) 876–0081 or (888) 660–7678, combines the best of old and new, with luxury rooms in a historic building. Expensive.

L'Hôtel de la Montagne, 1430, rue de la Montagne, (514) 288–5656, is an elegant hotel emphasizing the continental approach to personal service. It has one of the most splendid lobbies in Montréal—opulent Art Deco—and a "four star" restaurant, Lutetia. Thursday's disco is very popular. Moderate.

Holiday Inn Montréal Midtown, 420, rue Sherbrooke, ouest, (514) 842–6111 or (800) HOLIDAY, is the best Holiday Inn in the area, offering gourmet dining, an indoor pool, a sauna, and convention facilities. Moderate to expensive.

Quality Hôtel Dorval, 7700, côte de Liesse, Dorval Airport area, (514) 731–7821 or (800) 228–5151, a four-star hotel decorated in an Indian motif, provides shuttle service to business meetings within a 5-mile (8 km) radius. Expensive.

Hôtel Gouverneur Place Dupuis, 1415, rue Saint-Hubert, (514) 842–4881 or (888) 910–1111, features an indoor swimming pool, saunas, and several restaurants. Moderate to expensive.

Crowne Plaza Metro Centre, 505, rue Sherbrooke, est, (514) 842–8581 or (800) 561–4644, provides a swimming pool and sauna, connections to the underground city, restaurants, and a bar. Moderate to expensive.

Delta Montréal, 450, rue Sherbrooke, ouest, (514) 286–1986, excellent downtown location; good accommodations, dining, and amenities. Expensive.

Ruby Foo's Hotel, 7655, boulevard Décarie, (514) 731–7701, features excellent accommodations. Moderate.

La Tour Centre-Ville, 400, boulevard René-Lévesque, ouest, (514) 866–8861 or (800) 361–2790. Luxury furnished apartments available by the week or the month are close to everything downtown. Apartments have kitchens and dining rooms. There is a swimming pool on premises. Moderate.

Bed and Breakfast Downtown Network, 3458, avenue Laval, (514) 289–9749 or (800) 267–5180. Run by expatriate American Bob Finkelstein, this is the oldest of the city's B&B networks. The booking service has a large selection of homes, from grand Victorian town houses to historic homes in Old Montréal and the Latin Quarter. Rates are reasonable and include breakfast.

Dining

For many travelers, the whole point of a visit to Montréal is the food. Art museums, historic sites, theater, and music just fill in the time between meals. Flaky croissants or rich cretons on a baguette with a boule at Atwater Market might begin the day. Lunch will be leisurely, in a chic little bistro or in one of the many ethnic enclaves. Dinner will be at a bastion of fine cuisine, perhaps Toqué,

Les Ramparts, or Nuances. Visitors could repeat this easy routine each weekend for a year and never exhaust the options.

Dining is looked upon as a fine art. The most predominant influence is classic French cuisine, tempered mightily by the modern trends toward lighter dishes. With the gardens of Laval right next door, chefs in Montréal have the freshest of ingredients available year-round, and they take full advantage of them.

Nearly every cuisine in the world is available at Montréal restaurants, reflecting the many peoples that have immigrated to the city over its long history. About the only style of cooking you may have trouble finding in restaurants is indigenous habitant cuisine. To sample the down-home traditional Québec dishes such as tourtiere, fricot, and sugar pie, you may have to leave the city and head for a *cabine de sucre*, a sugar house in the countryside, where they serve traditional meals.

Montréal has its own special variety of fast food, called smoked meat. This delectable, thinly sliced cured meat is eaten stacked thickly on a crusty bun or sturdy bread, served with french fries and dill pickles. Similar to pastrami, it is a legacy of Jewish immigrants from Romania. Don't leave Montréal without sampling it.

The cost of dining in Montréal can easily equal the cost of a fine dinner in any other North American city. But it doesn't have to. Most restaurants offer a table d'hôte menu at more reasonable prices. As in most cities, small ethnic restaurants and neighborhood bistros are much less costly than the big-name restaurants.

Reservations are essential in better-known restaurants, especially on weekends or during festivals. Evening dining begins at about 7:00 P.M. and restaurants stay open quite late. Montréalers dress very well, and you will feel out of place (not to mention where you'll be seated) if you do not. Except at brasseries and neighborhood bistros and cafes, jeans are not appropriate dinner wear.

The choice of wines will be good and mostly from France. Prices will vary with the prices on the rest of the menu. In some restaurants, especially on rues Duluth and Arthur, est, you can bring your own wines.

Montréal is a night city, where you can dine, attend a concert or sports event, go out dancing or listen to music at a club, have an early morning snack at a bistro, and turn in at 4:00 or 5:00 A.M. The city is refreshingly free of the puritan (here more usually Presbyterian) disapproval of pleasure that you will find in many other Canadian cities.

Liquor (including beer and wine) may be purchased in government stores from 9:00 A.M. to 5:00 P.M. Monday through Saturday. Some of these are open later hours and even on Sunday. In addition, many grocery stores sell wine, beer, and alcoholic cider seven days a week. Many bars and restaurants serve until 3:00 A.M. seven days a week. The legal drinking age is eighteen. For more information on restaurants, visit www.montrealplus.ca.

Even if we could name all the good restaurants in Montréal, the list would be incomplete by the time the book reaches your hands. New chefs are coming to the city, current chefs are opening new restaurants, others are changing kitchens, so that the restaurant scene is in a constant state of change. We can only select a few of our own favorites and suggest that you ask local people to recommend others. Montréalers are passionate about food and will expound on it at length; they all want to share the wonderful new places they have discovered.

Old Montréal

Gibby's, 298, Place d'Youville, (514) 282–1837, is a popular steakhouse in historic Youville Stables (circa 1716). Expensive.

L'Arrivage, 350, Place Royale, (514) 872–9128. Situated in the stunning Museum of Archeology, this chic, glass-walled eatery has a great view of the bustling Old Port (Vieux Port). Closed Monday. Daily specials with fresh and interesting ingredients. Open for lunch only. Moderate.

Restaurant Union, 600, Place d'Youville, (514) 286–9851, is a very trendy place to go for early evening drinks and for the international cuisine. Expensive.

Les Ramparts, 97, de la Commune, est, (514) 876–0081 or (888) 660–7678, serves elegantly creative dishes. Expensive.

Le Saint Amable, 188, rue Saint-Amable, (514) 866–3471, is considered one of Montréal's finest continental restaurants, offering lobster Victoria, sole soufflé, and tournedos opera. Expensive.

La Marée, 404, Place Jacques-Cartier, (514) 861–9794, serves fine cuisine in an elegant eighteenth-century house. Expensive.

Le Fripon, 436, Place Jacques-Cartier, (514) 861–1386. A good spot from which to enjoy the street musicians and artists that enliven the square during the summer. The menu varies with the season. Seafood is a specialty. Moderate.

Bonaparte, 443, rue Saint-François-Xavier, (514) 844–4368. This classical French restaurant draws a dressy theater-going crowd. It's practically next door to the Centaur, Montréal's English-language theater. Moderate to expensive.

Central Downtown

Restaurant Toqué, 3842, Saint-Denis, (514) 499–2084. Situated on lively Saint-Denis in the Latin Quarter, this stark but elegant eatery looks more like an art gallery than a restaurant. The food, too, is a feast for the eyes. The colors and textures are arranged on the plate as if they are part of a painting. Chef Normand Laprise uses only fresh ingredients. Expensive.

Les Halles, 1450, rue Crescent, (514) 844–2328, is a premier French restaurant, located near the Ritz-Carlton Hotel, exclusive shops, and art galleries. Trout with sorrel in pastry, pike soufflé, chateaubriand with béarnaise, and veal Normande are specialties. Expensive.

Misto, 929, avenue Mont-Royal, est, (514) 526–5043, serves fine Italian food. Moderate.

Katsura, 2170, rue de la Montagne, (514) 849–1172, offers fine Japanese food in a beautiful contemporary interior. Japanese-style room with tatami mats, sushi bar, and waitresses clad in kimono. Expensive.

Ouelli Della Notte, 6834, boulevard Saint-Laurent, (514) 271–3929, offers both Italian food and a sushi bar. Expensive.

Beaver Club at the Queen Elizabeth Hotel, 900, boulevard René-Lévesque, ouest, (514) 861–3511, presents excellent French cuisine. Expensive.

La Minerva, 17 Prince Arthur, (514) 842–5451. One of several Greek eateries on a pedestrians-only street known for "bring-your-own-bottle" restaurants, this large taverna specializes in Mediterranean-style seafood dishes. Moderate

Ferreira Café Trattoria, 1446, rue Peel, (514) 848–0988, offers Portuguese fare, specializing in fresh fish dishes reminiscent of the Mediterranean. Inexpensive to moderate.

Alexandre Restaurant, 1454, rue Peel, (514) 288–5105. Step into this place and you'll think you've been transported to Paris. Many of the waiters come from France, and the furnishings—cane chairs and tiny round tables—will remind you of the Left Bank cafes. Tasty, reasonably priced food.

Le Caveau, 2063, rue Victoria, (514) 844–1624, is an inti-

Montréal Markets

The two largest city markets are Atwater, near the Lachine Canal, and Jean-Talon, in the heart of Little Italy. Shops inside the markets and outdoor stalls sell farm produce, meat, fresh fish, and other foods. One shop in Atwater sells nothing but cheese, another only oils and vinegars. In each of these, a cafe attracts locals on Sunday mornings for a breakfast of pastry or a fresh crusty baguette with cretons (a pâté made of spiced pork), accompanied by a boule, a soup bowl–size cup of coffee.

mate French restaurant with good food. Moderate to expensive.

Vieux Kitzbuhel, 505, boulevard Perrot, (514) 453–5521, is the place to go for Wiener schnitzel, Tiroler röstbraten, dorschfilet mit mandeln, kalbsschnitzel cordon bleu, and other good things to eat à la Austria. Moderate.

Hostaria Romano, 2044, rue Metcalfe, (514) 849–1389. Fine Italian cuisine to the sound of popular songs, performed by Toni, the owner. Moderate to expensive.

Schwartz's Montréal Hebrew Delicatessen, 3895, boulevard Saint-Laurent, (514) 842–4813, is perhaps the best deli in French Canada. Schwartz's smoked-meat sandwiches, washed down with Dr. Brown's soda, bring tears of joy to the eyes of deli addicts. Inexpensive.

Les Chenets, 2075, rue Bishop, (514) 844–1842, features a multicourse gastronomic dinner, a special dining experience rare in North America. The restaurant is also famous for its extensive wine list, with some bottles priced in the high four figures. Expensive.

Troika Restaurant, 2171, rue Crescent, (514) 849–9333, is one of Montréal's few Russian restaurants, in business since 1962. It features fresh Russian caviar, roast rack of lamb, beef stroganoff, and Russian vodkas and brandies. Strolling musicians play sentimental songs while you spoon your borscht. Expensive.

Nuances, 1, avenue du Casino, (514) 392–2708. One of Montréal's classiest newer places is in an unlikely venue: the Casino. It has elegant surroundings and an even more elegant clientele; its decor is of burnished rosewood paneling, dusky pink upholstery, and ultra-modern wrought-iron chandeliers. The fare is strictly gourmet—venison pâté, mussel soup, coriander-flavored rabbit, smoked duck. Jacket and tie. Expensive.

Entertainment

Fine dining certainly serves as a major form of entertainment in Montréal, but there are other forms too. The discothèque was well established in Montréal long before it became the rage in the United States and elsewhere. Montréalers are avid patrons of the symphony, opera, ballet, and live theater. The city attracts star entertainers and touring groups from all over the world. The Canadiens and the Expos make Montréal a big-league professional sports city. There are boîtes à chansons in Old Montréal, where folksingers serenade you with the ballads of Québec. Movie theaters can be found in every section of the city, featuring the latest major productions from Hollywood and, yes, from Montréal. Montréal is one of the filmmaking centers of Canada, and its productions have won top awards at Cannes and other film festivals. And there is jazz in Old Montréal, downtown, and along rue Saint-Denis.

The only problem you'll have is to make a choice: The entertainment possibilities in Montréal, on any given day, are quite extensive.

Ask your concierge or the coordinator of visitor services at your hotel for suggestions and help in making reservations. You can purchase tickets to major cultural events—such as a performance of the marvelous Les Grands Ballets Canadiens or the Montréal Symphony Orchestra—and for sporting events over the phone by calling Montréal Reservations Centre, (514) 284–2277. Tickets for dinner theaters may also be purchased over the phone by calling Voyage Astral, (514) 866–1001. Various free brochures and magazines that may list special events are available at your hotel. If you would like more information on arts entertainment, contact Info Art Bell at (514) 790–ARTS or (800) 203–ARTS.

English-language theater is presented at the Centaur Theatre, 453, rue Saint-François Xavier, (514) 288–3161. Theatre du Nouveau Monde stages French-language productions near the Place des Arts, (514) 866–8667.

For an evening of free entertainment, go walking and people-watching along rue Sainte-Catherine and in the rue Crescent area and rue Saint-Denis. These streets and those in Old Montréal never seem empty of people, even in the early morning hours.

Thursday's, 1449, rue Crescent, (514) 288–5656, is Montréal's top bar for cruising. The well-heeled yuppie crowd considers Thursday's its chic watering hole, at least as of this writing. Expensive.

Biddle's, 2060, rue Aylmer, (514) 842–8656, is Montréal's place for jazz.

Le Festin du Gouverneur, at the Old Fort on Île Ste Hélène, (514) 879–1141, is an unusual dinner theater, where you are part of the cast. You take part in a seventeenth-century banquet in old Québec. It is a lot of fun.

L'Air du Temps, 191, rue Saint-Paul, (514) 842–2003, offers jazz in a quasi-Victorian setting. A popular, sophisticated night spot.

Shopping

There are thousands of stores in Montréal—1,700 shops just within the underground city—enough to fill several days of serious browsing. You can find some good values in Canadian-made clothing and furs as well as Canadian arts and crafts. If money is not a pressing concern, Montréal offers high-fashion clothing, jewelry, furs, and cosmetics from the world's leading designers and makers. Montréal is Canada's haute couture capital, with highly talented Québécois designers, not just French-inspired but also Italian. The Québécois, regardless of their ethnicity, adore glamour and pay top dollar to look their best.

The huge, enclosed shopping complexes—Place Ville-Marie, Place Bonaventure, Complexe Desjardins, Place du Parc, Plaza Alexis Nihon, and Westmount Square, as well as the underground areas Les Cours Mont-Royal, Place Montréal Trust, Le Centre Eaton, and Promenade de la Cathedrale—offer a tremendous variety of specialty shops and boutiques in glamorous environments. Rue Sainte-Catherine features large department stores, such as Simon's and the Bay. The rue Crescent area sparkles with many boutiques offering dresses, shoes, jewelry, and other attractive, expensive goods.

Le Faubourg Sainte-Catherine is a colorful marketplace selling fresh and prepared gourmet foods. This is a wonderful area to stroll about and sample all the good things to eat. Prince Arthur Street is an enclave of ethnic restaurants and small shops, and on Laurier Street you'll find Greek goods and food. St. Lawrence Boulevard, also called "The Main," is another area of ethnic shops and restaurants. It seems that almost every nationality has a bit of commercial turf here—Jewish, Polish, Hungarian, Spanish, Portuguese, and so on. Mont-Royal Avenue has seventeen blocks of shopping from Avenue du Parc to rue Papineau, offering just about every kind of merchandise, many at bargain prices. In addition, there are many interesting shops in Chinatown and in Old Montréal. Antiques shops are found on rue Saint-Denis, north of Sherbrooke; rue Sherbrooke ouest, near the Museum of Fine Arts, and side streets in this area; and rue Notre Dame ouest, from rue Guy to Atwater Market. There are dozens of galleries in Montréal. Most of them are in the rue Sherbrooke ouest area, and in Old Montréal.

You can get a shopping guide from the Greater Montreal Convention and Business Bureau. Visit the Infotouriste Centre or call (877) BONJOUR. If you are really into shopping in Montréal, look for *Smart Shopping Montréal* by Sandra Philips; it is a highly regarded guide. E-mail sandra@smartshopping.net for more information or to find out how to order.

CHAPTER 8

Québec City

One word best describes Québec City: romantic. Old Québec City looks as if it had been plucked from some charming area in France and gently reassembled on and around an imposing, high-cliffed headland jutting into the powerful Saint Lawrence River.

Québec City is an eminently human habitation of winding streets and venerable buildings that exude more than four centuries of history. Unlike flashy and frenetic Montréal, Québec City is sedate, elegant, and completely secure in its position as the spiritual and political capital of French Canada.

Some 95 percent of its half million people are of French descent. Not many years ago, the city's elite were mostly of Anglo-Saxon stock, but their number has greatly diminished with the rise of the Québécois and the assertion of their right to be "masters of their own house." Luckily for the visitor, most of the people who work in the city will try to help you in your own language.

Winston Churchill, who visited Québec City in the early 1940s to plan the Allied invasion of France, called this ancient settlement the "Gibraltar of North America." Churchill was not just being kind to his hosts but was precisely describing the city's terrain and military history. Québec City is built on and around a steep palisade that juts into the Saint Lawrence River like a sharp spear, poised to thrust into any enemy daring to pass into the hinterland of Canada. In the seventeenth and eighteenth centuries, Québec City was of such strategic importance that no invader could hope to win the northern half of the continent until it was taken. This is why Québec City was a prime target for Britain's General James Wolfe in 1759. Once his forces were victorious on

The St. Louis Gate is one of four gates to Vieux-Québec.

the Plains of Abraham, New France became part of British North America.

As the capital of Québec, the city's main business is government: Several thousand civil employees work here. While most people think of Québec City only as a historic town, the modern community encompasses a metropolitan area with several suburbs. It is a major educational center, with the sprawling campus of the Université Laval and its thousands of students, an important seaport, and a manufacturing and tourism center. Sometimes its romantic image clouds the fact that Québec City is one of Canada's most dynamic generators of economic activity.

But for the visitor, the economic life of Québec City is far less important than the pleasure of being in a city that hides its mundane business so well. Québec City is one of those special places where you would like to stay a bit longer—to have a romantic affair, to paint lovely pictures, or to write a novel. In Québec City the air always seems clear and fresh. The slower pace of life can be savored like old brandy. Magnificent vistas of river, mountains, cliffs, and islands appear in every direction. In Québec City the illustrious ghosts of the past seem to whisper with every step you take: "Here I governed a people, here I fought my enemy, here I set out to explore a wilderness, here I prayed, and here I died." To fall in love with Québec City is not unusual—it is expected.

In 1985 UNESCO designated the historic district of Old Québec City as a World Heritage site. Québec City is the first North American city to be so honored. A monument commemorating this honor is located on the Dufferin Terrace.

How to Get to Québec City

By Car

Most traffic to Québec City originates in Montréal. The quickest route from Montréal, a distance of 240 miles (384 km), is to take the Louis-Hippolyte-Lafontaine Tunnel, east of Montréal's center, which crosses the Saint Lawrence River and immediately connects with Autoroute 20, the highway to Québec City. Near the city, cross back over the Saint Lawrence River via the Québec or Laporte Bridge, which will bring you into Sainte-Foy, the western suburb of Québec City. Boulevard Laurier takes you right into the heart of the city.

A slower but more scenic route is to follow the north shore of the Saint Lawrence River via Highway 138, which passes through pleasant farm country, lovely small villages and towns, and the historic city of Trois-Rivières. Some of the river views along this route are splendid. This trip can be shortened, without sacrificing scenery, by taking Autoroute 40 from Montréal to Trois-Rivières, then scenic Highway 138 to Donnacona, and from there Autoroute 40 again to Sainte-Foy and Québec City.

U.S. travelers coming directly to Québec City through Maine can take I–95 to Route 201 (just north of Waterville), which goes north and merges with Highway 173 at the border, near Jackman, Maine. Highway 173 goes through the Beauce region of Québec and connects with Autoroute 73 north of the town of Sainte-Marie. Autoroute 73 leads directly to the Québec or Laporte Bridge at Sainte-Foy.

Canadian and U.S. travelers coming from the Atlantic Canada provinces can follow the Trans-Canada Highway to Québec City.

By Air

Air Canada and other domestic airlines provide frequent daily service to Québec City. Québec Airport is located 14 miles (23 km) northwest of Québec City in Ancienne Lorette. Taxi and low-cost bus service is available to and from major hotels in the city.

Rental cars—Hertz, Tilden, Avis—are available at the airport and at other locations in Québec City.

By Rail

VIA Rail provides frequent daily service between Montréal and Québec City. The train makes a stop in the western suburb of Sainte-Foy, and at the Central Station in downtown. Call (418) 692–3940 for all train information in Québec City.

By Bus

Voyageur Lines provides hourly service between Montréal and Québec City. The bus terminal in Québec City is at 225, boulevard Charest, est; call (418) 525–3000 for information. Voyageur buses also make connections with buses at the New Brunswick border for those traveling into Atlantic Canada.

General Information

Time zone: Eastern
Telephone area code: 418
Police: (418) 691–6911

Medical emergencies: (418) 648–2626
Road condition information: (418) 643–6830

Tourist Information

Maps for walking tours, brochures on attractions, and other information can be obtained from the Greater Québec Area Tourism and Convention Bureau, 835, avenue Wilfred Laurier. Call (418) 649–2608 or visit www.quebecregion.com.

How to Get Around Québec City

The Central Area

Happily, you can see most of Québec City on foot. You can visualize the city as consisting of a level plain set high above the Saint Lawrence River (Upper Town), its steep cliffs skirted below by historic Lower Town. The massive Château Frontenac can be used as your central landmark. If you stand in front of the château on the Terrasse Dufferin (Dufferin Terrace), facing the Saint Lawrence River, Lower Town will be immediately below you. You can reach Lower Town by taking the elevator, located just a few steps away, or by walking down steep Côte de la Montagne. There are many important old buildings in Lower Town's Place Royale, including the historic church of Notre-Dame-des-Victoires.

Back on the Terrasse Dufferin, looking toward the château, you will see the Promenade des Gouverneurs, the Parc des Gouverneurs, and the Citadelle on your left. To your right are the Place d'Armes, rue du Trésor, the Quartier Latin (Latin Quarter), and Québec Seminary.

Walking west on rue Saint-Louis, away from the château, you will notice on both sides streets with many historic buildings, such as the Kent House and the Ursuline Convent. Continuing on rue Saint-Louis, you will pass through the old stone wall that encircles the historic area. To your left is access to the Citadelle, with its Changing of the Guard ceremony, and Battlefields Park, where you can stroll the famous Plains of Abraham. To your right are the handsome buildings of the Québec National Assembly.

Public Transportation

Québec City's buses will take you throughout the city and into nearby suburban communities, such as Sainte-Foy, which has the campus of the Université Laval, massive shopping malls, and

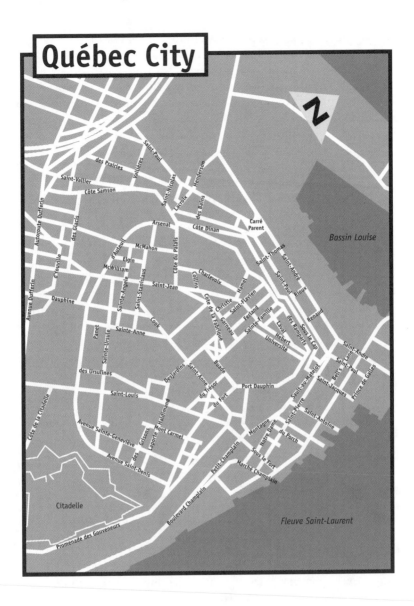

Québec City

Bassin Louise

Fleuve Saint-Laurent

Citadelle

Streets and locations:

Saint-Paul
des Prairies
Saint-Vallier
Côte Samson
Vallières
Saint-Nicolas
Larcroix
Henderson
des Bains
Autoroute Dufferin
des Glacis
Arsenal
Côte Dinan
Carré Parent
d'Youville
d'Auteuil
McMahon
Côte du Palais
Saint-Thomas
Saint-André
Avenue Dufferin
Elgin
McWilliam
Charlevoix
Saint-Paul
Rioux
Dauphine
Sainte-Angèle
Saint-Stanislaus
Saint-Jean
Collins
Hamel
Renaud
Côte de la Fabrique
Saint-Flavien
Ferland
des Remparts
Sous le Cap
Panet
Sainte-Anne
Cook
Garneau
Sainte-Famille
Laval
Hébert
Saint-André
Sainte-Ursule
Brade
Université
Saint-Louis
des Ursulines
Desjardins
Sainte-Anne
du Trésor
Port Dauphin
Sault-au-Matelot
Saint-Paul
Saint-Louis
Barts Lane
Saint-Jacques
Prince de Galles
du Fort
Saint-Pierre
Saint-Antoine
Avenue Sainte-Geneviève
des Grisons
Laporte
Haldimand
Mont Carmel
Montagne
Notre-Dame
du Porch
Avenue Saint-Denis
Petit-Champlain
Sous le Fort
Marché Champlain
Boulevard Champlain
Promenade des Gouverneurs

many motels. Taxis are available all over town, but they are rarely needed because of the close proximity of most attractions.

Calèches (horse-drawn carriages), with bilingual drivers who are knowledgeable tourist guides, offer a slow-paced, comfortable, and romantic way to see North America's most romantic city. Whereas automobiles seem out of place in Old Québec City, the calèches are as much a part of the tapestry as the venerable Château Frontenac itself. Calèches can be hired at Place d'Armes at any time of the year.

The ferry to and from the city of Lévis is an inexpensive cruise on the Saint Lawrence. It sails every half hour and takes passengers and cars. The terminal is located near Place Royale in Lower Town.

Guided Tours and Cruises

Guided bus tours of Québec City are provided by Grayline-de-Québec, (418) 523–9722 or (800) 217–9722. Old Québec Tours, (418) 664–0460 or (800) 267–TOUR.

Contact Québec, (418) 692–2801, and Les Tours Adlard, (418) 692–2358, provides guided tours through the city on foot.

The M/V *Louis-Jolliet*, (418) 692–1159 or (800) 563–4643, offers cruises from May to October on the Saint Lawrence River to Île d'Orléans, Montmorency Falls, and the Québec Bridge. It also offers night cruises with music and dancing. The boarding point is in front of Place Royale.

Héli-Express, (418) 877–5890, provides flights over Québec City and the nearby countryside.

Major Events

For more information on the following events, contact the Greater Québec Area Tourism and Convention Bureau (see "Tourist Information").

Carnaval de Québec (Winter Carnival) starts the first Thursday in February and lasts ten days. The only winter bash comparable to Québec's carnival is the Mardi Gras in New Orleans. Carnaval de Québec is a joyous celebration of the human spirit over the harshness of the winter season; it is also the last bacchanal before the somber season of Lent. Perhaps at no other time of the year do so many thousands of people pack into the city. The carnival attracts visitors from all over Canada and the United States and even from Europe. Even if the temperature plunges way below zero and Québec City is blanketed by a snowstorm, the carnival goes on, and whatever nature hands out only makes Québec City more lovely. As a matter of fact, Québec City is at its most beautiful in the snows of winter.

The carnival features glittering parades in both Upper and Lower Town, a snow-sculpture competition, grand balls, the crowning of a queen, fireworks, canoe races across the half-frozen Saint Lawrence, and much more. Le Bonhomme Carnaval, the giant snowman figure, is the official host, delighting all ages. Chefs go out of their way to show Québec's cuisine at its best. Streets, homes, and hotels are decorated with bright colors, and there are singing, dancing, hugging, and kissing in the streets. Wine and spirits never cease to flow—to keep out the cold and to enhance the joy of the moment. In short, there's nothing like Québec's carnival anywhere.

Plan ahead if you would like to attend. Some of the best space (such as the Château Frontenac, which is at the center of many events) is reserved a year in advance. Call at least several months ahead of time for reservations, before accommodations become scarce.

Le Festival d'Été de Québec (Summer Festival) takes place in early July and is the largest Francophone cultural event in North America. It features folksinging and dancing, art exhibitions, theater, sports events, and many other entertainments.

Expo Québec (Provincial Exhibition) is held in mid-August at Exhibition Park. This is an agricultural and industrial fair with a midway, live entertainment, and contests. Québécois farmers display their prize animals and produce.

Attractions

Québec City is the only walled city in North America. Walls have protected it from unwanted intruders ever since Samuel de Champlain's settlement. The walls you see today were built by the British in the early nineteenth century to protect Québec City from invading American armies. Although American forces, under generals Benedict Arnold and Richard Montgomery, unsuccessfully assaulted the earlier log walls at the beginning of the American War of Independence, no defender has ever shot at an enemy from these present granite ramparts. To the contrary, these old walls have welcomed millions of visitors into the most charming and romantic human habitation in all of North America through the historic Saint-Louis Gate.

Québec City is the only walled city in North America. The stone walls were constructed by the British as a defense against possible invasion of Canada from the United States. One of the best ways to see this historic city is to be driven in a calèche.

Lower Town

During the 1759 British siege of Québec City, most of its buildings were destroyed by artillery fire. Old engravings show Lower Town, in the area of Notre-Dame-des-Victoires, filled with ragged shells of buildings, rubble, and despondency everywhere. But a great human habitation, like the mythical phoenix, arises from its ashes and despair, rebuilds an even better place, and re-creates the best of its former glory.

Place Royale, on the site of Champlain's 1608 settlement, is an outstanding example of modern archaeologists, architects, builders, historians, and artisans working together to bring back the seventeenth- and eighteenth-century beauty and ambience in what had become a run-down section. Open daily from June through September, and October through May by appointment. Call (418) 643-6631. Free. There are a number of good restaurants and gift shops in the Place Royale area. The car and passenger ferry for Lévis operates from its nearby terminal.

Notre-Dame-des-Victoires (Our Lady of Victories), named to honor the people's faith and ability to survive, is the gem of Place Royale. It is an exquisite little church, with an attractive facade and a bright interior decorated with gold and many religious statues and paintings. Be sure to see the Chapel of Sainte-Geneviève and the model of an eighteenth-century sailing vessel hanging from the ceiling of the nave. The oldest stone church in Québec (circa 1688), it continues to be an active parish throughout the year. In the wide cobblestone square in front of the church, frequently used for folk singing and dancing, is a fine bust of King Louis XIV, one of the last remaining relics of the French monarchy. Free.

Maison-des-Vins, across the square from the church, sells fine wines and lets you see its wine cellars, brick vaults illuminated with candles. Free access.

Maison Jolliet was the home of Louis Jolliet, who along with Father Jacques Marquette explored the Mississippi River in the late seventeenth century. In his house is the *ascenseur* or funicular that, for a small price, will take you up to the Terrasse Dufferin at the Château Frontenac.

Maison Fornel has foundations constructed in 1658 and vaulted cellars built in 1735. Exhibits show the mechanics of the Place Royale restoration project: the methods used and the findings revealed through the digs and examinations of the old buildings. Free.

Maison Chevalier, a seventeenth- and eighteenth-century complex built for entrepreneur Jean Baptiste Chevalier, now serves as a very interesting and attractive museum of Québec historical artifacts, furniture, and works of art. Free.

Quartier Petit-Champlain is considered one of the oldest residential and commercial districts in North America. In the early seventeenth century, it was a place of elegant homes and diverse shops. Over the years it became a rather squalid area until recent renovations turned it into a charming riverside village in the heart of the city, a special place of flowers, restored homes, street musicians, clowns, jugglers, fine restaurants, and handcraft shops. Open all the time; free access.

Musée de la Civilisation has exhibits on various aspects of culture and also features musical and theatrical performances. Closed Monday. Admission charge.

Upper Town

Hotel **Château Frontenac** stands on the site where Governor Louis de Frontenac and subsequent governors lived in the Château Saint-Louis. The Norman-style château, with its slanted green copper roofs, has dominated Québec City since the late 1800s, and it is one of Canada's most beloved landmarks. Almost every visitor to the city takes a stroll through its beautiful dark-paneled lobby.

Terrasse Dufferin, in front of the hotel, is an extensive boardwalk set on the edge of the high cliffs overlooking Lower Town. The terrace offers excellent views of the high cliffs of Lévis, the broadening Saint Lawrence River, the tip of Île d'Orléans and the peaks of the Laurentians in the distance, and the quaint rooftops of Lower Town below. It displays a heroic statue of Samuel de Champlain. The elevator takes you down to Lower Town and a large congregation of calèche drivers hawking their tours of Vieux

Québec City. The Terrasse Dufferin was designed so that people could enjoy strolling in an inspiring setting high above the river. Often during the summer season and the winter carnival, singers and musicians provide free entertainment.

Parc des Gouverneurs, off the terrace and next to the château, was once a private garden and is now a public park. It contains a significant monument to Generals James Wolfe and Louis-Joseph de Montcalm, with a memorable inscription: THEIR COURAGE GAVE THEM THE SAME LOT; HISTORY THE SAME FAME; POSTERITY THE SAME MONUMENT.

Promenade des Gouverneurs merges with the Terrasse Dufferin beyond the Parc des Gouverneurs. The promenade is a protected walkway that skirts the cliffs of Cap Diamant and the walls of the formidable Citadelle, rising to the Plains of Abraham near the site of the fateful battle between Wolfe and Montcalm. It offers an exceptional view of the Saint Lawrence River and the steep cliffs of its southern shore. Climbing this path to the Plains of Abraham can be strenuous. For an easier walk, start the walk atop the Plains and stroll down to the Terrasse Dufferin.

Place d'Armes, across rue Saint-Louis from the château, holds an impressive monument in honor of the Recollet missionaries who came to New France in 1615.

Holy Trinity Anglican Cathedral, 31, rue Desjardins, nearby across rue du Trésor, was built in 1804, the first Anglican cathedral to be built outside the British Isles. This structure has beautiful stained-glass windows and historic memorials along its interior walls. A special pew is reserved for the British monarch. Although Québec City's Anglophone population has dwindled considerably, the cathedral continues to hold worship throughout the year.

Rue du Trésor, the street of treasury, is one of Québec City's more interesting streets. Located across from Anglican Cathedral, it is inhabited by a flock of artists who display their paintings and drawings on the walls of flanking buildings and create a festive atmosphere. There is something here for everyone, and the prices are quite inexpensive.

Musée du Fort, near the Champlain statue on the Terrasse Dufferin, features a light and sound show depicting the various sieges of Québec City and the battle on the Plains of Abraham. This is a good place to get a quick and interesting history of the city. Open throughout the year. Admission charge.

Basilica of Notre Dame, a gray baroque edifice in the so-called Quartier Latin (Latin Quarter), is the ecclesiastical seat of the archdiocese of Québec City. It was once responsible for the religious administration of all of New France, stretching to the Mississippi River. The interior of the basilica is lavishly decorated, albeit a bit gloomily for some tastes.

Québec Seminary, adjacent to the basilica, was founded by Québec's first bishop, François de Montmorency Laval, in 1663. Here was the original campus of the Université Laval, which now occupies its own contemporary academic city in Sainte-Foy. Within the seminary is an exquisite Jesuit chapel (Laval brought in the Jesuits in preference to the original Sulpician missionaries), a hidden treasure of which many visitors are unaware. The chapel contains the tomb of Bishop Laval, covered in a marble effigy. Pope John Paul II pronounced Laval "Blessed," a step toward sainthood in the Roman Catholic Church. The spires and buildings of the Québec Seminary have been distinctive features of the city's skyline since its early years. Of the old buildings, only the Château Frontenac and the Citadelle on Cap Diamant are more prominent. The seminary, built when most of North America was sparsely settled, imposed highly sophisticated European architecture on an entirely new landscape. The only counterpart at that time was hundreds of miles south in Spanish-controlled Mexico City. Within the seminary the University Museum houses an eclectic collection of religious items, historical artifacts, old coins, and even an Egyptian mummy. Open throughout the year. Admission charge.

Rue des Ramparts, behind the seminary, has stone fortifications on the high ground overlooking the harbor. Ancient pieces of artillery, poking their muzzles out of the ramparts, are today nice decorative touches in a city that has known mostly peace since the late eighteenth century.

Parc Montmorency is also near the Québec Seminary and borders Côte de la Montagne. Artists and young people congregate in this small park, graced with statues (such as that of nineteenth-century politican Sir Georges Étienne Cartier) and more artillery. Across from Montmorency Park, on Côte de la Montagne, is a heroic statue of Bishop Laval.

Côte de la Montagne, a steep street, winds down to Lower Town, past some intimate French restaurants and shops selling the creative work of artists and artisans (much better, but also much more expensive, than those on rue du Trésor). Côte de la Montagne will bring you to the Breakheart Stairs, which lead to the special world of Place Royale Lower Town.

The Quartier Latin has many good restaurants, lounges, cafes, fashionable boutiques, department stores, and Libraire Garneau, an excellent French-language bookshop. The area is compact, and every place is easy to reach on foot. If you must bring a car into this congested area, there is underground parking at the Hôtel de Ville (City Hall), and space is sometimes available at the Château Frontenac's garage.

The area west of the Château Frontenac and the Quartier Latin, toward the wall and its Saint-Louis and Saint-Jean Gates, is a mélange of narrow streets flanked by old buildings that exude the atmosphere of past centuries. It's fascinating to explore these streets to the accompaniment of the clopping, reverberating sounds of the hooves of calèche horses. Rue Saint-Louis, as an example of what is available in this area, has several good hotels and good restaurants.

The Ursuline Convent, 12, rue Donnacona, was founded in the seventeenth century by the immortal Blessed Marie de l'Incarnation. The convent is an important place of worship for pilgrims. The chapel, which is open to the public, is the most elegant house of prayer in the city. In an adjacent building the Ursuline nuns operate a historical museum that houses General Montcalm's skull. Montcalm's body is buried in the chapel, as is Marie de l'Incarnation's. Open January through November, Tuesday to Saturday. Admission charge.

Outside the Central Section

The Citadelle is on the tip of Cap Diamant. The current fortress, built by order of the Duke of Wellington, of Waterloo fame, superseded earlier French fortifications here. The Citadelle continues to be an active military installation, manned by members of the Canadian armed forces. Although built to repulse American invaders, its great moment in history came during World War II, when Winston Churchill and Franklin Roosevelt resided here for a time and planned the invasion of France. Inside the Citadelle is a military museum that displays a good collection of uniforms, weapons, decorations, documents, and insignia. The highlight of a visit to the Citadelle takes place on the main parade, where the colorful and exciting Changing of the Guard ceremony is performed daily at 10:00 A.M. from mid-June until Labour Day. The Beating the Retreat ceremony is also held daily during the summer at 6:00 P.M., except when it rains. A tour of the Citadelle is a must when in Québec City. Admission charge. Call (418) 694–2815 or visit www.qbc.clic.net/~citadel.

Québec Fortifications National Historic Park has pedestrian paths so that visitors can walk along and inspect these walls and their decorative gates. There is nothing else like them in North America. The powder magazine is open to the public. The fortifications also make a dramatic background for photos of yourself and your companions. Call (418) 648–7016 or visit parkscanada.risq.qc.ca/fortifications.

Artillery Park consists of barracks and other buildings used by the British and Canadian armies on a site formerly used by the French King's army. There are an interpretation center and an exhibition of early Québec fortifications. Open July through Labour Day. Call (418) 648–4205 or visit parkscanada.risq.qc.ca/artillerie. Admission charge.

Plains of Abraham Battlefields Park (Parc-des-Champs-de-Bataille) is an extensive park running along the southern edge of the city, high above the Saint Lawrence River, beginning just west of the Citadelle. Here is where the fate of Canada was decided in 1759 and where both Wolfe and Montcalm received their mortal wounds. Signs throughout the battlefield indicate the positions of the military forces and where the important engagements took place. Other monuments here (for example, a beautiful rose garden and a magnificent equestrian statue of Jeanne d'Arc) honor famous moments and personages in French or Québec history. Passenger cars are permitted on park roadways. It is a romantic place for walking and lounging during the warm days and evenings of summer, for pushing a baby carriage, or for jogging. In the winter the Québécois use its rolling terrain for cross-country skiing and sledding. During Carnaval, you can even ride a dogsled here. Open daily mid-May through Labour Day, Tuesday through Sunday the rest of the year. Admission charge. Call (418) 648–4071 for a schedule of special events.

Musée du Québec, at the western end of the Plains of Abraham, has a large permanent collection of paintings, sculpture, prints, furnishings, and religious objects relating to the history of the province. In addition, galleries feature the works of contemporary Québec artists. The museum is a major showplace for new and established talent and plays an important role in the development of the people's culture. Open throughout the year. Admission charge.

Cartier-Brébeuf Park, 175, rue de l'Espinay, is where Jacques Cartier had his winter encampment in 1535–36 and where the Jesuits established their first mission in 1626. You can visit a full-size replica of Cartier's ship *La Grande Hermine* and an interpretation center where you can learn more about Cartier and the early history of Québec. Open throughout the year. Admission charge.

Hôtel du Parlement, Québec National Assembly, just west of the Saint-Louis Gate and near the Québec Hilton, houses the provincial government. Bronze statues of famous persons in Québec history, such as Cartier and Champlain, decorate the facade. The richly decorated legislative chambers contain oil paintings of scenes from Québec's history and beautifully carved wood paneling and furnishings. The public can dine in the excellent Parliament Buildings Restaurant, where you can rub elbows with the politicians. Free guided tours are available. Open throughout the year. Call (418) 643–7239.

Galerie Anima G, 1037, rue de la Chevrotière, is the tallest government building in the city. From an observatory on the thirty-first floor you can see the panorama of Québec City, the river, and mountains. Open throughout the year. Free.

Grand Théâtre de Québec, 269, boulevard Saint-Cyrille, est, a handsome contemporary building both inside and out, is noted for its Louis Frechette and Octave Cremazie Halls. You can see Jordi Bonet's stunning mural, which shocked some conservative citizens when it was first unveiled. Here you can enjoy the symphony, ballet, opera, live theater, and top entertainers from all over the world. Tours are held year-round, with a small admission fee. Events are held throughout the year. Call (418) 643–8131 for a schedule of events and ticket information.

Université Laval is the first French-language Catholic institution of higher learning in North America. Its new campus is actually a city in itself, located on a 500-acre site in the suburb of Sainte-Foy. Though mainly a secular university today, it was founded by Bishop Laval in the seventeenth century and remained a stronghold of the Roman Catholic faith for many generations. The beautiful chapel in the center of the campus is a reminder of this heritage. The university has an enrollment of more than 24,000 full-time students. Of particular interest on campus is the sports complex, whose Olympic-size pool is open to the public. Laval's buildings interconnect through underground tunnels, and students often roller-skate to cover long distances quickly. Laval offers an excellent intensive French-language course in the summer for non-French-speaking students. Laval is close to Sainte-Foy's several huge and very attractive enclosed shopping malls, which you might want to visit after touring the campus.

Québec Aquarium, 1675, avenue du Parc, in Sainte-Foy, has a good collection of fish and other marine life. Open throughout the year. Admission charge.

Québec Hôtel Dieu Museum Les Augustines, 32, rue

Charlevoix, in Québec City, has an important historical collection of art and objects relating to Québec and the first hospital in America north of Mexico City. Open throughout the year. Free. **Maison des Jesuites,** 2320, chemin du Foulon, in the Sillery section, dates back to the beginning of the eighteenth century and is one of the oldest historic sites in North America. The first Jesuit mission was founded in 1637.

Chapelle des Jesuites, 20, rue Dauphine, is dedicated to the Roman Catholic religious martyrs of Canada. It contains relics of several saints. The chapel features beautiful sculptures and a high altar made from native pine. Open daily. Free.

Port of Québec National Historic Park, 100, rue Saint-André, has interesting exhibits that tell stories of early shipbuilding and timber trading in this important seaport.

Chalmers Wesley United Church, 78, rue Sainte-Ursule, is one of the most beautiful neo-Gothic structures in the city. It has superb stained-glass windows and handcrafted woodwork as well as a century-old organ. Evening concerts are held during the summer months.

Outside Québec City

Québec Zoological Park, via Highway 15, has more than 564 birds, representing 165 species, and some 214 mammals of 57 different species. There are lions, tigers, bears, camels, owls, eagles, beavers, wolves—more than enough wildlife, exotic and domestic, to delight everyone. The grounds of the zoo are nicely landscaped. Open throughout the year. Admission charge.

Montmorency Falls, via Highway 138, is on your way to Île d'Orléans and Sainte-Anne-de-Beaupré. You can't miss them because the falls are so near the highways and so awesome that the plunging water seems about to deluge the road. Montmorency Falls are almost as famous as those at Niagara. In the winter the surface freezes and forms a huge cone of ice. You can view the thundering water from the bottom or the top at a park, which can be reached via stairs or an aerial tramway. Those who do not suffer from vertigo can walk across the top of the falls on a suspension bridge. There are hiking trails, an interpretation center, and picnic areas.

Île d'Orléans, via Highway 138 through Beauport (or Autoroute Dufferin-Montmorency), is a special place for Québécois. Its rural beauty and simplicity remind them of their past seen through romantic perspectives. The towns display some superb examples of old Québec architecture, and the little eighteenth-century churches, such as those in Sainte-Famille and in Saint-

François, are gems. This is a great place to picnic in a meadow or on the bank of the Saint Lawrence, to read poetry and be in love. Saint-Petronille offers the best view of Québec City across the water. There are several excellent and unusual restaurants on the island and many places where you can buy fresh vegetables and fruits (strawberries), delicious maple syrup, and long loaves of fresh, crusty bread.

Sainte-Anne-de-Beaupré, via Highway 138, is the most important Roman Catholic shrine in all of Canada. Through the decades millions of pilgrims have come here from all over the world to pray and to seek relief from their suffering. A large number of miraculous cures have been attributed to Saint Anne here. The massive and magnificent basilica has hundreds of crutches left behind as evidence of cures. Like Lourdes, Sainte-Anne-de-Beaupré holds candlelight processions during summer evenings. Masses are held every day at the basilica. On a nearby hillside are the Fountain of Saint Anne; The Holy Stairs, where the pilgrims climb on their knees in prayer; beautiful little chapels (Scala Santa Chapel and the Old Chapel); and the Stations of the Cross set in a grove of trees. The Cyclorama presents biblical Jerusalem in a 360-degree painting. Admission charge. There are accommodations and restaurants in the area, although most people stay in Québec City. Facilities for persons with limited mobility are excellent here, including ramps, special rest rooms, and medical assistance.

Recreational Sports

This area has plenty of recreation at hand, with a wide variety of services and natural sites. In the winter you may enjoy cross-country skiing, sledding, or ice-skating at one of the local parks, or maybe try your hand at curling, popular at the Québec International Bonspiel, (418) 681–1221. Golf enthusiasts will also be pleased with a selection of more than twenty golf courses in the metropolitan area, and there are several spots where you can keep up on your tennis game.

You can also find several places in the area to enjoy more active sports. For river rafting on the Jacques-Cartier River, call Excursions Jacques-Cartier at (418) 848–7238, or Village Vacances Valcartier at (418) 844–2200. If you prefer the gentler ride of a canoe, try the Saint Anne River; call (800) 321–4992 for more information.

Horse lovers will find many places to ride, and those interested in cycling or mountain biking will find plenty of places to rent equipment. For good trail recommendations, ask the attendant when you rent, or call Promo Vélo at (418) 522–0087. For rentals of bikes and other outdoor sports equipment, try Cyclo Services, (418) 692–4052; Les Escursions Jacques-Cartier, (418) 848–7238; or Vélo Passe-Sport Plein Air, (418) 692–3643.

Professional Sports

The Rafales, of the National Hockey League, play home games at the Colisée. Call (418) 691–7211 for information. Harness races are held at the Québec Hippodrome on the Exposition grounds, 2205, avenue du Colisée, throughout the year. Call (418) 524–5283 for information.

Accommodations

Québec City offers accommodations in every range and for every taste. Inquire about special rates for seniors, commercial travelers, families, and for off-season periods. One period of the year when accommodations are almost impossible to book is during Carnaval, in February. The better places, such as the Château Frontenac, are usually booked a year in advance, although even this famed hotel might have some space for late reservations.

Québec City

Québec Hilton, 3, Place Québec, (418) 647–2411, is a large, modern, and complete hotel catering to conventions, touring groups, and individual travelers. Located next to key government offices and overlooking the old city, the hotel has many fine facilities, including a heated outdoor pool, sauna, health club, gourmet restaurants, and lounges. Le Caucus is this hotel's top restaurant. It is connected to the Convention Centre via an arcade of expensive boutiques. Expensive.

Le Château Frontenac, 1, rue des Carrières, (418) 692–3861, is more than a great hotel—it is Québec City's most important landmark and symbol. Every visitor to Québec City stops here. Through its long history the Château Frontenac has played host to royalty from many countries and the famous from all walks of life. During World War II, while Churchill and Roosevelt stayed in the nearby Citadelle, it accommodated the Allied officers who planned the invasion of France. Today it offers fine accommodations, excellent service, and gourmet dining to the discriminating traveler. Expensive.

Loews Le Concorde, 1225, Place Montcalm, (418) 647–2222, is one of the best hotels in Québec City. It offers spacious rooms with highly contemporary furnishings. Most of the rooms have splendid views of the old city, the Plains of Abraham, or the Saint Lawrence River. This hotel is across the street from the Plains of Abraham, with its beautiful green areas, gardens, and vistas. Le Concorde features an outdoor heated pool, sauna, gym, a rooftop revolving restaurant, and lounges. Expensive.

Radisson Hôtel des Gouverneurs, 690, Saint-Cyrille, est, (418) 647–1717, is next to the Parliament buildings and historic Vieux Québec City. This beautiful high-rise hotel offers excellent accommodations, services, gourmet dining, lounges, and a disco. It also has a heated outdoor pool and is connected to the Convention Centre. Expensive.

Ramada Downtown, 395, rue de la Couronne, (418) 647–2611, offers a central location convenient to attractions, restaurants, and lounges. Expensive.

Hôtel Clarendon, 57, rue Sainte-Anne, (418) 692–2480, features an excellent restaurant. Moderate.

Hôtel Château Laurier, 695, rue Grande Allee, est, (418) 522–8108. Moderate.

Sainte-Foy

Auberge Sainte-Foy, 1200, rue Lavigerie, (418) 651–2440, offers a swimming pool and an excellent restaurant. Moderate.

Château Bonne-Entente, 3400, chemin Sainte-Foy, (418) 653–5221, has a swimming pool, tennis courts, and a good restaurant. Moderate to expensive.

Auberge Universel Wandlyn, 2955, boulevard Laurier, (418) 650–1616. Moderate to expensive.

Hôtel des Gouverneurs Sainte-Foy, 3030, boulevard Laurier, (418) 651–3030, offers a terraced garden, outdoor pool, gourmet restaurant, and disco. Expensive.

Sainte-Anne-de-Beaupré and Mont Sainte-Anne

Sainte-Anne, said to be the mother of the Virgin Mary, attracts thousands of pilgrims to this town and its imposing basilica, built in her honor, a half-hour drive from Québec City. Accommodations can be hard to come by, especially during important days in the religious calendar, but there is a good selection of hotels in and around town.

Motel Spring & Restaurant Lainé, 8520, boulevard Sainte-Anne, Château-Richer, (418) 824–4953, includes a family-style restaurant. Close to Montmorency Falls and an eighteen-hole golf course. Moderate.

Auberge La Bécassine, 9341, boulevard Sainte-Anne, (418) 827–4988, is a small (16 rooms) and inexpensive hostelry.

Serious skiers consider Mont Sainte-Anne, a thirty-minute drive from Québec City, via Highway 138, est, the province's best downhill venue. This super facility has fifty-one trails spread over three sides of the mountain, and twelve ski lifts that can serve almost 18,000 skiers per hour. Eighty-five percent of the total skiable surface on the mountain is backed by a snowmaking system, although this area is heavy snow country in the winter. Thirteen night-skiing trails offer the highest vertical drop for night skiing in Canada. Mont Sainte-Anne is known for its ski and snowboard school and its state-of-the-art lifts, which include a gondola. Ride this to the summit in the summer just for the views of the Saint Lawrence valley and Québec City. During the summer, Mont Sainte-Anne also offers two eighteen-hole golf courses, a golf school, hiking and mountain cycling trails, and many other recreational activities.

This is an area of many fine accommodations, restaurants, and lounges. Accommodations range in price from moderate to expensive. Package plans are available. You can get more information on accommodations and make reservations throughout the year by calling toll-free (800) 463–1568 (accessible from the rest of Québec and the eastern United States), or call Tourisme Québec (see the beginning of this chapter). For more information on the park, call (418) 827–4561. For the latest ski conditions at Mont Sainte-Anne, call (418) 827–4579.

North of Québec City

Manoir du Lac Delage, 40, avenue du Lac, Lac Delage, (418) 848–2551, is a complete resort about twenty minutes from Québec City via Highway 175. It features a heated pool, tennis courts, badminton, volleyball, a golf course, horseback riding, boats, skiing, skating, and sleigh riding, as well as a fine dining room and cocktail lounge. Expensive.

Auberge Les Quatre-Temps, 161, chemin du Tour du Lac, Lac Beauport, (418) 849–4486, has an indoor pool, nice views, and skiing. Moderate to expensive.

Hôtel Château Lac-Beauport, 154, chemin du Tour du Lac, Lac Beauport, (418) 849–1811, has an outdoor pool, tennis, skiing, and nice views. Moderate to expensive.

Dining

The emphasis in Québec's capital is on French, Québécois, and Canadian-American cuisine. The top restaurants here are a match for the best in Montréal—in all of North America, for that matter. The people of Québec City, like those in Montréal, consider fine dining an art and demand perfection from their chefs. The price for a fine meal, with wine, tips, and taxes, is similar to what you'd pay in Montréal. People dress for dinner in their best and latest fashions. Dinner, which starts at 7:00 P.M. or later, often lasts a good part of the evening.

Québec City

Le Champlain, Château Frontenac, 1, rue des Carrières, (418) 692–3861, offers elegant, gourmet dining (under crystal chandeliers and to live harp and violin music). One of the best places in the city. Expensive.

La Crémaillère, 21, rue Saint-Stanislas, (418) 692–2216, prides itself on its European cuisine and fine service. Moderate to expensive.

Café de Paris, 66, rue Saint-Louis, (418) 694–9626, has a menu of French and Italian specialties, also beef Wellington and rack of lamb. Moderate to expensive.

Aux Anciens Canadiens, 34, rue Saint-Louis, (418) 692–1627, serves Québec meat pie and rabbit stew in one of Québec's oldest houses. Moderate.

La Caravelle, 68½, rue Saint-Louis, (418) 694–9022, is a Spanish restaurant, unique in Québec City, specializing in seafood, paella, and gazpacho andalouse. Moderate to expensive.

Laurie Raphael, 117, rue Dalhousie, (418) 692–4555. This trendy and sophisticated eatery serves fresh meats, fish, and vegetables, flavored with unusual herbs and spices. Moderate to expensive.

Le Saint-Amour, 48, rue Sainte-Ursule, (418) 694–0667, is considered by many Québécois to be one of the finest restaurants in the city. Specialties include fillets of sole with salmon stuffing and shrimp sauce, grilled lamb cutlets cooked with split garlic buds and marinated in olive oil, a special chicken pâté, and fish soup with garlic toast. There is dining in an outdoor garden—with a retractable roof. Moderate.

Serge Bruyère, 1200, rue Saint-Jean, (418) 694–0618, near the Latin Quarter, is noted for superb continental cuisine. Expensive.

Le Marie Clarisse, 12, Petit-Champlain, (418) 692–0857, offers fine dining in a comfortable and classy atmosphere. Expensive.

Café d'Europe, 27, rue Sainte-Angèle, (418) 692–3835, serves Italian and French cuisine, specializing in seasonal dishes. Moderate.

Au Petit Coin Breton, 1029, rue Saint-Jean, (418) 694–0758. The wait staff here serves you in Brittany period costumes to match the food. Moderate.

Sucrerie Blouin, 2967, Chemin Royal, (418) 829–2903, is a traditional sugar house with Québécois food specialties and fiddle music. Moderate.

Le Poisson d'Avril, 115, Quai Saint-André, (418) 692–1010, features an informal atmosphere and excellent seafood in the Lower Town. Mussels are divine. Moderate.

Restaurant Continental, 26, rue Saint-Louis, (418) 694–9995, serves Classical French cuisine, brilliantly updated. Expensive.

Île d'Orléans (Orleans Island)

L'Atre, 4403, Chemin Royal, Sainte-Famille, (418) 829–2474, prepares old-fashioned Québec dishes and serves them in traditional style in an ancient farmhouse (circa 1680) with an open hearth. You are brought to the door by a horse-drawn carriage. Expensive.

Auberge Chaumonot, 425, Chemin Royal, Saint-François, (418) 829–2735, offers regional cuisine in a beautiful setting on the banks of the Saint Lawrence. Moderate to expensive.

Le Moulin de Saint-Laurent, 754, Chemin Royal, Saint-Laurent, (418) 829–3888, serves French and Québécois dishes. Live entertainment on weekends. Expensive.

Outside Québec City

La Maison Deschambault, 128, Chemin du Roy, in Deschambault, (418) 286–3386. Fine dining in a setting that is hard to beat: a 1790 stone Québécois house overlooking a tranquil pond in a village dating back several centuries. Moderate to expensive.

Entertainment

Québec City's best entertainment in the evening is its own romantic ambience. Stroll through historic Upper and Lower Town, along the Terrasse Dufferin and onto the green fields of the Plains of Abraham, or dine elegantly in a fine gourmet restaurant and then linger over old brandy to savor the romantic essence of Québec City.

Most of the better hotels and motels feature live entertainment and dancing in their dining rooms and lounges. Ask the concierge at your place of accommodation for suggestions for taking in the current hot spots in town.

There is music everywhere in Québec City—in the streets, on city squares and in parks, especially during the summer. There are several venues for concerts and plays. They include Grande Théâtre de Québec, 269, boulevard Saint-Cyrille, est, (418) 643–8131; Palais Montcalm, 995, place d'Youville, (418) 691–2399; and the recently restored Théâtre Capitole, 972, rue Saint-Jean, (418) 694–4444.

Shopping

If you would like souvenirs, your best bet is to patronize the young artists who display their paintings and drawings in rue du Trésor. Their work is inexpensive, and you will go home with something original and the memory of the person who created it. Within the Quartier Latin are gift shops selling wood carvings from Saint-Jean-Port-Joli and soapstone carvings from the far north, bookshops, boutiques, and department stores. There is also a complex of very expensive boutiques in the small underground city at the Québec Hilton and Convention Centre. Sainte-Foy's boulevard Wilfrid Laurier has several enclosed shopping malls.

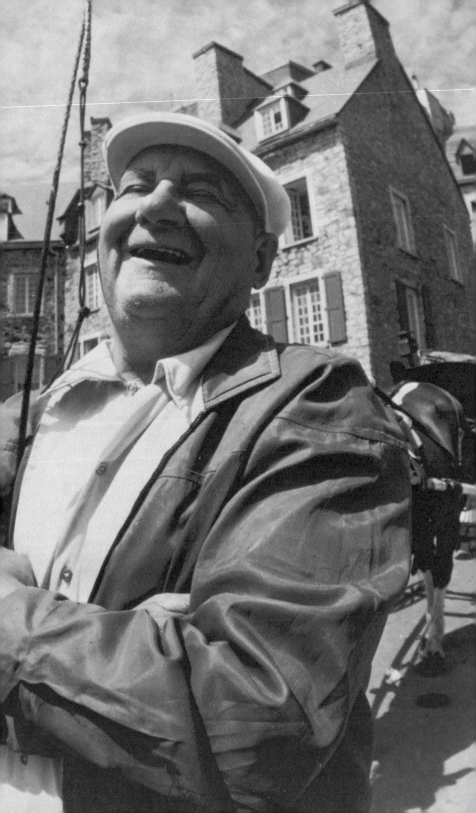

Other Popular Vacation Regions in Québec

Québec is Canada's largest province in terms of territory. It is so big that several European countries could be placed within Québec and still have room left over for more. It would be impossible to visit most of Québec during one trip. This is good because you will want to return again and again to see what you have missed. Many visitors to the province spend most of their time in Montréal and Québec City. This is a shame because they could easily add a whole new dimension to a trip by traveling out into the nearby countryside. There are other fascinating vacation regions that can be experienced within one visit.

Just a short drive to the north of Montréal is the Laurentian mountain resort region, a four-season area you can hike, swim, ride a horse, kayak, or canoe during the summer, and ski some of the finest downhill or cross-country trails in winter. The resorts here are world famous for their accommodations, service, and especially their cuisine and après-ski fun.

South of Montréal, in the Eastern Townships, there are picturesque towns, fine inns, an imposing monastery overlooking a majestic lake, and pleasant countryside. The Eastern Townships (Cantons-de-l'est, in French) is also popular for winter sports.

Between Montréal and Québec City is the "Heart of Québec." Deep in this heart are the historic cities of Trois-Rivières and

Ah, Québec; c'est magnifique!

Drummondville with their own attractions, parks, and religious shrines.

Along the north shore of the Saint Lawrence River to the east of Québec are the regions of Charlevoix, Manicouagan, and Duplessis. On this side of the river is Mont Sainte-Anne ski center, one of the finest winter sports facilities in North America. There are challenging downhill runs and extensive trails for cross-country ski touring. Summer brings hiking, swimming, and boating.

The Saint Lawrence River continues to widen as you travel farther east, and the mountain slopes plunge dramatically into the water. Wonderful inns and famous resorts are scattered throughout Charlevoix, whose quaint villages have become favorite haunts of artists. In the regions of Manicouagan and Duplessis, you enter a special world of small fishing settlements, traditional values, and a way of life reminiscent of earlier decades.

On the south side of the Saint Lawrence is one of the best-known road tours in all of Canada, around the Gaspé Peninsula, with mountains dropping to the broadening river as it becomes the sealike Gulf of Saint Lawrence. Here are the traditional fishing villages of Québec, places of strong family and community ties and a history that begins with the earliest European exploration of this continent. Parks showcase and protect the ecological wonders of this region, its wildlife, birds, and marine life. Gaspé offers good dining and excellent accommodations.

For more information on the Québec vacation regions described below, call Tourisme Québec: from the United States and Canada, (800) 363–7777; from Montréal, (514) 873–2015. Or write Tourisme Québec at P.O. Box 979, Montréal, Québec H36 2W3.

The Laurentians

As the Catskills are to New York City, the Laurentians (Laurentides, in French) are to Montréal. The Laurentians are a four-season recreational region of steep mountains, beautiful lakes, deep forests, and cozy valleys. This terrain provides the best Alpine and

cross-country skiing in Eastern Canada, plus every other winter sport you can think of, topped off by lively Québécois après-ski fun. During the summer and fall the region becomes a playground for camping, canoeing, sailing, hiking, rock climbing, auto touring, horseback riding, swimming, golf, and tennis. Laurentians resorts are known for luxurious accommodations, fine dining, and top star entertainment. Only an hour's drive from the central city, the Laurentians are close enough that you can enjoy them on a day trip from the city or vice-versa. You can come up here just for the day or stay an entire season.

The Laurentians are part of the Canadian Shield, a vast, relatively uninhabited area north of the Saint Lawrence River Valley and the Great Lakes, composed of rugged mountains, thousands of waterways, and endless forests. Agriculture and forestry, once the backbone of the Laurentian economy, are still important, but leisure-time businesses now provide a substantial portion of the region's employment and income. The Laurentians have achieved near-perfect balance between nature and the out-of-doors and the sybaritic urban pleasures. In the Laurentians you can really rough it in the wilderness—or you can live it up in style.

The Laurentians were settled by French-speaking Roman Catholics, and the towns of this region continue to reflect this heritage. But because of their proximity to Montréal and major cities in the eastern United States, affluent English-speaking Canadians and Americans have also made this area into a popular vacation refuge. So, though French in flavor, the Laurentians are cosmopolitan enough for everyone.

For more information on this vacationland, contact the Association touristique des Laurentides, 14 142, rue de la Chapelle, Mirabel, Québec City J7J 2C8; call (450) 436–8532 or (800) 561–6673.

The fastest highway access to the Laurentians from Montréal is Autoroute-des-Laurentides 15, a road that ends in Sainte-Agathe-des-Monts. From Sainte-Agathe to Saint-Jovite and Mont-Tremblant, Highway 117 is the main access road. From the Ottawa-Hull area, take Highway 105 to 117 at Mont-Laurier.

Limocar Laurentides, operating from Terminus Voyageur in Montréal, services the Laurentians with several runs a day; call (514) 842–2281.

Highway 15 passes through **Saint-Jérôme**, the "Gateway to the Laurentians." A bronze monument in town honors Father Labelle, an inspiring force in the economic development of this area in the nineteenth century. Also in Saint-Jérôme is the Vieux Palais

Art Gallery, which features works by artists living in the region. Open throughout the year.

At the municipality of **Prévost**, secondary roads lead to Echo, Connelly, and de l'Achigan Lakes.

The valley of **Saint-Sauveur** has several resorts, five ski centers, ninety-six slopes—some with 700-foot (213 m) vertical drops—and sixteen chairlifts. Saint-Sauveur has live theater, craft shops, antique boutiques, and good restaurants. Accommodations and dining are available at the Reláis Saint-Denis, 61, rue Saint-Denis, (450) 227–4766, moderate, and Auberge le Relais des Monts, on Highway 117, Piedmont, (450) 227–5181, with a swimming pool and skiing nearby, moderate. Motel Mont Habitant, 12, boulevard des Skieurs, Saint-Sauveur, (450) 227–2637, has a swimming pool, skiing on site, tennis, and access to a lake. Some rooms have fireplaces. Moderate.

Sainte-Adèle is another popular vacation center, featuring several downhill ski centers and miles of cross-country trails. There are also several studios in town where you can watch artisans make beautiful handicrafts, which you can buy.

Accommodations and dining around Saint-Adèle include:

Hôtel L'Eau à la Bouche, Highway 117, (450) 229–2991, is an elegant hostelry with one of the best dining rooms in the province. Expensive.

Auberge Champêtre, 1435, boulevard Sainte-Adèle, (450) 229–3533, has a swimming pool. Moderate to expensive.

Hôtel Le Chantecler, chemin du Chantecler, Lac Rond, (450) 229–3555, is a famous resort that offers good accommodations and dining, golf, tennis, swimming pools, lake beaches, boats, skiing on-site, and tennis. Moderate to expensive.

Highway 370 continues to **L'Estérel Resort and Convention Center**, boulevard Fridolin Simard, (450) 228–2571, one of the best resorts in the Laurentians. At L'Estérel you can ski cross country, sail and swim on a beautiful lake, play tennis and golf, work out in a health club, and enjoy the magnificent scenery around you; moderate (Modified American Plan).

Back via Highway 15 are the villages of **Val-Morin** and **Val-David**, noted for their artisans. Nearby Mont Condor attracts expert rock climbers from throughout North America. At Val-David is Santa Claus Village, exit 76 on Highway 15, an entertaining theme park for young children. Open the end of May to August. Admission charge.

In this area, you can find accommodations and dining at:

Hôtel La Sapinière, Highway 117, Val-David, (819)

322–2020, is a superb resort with outstanding cuisine (its wine cellar has 25,000 bottles, featuring 200 different labels), a swimming pool, cross-country skiing, tennis, and other recreational facilities; expensive, but packages are available. In 1982 this resort was the site for NATO's first meeting in Canada.

Auberge du Vieux Foyer, 3167, chemin Doncaster, Val-David, (819) 322–2686, has a good restaurant and accommodations, moderate.

Hotel Far Hills, rue Far Hills, Val-Morin, (450) 322–2014, is an excellent resort with cross-country skiing, swimming, sailing, tennis, and other sports, as well as an excellent dining room; expensive.

Sainte-Agathe, on Lac des Sables, has beaches, swimming, and boats for rent. Théâtre Le Patriote, chemin Tour du Lac, presents live French-language drama and exhibits handicrafts in a tourist pavilion. The scenic Linear Park, converted from a former railway line, "P'tit Train du Nord" passes through Sainte-Agathe. The trail stretches for 124 miles, from Saint-Jérôme in the south, to Mount-Laurier. Here you can stay at:

Motel Sainte-Agathe, 1000, rue Principale, (819) 326–2622, inexpensive.

Motel Saint-Moritz, 1580, rue Principale, (819) 326–3444, moderate.

Chalets Chanteclair, on Highway 117, (819) 326–5922, expensive.

Auberge Watel, 250, rue Saint-Venant, (800) 363–6478. Moderate.

Auberge du Lac des Sables, 230, rue Saint-Venant, (800) 567–8329. Moderate

Highway 117 takes you to **Saint-Jovite.** From here, a secondary road, Highway 327, takes you to the best-known and most popular recreational area in the Laurentians, **Mont Tremblant Provincial Park.** Here you can downhill ski on the highest mountain in the region, cross-country ski, ice-skate, snowshoe, camp, canoe, rock climb, swim, auto-tour, and hike. Fall foliage touring through the park is a favorite way for Montréalers and visitors to spend weekends.

The Mont-Tremblant area has the largest concentration of top-notch resorts and motels in the Laurentians. For additional information and reservations, call (888) 668–8008.

Auberge Gray Rocks Inn, located on the shore of Lac Ouimet, Highway 320, nord, Saint-Jovite, (819) 425–2771, is one of the best-known of the great Laurentian resorts, particularly popular with U.S. visitors. It offers excellent accommodations and dining and a wide variety of recreational facilities: skiing on-site, swimming in an indoor pool and at the lake, tennis, golf, seaplane rides, and much more. It has an indoor sports and fitness complex. Moderate.

Hôtel Club Tremblant, on Lac Tremblant, (819) 425–2731, provides excellent accommodations and dining, cross-country skiing, golf, tennis, sailing, and swimming. Expensive.

Hôtel Mont Tremblant, 1900, rue Principale, Mont-Tremblant, (819) 425–3232. Situated in the village, this hotel is a short drive from the ski slopes and other sporting facilities, including tennis, horseback riding, and cycling. Moderate.

Tremblant, (450) 476–9552 from Montréal, or (800) 461–8711 outside the city. This four-season resort has undergone an amazing transformation during the past several years. Vancouver-based Intrawest, a major ski resort operator, has poured more than $800 million into upgrading the center, adding condominiums, hotels, hiking trails, improved ski runs, and two eighteen-hole golf courses. At the foot of Mont Tremblant, there is now a pedestrians-only holiday village. Built in the style of Old Québec City, it is a complex of brightly colored buildings with steep roofs and dormer windows, housing restaurants, cafes, bars, boutiques, a movie theater, and numerous specialty stores. Activities available on-site or nearby include biking, swimming, hiking, horseback riding, boating, and downhill and cross-country skiing. Moderate to expensive.

From Saint-Jovite and the Mont-Tremblant area, Highway 117 continues on to the town of **Mont-Laurier,** where it meets Highway 105 from Ottawa-Hull. Highway 117 leads to La Vérendrye Provincial Park, an extensive wildlife refuge. **La Vérendrye Wildlife Reserve** offers camping, canoeing, fishing, moose hunting, cottages, and cross-country skiing.

Skiing the Laurentians

With five months of ice and snow each year, winter sports and Québec go together. Québec has the best skiing in Canada east of the Rockies. Excellent ski centers, with good facilities and well-tended slopes, are located close to Montréal—only an hour's drive away. What makes skiing in Québec different is the special liveliness of the Québécois themselves. Not only do they survive the long winter months, but they also make a joyful art out of living in a frigid zone. You'll feel their *joie de vivre* out on the slopes and especially at the many après-ski activities. Skiing in Québec also means having superb accommodations and dining, and easy access to Montréal. When you get tired of the downhill runs, you can ice-skate, ski cross-country, snowshoe, ice fish, or snowmobile amid magnificent winter scenery. •

Alpine Ski Centers
Mont Avila, in Saint-Sauveur, (450) 227–4671
Mont Olympia, Piedmont, (450) 227–3523
Mont Saint-Sauveur, Saint-Sauveur, (450) 227–4671
Mont Habitant, Saint-Sauveur, (450) 227–2637
Ski Morin Heights, Morin Heights, (450) 227–2020
Mont Gabriel, Mont-Rolland, (450) 227–1100
Le Chantecler, in Sainte-Adéle, (450) 229–3555
Belle Neige, Val-Morin, (819) 322–3311
Vallée Bleue, Val-David, (819) 322–3427
Mont Alta, Val-David, (819) 322–3206
Mont Blanc, Saint-Faustin, (819) 688–2444
Gray Rocks, Saint-Jovite, (819) 425–2771
Tremblant, Mont-Tremblant, (819) 425–8711
Mont Daniel, Saint-Aimé-du-lac-des-Îles, (819) 597–2388

The Eastern Townships

The Eastern Townships make up an extensive rural area southeast of Montréal, near the Vermont border, with rolling farmland, charming small towns, sparkling lakes, and medium-size mountains. About an hour's drive from downtown Montréal, the Townships (as locals call the region) has long been a favorite vacation haunt. During the summer the Townships is a tranquil haven for artists, writers, musicians, and actors, who contribute to the regions rich cultural life.

Much of the region was originally settled by Loyalists after the American Revolution and by British soldiers who were given land grants by the Crown. Because of this heritage, some of the communities resemble those in nearby New England. The fields are broad, in the English manner, while those in other parts of the province, notably around the shores of the Saint Lawrence River, are long and narrow strips, in the French tradition. In recent years the Anglo-Saxon population has declined, and French-speaking Québécois have come to dominate the towns. A few farmers from Switzerland and Germany have moved into the region, bringing their agricultural expertise and new cultural traditions.

The Townships nourish the fattest milk cows in the province. A congregation of monks living above Lac Memphremagog has become world famous for its cheeses. Some of the lushest apple orchards in Canada thrive here, their fruits making a delicious but potent cider. Ducks grow plump on local farms. Vast stands of sugar maples are tapped in the spring, producing some of the best maple syrup made in North America (despite what Vermonters will tell you).

The Townships is a four-season vacation area. In winter it offers great downhill and cross-country skiing. In spring you can tour a countryside awakening from the deep sleep of winter and bursting with life and color. Summer days are kept busy with swimming, golf, hiking, horseback riding, cycling on off-road trails, art, music, and theater. In autumn landscapes become scarlet, gold, and tan. You can visit country harvest fairs and sample from the bountiful fruit and vegetable harvests at roadside stands.

The Townships is easily reached by taking Autoroute 10, east toward Sherbrooke, the largest city in the region. From Vermont, I–91 and then Highway 55 take you right into the heart of the region, at Magog and Sherbrooke. If you are driving back into New England after visiting Montréal and Québec City, you can extend your trip by traveling through this lovely region.

On the way to the Townships, Highway 10 crosses the Richelieu River just south of **Chambly**. In early colonial days the Richelieu was an important waterway, giving Montréal and Québec City easy access to Lake Champlain and the English settlements in New York State and New England. General Montcalm and his French forces made frequent use of this route for his attacks during the Seven Years' (French and Indian) War. The Richelieu was also used by General Benedict Arnold and his American troops in their retreat from Québec. See old Fort Chambly, which played an important role in the early history of Canada and in Papineau's rebellion in the mid-nineteenth century. Open during the summer. Free.

Granby

The gateway city to the Townships is Granby, well known for its fine restaurants, and its fountains. Estriade, an off-road bike trail that was once a railway line, runs to the village of Waterloo. The Granby Song Festival, is held in mid-September. Many famous Québec performers make their names here.

Granby Zoo, 347, rue Bourget, a ninety-five-acre park with animals from all continents and a farm where children can pet tame animals is open May to mid-October. Admission charge.

Some accommodations in the Granby area are:

The Hôtel Le Castel de l'Estrie, 901, rue Principale, (450) 378–9071, is especially known for its cuisine. Moderate.

Hotel Le Granbyen, 700, rue Principale, (450) 378–8406, also has fine dining. Moderate.

Le Monde, 400, rue Principale, (514) 372–1705, offers inexpensive accommodations in two rooms.

As a side trip, take Highway 139 and explore the countryside down to Cowansville, and then take Highway 104 to Knowlton, where they raise ducks for restaurants. An interesting museum of local history is in the village, and an annual duck festival is held here, from mid-October to early November. There are numerous boutiques, pubs, and factory outlets.

Bromont, also near Granby, is ski country and draws horse-lovers as well. The site of the equestrian events during the Olympic Games of 1967, this community hosts a major horse show every year at the end of June. Château Bromont Hotel Spa, 90, rue Stanstead, (514) 534–3433, is a modern resort near the ski slopes with a health center. Moderate to expensive.

Magog and Mont-Orford

These are the prime recreational areas in the Eastern Townships. Magog is on the northern tip of Lac Memphremagog, a large body of water that extends well into Vermont. There are public beaches on Lac Memphremagog and cruises.

Mont-Orford Provincial Park offers all kinds of recreational activities—the best downhill skiing in the region, cross-country skiing, camping, hiking, biking, and swimming. Admission charge.

The Orford Art Centre, located off Highway 10, is well known for its summer educational program in music, art, and theater, especially for young talent. Its season runs from May to September. In July and August, the faculty and students hold their Festival of Music, during which the public may attend recitals and concerts.

Benedictine Abbey of Saint-Benoît-du-Lac is dramatically set on a peninsula overlooking Lac Memphremagog. To reach Saint-Benoît from Magog, take the road to Austin and then follow the signs to the abbey, which is at the end of a side road. A stunning sight when you come upon it at the end of a tree-lined cul-de-sac, the building is nestled among orchards and rolling, fertile fields. The abbey, which has recently been enlarged, was designed by Dom Bellot (1878–1944), who, as well as being an internationally renowned architect, was once the abbot. Men and women can take retreats at this tranquil and lovely place, home to some sixty Benedictine monks. Daily Eucharist is celebrated in Gregorian chant at 11:00 A.M. Call the monastery at (819) 843-4080 or, for women's lodging, (819) 843-2340; www.st-benoit-du-lac.com.

Accommodations and dining here include:

Hotel Chéribourg, on Highway 141 en route to Mont Orford, (819) 843-3308. Moderate.

Auberge L'Étoile sur le Lac, 1150, rue Principale, ouest, (819) 843-6521 or (800) 567-2727, serves three meals daily and has rooms overlooking Lac Memphremagog. Moderate.

At nearby Lake Massawippi are three of the Townships' finest inns: Hovey Manor, in North Hatley, (819) 842-2421 or (800) 661-2421, www.hoveymanor.com; Ripplecove Inn, in Ayer's Cliff, (819) 838-4296 or (800) 668-4296, www.ripplecove.com; and the Hatley Inn, in North Hatley, (819) 842-2451 or (800) 336-2451. These inns offer superb accommodations, dining, recreation, and guest amenities. Hovey Manor, within a secluded lakefront area, has English gardens. Ripplecove Inn, also on the lake, has one of the best dining rooms in the entire region. Hatley Inn overlooks the lake and is decorated with antiques. Some rooms have a fireplace and Jacuzzi. All three are expensive, but packages are available.

Sherbrooke

The largest city in the Townships, Sherbrooke is located on the Saint-François River. Sherbrooke's economy is based on forest products and other forms of manufacturing. In the spring, summer, and fall, stop to admire the thousands of plants in its gardens. These are arranged in intricate designs, a beautiful and colorful sight.

The Museum of Fine Arts, 241 Dufferin Street, is housed in the former Eastern Townships Bank, a historic landmark. It exhibits paintings, drawings, and sculpture. Open throughout the year. Admission charge.

Sherbrooke Seminary Museum, 222, rue Frontenac, has an extensive natural history collection, antiques, paintings, coins, medals, and firearms. Open throughout the year, afternoons only. Admission charge.

Also worth seeing is **Saint-Michel Cathédrale,** on rue de la Cathedrale, and the **Beauvoir Shrine.** In August Sherbrooke holds its Agricultural Exhibition, one of the largest in the province.

Here are some ideas for accommodations and dining:

Hôtel des Gouverneurs, 3131, rue King, ouest, (819)

565–0464, is one of the best in town for accommodations and dining. Moderate.

Hôtel Le Président, 3535, rue King, ouest, (819) 563–2941, is a motel-style lodging with an indoor pool and restaurant. Moderate to expensive.

Delta Hotel & Congress Centre, 2685 rue King, ouest, (800) 268–1133 or (819) 822–1989. This modern, comfortable hotel is one of the few in the area that allow pets. Indoor swimming pool and fitness center. Moderate to expensive.

To the south of Sherbrooke is **Lennoxville,** via Highway 147, the site of Bishop's University, founded in 1843. You are welcome to stroll the lovely campus and visit the internationally known experimental farm next door. Open May through early September. Lennoxville is also known for its antiques shops. Recommended accommodations and dining include the Motel La Paysanne, 42, rue Queen, (819) 569–5585, noted for its cuisine, moderate, and Motel La Marquise, 350, rue Queen, (800) 563–2411, moderate.

Eastern Townships Area Alpine Ski Centers

Mont Orford, Magog, (819) 843–6548
Owl's Head, Mansonville, (514) 292–3342
Mont Sutton, Sutton, (514) 538–2545
Bromont Ski Centre, Bromont, (514) 534–2200

For more detailed information on accommodations, dining, and recreation in the Eastern Townships, contact Tourisme Cantons-de-l'Est, 20 Don-Bosco Street South, Sherbrooke, Québec, J1L 1W4; (819) 820–2020 or 800–355–5755.

Centre-du-Québec and Mauricie

In haste to travel between Montréal and Québec City, many visitors miss the attractions of Trois-Rivières and Drummondville; two cities in the tourism region that is known as centre-du-Québec and Mauricie. Trois-Rivières is midway between Montréal and Québec City on the northern route (via Highways 40 and 138). Drummondville is midway on the southern route (via Highway 20).

Trois-Rivières

A venerable city that was an important industrial center for the early French, Trois-Riviéres has many historical attractions.

The **Saint-Maurice Ironworks** (Les-Forges-du-Saint-Maurice), 10,000, boulevard des Forges, is where the Canadian iron industry began under the French. Open May to September. Admission charge.

Pierre Boucher Museum at the Séminaire Saint-Joseph, 858, rue Laviolette, features art exhibitions throughout the year. Free.

The Museum of Archaeology of the Université du Québec, 3351, boulevard des Forges, has a collection of fossils and artifacts from Indian and European settlements in the region. Open throughout the year. Free.

Other walking tour attractions in the center of the city include the Museum of the Ursulines; St. James Anglican Church; the Roman Catholic cathedral, the only Westminster-style church in North America; statue of Maurice Duplessis, a legendary and controversial premier of Québec; the eighteenth century Manoir de Tonnancour; and Maison Hertel-de-la-Fresnière. There are also several art galleries and antiques shops in the city.

The **M/S *Jacques Cartier*** offers cruises on the Saint Lawrence River during the summer. Call (819) 375–3000 or (800) 567–3737.

Notre-Dame-du-Cap, adjacent to Trois-Rivières, at Cap-de-la-Madeleine, is an important religious shrine. It features a huge circular basilica decorated with beautiful stained-glass windows, an old historic chapel, and a large outdoor area for worship, including the Stations of the Cross and a gigantic rosary carved out of granite. Call (819) 374–2441.

Accommodations and dining here can be found at:

Hôtel des Gouverneur, 975, rue Hart, (819) 379–4550, (888) 910–1111, or www.gouverneur.com, offers excellent accommodations and dining, and many conveniences. Expensive.

Delta Sherbrooke Hotel & Conference Centre, 1620, rue Notre-Dame, (819) 376–1991, (800) 377–1265, or www.delahotels.com. Recreational facilities include an indoor swimming pool, whirlpool bath, sauna, and a fitness center. Le Troquet restaurant serves regional cuisine. Special deals for children. (There's a childen's play center, games, and baby-sitting center.) Expensive.

Le Deauville Motel, 4691, boulevard Royal, (819) 375–9691 or (800) 354–3889. Air-conditioned, nonsmoking rooms available. Summer theater. Bike rentals. Moderate.

Best Western Trois Rivíeres, 3600, boulevard Royal, (819) 379–3232, (800) 528-1234, or www.bestwestern.com., is a large modern facility with a good dining room. Moderate to expensive.

Nearby Parks

Trois-Rivières is the gateway to the Mastigouche and Saint-Maurice Parks, north via Highway 55.

Shawinigan Falls. This 150-foot waterfall is particularly impressive in the spring, when it is swollen with melted snow. Cruises on the Saint-Maurice River are offered from May to October; call (819) 537-7444.

Mauricie National Park is a spectacular wilderness area with panoramic views. Fishing, swimming, camping, canoeing, and cross-country skiing.

Drummondville

Des Voltigeurs Park includes the Trent Manor House and Estate (circa 1836), which displays antiques and other historical artifacts in a lovely setting. Among its collections is its museum of cuisine. Admission charge. The park also offers camping, swimming, touring, cross-country skiing, and snowshoeing.

Le Village Québécois d'Antan is on rue Mont Plaisir, Highway 3. Buildings, costumed staff, and activities depict life in a nineteenth-century Québec community. Open June to Labour Day. Admission charge. The village is a major historical and cultural attraction in the province.

Accommodations and dining around Drummondville include:

Comfort Inn, 1055, rue Hains (819) 477-4000, moderate.

Hôtellerie Le Dauphin, 600, boulevard Saint-Joseph, (418) 478-4141 or (800) 567-0995, www.le-dauphin.com, has a good restaurant as well as attractive rooms. In town, moderate.

Charlevoix

The Charlevoix coast, via Highway 138, from Sainte-Anne-de-Beaupré to Saint-Simeon, offers one of the most scenic drives along the ever-widening Saint Lawrence River. Along this route the rugged Laurentians extend their fingers into the river. There are breathtaking vistas and many examples of traditional Québécois architecture (homes, barns, churches) along the way. This is a rich area for photographers.

Cap Tourmente National Wildlife Reserve, with 5,000 acres of mudflats, tidal marsh, farmland, and mixed forest on the north shore of the Saint Lawrence River, is habitat to 250 bird species, including the greater snow goose that can be seen by the thousands during spring and fall migration. The reserve includes a nature center and several miles of hiking trails. It is open to the public from mid-April to early November. Admission charge.

Baie-Saint-Paul is a pretty town favored by artists. The Galerie d'Art Clarence Gagnon has works by this great Québécois artist. His paintings of rural life in Québec are highly prized and in major museums throughout Canada. The artist A. Y. Jackson also liked Baie-Saint-Paul and did many paintings here. At Saint-Joseph-de-la-Rive you can take the short ferry ride to Île aux Coudres, which has charming inns for accommodations and dining, museums of local history, lovely churches, spots where you can see porpoises in the river, and friendly islanders who welcome visitors.

Back on the mainland at Pointe-au-Pic is one of Québec's most famous resorts, Manoir Richelieu, (418) 665–3703, which resembles a French château. The Manoir Richelieu offers golf, tennis, swimming, fishing, fine accommodations, gourmet dining, lounges, and a casino. This was once a popular watering hole for wealthy Americans and English-speaking Canadians. Today it is more egalitarian, but the quality remains high. The views of the Saint Lawrence River and surrounding mountains from the front are magnificent, especially when shafts of sunlight plunge dramatically from the clouds and spread over the water. Expensive.

Highway 138 continues up the Charlevoix coast to the mouth of the Saguenay River, which is a favorite cavorting area for whales. At Baie-Sainte-Catherine, you can take a ferry to the historic town of Tadoussac and continue on the north shore into the regions of Manicouagan and Duplessis; call (418) 235–4395. You can go on whale-watching trips sailing on the schooner *Marie Clarisse*, which departs from the Hôtel Tadoussac dock. More than just a whale watch, this is also a scenic cruise of the Saguenay Fjord.

Most people touring the Charlevoix coast from Québec City try to make it a one- or two-day trip, turning back at Pointe-au-Pic or continuing from Saint-Simeon to the Gaspé via the ferry to Rivière-du-Loup on the south shore, (418) 862–5094.

There are several excellent inns in the Charlevoix region.

Auberge les Sources, in Pointe-au-Pic, (418) 665–6952. Moderate.

Auberge des Peupliers, in Cap-a-l'Aigle, (418) 665–4423. Moderate.

Auberge La Pinsonnière, in Cap-a-l'Aigle, (418) 665–4431. Expensive.

Auberge Donohue, in Pointe-au-Pic, (418) 665–4377. Moderate.

Auberge des 3 Canards, in Pointe-au-Pic, (418) 665–3761. Moderate.

Hôtel Cap-aux-Pierres, on Île aux Coudres, (418) 438–2711. Moderate.

The North Shore

Manicouagan Region

The Manicouagan region goes along the Saint Lawrence River from Tadoussac on the east shore of the Saguenay River to Baie Trinité. Tadoussac, via Highway 138 from Québec City, is reached by ferry across the Saguenay. This portion of the north shore of the Saint Lawrence is connected to the south shore by ferries between Les Escoumins and Trois-Pistoles on the south shore, between Baie-Comeau, the principal community in this region, and Matane, and between Godbout and Matane. These ferries allow you to tour the north shore as far as Godbout and still have access to the Gaspé and the Atlantic provinces.

At Godbout, the Saint Lawrence River empties into the Gulf of Saint Lawrence. For students of natural history, north of Baie-Comeau is the site where a gigantic meteor smashed into Earth thousands of years ago. Some scientists believe that the impact of this meteor so changed the Earth's environment that it was a cause for the disappearance of many species of animal life on our planet, including the dinosaurs. You can see the circular shape of this meteor by looking at a map or space satellite photo, and you can drive up to this area on Highway 389, which goes past the mammoth hydroelectric complex called Manic Five, with its Daniel Johnson Dam. There's excellent fishing in the lake and rivers surrounding the meteor, which is now simply a mound topped with thick woods. There's also good hunting. The use of local outfitters and guides is required.

There are many good places of accommodation in the Manicouagan region, including the Hôtel Tadoussac, (418) 235–4421, in Tadoussac, and the Hôtel Le Manoir, (418) 296–3391, in Baie-Comeau. Both offer excellent accommodations and dining, and both are moderate in price. Be sure to book a room ahead of arrival.

Duplessis Region

Highway 138 continues northeast along the north coast of the Gulf of Saint Lawrence, through the Duplessis region, all the way to Natashquan The road stops at Natashquan There is no connecting road from here to the Québec and Labrador border at Blanc-Sablon. At Blanc-Sablon, a paved road does go a few miles east to the village of Vieux-Fort and west to Pinware, Labrador. A ferry, operating when the waters of the Strait of Belle Isle are free of ice, provides access between Blanc-Sablon and Sainte Barbe on the northern tip of the huge island of Newfoundland. Commercial aviation companies provide regularly scheduled flights to many of the communities along the north coast of the Gulf of Saint Lawrence, with the city of Sept-Îles (Seven Islands) being their principal destination. Sept-Îles is a major port for the ocean shipment of iron ore and is the largest and most important of the communities on the coast.

Ferries also provide service to the remote fishing communities along the coast. During the summer, travelers have enjoyed the leisurely cruises and the opportunity to visit the picturesque villages to meet the people and to purchase their local handicrafts. A number of these fishing villages, such as Harrington Harbour, are inhabited by English-speaking people.

A freighter from Sept-Îles also provides service to Anticosti Island, an extensive wilderness preserve in the Gulf of Saint Lawrence, and back west to the city of Rimouski on the south shore of the Saint Lawrence River and just a few hours' drive to Québec City. Duplessis is most famous for its salmon-fishing rivers and for hunting. Anticosti Island, once a private domain of one man and off-limits to casual visitors and sportsmen, is now a prime place for salmon fishing and deer hunting. You can also hike and camp on Anticosti. The hiring of local outfitters and guides is required.

There are good accommodations and restaurants in Sept-Îles, as well as bed-and-breakfasts. Try the Hôtel Gouverneur at 666, boulevard Laure, (418) 962–7071, or the Comfort Inn at 854, boulevard Laure, (418) 968–6005, both inexpensive to moderate.

The Gaspé Peninsula Tour

On a map the Gaspé looks like Québec's lower lip jutting into the Gulf of Saint Lawrence. With Montréal and Québec City, the Gaspé is one of the must-see areas in Canada.

The greatest delight of a Gaspésian trip is the feel of an ever-present sea; but the sea must contend with spectacular mountains, steep cliffs, the Saint Lawrence Gulf and River, the islands, snug valleys, picturesque villages, and a way of life that remains close to nature and to the traditions of an earlier time. The Gaspésian trip is a constantly changing panorama of the moods of nature and humanity.

Allow three to five days for your Gaspésian tour. You can do it in two days, but then your trip will be all driving. There are public and private picnic and camping areas along the entire route. If you find yourself in an interesting village and your French is rusty or nonexistent, don't worry—there's sure to be a bilingual person around to recommend points of interest, accommodations, and places to eat. The local shopkeeper and the parish priest should also be helpful.

The accommodations mentioned in the guide are in logical stopping points. By and large, the best dining on the Gaspé can also be found at these lodging places. It is recommended that you call ahead for reservations, especially in the popular tourist town of Percé.

Most people prefer to begin their Gaspésian tour from Québec City, traveling along the south shore of the Saint Lawrence River and around the peninsula in a clockwise direction, then entering the province of New Brunswick at Campbellton (the gateway to Atlantic Canada) around the Baie des Chaleurs. The total distance is about 665 miles (1,064 km). Alternatively, you can follow the Charlevoix coast on the north shore from Québec City to Saint-Siméon, where a ferry crosses to Rivière-du-Loup on the south shore. The Charlevoix coast route is far more scenic, but it also requires more time.

Experienced travelers have found that the best vistas of sea, mountains, fishing villages, and forests are seen by going around the Gaspé Peninsula clockwise. Stretches of the road are set on narrow terraces with steep cliffs rising on one side and the pounding waves of the Saint Lawrence below on the other. The clockwise direction gives you a greater sense of security because you are driving on the inside of the road, hugging the sides of mountains. Sometimes, when the gulf waters are particularly rough, waves smash against the low sea walls and send spray high into the air, so keep your window washers full of cleaning solution.

Our Gaspésian tour follows the south shore of the Saint Lawrence River from Québec City. You can leave Québec City via the Québec or Pierre Laporte Bridge at Sainte-Foy or cross over on the ferry to Lévis. Get on Highway 20, a superhighway, and continue until it merges with Highway 132, which goes around the peninsula.

Saint-Jean-Port-Joli, 64 miles (102 km) from Québec City, is a major hand crafts center of the province. Shops and studios managed by craftspeople working in wood sculpture, jewelry, textiles, graphic arts, and pottery abound. This little riverfront town was launched into the field of hand crafts by the famous Bourgault family, master woodcarvers and teachers. The Saint-Jean-Port-Joli artisans exhibit their work throughout town and offer it for sale at attractive prices. The Musée Les Retrouvailles houses a collection of weaving looms, spinning wheels, and other tools. Open end of June to mid-September. Admission charge. Visit the richly decorated wooden church built in 1776. Also visit the Musée des Anciens Canadiens with its exhibits of wood carvings. Open mid-May through October. Admission charge.

Rivière-du-Loup is a large community, where the Trans-Canada Highway turns inland toward Edmundston, New Brunswick, another gateway to Atlantic Canada, with access to eastern Maine at Fort Kent and Madawaska. Points of interest include the Seigniorial Manor of the Frasers on rue Fraser, the Park of the Luminous Cross, the lookout at the summit of Mont Citadelle, the beach at Côte-des-Bains, and the lighthouse on the Île Blanche. Also visit the Musée du Bas-Saint-Laurent, which has interesting art and ethnology exhibitions; open from the end of June to early September, at various hours. Admission charge. Les Carillons touristiques is a private collection of bells of different sizes; open from May to November. Admission charge. Ecotourism tours and whale-watching cruises are offered daily, departing from the marina of Rivière-du-Lays, from early June through September. Recommended accommodations include Hotel Universel, 311, boulevard Hôtel de Ville, (418) 862–9520, moderate to expensive; Hotel Lévesque, 171, rue Fraser, (418) 862–6927, moderate; and Motel Auberge-de-la-Pointe, Highway 132, (418) 862–3514, moderate. The Motel Lévesque and the Motel Auberge-de-la-Pointe have good dining rooms.

Trois-Pistoles is a popular resort town and port for fishing. Visit La Maison du Notaire, 168, rue Notre-Dame, a century-old home that contains a handicrafts boutique and art gallery. Open throughout the year. Free. Also visit the Musée Saint-Laurent for local history. Open June to mid-September. Admission charge. You can take a ferry from Trois-Pistoles to the north shore of the river at Escoumins. At Île Razades is a bird sanctuary, and Île-aux-Basques is said to have been used by Basque fishermen even before the time of Cartier.

Rimouski, the largest city east of Québec City, is a center of religious, educational, and commercial activity for the Bas-Saint-Laurent and Gaspé regions. Its facility of the Québec National Archives houses a collection of family records, legal documents, maps, engravings, and photos. Open throughout the year. Free. Visit the Rimouski Regional Museum, 35, rue Saint-Germain, which features a permanent collection and itinerant exhibitions of contemporary and traditional art. Open throughout the year.

Admission charge. An interesting way to explore Rimouski is to take an architectural walking tour highlighting the city's architecture and history; for information, call (418) 723–2322. Other footpaths wind along the Rimouski River. There are several art galleries in town, including Galerie Basque at 1402, boulevard Saint-Germain, ouest, and Rimouski-Est, 635, rue Saint-Germain, est, (418) 724–6469. Accommodations include Hôtel Gouverneur, 155, boulevard René-Lepage, est, (418) 723–4422, moderate; and Hotel Rimouski, 225, boulevard René-Lapage, est, (418) 725–5000. Both offer fine dining.

Reserve National de Faune in Pointe-au-Père, (418) 724–6214, is one of the best places in Québec to observe coastal flora and fauna. Guided tours are available from mid-June to early September. Nearby, the Musée de la Mer exhibits recall the shipwreck of the *Empress of Ireland,* which claimed 1,012 lives on May 29, 1914.

Grand Métis is the site of the Métis Floral Garden at the Reford Estate, off Highway 132. This exceptional garden, a major attraction on the Gaspé tour, covers forty acres and has more than 500 species of trees and shrubs and a large variety of flowers. Open June to mid-September. Admission charge.

Matane, famous in big-city restaurants for its shrimp, is a major fishing port, and you can hire boats and equipment here for catching salmon and other species. There are nice views of the river, the lighthouse, and the islands. Ferry service operates between Matane and Baie-Comeau and Godbout on the north shore.

Matane Wildlife Reserve, 25 miles (40 km) south of Matane via Highway 195, has camping, cottages, canoeing, fishing, nature interpretation, hiking, touring, moose and small-game hunting, and cross-country skiing. For information, call (418) 562–3700.

De la Gaspésie Park (now a national park) is a great favorite with the Québécois, 10 miles (16 km) south of the town of Sainte-Anne-des-Monts via Highway 299, features camping, cottages, salmon and other fishing, nature interpretation, hiking, touring, cross-country skiing, and snowshoeing. There are accommodations and exceptional dining at l'Auberge le Gîte du Mont-Albert (advance reservations are absolutely essential). For information and reservations, call (418) 763–2288. Open year-round.

Between Sainte-Anne-des-Monts and Cap-aux-Os, you drive along the base of steep mountain walls and next to the waters of the Gulf of Saint Lawrence, each turn of the road offering a breathtaking view of the meeting of land and sea. For a long stretch the road twists and turns on its flat narrow bed, but at times it climbs inland into forests and past rushing streams. Small fishing villages along the way, such as Mont-Saint-Pierre, Grand-Vallée, and l'Anse-à-Valleau, are a photographer's delight. Split cod can be seen drying outdoors on flakes (wooden beds), and some of the villages sell fresh-baked bread from ancient outdoor ovens. Be sure to notice the canals that enable fishermen to dock their boats near their homes, and stop at some of the lighthouses along the way to enjoy the vistas.

Take your time and stop also at Forillon National Park. Many people speed by this region, but this section offers more of the true spirit of Gaspé than any other.

Parc National Forillon is land's end on the Gaspé Peninsula, (418) 368–5505. The cliffs here rise more than 600 feet (183 m) above the sea. The arctic Alpine flora of Cap-Bon-Ami and the pioneer plants at Penouille are unique to the region. At the top of the Forillon Peninsula, whales can sometimes be seen cavorting and spouting in the gulf water; gray seals and common seals also can be seen. You can hike, swim, and picnic and arrange cruising and fishing expeditions and deep-water scuba-diving excursions. Campsites are available at Cap-Bon-Ami and Petit-Gaspé.

From the village of **Cap-aux-Os** to the city of Gaspé, the coastline (except for Forillon Park) is less dramatic but nevertheless lovely. The area's culture changes here. Between Québec City and Cap-aux-Os, you have driven through quintessential French communities, but from here to Matapédia you will pass through many communities that, although predominantly French, have sizable English-speaking populations. Anglican and United Church spires stand alongside the towers of the Roman Catholic churches. Many of these English-speaking people are descendants of the Revolutionary War Loyalists and British troops who took part in Wolfe's campaign against the French.

Gaspé, a city of around 17,000 inhabitants, is the administrative center for this end of the peninsula. A monument commemorates Cartier's landing and his claiming of all the land before him for his king. The Gaspé Museum, on Highway 132, features exhibits of local history, displays the work of area artists, and holds concerts of folk, popular, and classical music. Open all year at various hours. Admission charge. Also visit the contemporary Cathedral of Gaspé, in the center of town, and the fish hatchery, off Highway 132. Fishing trips and boat rides can be arranged in Gaspé. There is also direct air service to the Îles de la Madeleine (Magdalen Islands). Recommended accommodations and dining include Quality Inn Gaspé, 178, rue de la Reine, (418) 368–3355,

Traditional domestic Québécois architecture, pleasing to the eye and perfect for the climate and terrain.

moderate; and Motel Adams, 2, rue Adams, (418) 368–2244, moderate.

Fort Prével offers coveted accommodations, a superb dining room, and a fine golf course. Highly recommended. Call (418) 368–2281 for reservations.

Percé is the most popular resort community on the Gaspé. Besides a number of excellent vistas of Percé Rock, a famous Canadian landmark, and Île Bonaventure (both now a national park), daily cruises take passengers to and around Île Bonaventure, a well-known bird sanctuary, with a rookery for gannets, gulls, puffins, and other species, (418) 782–2240. In Percé itself there are live theater, folk-song and dance festivals, concerts, and so on. You can take a mini-bus ride around Mont Sainte-Anne, go deep-sea fishing, visit the exhibits of artisans and painters, and enjoy excellent French cuisine. Recommended accommodations and dining include:

Hôtel-Motel Le Bonaventure, Highway 132, (418) 782–2166. Excellent dining. Moderate.

Hôtel-Motel La Normandie, Highway 132, (418) 782–2112. Moderate.

Motel Manoir Percé, Highway 132, (418) 782–2022. Moderate.

Auberge du Gargantua, route des Failles, (418) 782–2852, considered to have the best restaurant in Percé. Moderate accommodations, expensive dining.

The coastline from Percé to Chandler begins to turn in a southwesterly direction and forms the north shore of the Baie des Chaleurs. You will pass through several interesting fishing villages such as l'Anse-à-Beaufils, Cap d'Espoir, and Grand Rivière, where more split cod can be seen drying on flakes. Chandler is a mostly English-speaking community, where the main industry is pulp and paper. It offers fishing, swimming, tennis, and golf.

Bonaventure is by the sea, but the Acadian pioneers who settled here chose to farm the land rather than earn their living from fishing. The Musée Acadien du Québec traces their history. Crafts shop. Open year-round. Admission charge.

Many of the towns along this part of the coast provide deep-sea fishing and boat cruises for tourists.

New Carlisle, the hometown of the late René Lévesque, Québec's controversial premier, is the administrative center for the Baie des Chaleurs area. Its population has a substantial Loyalist element. This section of the coast also has a large population of French-Acadians whose ancestors were expelled from Nova Scotia by the British, and several communities of Mi'kmaq Indians. At Maria, for example, you can purchase Indian baskets, weavings, and snowshoes and see a church shaped like a tepee.

In New Richmond, you can visit the Gaspésie British Heritage Center, which includes historic houses, period furnishings, walking trails, a gift shop, and a restaurant. Open June through mid-October. Admission charge.

At Saint-Siméon there is a panoramic view of the Baie des Chaleurs and the distant coast of New Brunswick.

When you reach Carleton, a pleasant resort town, you are near the end of your Gaspésian tour. The main attraction here is to drive to the top of 1,959-foot (555 m) Mont Saint-Joseph for great views of the bay, the New Brunswick shore, and the surrounding countryside. On the summit is the Notre Dame Oratory, a religious shrine noted for its colorful mosaics and stained-glass windows. Carleton also offers saltwater swimming, horseback riding, golf, tennis, windsurfing, fishing excursions, and handicrafts boutiques. Recommended accommodations and dining include Hostellerie Baie Bleue, 482, boulevard Perron, (418) 364–3355, the best accommodations and dining in town, moderate to expensive. Also in Carleton is Aqua Mer, Canada's first thalassotherapy center, offering various water therapies for tired bodies, as well as fine lodging and dining, (418) 364–7055.

At the village of Miguasha is Parc National Miguasha, a rich reserve containing prehistoric fossils. Guided tours are given from early June to mid-October. Free. Continue farther to Pointe-à-la-Croix, where you can cross over on the bridge to Campbellton.

If you are going back to Québec City and points west, continue on to Matapédia, where Highway 132 cuts through the Matapédia Valley and comes out on the south shore of the Saint Lawrence River at Mont-Joli. Rimouski is just a few miles south of Mont-Joli, and Québec City is west beyond Rimouski.

Îles de la Madeleine (Magdalen Islands)

Souris, Prince Edward Island, is a terminus for the passenger and car ferry service, on the M/V *Madeline* to the Îles de la Madeleine (Magdalen Islands). It operates April 1 to the end of January, depending on weather and ice conditions. The crossing time is five hours. For more information, call (902) 687–2181, or Tourisme Québec. There is daily air service to the islands from Charlottetown, P.E.I., and the town of Gaspé. Tilden has a car rental agency on the islands. Make reservations before you go.

The Îles de la Madeleine are in the Gulf of Saint Lawrence, 180 miles (288 km) from the Gaspé, 70 miles (112 km) from Prince Edward Island, 55 miles (88 km) from Cape Breton. The archipelago's twelve islands are part of the Province of Québec. The main islands are Havre-Aubert, Étang-du-Nord, Havre-aux-Maisons, Grande-Entrée, Grosse-Île, Île d'Entrée, Île Brion, Île-aux-Cochons, and Rocher-aux-Oiseaux. On the seven inhabited islands, most of the residents are of French-Acadian stock, although there are about a thousand of English and Scottish descent. The Madelinots are fishing people who make their living from lobster, herring, and cod. They have formed cooperatives and operate the canneries, smokehouses, and freezing plants as owners.

The main reason for going to the Îles de la Madeleine is, quite frankly, to enjoy the pleasure of long sandy beaches, drawing closer to nature with its myriad seabirds, undulating dunes, and moody seas of the Gulf of Saint Lawrence. Bring a bike for transportation and a sleeping bag for accommodations. The islands also have organizations that provide diving expeditions, deep-sea fishing trips, land and air sightseeing, windsurfing and boat rentals, bike rentals, horseback riding, golf and tennis, and harness racing. There are history museums, nature preserves (seals, gannets, puffins), warm-water swimming areas, an aquarium, art galleries, and handicraft shops.

Almost all the restaurants here specialize in freshly caught seafood—lobster, cod, mussels, haddock. Recommended accommodations include Auberge Chez Denis François, in Havre-Aubert, (418) 937–2371, moderate; Hôtel Château Madelinot, in Cap-aux-Meules, (418) 986–3695, expensive; and Auberge Madeli in Cap-aux-Meules, (418) 986–2211, moderate. All offer fine dining. Tourisme Québec will provide you with information on bed-and-breakfast places and camping facilities, or call the tourism office on the islands direct at (418) 986–2245.

Part Three

Atlantic Canada

CHAPTER 10

New Brunswick

New Brunswick, the gateway to Atlantic Canada, is a province of brilliant contrasts. It is truly bilingual; both French and English are taught in public schools. And it is bicultural as well, with towns that have a distinctly different feel. You would never mistake the very British enclave of St. Andrews for French, nor Caraquet for English. But these are not the only flavors you will notice there.

New Brunswick has a large Irish population, especially along the Miramichi River, and an entire town, appropriately named New Denmark, is populated with Danish immigrants. A major Highland festival brings its many Scottish descendants to Fredericton each summer, and near Sussex are farms that are unmistakably German or Dutch. The province's Aboriginals—the term they have chosen as their official designation here—maintain their cultural traditions, which they are more than willing to share with visitors.

The Landscape

If New Brunswick's people represent a wide variety, its geography shows even more contrasts. New Brunswick hangs from the eastern edge of Canada's mainland, connected only by a short northwest land boundary with the province of Québec. Except for its border with Maine and the short marshy Isthmus of Chignecto that connects the province with Nova Scotia, all of the other edges of New Brunswick are washed by water. Its east and south sides face the Northumberland Strait (which separates it from Prince Edward Island) and the Bay of Fundy (which separates it from Nova Scotia), while its north is substantially bounded by the Bay

The Cabot Trail on dramatic Cape Breton Island in Nova Scotia is one of the most popular tourist attractions in all of Atlantic Canada.

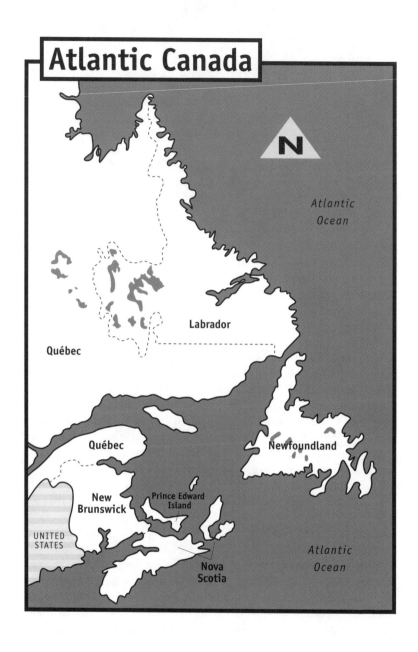

Atlantic Canada

N

*Atlantic
Ocean*

Labrador

Québec

Newfoundland

Québec

New
Brunswick

Prince Edward
Island

UNITED
STATES

Nova
Scotia

*Atlantic
Ocean*

of Chaleur. In the middle, and sometimes reaching right to the sea, New Brunswick has vast stretches of deep wilderness.

These two geographical features—its vast wilderness areas and its magnificent coastline—account for much of New Brunswick's tremendous appeal to travelers who stay long enough to appreciate it. But its mainland location means that many people do not. They see it as a bridge between the United States and the beaches of the two provinces to its east, and rush right through without ever opening their eyes to the land- and seascapes whizzing past.

The coastline they pass is one of the most beautiful and varied on the continent. Along the southern Fundy coast, the land is heavily indented. The St. Croix River enters Passamaquoddy Bay at the U.S. border, and Kennebacasis Bay, near St. John, is where the famed St. John River meets the sea. This ragged coastline is in places sheer cliff, and in others scattered with islands and skerries—mere outcrops of rock in the sea—where puffins, seals, gannets , and other wildlife make their homes.

For all its cities and sweeping agricultural lands, New Brunswick remains largely a place of wilderness forests and intimate connection with the sea. The only unsettled stretch of coastal wilderness left on the east coast of North America extends from St. Martins to Fundy National Park.

In sharp contrast to its tidy coastal towns, New Brunswick's wilderness is really wild. Few roads cut through its vast interior, where dense forests are broken only by rushing salmon rivers. No road at all penetrates the coastal wilderness between St. Martins and Fundy National Park, although a spectacular new scenic road from St. Martins gives visitors a hint of its grandeur.

A Brief History

Before the Europeans arrived, these were the lands of the Maliseet (also known as Malecite) and Mi'kmaq (also seen in its older spelling, Micmac) tribes of the First Nations.

The great explorer Samuel de Champlain and his associate, Sieur de Monts, attempted a settlement in 1604, choosing Dorchets Island in a river he named the St. Croix. The river, he thought, would provide protection, yet still allow trading with the native peoples. After a harsh winter devastated the group, Champlain moved his colony to the Fundy coast of Nova Scotia.

Apart from a few trading posts established at Saint John and elsewhere along the coast, little settlement took place during the following years. Franco-British wars over control of North America reached the region with the British capture of the small French Fort Beausejour at the head of the Bay of Fundy in 1755. When the British in Nova Scotia expelled the French-speaking Acadians, many of them escaped over the isthmus into the wilderness of the north coast, establishing small farms and the French Acadian heritage that enriches that coast today.

In 1763 Britain incorporated what is now New Brunswick into the colony of Nova Scotia. Coastal towns of New Brunswick became a haven for Loyalists fleeing the threats and land seizures that came with the American Revolution. More than 14,000 Loyalists settled along the shores of the St. Croix and St. John Rivers in the late 1770s and 1780s. Quickly establishing businesses, particularly in shipping, these new settlers dominated the area and succeeded in having the region declared a separate province in 1784.

The Napoleonic Wars in the early nineteenth century led to a British demand for timber products and the New Brunswick forest industry was born, an industry that is still crucial to the economy of the province. Timber and shipbuilding provided wealth to those regions where poor soils precluded large-scale agriculture.

The nineteenth century was good to the province, and England had allowed the colony a large measure of home rule, so it was with something less than enthusiasm that New Brunswick joined the Dominion of Canada at the time of Confederation in 1867.

New Brunswick was the home base for K. C. Irving, whose spectacular rise to wealth is legendary. He founded the Irving petroleum companies as well as operating a multitude of other business, such as paper plants, newspapers, radio stations, and lumbering. He and his family have also given back to their community by, among other things, creating the Irving Eco-Center la Dune de Bouctouche that is not only saving this fragile barrier dune but serving as a research and learning center as well.

Another well-known son of the province is William M. Aitken, who founded a publishing empire in Britain, served in England's wartime cabinet under Winston Churchill, and was granted the title of Lord Beaverbrook. He funded the Beaverbrook Art Gallery in Fredericton, one of the most important in the entire Atlantic region, as well as the Fredericton Playhouse and many of the buildings of the University of New Brunswick.

Travelers can learn about New Brunswick's rich past in many

New Brunswick

Campbellton •
Dalhousie •
• Charlo
Atholville •
• New Mills
Petit-Rocher •
Beresford •
Bathurst •
Caraquet •
Village Historique Acadien
• Shippagan
Restigouche Region
Tracadie •
Gulf of St. Lawrence
St. Jacques
• Edmundston
• St. Basile
• St. Quentin
Mount Carleton Provincial Park
Neguac •
• St. Leonard
Newcastle •
Kouchibouguac National Park
• Grand Falls
• Chatham
Prince Edward Island
New Denmark
Miramichi Region
St. Louis-de-Kent •
Richibucto •
Perth-Andover •
• Rexton
Buctouche •
N
• Florenceville
• Hartland
Cocagne
St. John River Region
Shediac •
Woodstock
Moncton •
Cap-Pelé
Mactaquac Provincial Park •
Fredericton
• Dieppe
Sackville •
Kings Landing •
Dorchester —
Oromocto
Hopewell Cape •
Fort Beausejour
• McAdam
Gagetown •
Sussex •
Nova Scotia
MAINE
Alma
Fundy National Park
Fundy Tidal Region
St. Stephen
St. •
John
St. George
Bay of Fundy
St. Andrews •
Black's Harbor
Deer Island
Campobello Island
Grand Manan Island

ways. For the Loyalist and English story, visit King's Landing off of the Trans-Canada Highway 2 just west of Fredericton. Here an entire Loyalist settlement of period homes and shops, saved from an area to be flooded by a dam, have been assembled in a rural nineteenth century community. On the north coast, don't miss Village Historique Acadian at Grand Anse, west of Caraquet, where the story of early Acadian life is told by costumed interpreters in original buildings. A totally different approach to Acadian culture can be found at La Pays de la Sagouine at Bouctouche. Here role-playing docents and live dinner theater tell the tale of early twentieth century Acadian life, drawn from the pages of New Brunswick author Antoine Maillet.

But you don't have to go to a museum to experience Acadian

culture; in community after community it is vibrant and very visible. The widespread display of the red, white, and blue Acadian Stella Maris flag with its single gold star is a point of French cultural pride (but is not a symbol of separatist sentiment).

New Brunswick is noted for the quality of crafts produced by its many artisans. Look for pewter, weaving, knitted clothing, pottery, woodcarving, and glassware. On a more practical level, look for fine home-made jams and jellies, farmstead cheeses, handcrafted soaps, and needlework such as handmade quilts and hooked rugs. You will find a good selection at local farmers' markets in Bathurst, Saint John, Fredericton, and Moncton. Look for signs for shops, studios, and farms along the roadside, especially on theTrans-Canada Highway 2, which follows the St. John River to Edmundston.

The Fundy Tides

The world's highest tides are in the Bay of Fundy. Within six hours, a busy harbor filled with bobbing boats can turn into a mudflat, with the same boats sitting at odd angles below very tall wharf pilings. At its highest, the difference between low and high tide has been measured at more than 50 feet.

As you might imagine, the speed and force of these tides wears hard upon the shore. Their constant motion has sculpted fantastic shapes, wearing away softer earth and rocks at a faster rate than harder ones to form caves, sea arches, bluffs, sea stacks, and entire beaches of almost perfectly rounded waterworn pebbles and rocks.

The tides also make the Bay of Fundy one of the most nutrient-rich bodies of water on earth. These feeding grounds bring a wide variety of sea life and their predators, including whales. You can see more varieties of whales in greater numbers here than in any other place on earth. Whale-watch boats leave from harbors all along the Fundy Coast, and you are almost certain to find these magnificent creatures.

For those interested in water sports, New Brunswick's shore is a paradise. But be sure to check with locals who know the waters, and keep a tide chart handy (they're in all the newspapers and at tourist offices) to avoid being left high and dry in the mud. Be especially careful of open waters here; the sudden changes create violent whirlpools and tidal currents.

How to Get to New Brunswick

By Car

From the state of Maine, the most widely used route takes I–95 to Houlton and connects with the Trans-Canada Highway 2. For a more scenic but longer ride, take Route 9 from Bangor to St. Stephen or Route 1 along the coast of Maine to St. Stephen, with a side trip to Campobello Island.

From western Canada, take the Trans-Canada Highway 2, which brings you to Edmundston. From Québec's Gaspé region, cross into the province from Matapédia, and head toward Campbellton on Highway 11, which will take you south toward Moncton. From Prince Edward Island, drive to Borden-Carleton and take the recently opened Confederation Bridge, which spans the Northumberland Straits.

New Brunswick's roads and highways are well maintained and marked. Some secondary roads are unpaved, but they invite exploration, particularly along the coasts. Be careful on the unpaved roads in the interior, as many are used by heavy trucks in lumbering, farming, and mining operations.

Rental cars—Hertz, Avis, Budget, and Tilden—are available at major airports and cities.

By Ship

From Digby, Nova Scotia, to Saint John, take the M/V *Princess of Acadia* (see page 264). You can also arrive by ferry from Eastport, Maine, or from Campobello Island via Deer Island by two ferries.

By Air

Air Canada and Canadian Airlines International serve New Brunswick. The major airports are located in Saint John, Fredericton, Charlo, and Moncton. Rental cars are available there.

By Bus

Increasingly, people are visiting the province on tour buses. Check with your own travel agent for details on these comprehensive tours.

There is daily bus service to St. Stephen from the United States through Maine on Greyhound and from the Québec area on Voyageur buses. SMT buses, (506) 648–3500 in Saint John, will transport you within New Brunswick.

By Rail

VIA Rail service goes along the eastern coast of New Brunswick
from Rivière-du-Loup to Matapédia to Moncton.

General Information

Time zone: Atlantic
Telephone area code: 506
Police and medical emergencies: dial 911

Climate and Clothing

Wherever you have a seacoast in a temperate latitude, you can depend on one thing: undependable weather. One day may dawn in
a chowder of fog, which burns off by midmorning to reveal a glorious sunny day, only to have a sea wind blow in with rain in the
late afternoon. But for the most part, summer days are warm but
not humid—perfect for active sports and for swimming in the
warmest seawaters north of Virginia. June through mid-October
are the best times to visit, when days tend to be sunny and
evenings cool. You should bring light jackets and sweaters for
evenings and the occasional rainy day. If coastal fogs cover the
sun in May and June, as they often do, head inland, where you
will likely find glorious weather.

Autumn weather is cooler, but days are still warm. As they
grow shorter (remember you are north of the forty-fifth parallel
all over Atlantic Canada), evenings become cooler, sometimes
downright chilly. But with those shorter days come some of the
northeast's most glorious fall foliage. The St. John River Valley
and the area around Sussex and the Fundy shore are simply
breathtaking in the fall.

Winters are cold, sometimes very cold, and snow is frequent
and plentiful, which is just the way those travelers who come to
New Brunswick for its abundant winter sports like it. Snowmobiling, dogsledding, ice-skating, sledding, and skiing, both downhill
and cross-country, are popular with locals, so winter is a good
time to meet the hospitable people who live here, and to join them
at play. Just be sure to bring your mittens and earmuffs.

Although you will be welcomed warmly no matter how you dress (New Brunswick is the very soul of good manners and hospitality) in a few places you will feel more comfortable in dressy clothes. In dining rooms of large upscale hotels, such as the Algonquin, and nicer restaurants, men will want to wear a jacket and tie. But for the most part, casual clothing is acceptable everywhere.

Tourist Information

You can receive free travel literature before you leave home by calling New Brunswick's Department of Tourism toll-free at (800) 561–0123, visiting www.tourismnbcanada.com, or writing it at P.O. Box 12345, Woodstock, New Brunswick E7M 5C3.

Major Events

Summer is festival time in New Brunswick, when residents pull out all stops to celebrate everything from their heritages to the lobster.

June
Salmon Festival, Campbellton, late June to early July
International Francophone Festival, Tracadie-Shiela
Festival Moncton (jazz and blues), late June to early July

July
Shediac Lobster Festival, Shediac
Peat Moss Festival, Lamèque
Canada's Irish Festival on the Miramichi (largest in the country), Chatham
Lamèque International Festival of Baroque Music, Lamèque
Fisheries Festival, Shippagan
Loyalist Days, Saint John
Festival Western de Saint-Quentin, Saint-Quentina
Woodstock Old Home Week, Woodstock
New Brunswick Highland Games and Scottish Festival, Fredericton
Festival Bon Ami Get Together, Dalhousie
Miramichi Folk Song Festival, Newcastle
La Foire Brayonne, Edmundston

August
Victoria Park Arts and Crafts Fair, Moncton
Le Festival Acadian de Caraquet, Caraquet
Festival by the Sea, Saint John

Chocolate Festival, Saint Stephen
Sand Sculpture Contest, Parlée Beach
Grand Ole, Atlantic National Exhibition, Saint John

September
Fredericton Festival of Fine Crafts, Labour Day weekend
Mactaquac Craft Festival, Mactaquac
Fredericton Exhibition and Provincial Livestock Show, Fredericton
Harvest Jazz and Blues Festival, Fredericton
Festival international du drama Francophone en Acadie, Moncton
Atlantic Balloon Festival, Sussex

Accommodations are difficult to book in the host communities during popular festivals. Make reservations in advance.

Easy-to-Book Adventures

New Brunswick has been innovative in developing special-interest vacation packages. These packages, which are promoted under a program called "Day Adventures," include accommodations and activities. Some also include meals and entertainment. For more information, call the listed organization or the New Brunswick Department of Tourism. Although the actual packages may change from year to year, these are those most frequently offered.

Canoeing on the Restigouche River, with crackling campfires, home-cooked meals, and a scenic waterway; (506) 684–2120.

Whale-watching in Passamaquoddy Bay and staying at an island B&B, (506) 747–2946, or at a family-run hotel at historic St. Andrews-by-the-Sea, (506) 529–8877.

Whitewater canoeing weekends on the St. Croix River, combined with fishing and swimming; (506) 466–1240.

Romantic getaway with candlelight dinners, champagne, picnic lunches, and carriage rides through covered bridges at the coastal village of St. Martins; (506) 833–4772.

Golfing at the Algonquin Resort's eighteen-hole signature-course, (506) 529–8823, and at Royal Oaks, another signature course in Moncton, (506) 384–3330.

Horseback riding along the wooded trails of Albert County near Moncton; (506) 382–2587.

Painting workshops in Gagetown, at a historic community in the Saint John River Valley; (506) 488–1116.

Kayaking among the islands in the Bay of Fundy: (800) 640–8944.

Hunting and Fishing

New Brunswick has long been popular with hunters and anglers from around the world. The province is easily accessible and has many miles of wilderness and waterways for both game and fish. New Brunswick has good hunting for black bear, deer, grouse, woodcock, and many species of duck. All nonresident hunters are required by law to hire licensed guides. There is also excellent fishing, and the province is famous for its Atlantic salmon, which can be caught in its Miramichi and Restigouche Rivers. Salmon fishing is restricted to fly fishing only, and you must hire a licensed guide. You can also fish for trout and bass in inland waters and hire boats and gear for exciting deep-sea fishing excursions. A list of outfitters and information on hunting and fishing are available from New Brunswick's Department of Tourism.

Provincial Parks and Campgrounds

Parks and campgrounds (both government and private) are located throughout New Brunswick. All parks are open during the summer and a few (such as Mactaquac, Sugarloaf, and Mount Carleton) are open throughout the year. No reservations for campsites at provincial parks are accepted: Spaces are allotted on a first-come/first-served basis. The maximum stay at a provincial campsite is fourteen days. There are also two national parks in New Brunswick, Fundy, and Kouchibouguac.

Most parks have recreational activities, such as swimming, nature trails, canoeing, fishing, and playgrounds. For more information on provincial and private campgrounds, contact New Brunswick's Department of Tourism.

Accommodations

New Brunswick offers some of Eastern Canada's finest inns, several of them in the seaside town of St. Andrews alone. Advance reservations are recommended from about the end of June through Labour Day.

Take advantage of the free Dial-a-Nite service, which connects you with hotels, motels, farm vacation hosts, and privately operated campgrounds throughout the province. You are encouraged to use this service at all government-operated Tourist Information Centres, which are strategically located at border crossings, such as St. Stephen and Woodstock.

If you have any complaints concerning accommodations, contact the New Brunswick Department of Tourism, (800) 561–0123, or write to P.O. Box 12345, Woodstock, New Brunswick E7M 5C3.

New Brunswick Farm Vacations

If you want to get to know real New Brunswickers, live with them on their farms. You will get a clean, cozy bedroom, wholesome meals, plenty of fresh air, and a chance to take part in the activities of the farm, the family, and the local community. Best of all, it's a high-value vacation at an outrageously inexpensive price. For full details on New Brunswick farm vacations, contact the New Brunswick Department of Tourism.

Dining

The native foods of New Brunswick present the traveler with some delicious treats: potatoes from the St. John River Valley, fiddleheads (the first buds of certain ferns, used as a vegetable), mushrooms from the Tantramar area, lobster from Shediac and the Northumberland shore, herring and sardines from Blacks Harbour, Miramichi salmon, oysters and crabs from Caraquet and Shippegan.

There is a good choice of restaurants in most areas: Some, such as Shadow Lawn in Rothesay and San Martello Dining Room in Saint John, have achieved an excellent reputation far beyond New Brunswick's borders.

Liquor by the bottle is sold in government stores and in a few privately operated stores that act as agencies of the New Brunswick Liquor Corporation. Government liquor stores, located in major cities and towns, are open Monday through Saturday. Liquor is also sold by the glass in licensed restaurants, dining rooms, and lounges. The legal drinking age is nineteen.

What's in a Name?

Quite a lot in Atlantic Canada, when the name is St. John, Saint John, or St. John's. They are not interchangeable. Saint John is the largest city in New Brunswick, and it sits on the St. John River. The capital of Newfoundland is St. John's, a fact it is wise to remember when you are reading the flight screens in an airport. Forgetting that distinction could take you to the wrong province.

Touring New Brunswick

Although there is so much to see and do in New Brunswick by following the established tourist routes, be adventuresome and take the less traveled roads. You will be surprised at some of your discoveries: a hidden cove, perfect for a picnic; a majestic Victorian farmhouse gracing a gentle, sloping hill; a country store, children drying dulse on the ground and offering you a bit of this sea tang to chew. The possibilities are endless because of New Brunswick's great variety. Don't be in a rush to pass through this beautiful province.

To make it easy for visitors to plan driving tours, the New Brunswick government has organized the province into picturesque driving routes such as the River Valley Scenic Drive, which follows the St. John River from Edmundston, through Hartland and Fredericton, to Saint John. The Fundy Coastal Drive, from St. Stephen on the Maine border embraces the islands of Passamaquoddy Bay to Moncton. The Acadian Coastal Drive snakes around the scenic east coast from Aulac in the south, through Bouctouche, Caraquet, and on to the Bay of Chaleur. The Miramichi River Route runs from Fredericton to Chatham, along what is considered to be one of Canada's best salmon rivers.

The Upper River Valley

The St. John River rises in the northern wilderness of Maine, forming the upper western border between that state and New Brunswick (also the international border between the United States and Canada). The river moves into the heartland of the province, past the provincial capital of Fredericton, and rushes out to sea into the Bay of Fundy at New Brunswick's largest city, Saint John. Most of the land in the river valley is devoted to agriculture: potatoes, other vegetable crops, dairy and beef cattle. The scenery along the entire valley is exceptionally beautiful. It is often called the "Rhine of Canada," albeit without castles and vineyards.

Most Canadians enter New Brunswick via the Trans-Canada Highway 2, a few miles north of **Edmundston.** There is a border crossing here for Americans from Madawaska, Maine. Edmundston is a large city; its principal economic activities are lumbering, paper, and pulp. The majority of residents speak French, as do most of the people in this region on both sides of the international border. In the nineteenth century the residents here became fed up with the squabble between the United States and Great Britain over the location of the international border and decided to form their own "Republique de Madawaska." This idea continues in the mythology of the region.

While in Edmundston visit the Madawaska Museum, featuring the history and development of this part of the St. John River Valley. Open all year. Admission charge. Near Edmundston is Les-Jardins-de-la-République Provincial Park with an outstanding botanic and show garden. Admission charge. Also at the park is the Antique Automobile Museum, a collection of classic cars. Open mid-June to Labour Day. Admission charge. This park itself is a major recreational facility offering swimming, tennis, and other activities.

The skyline of Edmundston is dominated by the Cathedral of the Immaculate Conception.

Accommodations and dining in this area can be found at:

Hotel République City Hotels, south of the city heading toward Fredericton, on the Trans-Canada Highway, (506) 735–5525, has an indoor pool, dining room, and lounge. Moderate.

Le Fief, 87 Church Street, (507) 735–0400, is a country inn with an outstanding dining room. The menu here, along with the crystal-and-linens atmosphere, would be a standout in Montréal.

Praga Hotel, 127 Victoria Street, (506) 735–5567, is comfortable and has a dining room and lounge. Inexpensive.

Howard Johnson Hotel & Convention Centre, 100 Rice Street, (506) 739–7321, in the city center, has an indoor pool and dining room. Moderate.

At the town of **Saint Basile,** just south of Edmundston on the Trans-Canada, is the Saint Basile Chapel Museum, a replica of a chapel built in the early 1800s, and a nearby cemetery dating back

New Brunswick has some of the richest farmland in all of Eastern Canada. Consider a farm vacation in this province, where you can share in the everyday life of a farm family or relax as you see fit. Excellent meals and accommodations are offered at a price you cannot afford to pass up.

to 1785. Open July and August. Admission charge.

Saint Leonard, on the Trans-Canada, is the home of the internationally famous Madawaska weavers. You can visit their gift shop and select choice knitted woolen goods of exquisite patterns and colors. There is a border crossing here from Van Buren, Maine. You can also go up to Campbellton via Highway 17 from here. You can stay at Daigle's Motel, off the Trans-Canada on Highway 17, (506) 423–6351, with an outdoor pool and reliable dining room, moderate.

Grand Falls is where the St. John River becomes a miniature Niagara Falls, plunging over craggy rocks into a gorge. Scenic lookouts provide good views of both. Visit the Grand Falls Historical Museum. Open July to September. For accommodations and dining, try the Best Western Près-du-lac, on the Trans-Canada, (506) 473–1300, with a heated pool, dining room, and lounge, moderate; or the Coastal Inns Motel Leo, on the Trans-Canada, (506) 473–2090, which welcomes pets and has a dining room, moderate.

Take a side trip, via Highway 108, to **New Denmark,** founded by Danish settlers, and visit their museum of pioneering history. Open mid-June to Labour Day. Free.

Perth-Andover, off the Trans-Canada, is the home to the Southern Victoria Historical Museum. (Americans can enter the province here from Fort Fairfield, Maine.) Nine miles (14.5 km) to the south of Perth-Andover, on Highway 105, is Muniac Provincial Park.

At **Florenceville** there is a covered bridge spanning the St. John River. **Hartland,** to the south, has no fewer than four. The most interesting is the one between Routes 103 and 105. Hartland Covered Bridge, as it is called, is the longest in the world, measuring 1,282 feet (391 m).The bridge marks its one-hundreth birthday in 2001.

Woodstock is where many U.S. residents enter the province, via I–95 from Houlton, Maine. Here you can visit the Old Carleton County Court House (circa 1833), on Highway 560, in Upper Woodstock, used as a seat of justice and a stagecoach stop.

Open July to Labour Day. Donations. For accommodations and dining, try Stiles Motel, 827 Main Street, (506) 328–6671, which has a dining room, moderate; Auberge Wandlyn Inn, on the Trans-Canada and I–95, (506) 328–8876, with many conveniences, a swimming pool, and dining room, moderate to expensive; or Panorama Motel, Trans-Canada and I–95, (506) 328–3315, a good value, with an indoor pool, dining room, and lounge, moderate.

Kings Landing Historical Settlement, at **Prince William,** via the Trans-Canada, is one of Canada's top attractions and has something of interest for the entire family. Kings Landing depicts the life of a Loyalist settlement in the river valley from the late eighteenth through the nineteenth centuries: how the people lived, worked, worshipped, and entertained themselves. This large site has sixty buildings (including homes, farmhouses, barns, workshops, and an Anglican chapel where services are still held). More than a hundred people dressed in period costumes do the chores of an earlier time while answering visitors' questions. Kings Landing has a beautiful setting high above the St. John River, and the only traffic in the settlement consists of visitors and horses. The Kings Head Inn offers hearty traditional meals in a historic environment. Live, professional entertainment is presented at the King's Theatre, and tours for children and special events for all ages occur throughout the summer. Open June to November. Admission charge. Special family rates. Call (506) 363–5090.

Also in this area and convenient to the Trans-Canada is **Mactaquac Park,** open throughout the year. Mactaquac has everything: swimming, boating, an eighteen-hole golf course, a dining facility in an elegant lodge, hiking, camping, nature trails, entertainment, and much more. If you intend to camp there, however, be warned that during the summer season this is one of the most popular provincial parks in all of Atlantic Canada, and on weekends it is best to arrive before noon. But give it a try anyway, or use private campgrounds and then the public facilities of the park. There is a dining room at Mactaquac Lodge.

Fredericton, the "city of stately elms," became the capital of New Brunswick in 1785. Lying along the west bank of the gently flowing St. John, Fredericton may be the most beautiful city in Atlantic Canada, with its river, elms, and large Victorian mansions. Fredericton has generally escaped the ugly wounds of industrialization by remaining a place where the main activity is essentially that of the mind—scholarship and politics.

There are plenty of self-guided tours that you can find out

about in *Touriffic Tours*, a pamphlet that includes tour ideas and several coupons. For more information, stop by Fredericton Tourism at 11 Carleton Street, phone (506) 460–2041 or (888) 888–4768, or visit www.city.fredericton.nb.ca. Here you can also find out about the Canada Day Celebrations in the beginning of July, with all sorts of festivities including fireworks over the St. John River.

Christ Church Cathedral, Brunswick and Church Streets, was built in the mid-1800s. The first cathedral foundation on British soil since the Norman Conquest, architecturally this is perhaps the finest Anglican cathedral in all of Canada. Its landscape is graced by tall elms, and the building resembles Salisbury Cathedral. Tours during the summer months. Free.

Legislative Assembly Building, on Queen Street, the province's seat of government, has a stunning, ornate interior and houses an excellent portrait of King George III, a collection of Audubon bird prints, Hogarth prints, and a copy of the original Domesday Book (1087) printed in 1783. Tours are available. Free.

Guard House, off Carleton Street, within a military compound, is a restored military post, with a costumed guard on duty. Open June to Labour Day. Free.

Soldiers Barracks, also within the military compound, is a three-story building that has been restored and furnished to show what barracks life was like in the mid-1800s. Open June to Labour Day. Free.

The Carlton II provides scenic cruises along the beautiful St. John River. It sails from Regent Street Wharf, which is located near the back of the Beaverbrook Hotel. Call (506) 454–2628.

Officers' Square, in the center of the city, features the Old Officers' Quarters, which houses the York-Sunbury Historical Society Museum. This fine museum has many interesting displays from Fredericton's military and civilian past, including items from the Boer War and World Wars I and II, colonial furniture, and Indian artifacts. Open all year. Admission charge. At 11:00 A.M. and 7:00 P.M. Tuesday through Saturday from July to late August, the colorful Changing of the Guard ceremony takes place in the square. The guards wear scarlet tunics, blue pants, and white pith helmets, and they are usually inspected by some distinguished citizen or guest. The square contains a statue to Lord Beaverbrook, the city's great benefactor.

Saint Dunstan's Church, on Regent Street between King and Brunswick, is on the site of the first Roman Catholic cathedral built in New Brunswick. The original cathedral was demolished and replaced by the current structure. The episcopal throne of the first bishop has been preserved, and there is a beautiful painting entitled *The Crucifixion.*

The Playhouse, on Queen Street directly opposite the Lord Beaverbrook Hotel, is the center of the performing arts in the Maritime Provinces. It is home for Theatre New Brunswick, a professional company that plays locally and tours the region. It also features symphony concerts, ballet, and special guest performers. Call (506) 458–8344.

Science East Science Center, at the Old County Jail, Brunswick Street, offers a great diversion for families with children. More than fifty interactive exhibits allow children (and curious adults) to explore how the world works around us.

Beaverbrook Art Gallery, on Queen Street, is the finest facility of its kind in Atlantic Canada, featuring Salvador Dali's massive *Santiago el Grande* and works by Sir Joshua Reynolds, Thomas Gainsborough, John Constable, William Hogarth, Graham Sutherland, Walter Richard Sickert, Augustus John, and others. The gallery has the largest single collection of the nineteenth-century Canadian artist Cornelius Krieghoff. In addition to this permanent collection, the gallery has changing shows featuring the works of contemporary artists from New Brunswick and other parts of Canada. Open throughout the year. Admission charge. Call (506) 458–8545.

The Green, next to the Beaverbrook Gallery, is a lovely grassy, tree-shaded area along the bank of the St. John River. A statue of the poet Robert Burns, a fine marble fountain donated by Lord Beaverbrook, and a memorial to the Loyalists who settled Fredericton grace the green.

University of New Brunswick, on University Avenue, overlooks the city and the river. Its many historic buildings and their exhibitions are open to the public, free. You can arrange a tour of the Brydone Jack Observatory, the first astronomical observatory in Canada. Visit the old Burden Academy on campus, a one-room schoolhouse of the mid-1800s. At Head Hall see an exhibit of early electrical implements. The Old Arts Building is the oldest university building (circa 1825) still in use on any campus in Canada. The Provincial Archives, of historical records, maps, photographs, plans, and drawings relating to the history and development of New Brunswick, are located in the Bonar Law–Bennett Building, open every weekday. Sports events, concerts, and conventions are held at the modern Aitken Centre. Saint Thomas University, which grants its own degrees, uses many of the Univer-

sity of New Brunswick's facilities.

Be in Fredericton on Saturday morning and visit the **Boyce Farmers' Market,** which operates from 6:00 A.M. to 6:00 P.M.. Farmers, artisans, and others offer all kinds of good things for sale: fresh fruits and vegetables, homemade baked goods and relishes, maple syrup, unique pottery, flowers, and more. The browsing is free, and no doubt you'll find something to buy.

Fredericton also has public tennis courts and swimming and wading pools. Call the Recreation Department, (506) 460–2230, for locations and hours of operation. If you're the betting type, there's harness racing at the Fredericton Raceway. Call (506) 458–8819 for a schedule.

The **Summer Music Series** offers a variety of local talent that ranges from jazz, blues, pop, and folk to concert bands. The concerts are offered every Tuesday and Thursday evening in July and August.

The city has a number of modern shopping centers: Fredericton Shopping Mall, Brookside Mall, Regent Mall, and Kings Place are enclosed and have all sorts of boutiques, gift shops, and clothing stores.

The following is a listing of accommodations in the Fredericton area:

Prospect Inn, at the junction of Woodstock Road and Route 102, (506) 450–9911, has a swimming pool and dining room. Moderate.

Sheraton Inn Fredericton, 225 Woodstock Road, (506) 457–7000, is a modern four-star property with elegant bedrooms that is one of the best hotels in town. Moderate to expensive.

Carriage House Inn, 230 University Avenue, (506) 452–9924, an imposing Victorian home located near the cathedral, art gallery, shops, and restaurants, serves home-style breakfasts. Moderate to expensive.

Lord Beaverbrook Hotel, 659 Queen Street in the center of the city, (506) 455–3371, is an "establishment" place, close to everything, with an indoor swimming pool, restaurants, and lounges. Moderate to expensive.

Fredericton Inn, 1315 Regent Street, (506) 455–1430, has a swimming pool, a restaurant, and a lounge. Moderate to expensive.

City Motel, 1216 Regent Street, (506) 450–9900, has newly furnished rooms, a restaurant, and lounge. Moderate to expensive.

Auberge Wandlyn Inn, 958 West Prospect Street, (506) 462–4444, features many conveniences, including a swimming pool, restaurant, and lounge. Moderate to expensive.

University of New Brunswick, off Highway 2, (506) 453–4891, offers dormitory rooms during the summer. Inexpensive.

Howard Johnson's Hotel & Restaurant, Lower Saint Mary's on the Trans-Canada south of the city, (506) 460–5500, has the usual Howard Johnson conveniences, including a restaurant and pool. Moderate.

Dining places in Fredricton are:

Luna Pizza, 168 Dundonald Street, (506) 455–4020, features live lobsters as well as Italian and Greek dishes. It has an outside patio. Inexpensive.

Prospect Street Restaurant, 958 Prospect, (506) 452–8937, features continental cuisine and a dinner theater. Moderate.

Schade's Restaurant, 536 Queen Street, (506) 450–3341, is a bright, cheery family-style eatery serving German food. Schnitzels are a house specialty. Moderate

Hilltop Pub, 1034 Prospect Street, (506) 458–9057, has good steaks and a daily buffet. Moderate.

Dolan's Pub, 349 King Street, Piper's Lane, (506) 454–7474, offers a traditional pub menu for lunch and dinner, and live entertainment Thursday through Saturday. Inexpensive.

The Lobster Hut, 1216 Regent Street, at the City Motel, (506) 455–4413, serves seafood Canadian style. Moderate.

The Cabin, 723 Woodstock Road, (506) 459–0094, has a traditional diner menu and atmosphere, offering plenty of classic favorites. Inexpensive.

The Lunar Rogue Pub, 652 King Street, (506) 450–2065. Patio bar. Daily food specials and themed ethnic food on certain days, such as nachos (Tuesday night), samosas (Wednesday), etc. Moderate.

Crispins, King Place, (506) 459–1165, has a salad bar, light meals, and a deli. Inexpensive.

Season's Restaurant, 369 Lincoln Road, (506) 451–0081, serves steaks, chicken, and seafood; diners have a view overlooking the St. John River. Moderate.

Joe's Diner, 817 Devon Avenue, (506) 472–3168, is one of the local favorites. Inexpensive.

The Lower St. John River

To see more of the St. John River Valley, take Highway 102 south from Fredericton. This leisurely drive along the river to the city of Saint John offers the best scenery in this valley. Several river ferries cross the river along the way. At **Oromocto** you are welcome to enter the huge Canadian Forces Base and visit its Gagetown Military Museum. It has exhibits relating to the Royal Canadian Dragoons, the Black Watch, and the Eighth Canadian Hussars. Open throughout the year. Free. Also in Oromocto is the Fort Hughes Blockhouse, a historical reconstruction. Open end of June to Labour Day. Free. The place to stay is the Oromocto Hotel, 100 Hersey Street, (506) 357-8424, moderate to expensive.

The village of **Gagetown** is a charming, historic riverside community. The Queens County Museum, with many Loyalist furnishings, is housed in the birthplace of Sir Leonard Tilley, a Father of Canadian Confederation. Open mid-June to mid-September. Admission charge. Here also is the workshop of the Loomcrafters, well-known artisan weavers of fine woolen goods and tartans. Their studio is in the oldest building on the St. John River, built in 1761 by the British as a trading post. You can buy tartans, ties, linens, and suitings here or have something woven to order. Open mid-May to the end of September. Free. There are also several other craftspersons in the area.

Steamers Stop Inn, Front Street, (506) 488-2903, is a charming country inn, serving hearty home cooking at moderate prices. There is a sailing school at Colpitt's Marina. A free ferry at Gagetown takes you across the river to explore the lovely countryside around Grand Lake and the Kingston Peninsula.

Highway 102 continues along the west bank of the river. At **Oak Point** the river broadens at Long Reach. Many of the houses along this route were built by Loyalists in the early 1800s. And at **Westfield** it begins to widen even more into Grand Bay. Highway 102 connects with Highway 7, which leads to the city of **Saint John,** at the southern end of Grand Bay. The St. John River flows through the narrow Reversing Falls Rapids section at low tide into Saint John Harbour and ultimately into the Bay of Fundy.

The Lower Fundy Coast

The Fundy Coast extends from Passamaquoddy Bay to beyond Fundy National Park, and in this region of Saint John are the islands of Grand Manan and Campobello, affluent resort towns, and natural curiosities. Highway 1 begins at the U.S. border, connecting St. Stephen with Saint John.

This is the most dramatic coast in New Brunswick—high

cliffs, intriguing coves, fascinating islands steeped in history, rookeries for puffins, the highest tides in the world, and picturesque fishing villages. You can hire boats and gear for fishing expeditions from several harbors.

Campobello Island, on Passamaquoddy Bay, is where Franklin Delano Roosevelt had his summer home. His cottage and estate are part of the Roosevelt-Campobello International Park, jointly administered by the federal governments of the United States and Canada. This surprisingly modest home was FDR's retreat, and has no office, just the family's well-loved rooms, which your entire family will find fascinating, with every detail preserved. Open late May to mid-October. Free. Also visit the Campobello Island Library and Museum, which contains Roosevelt memorabilia and artifacts of the Owen family, early settlers. Open all year. Free.

Take the time to explore the rest of the island. Herring Cove Provincial Park offers a nine-hole golf course and camping. Farther east, beyond the loop of Route 127 to St. Andrews (covered separately below), is **St. George.** This friendly old quarry town sits astride a waterfall and has an excellent Adventure Centre along its waterfront. Here you can make reservations for whale watches or any of the other "Day Adventures" experiences offered all over the province. Or visit with the local outfitters who have their headquarters in this pleasant park. Piskahegan River Company, (506) 755-6269 or (800) 640-8944, operates some of the province's best kayak excursions from here, providing all equipment and complete instruction. It's a good place to try the sport, which is surprisingly easy to learn and enjoy immediately. Accommodations and dining are available at Friar's Bay Motor Lodge, in Welshpool, (506) 752–2056, moderate; and Owen House, in Welshpool, (506) 752–2977, moderate, once the home of some of the island's original settlers. The Lodge at Herring Cove serves seafood, freshly caught from local waters. The only land access to Campobello Island is through Lubec, Maine, from U.S. Highway 1 to 189.

A ferry connects Campobello to Deer Island, and then a free ferry takes you to the New Brunswick mainland. This is a satisfying ride among the islands in the bay. Only a limited number of autos can be transported per sailing, so plan your itinerary accordingly.

St. Stephen is the principal entry point for travelers coming up the Maine coast via U.S. Highway 1 or from Bangor, Maine, via

U.S. Highway 9. While in town visit the Charlotte County Historical Society Museum. Open June to early September. Donations accepted. One of St. Stephen's main attractions is Ganong's Candy Factory and Shop. It was the first to make lollipops in Canada and the first to sell chocolates in Valentine heart packages. A new Chocolate Museum opened in 1999, where you can watch the process. Watch chocolate-dipping demonstrations and see the world's tallest jelly bean display. Ganongs chocolatier shop is located on Milltown Boulevard. St. Stephen's annual Chocolate Festival takes place in early August. Also held in early August, the International Festival celebrates many generations of friendship between St. Stephen and Calais, Maine.

Accommodations and dining are available at Winsome Inn, 198 King Street, on Highway 1, (506) 466–2130, comfortable, with a coffee shop, moderate; and Scoodic Motel, on Highway 1, (506) 466–1540, inexpensive to moderate.

At **Lepreau,** on Highway 1, en route to Saint John, take Highway 790, and explore a peninsula of fishing villages: Maces Bay, Dipper Harbour, and Chance Harbour. This is a prime area for photography and picnics.

Take Highway 127, off Highway 1, to reach the resort community of St. Andrews, overlooking Passamaquoddy Bay. One of New Brunswick's most beautiful towns, St. Andrews was founded in 1783 by Loyalists, some of whom floated their homes here from Castine, Maine. The town has an early-nineteenth-century New England look and has long been a popular summer vacation place. It has several attractions other than browsing in its shops. The **Huntsman Marine Science Centre and Aquarium** has live marine specimens and displays and films on marine ecology. Open the end of May to October. Admission charge.

Henry Phipps Ross and Sarah Juliette Ross Memorial Museum, in an 1800s Georgian-style home, exhibits a collection of Chinese porcelains and other antiques. Open mid-May to early October. Free.

St. Andrews Blockhouse National Historic Site, a War of 1812 fortification, has displays and tours. Open June to mid-September. Free.

Kingsbrae Horticultural Garden, (506) 529–3335, kinghort@ nbnet.nb.ca, is an exciting new garden and arboretum that has opened on King Street, set on twenty-seven acres of a former private estate. The garden has hundreds of varieties of perennial flowers.

The town invites strolling its tree-lined streets and browsing in its many gift and handicraft shops. St. Andrews has one of the best golf courses in the province; also tennis, beaches, boat tours, fishing, whale-watching cruises, and many other recreational opportunities. Go to the town dock to book cruises, kayak trips, and other adventures.

Accommodations and dining are available at the following:

Algonquin Hotel and Resort, which dominates the hill in the center of town, (506) 529-8823, is one of the premier resorts in Atlantic Canada, with a golf course, tennis courts, swimming pool, excellent dining room, a lounge with live entertainment, and many services and conveniences. Expensive.

A Hiram Walker Estate Heritage Inn, 109 Reed Avenue, (506) 529-4210, is the elegant former summer home of Edward Chandler Walker, a member of the famous whiskey family that invented "Canadian Club." Luxurious rooms furnished with antiques. Next door to St. Andrews eighteen-hole golf course. Expensive.

Kingsbrae Arms Relais and Chateaux, 219 King Street, (506) 529-1897. A recently opened five-star hostelry with fireplaces, right next door to a twenty-seven-acre horticultural garden. Expensive.

Windsor House of St. Andrews, Water Street, (506) 529-3330, is a magnificently restored building furnished in rare antiques and custom crafted pieces Windsor House's dining room is every inch the equal of its elegant rooms. Expensive.

Garden Gate Bed & Breakfast, 364 Montague Street, (506) 529-4453, is a four-bedroom hostelry, open during the summer. Moderate.

Rossmount Inn, on Highway 127, (506) 529-3351, is a favorite of knowledgeable travelers. It has a good dining room. Moderate to expensive.

Smugglers Wharf Restaurant, 225 Water Street, (506) 529-3554, offers seafood and a nice view of the bay. Moderate.

St. Andrew's Lighthouse Restaurant, Patrick Street, (506) 529-3082, located right on the wharf, serves reliably good seafood. Moderate.

Blue Moon Motel, 310 Mowat Drive on Highway 127, (506) 529-3245. Moderate.

Tara Manor Inn, 559 Mowat Drive on Highway 127, (506) 529-3304, has a heated pool, dining room. Moderate to expensive.

To get to **Grand Manan Island** take Highway 776, off Highway 1, to **Blacks Harbour** ferry terminal, (506) 662-3724. Ferries sail throughout the year, making six trips each way daily during the summer months; a reduced schedule is followed the rest of the

The fishing villages along the Fundy coast offer perfect scences for pictures, whether on canvas, watercolor paper, or film. Here you have everything—seagulls, floating mists, rock headlands, charming villages, and the ever-present sea.

year. Crossing time is two hours. Vessels hold a hundred passengers and twenty-five autos. During the peak vacation period, there is often a wait to get on board.

Grand Manan is a large island located closer to the U.S. coast at Maine than to Canada's. A favorite vacation island, it is a prize birding area for ornithologists.

Visit the **Grand Manan Museum and Walter B. McLaughlin Marine Gallery,** featuring local history, geology, ornithology, and marine lore. Open mid-June to mid-September. Free.

You can arrange for tours of the puffin and tern rookeries. For cruises to see the whales, contact Grand Manan Sea-Land Adventures, P.O. Box 86. Grand Manan Island, New Brunswick E0G 1L0, (506)662–8997. To learn kayaking or tour the coast by kayak, reserve a space with Adventure High in North Head, (506) 662–3563. You can end afternoon tours with a sunset lobster dinner on the beach. In addition to its many nature trails, the island also is a perfect place for beachcombing. And try dulse here—the dried seaweed is an acquired taste but healthful. The best part of Grand Manan, however, is that you can get away from the cares and pressures of the modern world.

The **Marathon Inn,** North Head, (506) 662–8488, has rooms and very good dining. Expensive.

The **Compass Rose,** (506) 662–8570, is a cozy inn with delicious home cooking, breakfast included. Moderate.

Shorecrest Lodge, (506) 662–3216, is a comfortable lodge with good home-cooked meals. Moderate.

Reservations for accommodations on the island are essential.

Saint John

Saint John was incorporated as Canada's first city in 1785, and is now New Brunswick's largest industrialized urban area. The city has always been an important seaport and shipbuilding and repair center. The people of Saint John celebrate their heritage on Loyalist Day (May 18) and during Loyalist Days (mid-July). In August there's the Festival by the Sea, a national performing-arts festival with hundreds of shows and performers. Saint John is an attractive city with many new developments such as Market Square and a revitalized waterfront. Saint John is a departure point for Nova Scotia across the Bay of Fundy (see page 264).

To get more information, call the Route 1 Information Center at (506) 658-2940, or stop by their Reversing Falls or Market Square locations. Saint John's Tourist Information Center, located in Market Square, (506) 658-2855, provides maps and brochures and conducts tours of the city during the summer.

King's Square, in the center of the city, is laid out in the pattern of the British Union Jack. It is a pleasant park for a stroll, and band concerts are occasionally performed.

Barbour's General Store, at the foot of King Street, is a historic building filled with merchandise of the nineteenth century. Open mid-May to mid-October. Free.

Pleasant Villa School (Little Red Schoolhouse), next to Barbour's Store, is an 1876 schoolhouse furnished with original furniture. Open mid-May to mid-October. Free.

The Old Loyalist Burial Ground, east of King's Square, with graves dating to the 1700s, is located near Barbour's Store.

Carleton Martello Tower National Historic Site, on Fundy Drive at Whipple Street, is a circular stone fortification housing a military museum. Open mid-June to mid-October. Free.

Fort Howe Blockhouse (circa 1777), on Magazine Street, offers an excellent view of Saint John Harbour.

Prince William Street is famous for its many crafts stores, antiques shops, and art galleries. This street has been designated a National Historic Site.

New Brunswick Museum (Canada's first museum, founded in 1842), next to Market Square, is the province's main showcase for exhibits on its heritage (especially its collection on early Indian cultures) and natural history. Open throughout the year. Admission charge.

Market Square, at the foot of King Street, is a handsome complex consisting of a 45,000-square-foot (4,180 sq m) Trade and Convention Centre, a civic and regional library (there is an art gallery in the library), an enclosed retail mall (with more than seventy shops, restaurants, and lounges), two full-facility hotels (Hilton and Delta), and a series of enclosed overhead walkways that connect with other buildings in the commercial core of the city. The waterfront area adjacent to Market Square has been made into pleasant promenades.

Reversing Falls Rapids is where the St. John River empties into the harbor. At high tide in the harbor, the flow of water reverses itself. This phenomenon can be viewed from the gorge above, where there is parking and a Tourism Information Centre.

Trinity Church (Anglican), 115 Charlotte Street, has over its west door a replica of the British royal arms carved in 1714, brought here by Boston Loyalists and placed in this church in 1791.

St. John's Stone Church, 87 Carleton Street, was built in 1825 from ballast brought in English ships. This is the only house of worship in the area designated a "garrison church."

Old City Market, which spans an entire block between Charlotte and Germain Streets, is a colorful, frenetic bazaar where merchants show their meats, fruits, vegetables, baked goods, and crafts. It's also a good place to have lunch. Open Monday through Saturday, except holidays.

Cherry Brook Zoo, in Rockwood Park, via Highway 100, northeast of the city center, has a collection of live animals from around the world, a nice treat for the kids. Open during the summer. Admission charge.

Old County Courthouse, on Sydney Street, next to the tourist bureau, has an elegant spiral stairway. Open during the summer. Free.

Accommodations in the Saint John area include the following:

Shadow Lawn Country Inn, 3180 Rothesay Road, Rothesay, via Highway 100, is about fifteen minutes from Saint John, (506) 847–7539. Shadow Lawn, a top choice for excellent accommodations and superb dining in the Saint John area, is located in a pretty private-school town and is well known throughout Canada. Reservations are a must. You might very well rub elbows with a prime minister or premier here. Moderate to expensive.

Hilton Saint John, next to Market Square, on the waterfront, (506) 693–8484, has a hard-to-beat location with sweeping harbor views, swimming pool, sauna, lounge, and a dining room that features New Brunswick specialties, such as lobster and fiddleheads. The Hilton is the best hotel in town. Expensive.

Fundy Line Motel, 532 Rothesay Avenue, (506) 633–7733. Moderate.

Island View Motel, 1726 Manawagonish Road, (506) 672–1381. Moderate.

EconoLodge, 1441 Manawagonish Road, (506) 635–8700. Moderate.

Hillside Motel, 1131 Manawagonish Road, (506) 672–1273. Moderate.

Hillcrest Motel, 1315 Manawagonish Road, (506) 672–5310. Moderate.

Balmoral Court Motel, 1284 Manawagonish Road, (506) 672–3019. Moderate.

Howard Johnson Hotel, off Highways 1 and 100, (506) 642–2622, offers many conveniences, including a swimming pool, dining room, and lounge. Moderate.

Coastal Inn Fort Howe Hotel, Main and Portland Streets, (506) 657–7320, popular with travelers, features a swimming pool and a good restaurant. Moderate.

The Delta Brunswick Inn, 39 King Street (downtown), (506) 648–1981, has fine accommodations, a dining room, lounge, sauna, swimming pool, and perfect location. Moderate to expensive.

Fairport Motel & Restaurant, 1360 Manawagonish Road, (506) 672–9700. Licensed. Moderate.

Park Plaza Motel, 607 Rothesay Avenue, (506) 633–4100. Moderate.

Dining possibilities in Saint John include the following choices.

The Martello Dining Room, 357 Dufferin Row, (506) 635–5968, is outstanding. The chef serves the freshest of local ingredients with a distinct continental flair. Expensive.

Beatty and the Beastro, 60 Charlotte Street, (506) 652–3888, is an informal, upbeat restaurant with the air of a cafe. Moderate.

Grannan's, in Market Square, (506) 634–1555, has a fine reputation for serving excellent seafood. Moderate to expensive.

Turn of the Tide, in the Hilton Hotel, (506) 693–8484, highlights seafood, and it has an excellent brunch feast. Expensive.

Top of the Town, Coastal Inn Fort Howe Hotel, off Highway 1 on 100, (506) 657–7320, lets you dine high above the city. Moderate to expensive.

Mediterranean, 419 Rothesay Avenue, (506) 634–3183, serves good Greek food. Moderate.

The Upper Fundy Coast

In the town of Hampton, en route from Saint John to Sussex via Highway 1, is the Kings County Historical Society Museum. Open mid-June to the end of September. Admission charge. In Sussex visit the Agricultural Museum of New Brunswick. Open mid-June to September. Admission charge. Near the museum is a farmers' market.

Because the Trans-Canada and Highway 1 converge in Sussex, many travelers stop here overnight. Quality Inn, on the Trans-Canada, (506) 433–3470, and Timberland Motor Inn, in Penobsquis, (506) 433–2480, both have dining rooms and moderate rates.

Take Highway 111 from Sussex to **St. Martins,** a charming, historic shipbuilding town during the "age of sail" on the Bay of Fundy. Visit the Quaco Museum here. Open June to September. Admission charge. Stay at the Weslan Inn, 45 Main Street, (506) 833–2351, where spacious rooms are furnished with antiques. It serves hearty breakfasts and excellent dinners by reservation. Moderate.

The province has completed an ambitious project with the **Fundy Trail Parkway,** reached from St. Martins. Taking walkers, drivers, and cyclists into the otherwise undeveloped coastal wilderness as far as Big Salmon River, a paved multipurpose trail and, parallel to it, the auto parkway skirt the coast and open out to observation points with stunning coastal views. At the river is an interpretation center that describes the wilderness and the town that was once at the site. Visit www.fundytrailparkway.com for more information.

From Sussex you can take the Trans-Canada to Moncton or take a more interesting route, via Highway 114, through **Fundy National Park,** (506) 887–6000, which calls itself the "sea-conditioned" playground. This 80-square-mile (205 sq km) area features camping facilities, picnicking, swimming in a heated pool or in the Bay of Fundy, nature and hiking trails, fishing, boating, golf, extensive interpretation programs, tennis, playgrounds, bowling greens, and many other cultural and recreational programs. Within the park you can stay at Caledonia Highlands Inn and Chalets, (506) 887–2930, and at the Fundy Park Chalets, (506) 887–2808, which has a dining room. Both are moderate in price.

Follow Highway 114 to **Hopewell Cape,** where you can see Hopewell Rocks, giant sea stacks shaped like flowerpots, with trees growing on top of them. An interpretive center (www.hopewellrocks.com) explains the entire coastal ecology. Stairs take you to an overlook if the tide is high, or onto the ocean floor if the tide is out. Here you can walk among these stone giants. Or you can kayak around them at high tide with Baymount Outdoor Adventures, (506) 734–2660. Also in this area is the Albert County Museum and the County Court House (local history, agricultural and nautical lore). Open mid-May to mid-October. Admission charge.

Hillsborough, farther along Highway 114, is the site of the William Henry Steeves House, home of one of the Fathers of the Confederation. The highlight of the house is one of the finest handmade appliquéd quilts in existence anywhere. Open mid-June to mid-September. Admission charge. A hand-carved cross at St. Mary's Anglican Church, opposite the Steeves House, was made from the remains of another recovered from London's Great Fire of 1666. Another reason to visit Hillsboro is to stay and dine at The Ship's Lantern, (506) 734–3221, www.shipslantern.com, a beautifully restored mansion in the center of town. The dining room is outstanding. Moderate.

Moncton

Highway 114 will take you right into the center of Moncton, the telecommunications hub of Atlantic Canada. It is a lively, business-oriented city that has forged an optimistic economic future, largely because of its well-educated, bilingual population.

Moncton is the jumping-off point for two of the province's scenic drives: the Fundy Coastal and the Acadian Drive. This is a university town with a thriving cultural life. In 1994 Moncton played host to the Congress Mondial Acadian, a gathering of Acadians from around the world.

One of the most curious tourist attractions is Magnetic Hill, via Highway 126 and the Trans-Canada (watch for signs). An optical illusion, it makes motorists think that their cars are being pulled backward by a giant magnet. Take the kids to the Magic Mountain Water Theme Park and Magnetic Hill Zoo, the largest zoo in Atlantic Canada. Admission charge. Take them also to Crystal Palace, an indoor/outdoor themed attraction with rides, attached to a Best Western hotel. Reasonably priced family packages. For information, call (506) 858–8584.

Acadian Museum, located in the Clement Cormier building on the modern campus of the University of Moncton (the only degree-granting university outside Québec), has an interesting collection of Acadian artifacts and documents. It has become the premier research center for Acadian studies. Open throughout the year. Free.

Bore View Park, on Main Street in the center of the city, is where you can see the tidal bore (the rippling of water heralding the coming of the high tide) rushing up the Petitcodiac River toward Moncton. A sign in the park tells the times the tidal bore arrives from the Bay of Fundy.

Moncton is a popular stopover for those traveling to Nova Scotia, Prince Edward Island, and Québec's Gaspé region. It is also near the province's best warm-water beaches. It is a good idea to make advance reservations for Moncton.

Accommodations and dining include the following:

Mountain Top Motor Inn, Trans-Canada, (506) 858–9080, features a dining room. Moderate.

Holiday Inn Express, Highways 2 and 126, (506) 384–1050, features many conveniences, a swimming pool, dining room, and lounge. Moderate to expensive.

Keddy's Motor Inn, Trans-Canada, (506) 854–2210, on the road to warm-water beaches, has a swimming pool. Moderate to expensive.

Elmwood Motel, 401 Elmwood Drive, (506) 856–5096, offers housekeeping suites. Moderate.

Nor-WesCourt, 1325 Mountain Road, (506) 384–1222. Inexpensive to moderate.

Brunswick Hotel, 1005 Main Street, (506) 854–6340, a renovated accommodation with many hotel services, a swimming pool, and a good location. Moderate to expensive.

Delta Beausejour, 750 Main Street, (506) 854–4344, provides excellent accommodations, services, and restaurants in a convenient location. Expensive.

Rodd Parkhouse Inn, 434 Main Street, next to Bore View Park, (506) 382–1664, offers a good location, dining room, lounge, and swimming pool. Moderate to expensive.

Dining spots in Moncton include the following:

Fisherman's Paradise, 367 Dieppe Boulevard, (506) 859–4388. A seafood tradition in the greater Moncton area. Moderate to expensive.

L'Auberge, Delta Beausejour, 750 Main Street, (506) 854–4344, serves seafood, coq au vin, and other specialties. Moderate.

Windjammer, Delta Beausejour, 750 Main Street, (506) 854–4344, elegantly prepares roast beef, Cornish hen, lobster, and fiddleheads. Expensive.

Vito's, 726 Mountain Road, (506) 858–5000, serves pizza and pasta, chicken cacciatore, and other Italian dishes; it is popular with residents and travelers. Inexpensive.

Boomerang's Steak House, 130 Westmorland Street, (506) 857–8325. This is the place to go if you're hungry. Huge helpings. The Australian-themed restaurant specializes in barbecued steaks. Moderate.

Toward Nova Scotia

Highway 106 from Moncton to **Dorchester** is an interesting and scenic drive to the Nova Scotia border or to the Confederation

Bridge to Prince Edward Island ferry. En route you will pass through the lovely Acadian villages of Memramcook and Saint Joseph. In Saint Joseph the Survival of the Acadians National Historic Site has a visitor's center with exhibits on Acadian survival after their deportation in 1755. Open mid-May to mid-October. Free.

Dorchester has the Bell Inn (circa 1811), the oldest stone building in New Brunswick. Open June to September. Free. In the center of the village are Keillor House, built in 1813 and furnished with antiques, a carriage house, and a general store. Open June to mid-September. Free. Stay at the Rocklyn Inn B&B, (506) 379–2205. This elegant old home serves a full English breakfast. Inexpensive.

Highway 106 leads to **Sackville,** a pleasant community and home of Mount Allison University, whose campus is the most beautiful in the province. Be sure to visit its Owens Art Gallery. Open all year. Free. During the summer Mount Allison offers inexpensive accommodations and dining on campus. Call (506) 364–2255. In Sackville you can also visit the nearby Canadian Broadcasting Corporation's international-transmitting facilities. See Sackville's Harness Shop, which claims to be the only one in North America still making horse collars by hand. Sackville is where the first Baptist church in Canada was organized. The famous Tantramar Marshes are in this area. These marshes, producing salt-meadow hay for cattle feed, were reclaimed from the sea by the early Acadian dike system.

One treat of visiting Sackville is to stay and eat at the Marshlands Inn, 59 Bridge Street, (506) 536–0170, an elegant Victorian mansion that serves good dinners. The bedrooms offer old-fashioned luxury. This is a very popular place for both accommodations and dinner; reservations are essential. Accommodations are moderate; dinner is moderate to expensive. Also in Sackville is the Savoy Arms B&B, 55 Bridge Street, (506) 536–0790, moderate; the Different Drummer B&B, 82 West Main Street, (506) 536–1291, moderate; and Borden's Restaurant and Motel, off the Trans-Canada, (506) 536–1066, inexpensive to moderate.

At **Aulac,** off the Trans-Canada, is Fort Beausejour National Historic Park. Here are the remains of an eighteenth-century military fortification that was of strategic importance to both the French and the English in their struggle over North America. Open mid-May to mid-October. Free. There is an excellent view from here of the Cumberland Basin. Nearby is the Drury Lane Steak House, off the Trans-Canada, (506) 536–1252, famous in

Atlantic Canada for its beef dishes. Moderate to expensive.

If you are heading for Prince Edward Island, take Highway 16 (a section of the Trans-Canada) to the Confederation Bridge at Cape Tormentine.

Acadian Coastal Drive

Most of the communities in this region are French-Acadian, although a number of English-speaking towns are sprinkled throughout. Because most of the people here are fluently bilingual, you should have no language problem. This coast has the best beaches and saltwater swimming in the province. The sand is soft, the water warm. This region is a very engaging part of the province, where the air and sun invite the pleasure of relaxing indolence.

Highways 15 and 134 take you to the popular coastal town of **Shediac,** which calls itself the "lobster capital of the world" and features plenty of places where you can gorge on these succulent "homards." In July Shediac celebrates its Lobster Festival, but all summer long boat tours and fishing expeditions are available. Nearby Parlée Beach Park has sandy beaches, warm water, and camping, picnic, and recreational facilities. Parlée Beach is a good place for very small children, because the water is shallow and almost tepid. Other accommodations include the **Four Seas Restaurant and Motel,** 762 Main Street, (506) 532–2585. Inexpensive to moderate.

Chez-Françoise, 93 Main Street, (506) 532–4233, a lovely inn offering accommodations and excellent seafood. Inexpensive to moderate. **Neptune Motel,** (506) 532–4299. Inexpensive to moderate.

Farther south, via Highways 15 and 950, there are excellent beaches at Cap Pelé, off Highway 15. In nearby **Robichaud** on Highway 15 is the Sportsman's Museum, with exhibits on hunting, fishing, and trapping. Open May to September. Admission charge.

Highway 134 takes you up the Acadian Coast as far as Kouchibouguac. Highways 11 and 8 lead from there to the city of Campbellton, near the Québec border. If you want to really appreciate the Acadian region, get off the main highways for a while. Meander down the country roads that cobweb the coast. They'll take you off the beaten track, into villages where the same French-speaking families have lived for generations.

The Acadian Coastal Drive continues through **Bouctouche,** an attractive waterside town with at least two reasons to stop. The Irving Eco-Centre la Dune de Bouctouche, north of town, protects a fragile and essential coastal ecosystem where piping plover and terns nest. A wide boardwalk takes visitors across the area with an elevated view and access to the beach and dunes themselves. Free. Nearby KayaBeCano will take you to explore this same ecosystem or the shallow-water oyster beds by kayak or trimaran sailboat, (506) 743–6265 or (888) KAYABEC, www.sn2000.nb.ca/comp/kayabecano.

In the center of town, on an island created in the middle of the river, is the separate little world of La Pays de la Sagouine, (506) 743–1400, www.bouctouche.org. Although it's often described as a theme park, it is in reality quite different. Characters from Antonine Maillet's novels of Acadian life in the early twentieth century live in the homes described in the book (and become bilingual when they meet English-speaking tourists). Music, dance, food, and a lost way of life are part of the experience here.

Enjoy the lively dinner theater here (in French, but good acting is universally understood) or settle in for the evening at La Vieux Presbytère de Bouctouche, (506) 743–5568, www.sn2000.nb.ca/comp/presbytere. The seafood is superbly treated, always impeccably fresh, and presented with flair. Guest rooms are large and bright. Inexpensive to moderate.

Visit the Kent Museum, which displays local history and the works of area artists and a century-old restored convent. Open June to September. Admission charge.

Rexton was the birthplace of Andrew Bonar Law, the only colonial-born prime minister of Great Britain. His home is open to the public from the end of June to Labour Day. Free. Visit the Richibucto River Museum, with its exhibits of local history and Indian artifacts. Open July and August. Donation. There are accommodations in nearby Richibucto at Habitant Restaurant and Motel, (506) 523–4421, moderate.

Kouchibouguac National Park, via Highways 11 and 117, (506) 876–2443, offers an extensive area for recreation, with camping, sandy beaches, saltwater swimming, hiking, canoeing, and birding. Highway 117, which goes through the park and along the coast, is a scenic drive to the city of Miramichi. At Point Escuminac see the memorial sculpture of local fishermen who lost their lives in the Gulf of the Saint Lawrence.

The city of **Miramichi,** which can be reached more directly via Highway 11, is at the eastern end of the salmon-rich Miramichi River. The towns of Chatham and Newcastle, about 5 miles apart and separated by a wide river, along with several other smaller towns, have been combined by the federal government into the new city of Miramichi. Travelers still perceive this stretched-out, ungainly city as it is geographically: a series of separate smaller communities. Local people agree, and have wisely left the old town designations in their addresses, so you will always know where you are going. The provincial map does the same. Although road signs will point you to Miramichi City from afar, when you arrive, the locations are clear. Visit the Miramichi Natural History Museum in Chatham. Open July and August. Along with those interested in fishing, flora, and fauna, Miramichi draws many visitors who like Celtic music. The city plays host to one of North America's biggest Irish festivals, held in mid-July.

A couple of famous figures from the past are associated with Chatham. Viscount R. B. Bennet, prime minister of Canada and a New Brunswick son, had his law practice here. Joseph Cunard, brother of Sir Samuel Cunard, who founded the Cunard Steamship Company, operated a thriving lumber business. The name of the family lives on in Cunard Street. The Cunard Restaurant, 32 Cunard Street, Chatham, (506) 773–7107, serves Chinese and Canadian food. Inexpensive.

Highway 8, which takes you along the Miramichi River Route to the capital city of Fredericton, passes through the Newcastle part of the city, where Lord Beaverbrook, the famous newspaper baron, grew up. Beaverbrook House, his boyhood home, is in the center of town. Guided tours. Open all year. Free.

Ritchie Wharf, in Newcastle, is a center for waterfront and river activities, with a tourist information office, restaurants, shops, and kiosks where you can sign on for boat tours.

Highway 11 continues north along Miramichi Bay. At **Bartibog Bridge** is MacDonald Farm Historic Park, depicting agricultural life in New Brunswick in the nineteenth century. There is a handsome Georgian-style house, furnished with antiques and memorabilia of its builder, Alexander MacDonald, leader of the famed MacDonald's Highlanders during the American Revolutionary War. Visitors are invited to stroll the grounds and see the farming, lumbering, and fishing activities that were the backbone of the local economy. Open late June to Labour Day. Admission charge.

Beyond Miramichi City, Highway 11 enters what is considered the heart of French-Acadian country.

Tracadie, meaning "ideal place to camp" in Mi'kmaq, is the site of the unusual Tracadie Historical Museum at Academie Sainte-Famille, which tells the story of those who dedicated their lives to a leper colony that was once here. Open mid-June to mid-August. Admission charge. Accommodations in Tracadie include the Hotel Thomas, (506) 395–2216, moderate. There are fine beaches in a provincial park at nearby Val-Comeau.

Shippagan, an active fishing center, is set on the end of this large peninsula. The Shippagan Marine Center, off Second Avenue, opened in 1982 and features one of the largest aquariums in Eastern Canada, along with interactive displays on fishing, lighthouses, and boats. Open throughout the summer. Admission charge. Be sure to see the extensive peat-moss areas, where tours of cutting and processing operations are available during the week. You can also hire boats and gear for deep-sea fishing expeditions.

A bridge leads from Shippagan to **Lamèque Island,** where there is a new ecocenter with a boardwalk over the marsh, an observation tower, and benches on a woodland trail for serious bird viewing. Just over the bridge is Auberge des Compagnons, (506) 344–7766, www.sn2000.nb.ca/comp/auberge-des-compagnons, a beautiful new country inn with large, well-appointed rooms and a dining room overlooking the water. Moderate. From there you can take another bridge to **Miscou Island,** a tranquil island with peat bogs, a spectacular beach, and windswept sand dunes.

Caraquet, on Highway 11, is the site of Village Historique Acadien, a re-creation of eighteenth- and nineteenth-century French-Acadian life in Atlantic Canada. There are original homes, barns, and workshops saved from locations with accurate period furnishings. Workshops of a blacksmith, cobbler, printer, cartwright, weaver, and shingler are all in operation, with costumed staff working the traditional crafts and chores of their ancestors, and answering questions about early Acadian life. A visitors' center has a cafeteria serving Acadian dishes; it also has displays of artifacts and audiovisual presentations about the village and Acadian history. The treat is to be able to walk through the village streets and absorb the ambience of a time long gone. From 11:30 A.M. to 4:00 P.M. daily you can have an authentic and delicious lunch inside the historic village. The Village Historique Acadien is one of the highlights of New Brunswick. Open the beginning of June to the end of September. Admission charge. For more information, call (506) 726–2600. The nearby Boutique du Village sells Acadian handicrafts: weaving, pottery, sculpture, recorded music, books. Open mid-June to the end of September.

Also in Caraquet is the less ambitious but nonetheless interesting Acadian Museum. Open June to mid-September. Admission charge. Sainte-Anne-du-Bocage Shrine is a historic and religious monument to the Acadians who settled this area after their expulsion from Nova Scotia. Open throughout the year. Free. In August Caraquet is the site of the largest Acadian festival in Atlantic Canada, highlighted by the blessing of the fishing fleet, folksinging and dancing, traditional foods, a talent show, and the grand Evangeline and Gabriel Ball. Deep-sea fishing and boat tours can be arranged in Caraquet.

Accommodations in the area include:

Hotel Paulin, (506) 727–9981, small, warm, and comfortable. Inexpensive.

Maison Touristique Dugas B&B, (506) 727–3195. Inexpensive.

Motel Bel Air, (506) 727–3488. Inexpensive.

Motel Colibri, (506) 727–2222, also has entertainment. Moderate.

For fine dining, the Hotel Paulin is noted for its fresh seafood, especially its mussels, and desserts, including sugar pie. Moderate to expensive.

At Grand-Anse you can visit the Popes' Museum, where portraits of all the pontiffs are displayed, along with many religious objects of historic significance. Open June to early September. Admission charge.

From Caraquet follow Highway 11 to **Bathurst,** an attractive town and a convenient place to obtain accommodations for the Acadian Festival when the peninsula is all booked. Visit the farmers' market on Saturday morning, and the salt marshes of the Daly Point Reserve. Other points of interest in the Bathurst area are Pabineau Falls and Tetagouche Falls.

Accommodations and dining in the Bathurst region include the following:

Atlantic Host Inn, on Highway 11, (506) 548–3335, is one of the best in the area, with swimming pools and a very good dining room. Moderate.

Best Western Danny's Inn and Conference Centre, off Highways 11 and 134, (506) 546–6621, is popular with travelers and has the best dining room in town. Moderate to expensive.

Comfort Inn By Journey's End Motels, 1170 St. Peter Avenue, (506) 547–8000. Moderate.

Country Inn & Suites, 777 St. Peter Avenue, (506) 548–4949. Moderate.

The Harbour Inn Bed & Breakfast, 262 Main Street, (506)

546–4757. A small hostelry not far from the beach. Inexpensive.

Keddy's Le Chateau Hotel & Convention Centre, 80 Main Street, (506) 546–6691, offers a beach, dining room, and lounge. Moderate to expensive.

La Fine Grobe, in the village of Nigadoo, on Highway 134 just a few miles north of Bathurst, (506) 783–3138, is one of New Brunswick's most creative restaurants, operated by chef Georges Frachon, a native of Grenoble, France. Once you book a table, it is yours for the entire evening. All the ingredients of every dish are fresh, with herbs plucked from Frachon's own garden. The menu is broad—from chateaubriand to seafood caught in local waters—and so is the selection of wines. The restaurant is furnished Acadian style (blond pine) and overlooks the Bay of Chaleur. La Fine Grobe also has two modest guests rooms. Moderate.

At the extreme western end of the Acadian Coastal Drive, along the Bay of Chaleurs, is **Dalhousie,** site of one of New Brunswick's biggest paper mills. Visit its Restigouche Regional Museum, at the corner of George and Adelaide Streets. Open during the summer. Free. Inch Arran Park has swimming and a good information center for local activities.

Campbellton is the commercial center of this northern region of New Brunswick. See the cairn at Riverside Park, off Highway 134 on the Bay of Chaleur, commemorating the last naval battle of the Seven Years' War. And visit the Restigouche Gallery on Andrew Street. Open throughout the year. Free. **Sugarloaf Provincial Park,** near the city, has one of the few Alpine slides in eastern Canada—fun for all members of the family.

Accommodations and dining in Campbellton are available at:

Wandlyn/Maritime Inn, 26 Duke Street, (506) 753–7606. Moderate to expensive.

Aylesford Inn, a family-run, six-bedroom inn, 8 McMillan Avenue, (506) 759–7672. Moderate.

Howard Johnson Hotel, 157 Water Street, (506) 753–4133. Licensed dining room. Moderate.

Campbellton is the gateway to Québec's Gaspé region. A bridge here leads to Pointe-à-la-Croix, Québec.

Highway 134 takes you to Matapédia, Québec, where you can take Highway 132 across the Gaspé Peninsula to Mont-Joli on the Saint Lawrence River, which leads to Québec City.

Highway 17 west from Campbellton leads to access roads (from Saint-Quentin and Five Fingers) to **Mount Carleton Provincial Park,** a secluded natural area, rich in game and birds.

Highway 17 west continues to Saint-Leonard and the St. John River Valley.

The Miramichi River Route

Say the word Miramichi (pronouncing it properly, as *mir-a-ma-SHEE*) and you will see a glazed and dreamy look come into the eyes of New Brunswick natives. Visitors who buzz through may wonder what magic there is in this stretch of road through the woods along a river; those who stop to explore it even for a day will know. Anyone who travels the river by canoe or pauses to fish in its waters or hike the trails along its banks will certainly fall under its spell.

Attractions of the stop-and-visit variety are few, but outdoor activities are many. The main and often only road through the region is Highway 8, between Fredericton and Newcastle, in the city of Miramichi. In terms of the province's scenic drive designations, it connects the River Valley Scenic Drive with the Acadian Coastal Drive.

This area is famous for tall tales of extraordinary lumberjacks. At **Boiestown** visit the Central New Brunswick Woodmen's Museum, which depicts the life of early woodchoppers, hunters, and trappers. Open mid-May to end of September. Admission charge.

Stop to walk across the Priceville Swinging Bridge, on the Mc-Namee Road, between Boiestown and Doaktown. The Doak Historic Site, in **Doaktown,** is a living history museum in an original settler's farm. Docents demonstrate early rural skills using original furnishings of the farm. Open late June to early September. Free. Also in Doaktown is the Miramichi Salmon Museum, which examines the fish, its ecosystem, and the history of salmon fishing, especially in this legendary salmon river.

At the **Eel Ground** Micmac village, (506) 623–5488, you can visit Canada's oldest fish hatchery and learn how New Brunswick's Aboriginals have fished and protected the salmon for centuries. At **Red Bank** you can visit another Micmac village, (506) 836–6179, to sample native foods and see birch bark canoes under construction.

Those who want to spend a few days fishing themselves can settle into Miramichi Gray Rapids Lodge, which has prime waters, licensed guides, all equipment, instruction, and a convivial dining room. Reach them through the Day Adventures program at any of the twenty-five Adventure Centres throughout the province, or at (506) 357–9784, (800) 261–2330 in Canada, or (888) 818–4442 in the United States.

For lodging along the Miramichi, choose a rustic but very comfortable cabin overlooking the river at O'Donnell's Cottages, in Doaktown, (506) 365–7924, www.odonnellscottages.com. O'Donnell's also offers excellent guided canoe excursions, hikes, and campfire cookouts.

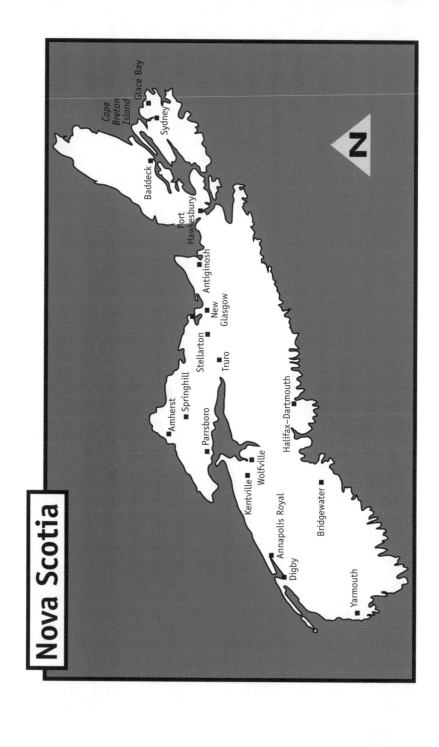

Nova Scotia

Cape Breton Island

Glace Bay
Sydney
Baddeck
Port Hawkesbury
Antiginosh
New Glasgow
Stellarton
Truro
Springhill
Amherst
Parrsboro
Halifax–Dartmouth
Wolfville
Kentville
Bridgewater
Annapolis Royal
Digby
Yarmouth

N

CHAPTER 11

Nova Scotia

Barely attached to Canada's mainland by a narrow strip of land, Nova Scotia is bounded by the major bodies of water that wash the shores of Maritime Canada: the Bay of Fundy, the Northumberland Strait, the Atlantic Ocean, and the Gulf of Saint Lawrence. From its earliest settlement, the main way of getting there was by sea, and many visitors from the United States and the rest of Canada still arrive that way. Ferries attach it to Portland and Bar Harbor in Maine, Saint John in New Brunswick, Wood Islands in Prince Edward Island, and two ports on Newfoundland. Cruise ships and giant freighters use the excellent harbor at Halifax. The sea is still very much a part of Nova Scotia life.

History

The earliest history of this "almost island" is the story of the battle between Britain and France for control of the New World. John Cabot, while out on his first voyage of exploration for Henry VIII, landed on Cape Breton and claimed it for England in 1497. No one actually settled here, however, until Samuel de Champlain and Sieur de Monts abandoned their New Brunswick island after a disastrous winter there and relocated to the north shore of what is now Nova Scotia, in 1605. To kill time during the long cold winters Champlain started a social club, L'Ordre de Bon Temps, which survives to this day.

In 1621 King James I of England made New Scotland, or Nova Scotia, Britain's first colony based on the Cabot claim, but the French ignored him and continued their settlement of the peninsula, particularly along the fertile north side of its Bay of

Fundy shore. The two countries fought each other until 1713, when French forces were driven onto Cape Breton and the English took control of the main peninsula. Since Cape Breton was the key to the control of the Gulf of Saint Lawrence and the interior of New France, the French strengthened their fortress at Louisbourg, spending so much money that the king was heard to quip that he expected to rise from his bed one morning and see its ramparts rising on the horizon.

England also anticipated the war, and built a fort and great naval base on a perfect inland harbor, naming it Halifax. Prince Edward, father of the future Queen Victoria, was its military commander from 1799 to 1802. While the fort at Louisbourg held off the British for a few years, the British prepared to drive the French from their last stronghold.

One of the unfortunate things that they did in anticipation of the war was to forcefully remove from Nova Scotia those French Acadian settlers who refused to become British subjects in 1755. War did come, and in 1758, spearheaded by a force of New Englanders, Fortress Louisbourg was captured by the British and razed. Britain finally had control of the gulf and within two years had driven France from North America. Originally part of the province of Nova Scotia, Prince Edward Island separated in 1767 and New Brunswick separated in 1784.

In order to populate the new province with loyal citizens, Britain began a program of offering land deals and incentives to New Englanders to come and settle here. Many did, and half of the population at the time of the American Revolution were former New Englanders. They actually sent four delegates to the Constitutional Convention in Philadelphia. During the revolution and its aftermath, 35,000 more Loyalist British subjects moved north and into the province.

Self-government through elected representatives was granted to the province in 1848 and, despite substantial opposition to union with the other provinces, Nova Scotia became part of the Dominion of Canada in 1867.

Only a small portion of the land of the province is suitable for farming and other agriculture. Although farms will be found scattered around the province, the most productive are those of the Annapolis Valley. In the beginning these were created by the Acadian French settlers who were later expelled. Many returned after peace in 1763 and French Acadians now represent about 12.5 percent of the population.

After the English gained control, they began an energetic program to populate the land with settlers. Primary among these were Scots who were being dispossessed by land-use shifts on the big estates of Scotland. They brought the province its name and a distinct character. See a bit of their history at Pictou and enjoy the culture at the Highland Festival at Antigonish.

The flow of settlers from New England swelled with Loyalists in the 1780s. They built Shelburne, where several of the houses were reconstructed here after having been taken down and shipped from Boston. Englishmen and the Irish, of course, also answered the call for settlers, and Germans settled the port town of Lunenburg. Following the British incursions into Maryland during the War of 1812, a number of former slaves were taken to Nova Scotia. Many escaped slaves also found their way there. There is a significant black population in the Halifax and Shelburne areas and near the coal mines of Sydney where many of the first black immigrants found work.

From the small subsistence farming communities of the Acadians, the economy of the province turned to the wealth of its forests and the sea around it. Fishing and timber products were major industries. With the abundance of timber, shipbuilding quickly became a major employer, particularly after the start of the American Revolution. Shipbuilding remained a strong part of the economy until the advent of iron and steel ships made wooden ones obsolete. Among the finest ships ever built were the famed Nova Scotia fishing schooners, the best-known of which is the *Bluenose,* the fastest schooner of its time. A replica can be seen berthed at Lunenberg or Halifax.

For Nova Scotia the advent of World War I meant that its position as a leading shipping center and naval base was important to England and to the Allies. Supplies and troops poured through its harbor. Barely more than twenty years later, as England and the rest of Europe once again geared up for war, Canada, and in particular the harbor at Halifax, became the center of the convoys that saved the British Isles as World War II engulfed the continent. Thousands of merchant ships and their escort vessels, many Canadian, jammed the harbor before they went off to run the U-boat gauntlet of the North Atlantic to England.

Timber, now used for the paper industry instead of shipbuilding, remains important. Mining has long played a role in the local economy, with major coal mines located all around Sydney, on Cape Breton. Many of the Sydney mines have closed, but the culture of the industry lives on in the Mining Museum. Although there is still some commercial fishing, particularly along the

First Prize

Nova Scotia may not be Canada's richest or most populous province, but it has honored itself by having the first Roman Catholic church in North America and the first drama written and staged in North America. It was the first British overseas colony with responsible government. It had the first school, common law courts, Protestant church (still used for worship), representative assembly, post office, newspaper and freedom of the press, circulating library, Masonic home, English university, legal trade union, and institute of science in Canada.

Atlantic Coast and off Digby, catches are down and aquaculture has become a strong presence. Look particularly for mussel and salmon farms as you pass protected coves and small harbors.

The traveler will have no trouble becoming immersed in Nova Scotia's culture. On the northwest coast from Yarmouth toward Annapolis Royal, there is a healthy Acadian culture with museums and shows based on Longfellow's *Evangeline*. Linger here and visit the churches, still the center of community in these towns. For the Loyalist experience, visit Shelburne and the living museum town of Sherbrooke. Halifax itself has its share of Loyalist connections. In fact, Royal Governor Benning Wentworth took over the post in Halifax after he lost the same job in New Hampshire, chased out by a revolutionary mob. You'll find the Scottish all over the island, but especially at Pictou, Tignish, Antigonish, and especially in the highlands of Cape Breton. Settle in with them for a Saturday night *ceilidh* (a sort of Scottish down-home party with fiddles) or make a special trip for Celtic Colours, a super-ceilidh held every autumn.

The Landscape

Nova Scotia lies in two distinct parts, the more populated and larger main peninsula and the island of Cape Breton, in the north. Cape Breton is noted for its rough granite mountains, particularly along the north and western sides where they fall dramatically into the sea. Cape Breton itself is nearly split in two on its east side by Bras d'Or Lake.

The main part of Nova Scotia attaches to mainland Canada over a low marshy isthmus near Amherst. The peninsula then runs southwest, roughly parallel to the east shore of New Brunswick, forming a shore of the Bay of Fundy, which scours it twice daily with the highest tides in the world. The stone cliffs along the bay are red sandstone.

The center of the province is made up of high but rolling mountains, heavily forested and containing the wilderness Kejimkujik National Park. The east coast is largely granite, fortunate for the province because it wears away less rapidly from the constant assaults of the open Atlantic Ocean. This shore is heavily scored by rocky inlets that can run inland for several miles, providing the setting for picturebook fishing villages.

How to Get to Nova Scotia

By Car

Take Trans-Canada Highway 2 from Moncton, New Brunswick, to Amherst, Nova Scotia. Nova Scotia's roads and highways are paved and well maintained, with good signs. The hundred-series highways are high-speed roads designed for commerce and quick travel.

To experience the real Nova Scotia, to see the scenery and historic sites, to experience the festivals, to find the country inns, antiques shops, parks, and campgrounds, motorists should leave the highways and drive the secondary roads, the seaside routes, even the unpaved country and coastal roads that frequently lead to interesting, off-the-beaten-track places.

Rental cars—Tilden, Hertz, Avis, Budget, and others—are available at Halifax Airport and ferry landings, as well as in Halifax.

By Ship

Car ferries operate from the following points to various parts of Nova Scotia (advance reservations are a must):

Portland, Maine (crossing time eleven hours). The M/S *Scotia Prince* is a cruise/car liner that sails every evening from Portland and arrives the following morning in Yarmouth; it departs Yarmouth in midmorning and arrives in Portland in early evening.

It operates from May through October. Boarding is at the International Ferry Terminal on Commercial Street in Portland. For more information and reservations, call Prince of Fundy Cruises toll-free: Maine, (800) 482–0955; the rest of the United States, (800) 341–7540; Nova Scotia, New Brunswick, Prince Edward Island, (800) 565–7900; for the rest of Canada, it's a toll call, (902) 742–5164.

Bar Harbor, Maine (crossing time two hours and forty-five minutes). *The Cat* sails out of Bar Harbor every morning (7:30 A.M.) and every afternoon except Wednesdays (3:30 P.M.) during July and August, with morning sailings in June and September as well. *The Cat* features cabin accommodations, comfortable lounges, sundecks, a cafeteria, bar, newsstand, casino, and duty-free shop. It accepts autos, campers, trailers, trucks, and bikes. For more information and reservations, call Bay Ferries at (902) 742–6800, or toll-free from the United States, (888) 249–SAIL, or visit www.nfl-bax.com.

Saint John, New Brunswick (crossing time two and a half to three hours). The M/V *Princess of Acadia* leaves downtown Saint John three times daily Monday through Saturday, two times on Sunday (with a reduced schedule in the winter), for Digby, Nova Scotia, across the Bay of Fundy. For more information and reservations, call Marine Atlantic at the numbers listed above.

Wood Islands, Prince Edward Island. Car ferries operate on this run from Wood Islands, Prince Edward Island, to Caribou (near Pictou), Nova Scotia, as long as the Northumberland Strait remains free of ice. Service is on a first-come basis (no reservations) and the trip takes 75 minutes.

By Air

Air Canada and its affiliate carrier, Air Nova, have daily service to Halifax, Yarmouth, and Sydney, Nova Scotia. Halifax has the only international airport, so flights from the United States and Europe arrive here. It is one of the most compact, friendly, and well-arranged airports on the continent, always a pleasure to pass through.

As you arrive by air, on your way into the center of the airport you will pass the tourism center, which is a gold mine of information. Stop here for maps, up-to-date provincial guides, and local newspaper-format listings of current events and festivals.

By Bus

You can travel from the United States to Nova Scotia on Greyhound; to Portland, Maine, and via the ferry M/S *Scotia Prince* to Yarmouth; to Bar Harbor, Maine, and via the ferry *Bluenose* to Yarmouth; to the New Brunswick border and via SMT Eastern Limited bus to Saint John and then on the *Princess of Acadia* to Digby, or on to Amherst for connection with Acadian Lines. From Québec, you can travel on Voyageur buses to New Brunswick, connect with SMT, and then with Acadian.

By Rail

Take Canada's VIA Rail service from Toronto, Montréal, or other cities to reach Halifax and other Nova Scotia points. There is service to Halifax every day except Tuesday.

General Information

Time zone: Atlantic
Telephone area code: 902
Emergency assistance: 911

Climate and Clothing

The usual tourist season in Nova Scotia is from late May to late October. The best period to visit the province is from late June to about mid-October. While July and August are the warmest months and the most popular with visitors, many people who know Nova Scotia feel that early September to mid-October is one of Nova Scotia's most glorious times. The days are usually warm and crystal clear, and the nights are cool. There is more color to the landscape, and the sea is a magnificent Prussian blue. Fewer tourists compete for choice accommodations and dining spots. One drawback of this season is that some attractions close down, and festivals diminish in number. But the off-season is harvest time, and the farms overflow with good things to eat. Nova Scotia is generally not a destination for winter vacationers, although Halifax has become the convention center of Atlantic Canada, drawing delegates to meetings throughout the year.

Nova Scotia has a temperate climate. The temperature in Halifax, for example, averages 72°F (22°C) in July and 31°F (0°C) in January. In the spring and early summer, there can be periods of fog along the immediate coast. If you do get caught in the coastal fog, try exploring the interior, although it is hard to get far from the coast on this almost island province.

You can rely on seasonal clothes, with warm sweaters and

Neil's Harbour is a quintessential Nova Scotia fishing village, located at the far end of Cape Breton Island. Not far from here John Cabot landed in 1497 and staked claim to Nova Scotia for the English king.

tweeds for cool evenings. Formal clothes are not necessary for evening dining, even at the better restaurants, but you will want dressier clothes for dining in some Halifax upscale dining rooms.

Tourist Information

For more information on Nova Scotia, including free brochures and maps (Tourism Nova Scotia will also help you book reservations for accommodations, ferries, and transportation), call Check-In, the Nova Scotia Reservation and Travel Information System: in the continental United States and Canada, (800) 565–0000; in Halifax and Dartmouth, (902) 425–5781.

Tourist information can be obtained at provincial information centers at Portland, Maine; Yarmouth, Amherst, Pictou, Antigonish, downtown Halifax, Port Hastings, Digby, Wood Island (Prince Edward Island), and the Halifax International Airport terminal.

Major Events

During the summer season all kinds of festivals and events happen in many communities almost every day; thus, Nova Scotia was appointed Canada's official "Festival Province." The list that follows is only partial. Most festivals consist of parades, theater, sporting events, handicrafts displays, music, games, and abundant offerings of local foods. These happy doings attract large crowds, and it is therefore necessary to book your lodgings (for example, in Antigonish during the Highland Games) well in advance. Reservations are also necessary for many theatrical and musical events where seating is limited. On the other hand, you need not stay overnight in a festival-crowded town: Just drop in for the day's events, enjoy, and then move on to your next destination. If you have trouble finding a place to sleep, most towns have a tourist bureau to solve your problems and make you feel welcome.

May
Apple Blossom Festival, Annapolis Valley

June
Country Fair, Windsor

Avon River Bluegrass and Oldtime Music Festival, Mount Denson
Canada Day Fireworks, Greenwood
Lobster Sports Fest, Yarmouth

July
Nova Scotia International Tattoo, Halifax
Canada Day Celebrations, throughout the province
Festival Acadien de Clare, Clare
Snow and Shine Car Show, Hantsport
Lobster Carnival, Pictou
Maritime Old Time Fiddling Contest, Dartmouth
Atlantic Jazz Festival, Halifax
Mayor's Tea, Yarmouth
Maritime Old Time Jamboree, Dartmouth
Chester Summer Festival, Chester
Strawberry Supper, Maitland Bridge
Centre Bras d'Or Festival of the Arts (mid-July to end August), Baddeck
Antigonish Festival, Antigonish
Cherry Carnival, Bear River
Seafest, Yarmouth
Pipe and Drums on Parade, New Glasgow
Acadian Days, Grand Pré
Nova Scotia Bluegrass and Oldtime Music Festival, Ardoise in Hants County

August
Digby Scallop Days, Digby
Yarmouth Cup/Ocean/Windsurfing races
Cape Breton Fiddlers Festival, St. Ann's
Lunenburg Folk Harbour Festival, Lunenburg
Downeast Fiddling Contest, Lower Sackville
International Buskers Festival, Halifax
Sand Castle and Sculpture Festival, Clam Harbour Beach
Nova Scotia Provincial Exhibition, Truro
Atlantic Fringe Festival, Halifax

West Kings Community Fair, Tremont
Nova Scotia International Air Show, Dartmouth
Oktoberfest, Tatamagouche and Lunenburg
Hants County Exhibition (agriculture), Windsor
South Shore Festival of the Arts, South Shore

Provincial Parks and Campgrounds

Parks for picnicking and other daytime activities are maintained by the government and local organizations. They are typically located off principal roads and highways throughout the province. Watch for the picnic table sign. Some of these wayside stops provide access to swimming and hiking areas; all have water, picnic tables, and toilet facilities.

Most government-operated campgrounds provide basic services (water, firewood, tables, toilets, and fireplaces). Some have more extensive services, such as electrical hookups, showers, sewage disposal, and organized activities. They are, by and large, situated in wooded areas or near the ocean. The camping season begins in early May and extends into October, although some campgrounds close after Labour Day. Fees are nominal. For more information on these and the large number of privately operated campgrounds in Nova Scotia, call Tourism Nova Scotia at (800) 565–0000 or (902) 425–5781.

Sports

For a moderate day rate, you can charter a boat for deep-sea fishing, with its skipper, bait, and gear provided. Tuna is a major sports fish off Nova Scotia's Atlantic coast. No licenses are required, except for sea trout, salmon, and striped bass. Licenses are required for all freshwater angling.

Hunting is also a passion: deer, black bear, partridge, pheasant, grouse, woodcock, and goose. All visiting hunters must employ guides. For complete information on regulations, licenses, and outfitters for both fishing and hunting, call Tourism Nova Scotia.

Nova Scotia also offers excellent canoeing, sailing, sea kayaking, windsurfing, golfing, shipwreck diving, river rafting, bike touring, hiking, swimming, downhill skiing, cross-country skiing, snowmobiling, and tennis.

Accommodations

Good accommodations are abundant throughout Nova Scotia. They range from plush hotels and world-famous resorts to hotels, motels, tourist homes, bed-and-breakfasts, farm vacations, and campgrounds. The provincial government inspects all accommodations, which must meet strict standards of cleanliness and safety.

During the summer tourist season, Nova Scotia accommodations do a brisk business. Advance reservations are a must, particularly for Halifax and those communities in which major festivals are taking place.

The government of Nova Scotia has established the Check-In service, where you can reserve accommodations by calling Tourism Nova Scotia toll-free at (800) 565–0000.

Nova Scotia Farm and Country Vacations

Here is your chance to live with Nova Scotia country people, to be part of their families. You are invited to eat at their tables, and their food is the best because they raise most of it. You can do chores and participate in the activities of the family and the local community. You can stay for a night or for the entire summer. You can come up yourself or with your family. The accommodations and the meals are inexpensive—the best value going. For more information on the location of the farms, contact Tourism Nova Scotia.

Dining

Nova Scotia's best cuisine is based on native foods: fresh fruits and vegetables, fish (salmon, halibut, swordfish, haddock, and flounder), shellfish (lobster, scallops, and clams), homemade soups and chowders, and hot-from-the-oven pies and bread. Occasionally you come across Scottish oatcakes, scones, shortbread, and French Acadian rapi-pie, a pork and potato dish. Halifax offers Nova Scotia's largest concentration of excellent restaurants, and there are many other restaurants with fine reputations scattered throughout the province, often in country inns, such as Cooper's Inn in Shelburne.

Pick up a copy of the booklet *Taste of Nova Scotia* and look for the restaurants listed there. This group of chefs has committed to using the freshest of locally grown vegetables and meats, along with locally caught or harvested products of the sea. Their logo will appear also on restaurants and on menus, a seal of quality wherever you see it. Those who love seafood will be happy to learn that Nova Scotia, along with neighboring provinces, is dedicated to encouraging seafood farming as a way of taking the pressure of diminishing wild sea life. Salmon and several varieties of shellfish are being farmed, and local chefs encourage this by choosing them for their menus.

Liquor can be purchased at government-operated stores in major towns and all cities Monday through Saturday. You can also buy liquor in restaurants and bars. The minimum drinking age is nineteen.

Touring Nova Scotia

Exploring

Although you will find a lot to keep you busy in Halifax and other cities and larger towns, be sure to visit the small coastal and rural villages. Many times this means traveling on narrow dirt roads, but the fine scenery and the quiet, simple, and unhurried way of life are worth the effort.

Talk to people and you will hear stories not told in any book, about ship disasters and valiant men and women. Find out who does the carving or weaving in the town or village—you may find some excellent values and will probably be able to watch them at work. In many communities you may also purchase fresh fish and lobster, home-baked cakes and breads, and newly harvested fruits and vegetables. These are personal discoveries that you will never find in any guidebook, no matter how comprehensive.

One of the most interesting aspects of talking with the local people is hearing the various English accents (and French in the Acadian towns). Some of them may sound like foreign or ancient languages. Many of the villages and the surrounding scenery are a feast for the eye; a camera or a sketch book is a must. It is also in the off-the-main-road places that you will find the undeveloped bits of coastline or the quiet nook where you can be by yourself in the midst of a magnificent natural world.

Nova Scotia's tourism is divided into geographical trails to make touring more convenient: the Evangeline Trail, the Glooscap Trail, the Lighthouse Route, the Sunrise Trail, the Marine Drive, the Cabot Trail, the Fleur-de-Lis Trail, the Marconi Trail, and the Ceilidh Trail. Each is well marked, and distinctive signs highlight major attractions en route. Halifax-Dartmouth, now a single city in two parts, is a separate tourism region.

Yarmouth to Annapolis Royal via the Evangeline Trail

The Evangeline Trail, Highway 1, from Yarmouth to Windsor, runs along the coast of the Bay of Fundy and through the Annapolis Valley. Here you can explore the English and the French Acadian fishing and farming settlements, with plenty of antiques shops along the way as well as places to buy local crafts, produce, and home-baked goods.

Yarmouth serves as terminal for the *Scotia Prince* and *The Cat* car ferries from Portland and Bar Harbor, Maine, and is thus a major gateway to and from the province for thousands of visitors each year. Settled in 1761 by New England families, it is western Nova Scotia's commercial center. You can visit the Fire Fighters Museum at 451 Main Street, which has thirty-four engines, including two 1840 Hunneman engines and an 1880 Silsby steamer. Open throughout the year. Admission charge. Take a walking tour past Yarmouth's handsome old captain's houses dating back to the Victorian era. Admission charge. Take the road out to Yarmouth Light on Cape Forchu, where you will go by some tiny fishing hamlets and end up at a dramatic granite headland marking the entrance to the harbor.

Because of the large number of people passing through Yarmouth, be sure to reserve lodgings ahead.

Capri Motel, 8 Herbert Street, (902) 742–7168, offers a swimming pool, dining room, and lounge. Moderate.

Rodd Colony Harbour Inn, adjacent to the ferry terminal, (902) 742–9194, offers a convenient location, good rooms, restaurant, and lounge. Moderate.

Rodd Grand Hotel, 417 Main Street, (902) 742–2446, provides full hotel services, one of the best in the area. A good dining room features beef and seafood dishes. Moderate to expensive.

Best Western Mermaid, 545 Main Street, (902) 742–7821, offers a swimming pool and restaurant. Moderate.

Lakelawn Motel, 641 Main Street, (902) 742–3588, serves breakfast. Moderate.

Victorian Vogue Bed and Breakfast, 109 Brunswick Street, (902) 742–6398. Historic home. Moderate.

Manor Inn, in Hebron, a few miles north of Yarmouth on Highway 1, (902) 742–2487, was once the grand lakeside mansion of a shipping tycoon. It has beautiful lawns, shade trees, and

At Grand Pré National Park, visit the old Acadian chapel (the Church of Saint Charles) and see the lovely statue of Evangeline, the heroine immortalized by Longfellow.

a rose garden. Rooms are available in the mansion and adjacent building. It offers an excellent dining room, lounges, and various recreations. A memorable place to stay. Expensive.

Captain Kelly's Kitchen, 557 Main Street, (902) 742–9191, a very popular restaurant, is conveniently located in an old mansion. Seafood and beef dishes are prepared with skill. Moderate.

Harris's Quick and Tasty, north of the center of town on Highway 1, (902) 742–3467, is open for lunch and dinner until 11:00 P.M. Moderate.

The Austrian Inn, in the Dayton area, (902) 742–6202, offers savory meat and seafood dishes. Moderate.

After leaving Yarmouth, you'll pass through **Hebron,** with marvelous displays of white, pink, and blue lupines growing alongside the highway in June. Then you'll enter a district known as **Clare** (or the **French Shore,** because of the string of French Acadian towns). Here you'll have sweeping views of the rural countryside and the waters of the Bay of Fundy; the French villages are charming and accented with large churches. Be on the lookout for places selling fresh bread and for side roads leading to the Fundy shore for a picnic.

In **Meteghan** visit La Vieille Maison, an eighteenth-century Acadian house, furnished with artifacts from that period. Open daily, late June to Labour Day. Admission charge.

Church Point claims to have the largest wooden church (Saint Mary's) in North America; inside is an excellent museum of early church vestments, furnishings, and historical documents. Open late June to about mid-September. Admission charge. The annual Acadian Festival of Clare in July is well worth attending. Two restaurants in town specializing in Acadian cuisine and seafood are Tides-Inn-Marée Haute Restaurant and Restaurant Le Casse-Croûte.

You won't miss seeing the great stone church in **Saint Bernard** because it so dominates the landscape. It was built by the parishioners and seats 1,000.

Digby is a popular town with tourists and an important shipping point. Its harbor opens on the Bay of Fundy. The car ferry *Princess of Acadia* provides a shortcut between Nova Scotia and Saint John, New Brunswick. Digby has one of the largest scallop

fleets in the world, and the tiny scallops they catch are absolutely delicious. If you're in Digby in early August, enjoy the Scallop Days Festival. For a good view of the Annapolis Basin, go to the top of the hill near the high school or to the lighthouse at Point Prim, north of town.

The Admiral Digby Museum has furnishings, maps, and photographs of local interest. Open Monday through Friday afternoons, mid-June to mid-September. Free. The area offers hunting, angling, saltwater fishing, and superb golf at the Pines Resort. Take a side trip to Smith's Cove, a favored resort area, or out to Brier's Island and Long Island (Route 217), where there are whale-watching boat tours. Humpback, finback, and the rare right whale congregate in the Bay of Fundy from July to September, and the whale-watching tours have a success rate of 90 percent. At the dam on the Great Basin of Annapolis, you can see a tidal rise of 21 to 28 feet (6.4 to 8.5 m) twice every twenty-four hours. For accommodations and dining, try the following suggestions.

Admiral Digby Inn, French Shore Road, (902) 245–2531, has a heated swimming pool, dining room, and lounge. Moderate to expensive.

Hedley House Inn by the Sea, at Smith's Cove, (902) 245–2585, offers various recreational facilities, including a beach. Moderate. Its dining room overlooks the water and provides good food and fine service. Moderate.

Mountain Gap Inn, at Smith's Cove, (902) 245–5841, features various recreational activities on twenty-five acres, plus a dining room and lounge. Moderate.

The Pines Resort Hotel, near the center of town, (902) 245–2511, is a complete resort, one of the best in Atlantic Canada. Expensive. Its main dining room serves well-executed, varied cuisine and is the best place in town to eat. Moderate to expensive.

Bear River calls itself the "Switzerland of Nova Scotia," a bit of exaggeration. At any rate, the town is well worth a visit to see its quaint shops (many of which sell local handcrafts) set on stilts on the Bear River, a prime striped-bass estuary. Don't miss the Dutch windmill, built by local artisans and featuring a tearoom. In July enjoy the Cherry Carnival.

Old Saint Edwards Church Museum in **Clementsport** is built like a wooden sailing ship, with hand-hewn timbers and wood peg fasteners, and was once used as a lighthouse. Open during the summer. Free.

Upper Clements has a wildlife park with lynx, fox, bear, and cougar. Open mid-May to mid-October. Free. Also visit Upper Clements Theme Park, with rides, attractions, crafts, restaurants, and Nova Scotia traditions.

Annapolis Royal and Port Royal

First settled in the seventeenth century, Annapolis Royal is one of the most charming towns in Nova Scotia. It has tree-lined streets and handsome old homes. The town's central attraction is **Fort Anne,** a national historic park with fortifications and ruins dating to 1710. Open April to late October. Admission charge for the display building.

A major renewal and redevelopment project has refurbished numerous historic attractions and created new ones at Annapolis Royal. Three museums—the **O'Dell Inn** (a Victorian stagecoach inn), the **Pickels and Mills** store, and **McNamara House**—have been refurbished. The **Adams-Ritchie House,** believed to be the oldest building of British origin in Canada (circa 1712), has been salvaged, and forty-nine other houses and buildings have been earmarked for restoration. A waterfront walkway has been constructed, a pleasant place for a stroll. The restored **King's Theatre,** on Saint George Street, produces comedies and musicals during the summer. The town was declared a National Historic Site in 1994.

The **Annapolis Royal Historic Gardens** are simply splendid. The ten-acre site fronting the Allain River features three theme areas designed and planted to represent seventeenth-century Acadian, eighteenth-century British, and Victorian periods of the community's past. Admission charge. An excellent Victorian-style dining room with a gazebo and patio overlooks the gardens.

Accommodations and dining can be found at the following places:

Annapolis Royal Inn, west of town on Highway 1, (902) 532–2323, has thirty units. Moderate.

English Oaks B&B, off Route 201, (902) 532–2066. Moderate.

Bread and Roses Country Inn, 82 Victoria Street, (902) 532–5727, is an excellent bed-and-breakfast place in a fine old home. Moderate.

Hillsdale House, 519 Saint George Street, (902) 532–2345. Moderate.

The Garrison House Inn, on St. George Street, (902) 532–5750, is a historic lodging offering fine accommodations and dining. Moderate.

Newman's Restaurant, on St. George Street, (902) 532–5502, is a top place for dinner. Moderate.

The Queen Ann Inn, 494 Upper St. George Street, (902) 532–7850, is a bed-and-breakfast with ten rooms, furnished with antiques. Moderate.

On the causeway between Annapolis Royal and Granville Ferry, Nova Scotia's massive tidal-power project is the only saltwater generating station in North America. This hydroelectric-power installation generates electricity from the tides of the Bay of Fundy. This power, approximately 50 million kilowatt hours of electricity per year, displacing about 80,000 barrels of foreign oil, is serving the needs of Nova Scotia.

In **Granville Ferry,** across the Annapolis River, visit the North Hills Museum, which has a fine collection of Georgian furniture, ceramics, silver, and glass. Open daily mid-May to mid-October. Free. From Granville Ferry watch for the signs to **Port Royal.** The Port Royal National Historic Park, a reconstruction of Champlain's 1605 settlement, at the exact location, is one of the most important historical sites in all of Atlantic Canada. It offers visitors a real sense of what life was like in this speck of European civilization set in a vast wilderness. Open April to the end of October. Admission charge.

Kejimkujik National Park

Located off Highway 8, which cuts across western Nova Scotia from Liverpool, on the south shore, to Annapolis Royal, Kejimkujik is a vast inland area of forest, lakes, and streams.

Unlike all the other national parks in Atlantic Canada, it is entirely inland (except for a detached piece on the southern coast at Port Mouton) without the beach and saltwater activities that characterize all the others. That's not to suggest it doesn't offer water sports. Plenty of lake and pond frontage provides swimming beaches and put-ins for canoes and other boats. You can rent canoes in the park at Jake's Landing. Bike rentals are also available in the park, where there are miles of paved and unpaved roads with relatively little traffic. Bikes are not allowed on the park's trails.

The campground is large, with wooded sites well separated and less crowded than most oceanside camping areas. A nature interpretation center has excellent publications about the park's wildlife and flora, as well as on its history as a First Nations site. Guided hikes, canoe trips, and nature programs are offered regularly, both in the main park and at the Seaside Adjunct area.

In the winter the park has ice-skating and three designated snowshoe trails, as well as 70 miles of cross-country ski trails, about half of them groomed. For the really hardy, the park also has winter camping, free of charge. Contact the park at (902) 682–2772.

Close to the park entrance on Highway 8 is the Whitman Inn, (902) 682–2226, with attractive rooms, dinners by reservation (for nonguests, as well), and an indoor pool. Moderate.

Annapolis to Halifax via the Evangeline Trail

The agriculturally rich **Annapolis Valley** is flanked on both sides by high hills (called mountains by Nova Scotians in this part of the province). Be on the lookout for the many roadside stands selling fresh fruits and vegetables, wonderful for munching while you travel or for the evening meal if you're bringing your own cooking gear. In season you can pick your own fruits and vegetables at some farms.

At **Bridgetown,** stop at the James House, circa 1837, for tea and a look at historical displays. Open July and August. Free. There's also a public swimming pool in town. Accommodations and dining are available at the Bridgetown Motor Inn, 396 Granville Street, East, (902) 665–4403, which features a pool, sauna, and dining room, moderate.

At **Middleton** visit the Annapolis Valley MacDonald Museum, which has a large collection of old clocks. In **Wilmot** some of the Loyalist descendants of John Alden and Priscilla Mullins (of *Mayflower* and Plymouth Colony fame) settled. **Kingston** is home for the Kingston Bible College and Nova Scotia's largest steer barbecue, held on the second Saturday of July. At **Auburn** is Saint Mary's Church, circa 1790, with walls plastered with mussel shells and windows carried by foot soldiers from Halifax.

Kentville is the shire town (administrative center) of Kings County and the largest community in the valley. The Canada Department of Agriculture Research Station, specializing in poultry and horticulture, is here, and you are welcome to visit its beautiful grounds. Open throughout the year. Free. The town also has a public swimming pool and tennis courts. The Annapolis Valley Apple Blossom Festival is centered in Kentville, and Rhododendron Sunday is celebrated here in June with magnificent floral displays. For accommodations and dining, try Allen's Motel, Highway 1, (902) 678–2683, with a dining room and picnic area, inexpensive; Sun Valley Motel, 905 Park Street, (902) 678–7368, featuring a coffee shop and convenience to recreational facilities, inexpensive; and Auberge Wandlyn Inn, in Colbrook, Highways 1 and 101, (902) 678–8311, the best in the area, with many facilities and services, including a dining room and lounge, moderate.

A few miles outside of Kentville is **Starr's Point,** which has the Prescott House, a fine example of Georgian architecture, with an exceptional garden. It's worth the side trip. **Blomidon Look Off** offers a spectacular panoramic view of Minas Basin and four Nova Scotia counties. The nature trail system at **Cape Split** is one of the most popular in Nova Scotia.

Lovely **Wolfville** is named after a Connecticut settler, Judge Elisha DeWolfe. In town is the well-known Acadia University, founded by the Nova Scotia Baptist Education Society in 1838. You will enjoy strolling through its tranquil campus. Visit the free Wolfville Historical Museum, with its collection of artifacts relating to the early New England Planters. Open mid-June to mid-September. Free. Wolfville was the center for the old Acadian country, before the Acadians were sent into exile after refusing to swear loyalty to the British government.

Area accommodations and dining facilities include:

Victoria's Historic Inn, 416 Main Street, Wolfville, (902) 542–5744, is a fine old inn near Acadia University with a dining room and tea garden. Moderate.

Blomidon Inn, 127 Main Street, Wolfville, (902) 542–2291, the home of a former shipowner, has seven fireplaces, four-poster mahogany beds, handcrafted quilts, and antiques. It also has a fine dining room. Moderate.

Old Orchard Inn, Highway 101, Greenwich, (902) 542–5751, features many recreational facilities, a fine dining room and lounge, entertainment. Expensive.

Roselawn Lodging, 32 Main Street, Wolfville, (902) 542–3420, has housekeeping cottages and efficiency units. Moderate.

Tattingstone Inn, 434 Main Street, (902) 542–7696, has ten rooms decorated in elegant Georgian style. Moderate to expensive.

Gingerbread House Inn, 8 Robie Tufts Drive, (902) 542–1458, with suites and rooms overlooking the water, has won an award for design and restoration. Candlelight breakfast, afternoon tea. Moderate.

Nearby are **Grand Pré** and **Grand Pré National Historic Park,** where a reconstruction of an old Acadian chapel (the Church of Saint Charles) holds a museum of artifacts and paintings commemorating the Acadian settlement and expulsion (1675–1755).

This beautifully landscaped site is pictured in Longfellow's poem *Evangeline,* and a stunning statue of the lovely lady stands in front of the chapel. A bust of Longfellow is nearby. Open early April until Labour Day. Free. Grounds open all year. On a nearby hill is the old Church of the Covenanters, which was built in the 1790s by New England Planters. It is noted for its unique pew boxes, sounding boards, and a pulpit that rises halfway to the ceiling. Be sure to explore the surrounding countryside to see the land that the Acadians reclaimed from the sea by constructing dikes. Through their system of dikes, they created extremely productive agricultural land from an area of wet marshes. Also here is the Grand Pré Estate Vineyard in the Annapolis Valley.

On the road from Grand Pré is the town of **Hantsport.** Here is the Churchill House and Maritime Museum, dating from 1860 and housing an excellent collection of shipwrights' tools, ship models, and other seafaring objects. Hantsport was the home of William Hall, R.M., son of a Virginia slave and the first Canadian black to win the Victoria Cross.

Windsor is the site of Fort Edward Blockhouse, the oldest such structure in Canada. Built in 1750, it was a major assembly point in the expulsion of the Acadians. Open June 1 to Labour Day. Free. Don't miss the Haliburton House, former home of Judge Thomas Chandler Haliburton, creator of the funny Sam Slick stories. His Victorian house is furnished with fine antiques and set on twenty-five beautifully landscaped acres, including gardens. Open mid-May to end of October. Admission by donation. Windsor is a pleasant town in which to relax before Halifax, your next major stop.

On your way to Halifax, you should consider visiting **Mount Uniacke,** which has the stately Uniacke House, one of the finest mansions in all of Atlantic Canada. Open June to mid-October. Admission by donation.

Yarmouth to Lunenburg via the Lighthouse Route

The other route from Yarmouth to Halifax, Highway 3, along the south coast of Nova Scotia, is known as the Lighthouse Route because of its numerous offshore lighthouses and beacons, which for centuries have guided the fishing boats and marine traffic safely along the indented shore. The Lighthouse Route signs point to the picturesque seafaring communities that are strung along the coast between Yarmouth and Halifax. Here one truly experiences the effects of the Atlantic Ocean on the Nova Scotian way of life, along with the province's highest concentration of tourist facilities.

The coastline here is famous for its many beaches, granite coves, beautiful fishing and sailing villages, and the hardy people who inhabit them. Explore the side roads to see all facets of the maritime way of life and the special environment of the sea.

Tusket, one of the first towns out of Yarmouth, was founded by Dutch Loyalists from New York and New Jersey. The Tusket Courthouse, built in 1804, is the oldest courthouse in Canada and is open June through October Admission charge. Accommodations in this area include Vaughan Lake Bed and Breakfast, in Gavelston, (902) 648–3122. Inexpensive.

Outside Tusket is the road that will take you down a scenic peninsula to **Wedgeport,** a port once famous for its tuna-fishing fleet and tuna tournaments. The peninsula is inhabited mainly by French Acadians. With the decline of the tuna, all that's left is a museum recalling the greats who once fished here. A nature trail leads along the estuary.

The **Pubnicos** (West, Middle West, Lower West, East, Middle East, and Lower East) are small farming and fishing towns, with an Acadian citizenry. See the Acadian Museum and Acadian Village in **West Pubnico.** Admission charge. Both are open during the summer.

Take a tour of **Cape Sable,** the most southerly area on Nova Scotia, via Highway 330. Visit the Archelaus Smith Museum of maritime lore. Open July to mid-September. Free. For accommodations, try the Penney Estate Bed and Breakfast, on Route 330, (902) 745–1516, moderate.

Barrington was settled by people from Cape Cod and Nantucket in 1760, many of them progeny of the *Mayflower* Pilgrims. Barrington has the oldest Nonconformist church in Canada. Visit the Old Meeting House, the only surviving New England–style meetinghouse in Nova Scotia. Open mid-June to late September. Free. The Barrington Woolen Mill Museum demonstrates hand spinning, June through September. Admission by donation.

Shelburne was one of the major Loyalist settlements. About 10,000 New Yorkers, most of them aristocrats, started a new life in Canada here, creating North America's fourth largest city in one settling. It's a lovely old town with many fine buildings. You'll want to linger a bit. Shelburne is also known as the birthplace of yachts. Donald MacKay, the great Boston clipper-ship builder, learned his craft in Shelburne. Visit the Ross Thompson House (circa 1784), a Loyalist-era store and home. Open mid-May to mid-October. Free. And see the shipbuilding and genealogical exhibits at the Shelburne County Museum. Open throughout the year. Admission charge.

A fascinating opportunity to see real wooden dories being crafted as they were in Shelburne's glory days is right down the street from the Cooper's Inn, at the Dory Shop Museum. Along with the workshop are displays about the dory and several vintage examples. Open June through September. Admission charge.

One of the province's best nature cruises combines the boat trip with an island exploration. McNutt's Island Coastal Encounters in Shelburne, (902) 875–4269 or 875–6177, operates May through October with a naturalist to guide a hike on the deserted island. A lobster, salmon, or steak dinner on the island follows the tour.

For accommodations and exceptional dining in Shelburne, try the Cooper's Inn & Restaurant, 36 Dock Street, (902) 857–4656. It is a restored 1785 Loyalist heritage home, overlooking the waterfront. Moderate. Also in Shelburne is the Loyalist Inn, 160 Water Street, (902) 875–2343, inexpensive, and the nearby Harbour House Bed & Breakfast, 187 Water Street, (902) 875–2074, inexpensive.

At **Jordan Falls** look for the road on the right that will take you to **Lockeport,** which has a fine beach. The town was founded by people from Plymouth, Massachusetts. Visit the Little School Museum, July to Labour Day. Free.

Port Mouton offers white sand beaches and seafood dining from local catches. Sieur de Monts gave the town its name because of sheep lost overboard during a visit in 1604. You can take boat tours here.

Liverpool has a swashbuckling past. It was a main port for privateers. There is good canoeing and salmon fishing in the nearby Medway River and a beach for swimming at Battery Point. Visit the Simeon Perkins House, featuring nineteenth-century furnishings. Open mid-May to the end of October. Free. The Perkins House, formerly a rectory, has demonstrations of early crafts. You can also explore Fort Point Lighthouse, open May through October. Free. Highway 8 from Liverpool leads to Kejimkujik National Park.

For accommodations and dining in the Liverpool area, try **Lane's Privateer Motor Inn,** at the east end of Liverpool Bridge, (902) 354–3456, which offers canoe rental, boat launching, and a dining room. Moderate.

White Point Beach Resort, on Highway 3, (902) 354–2711,

has good accommodations, dining, live entertainment, fishing, biking, swimming, and many other amenities and recreational activities. Moderate to expensive.

Ocean View Cottages, on Route 3, (902) 683–2012. Moderate.

Bridgewater is an industrial center and ships Christmas trees for the Canadian and U.S. markets. There are plenty of stores in town for shopping. Visit the DesBrisay Museum and Park, which has collections of pottery and painted china as well as natural history exhibits and artifacts of the early settlers. Open throughout the year. Admission charge in the summer. Also visit the Wile Carding Mill, a mid-nineteenth-century woolen mill with hands-on programs. Open mid-May to the end of September. Free. At **La Have,** a side trip via Highway 332, is the Fort Point Museum, part of the 1632 Fort Sainte-Marie-de-Grace National Historic Site. Open July and August. Free.

Bridgewater accommodations and dining include Bridgewater Motor Inn, 35 High Street, (902) 543–8171 or (800) 565–8171, with a swimming pool and dining room, moderate; Fairview Inn, 25 Queen Street, (902) 543–2233, a heritage country inn with some shared bathrooms, inexpensive; Auberge Wandlyn Inn, 50 North Street, (902) 543–7131, www.wandlyn.com, with a good dining room, lounge, and many conveniences, moderate to expensive.

Highway 332 also leads to **Riverport** and the **Ovens Natural Park.** In the mid-1800s there was a gold rush here, and you can see monuments, caverns, and a museum associated with that feverish period. The best part of the Ovens is hiking along the high cliffs with the sea crashing below. Sea cave boat tours run July and August. Well worth the side trip. Open the end of May to mid-October. Admission charge.

Take Highway 3 or continue on 332 to Lunenburg, the most important seafaring town on this coast outside of Halifax. This was the home of the famous racing schooner *Bluenose,* a replica of which you can usually see in Halifax from May to October and in Lunenburg during the rest of the year. The original *Bluenose* was champion (1921–1946) of the International Schooner Races. Settled by people from Germany, France, and Switzerland, Lunenburg still reflects the Germanic influence. The noteworthy Victorian architecture suggests that this is a hard-working and prosperous place.

Don't miss the **Fisheries Museum of the Atlantic,** which consists of two vessels that you can board: the dragger *Cape North* and the schooner *Theresa E. Connor*. This museum also has exhibits in various waterfront buildings and films in the Ice House Theatre. Open mid-May to end of October, (902) 634–4794. Admission charge. Poke around in the interesting shipyard where a replica of the HMS *Bounty* was built. Visit beautiful Saint John's Church (Anglican), founded by royal charter in 1754. The Nova Scotia Fisheries Exhibition and Fisherman's Reunion is held in September.

From Lunenburg, a nice, short drive via Highway 3 takes you to the fishing village of **Blue Rocks.** The entire route hugs a shoreline of tiny fishing harbors and interesting rock formations. The scenery around here is wonderful for the artist and the photographer, for picnickers and people in love.

In **Parkdale** via Highway 10 and New Germany, see the Parkdale-Maplewood Museum for historical artifacts and exhibits focusing on the German heritage of the area. Open during the summer. Free.

Accommodations and dining in Lunenburg include:

Atlantic View Motel and Cottages, R.R. 2, (902) 634–4545. Moderate.

Bluenose Lodge, 10 Falkland Street, (902) 634–8851, offers good accommodations and features a popular dining room specializing in heaping fisherman's platters. Moderate.

Compass Rose, 15 King Street, (902) 634–8509. Inexpensive to moderate.

Lion Inn, 33 Cornwallis Street, (902) 634–8988. Inexpensive to moderate.

Brigantine Inn, Bistro, and Coffee Shop, 82 Montague Street, (902) 634–3300. Inexpensive to moderate.

Boscowan Inn, 150 Cumberland Street, (902) 634–3325. Inexpensive to moderate.

Kaulbach House Historic Inn, 75 Pelham Street, (902) 634–8818. Inexpensive to moderate.

The Dolphin of Lunenburg, 90 Pelham Street, (902) 634–3546, serves lobster suppers. Moderate to expensive.

The Rum Runner Inn, 66 Montague Street, (902) 634–9200, overlooking the Fisheries Museum, serves lobster and other seafood. Moderate to expensive.

Old Fish Factory, 68 Bluenose Drive, (902) 634–3333, serves, as you might guess, seafood. Moderate.

Yellow Dragon, also on Montague Street, is the town's Chinese restaurant.

You can come on board these vessels when you visit the important fishing town of Lunenburg, where the famous racing schooner *Bluenose* was built.

Lunenburg to Halifax via the Lighthouse Route

In pretty **Mahone Bay,** via Highway 3, three churches stand side by side, a striking ecclesiastical formation that provides a perfect subject for your camera. In town are handicrafts shops: Shuttles and Seawinds, Birdsall and Worthington Pottery, The TeAzer, The Whirligig, and Amos Pewterers. Accommodations in Mahone Bay include the Bayview Pines Country Inn, Rural Road 2 at Indian Point, (902) 624–9970. Moderate. The Inlet Cafe, Edgewater Street, (902) 624–6363, serves very good seafood. Moderate.

In the bay itself is **Oak Island,** where the pirate Captain Kidd is supposed to have buried a treasure beyond imagining. Although people have dug on the island for decades (some quite scientifically), the treasure remains the old cutthroat's secret. Oak Island Inn and Marina, located between Mahone Bay and Chester, (902) 627–2600, offers fine accommodations and dining, also boat cruises to and tours of Oak Island. Moderate.

Chester, via Highway 3, set at the end of a peninsula, has long been a refuge for the affluent and retired high-ranking military. Chester is a pleasant, beautiful place, with a fine golf course and ferry trips to the Tancook Islands. As well as being a favorite spot for well-heeled retirees, Chester is a yachtsman's heaven. The waters around here, with their stiff sea breezes, provide perfect weather conditions for sailors, many of whom own boats that cost as much as (and in some cases more than) the large, elegant homes that are scattered around the shoreline. The Captain's House Inn, 129 Central Street, (902) 275–3501, is one such splendid building. Converted now to a restaurant with lodgings, it serves excellent seafood in a dining room overlooking the ocean. Other accommodations in town are at the Windjammer Motel, off Highway 3, (902) 275–3567, which has a well-known restaurant. Moderate. The Galley at South Shore Marine, at Marriotts Cove, (902) 275–4700, serves home-style cooking and seafood. Moderate. The Rope Loft Dining Room, (902) 275–3430, overlooks the harbor and offers seafood, steak, pasta, and salads. Moderate. There is an amusing story of how the women of Chester saved the town from an attacking U.S. ship in 1782. With their husbands absent, the women wore scarlet-lined skirts over their dresses and shouldered broomsticks and children played the drums, causing the ship to withdraw because they thought a full British garrison was there.

The Ross Farm, on Highway 12, north of Chester at **New Ross,** is Nova Scotia's official agricultural museum, designed to preserve the agricultural heritage of Nova Scotia and to foster an appreciation of early rural life. A restored nineteenth-century farm, Ross Farm uses the old methods of farming, including teams of oxen. Open mid-May to mid-October. Admission charge.

Back on Highway 103, turn off at Highway 333 to go directly to the Peggy's Cove area or stay on Highway 103 and be in Halifax in a few minutes.

Amherst to Halifax and Cape Breton Island

Amherst is the overland gateway from Canada and the United States into Nova Scotia and the geographical center of the Maritime Provinces. More people come into Nova Scotia through Amherst than through any other portal. If your route to the province is entirely by land (via New Brunswick), the Trans-Canada Highway will bring you through this nice community, with accommodations, shops, and restaurants.

The town is named after Baron Jeffrey Amherst, who also gave his name to a college in Massachusetts. Be sure to visit the Nova Scotia Tourist Bureau facility at the border, where a kilted bagpiper welcomes you. You can see the famous Tantramar Marshes from viewpoints in town. From Amherst it is easy to get to Cape Breton Island via the Trans-Canada Highway 104 or to Halifax via the Trans-Canada to Truro and then Highway 102.

Auberge Wandlyn Inn, at the Victoria Street exit of the Trans-Canada, (902) 667–3331, offers many conveniences, a dining room, and a lounge. Moderate.

Amherst Shore Country Inn, on Highway 366 in Lorneville, (902) 667–4800 or (800) 661–ASCI, www.ascinn.ns.ca, has elegant rooms and one of the best restaurants in this part of Nova Scotia—Spanish tomato soup, sole with rice and pecan filling, blueberry flan, fresh fruit Romanoff. Moderate to expensive.

At **Minudie,** via Highways 12 and 242, overlooking the Cumberland Basin and a short trip from Amherst, is the Amos Seaman School Museum, with its collection of memorabilia commemorating the life of a successful nineteenth-century merchant and industrialist. Open early July to early September. Free.

Also near Amherst, at **Nappan,** via Highway 302, is the Canada Department of Agriculture Experimental Farm. Open throughout the year, with picnic facilities. South of Nappan along Highway 302 a tidal bore, a singular wave in advance of the high tide, occurs on the Maccan River near the village of Maccan.

Highway 242 leads to the small Cumberland Basin community of **Joggins,** famous for its fossil fields and cliffs, where relics of prehistoric times may be picked up along the beach and in the fields, and fossilized plants may be seen embedded in the 150-foot (46 m) sandstone cliffs. This is a protected site, and interested parties must secure a permit (free of charge) from the Nova Scotia Museum in Halifax. The excellent displays at the Joggins Fossil Centre provide the geological background. Open June through September. Admission charge.

Via the Glooscap Trail (Glooscap is the man-god of the Mi'kmaq Indians), Highway 2, visit **Springhill,** exit 5 off the Trans-Canada. Springhill, in a beautiful location, is most widely known for the tragedies that have taken place in its coal mines. Its number 2 mine is the deepest in Canada. In 1881, 125 miners lost their lives, and in 1956, 39 miners died. In 1958 another Springhill disaster claimed 76 lives. You can tour a (safe) real coal mine, with experienced miners as guides, and see industry exhibits at the Miners Museum. Open May 1 to the end of November. Admission charge. Springhill is also the hometown of Anne Murray, one of North America's most popular singers. The Anne Murray Center tells the story of Anne's career.

Parrsboro, on the Minas Basin, via Glooscap, Highway 2, is a very pretty town of tree-shaded streets and the old homes of a hardy seafaring breed. This is a good place to see the Bay of Fundy's extreme tides (the highest in the world), with large cargo ships resting on the red muddy bottom at low water. The area around the town is a rock hound's haven, where amethysts, agates, and other minerals can be found with a little diligence. Visit the Fundy Geological Museum, with its impressive collection. Open all year. Admission charge. Take Highway 209 out to the beautiful headland of Cape Spencer for the scenery and perhaps the discovery of a rare gemstone. The Maple Inn, 17 Western Avenue, (902) 254–3735, offers accommodations and dining, as does the Sunshine Inn, on Highway 2, (902) 254–3135, which serves breakfast. Both are moderate. My Place Dining Room on Church Street serves home cooking, and so does the Stowaway on Main Street. Both are inexpensive.

Highway 2 from Parrsboro leads to the **Five Islands** area, five small islands in the Minas Basin. The scenery here is a photographer's delight. Overnight camping and a beach are at Five Islands Provincial Park. Five Islands Lighthouse is open July and August. Free.

Not far from Great Village, at **Londonderry,** on a side road off Highway 2, is the Miners Museum, showing artifacts of mining operations in that area. Open May 1 to the end of September. Free.

Highway 2 will take you into **Truro,** where you can connect with the Trans-Canada for Cape Breton Island or to Highway 102, the fast track to Halifax. But do take time to see Truro and stroll through beautiful Victoria Park to the impressive waterfall. Visit the Colchester Historical Society Museum (human and natural history). Open throughout the year. Admission charge.

Truro accommodations and dining are available at the following places:

Berry's Motel, 73 Robie Street, (902) 895–2823, is comfortable and serves breakfast. Moderate.

Best Western Glengarry Truro Trade and Convention Centre, 150 Willow Street, (902) 893–4311, features a swimming pool, spacious grounds, dining room, and lounge. Moderate.

Keddy's Motor Inn and Convention Centre, 437 Prince Street, downtown Truro, (902) 895–1651, has many conveniences, a dining room, and a lounge with entertainment. Moderate.

Palliser Resort, off Highway 102 at exit 14, (902) 893–8951, has good accommodations and dining. Moderate.

For delicious Italian specialties cooked to order, call the Paesanella, on Bible Hill, (902) 893–7011, for orders to go; for steaks, try the Best Western Glengarry Motel's dining room. Both are priced moderately.

Just below Truro off Highway 102, en route to Halifax, is a provincial wildlife park at **Shubenacadie,** which has many birds and animals common to Nova Scotia, including a small herd of Sable Island ponies. Because the animals are wild, parents should supervise their children so that they will not be injured or disturb the animals. There are picnic facilities here. Open mid-May to mid-October. Admission charge. Shubenacadie also has a Mi'kmaq reserve and roadside stands selling their crafts.

On Highway 215, in **Maitland,** is the Lawrence House, home of William D. Lawrence, builder of the largest full-rigged wooden ship in Canada, launched here in 1874. Open June through mid-October. Admission by donation. Highway 14, off Highway 102, leads to the South Rawdon Museum, in **South Rawdon,** which has exhibits of the local temperance movement and local life. Open mid-June to mid-September. Free.

If you're heading straight to Cape Breton Island from Amherst, you can take the Trans-Canada (Highway 104) to the causeway at the Canso Strait. However, a more scenic route is the

Sunrise Trail (Highway 6), which runs parallel to the Trans-Canada and along the Northumberland shore. The Sunrise Trail gives you access not only to interesting towns and villages, but also to beaches with the warmest water in Nova Scotia.

Highway 6 is a major road out of Amherst. It passes through **Pugwash,** the birthplace and summer home of industrialist Cyrus Eaton, and the original site of the internationally known Thinkers' Conferences, which brought outstanding people from all over the world to this lovely community. Pugwash offers good bathing in warm waters, fishing, and golf.

At **Tatamagouche** is the Sunrise Trail Museum, with artifacts of the Mi'Kmaq, the Acadians, and the giantess Anna Swann. Open throughout the summer. Admission charge. There are many fine beaches in this area.

Highway 311 will take you to the Balmoral Grist Mill at **Balmoral Mills,** a rare and fascinating chance to see nineteenth-century machinery grind wheat, oats, and barley into flour. Open mid-May to the end of October. Free. Nearby, on Highway 326 in **Denmark,** is the Sutherland Steam Mill (circa 1894), which manufactured carriages, wagons, doors, and window sashes. Open daily mid-May to mid-October. Free.

At **Pictou,** via Highway 6, take time to visit the Hector Heritage Quay, where exhibits show the settlement of Nova Scotia by Highland Scots. The *Hector,* a decrepit Dutch ship, is famous in Canadian and Scottish history for bringing thirty-three families and twenty-five unmarried men to start a new life in the New World of 1773. This was the time of the Highland clearances, when Scots were being evicted from their ancient lands and replaced with profitable sheep. The *Hector* settlers faced a difficult time in the hostile wilds of Nova Scotia (the plight of the *Mayflower* Pilgrims seems tame in comparison), but they survived, and their progeny have flourished in Canada. At the boatyard, part of the site, shipwrights are reconstructiong the *Hector,* using tools and shipbuilding methods of the nineteenth century. Guides in period dress explain the story of the ship's voyage and the early years of Scottish pioneers. Open mid-May to mid-October. Admission charge.

The Northumberland Fisheries Museum is located in the old Pictou railway station and features items relating to the Northumberland fisheries. Open during the summer. Admission charge. The 1806 Thomas McCulloch House is the former home of the Reverend T. McCulloch, minister, author, educator, ornithologist, and founder of Pictou Academy. Open mid-May to the end of

October. Free. In early July Pictou holds its Lobster Carnival. De-Coste Entertainment Centre on Water Street regularly features concerts, plays, and other performances during the summer.

In Pictou, accommodations are available at The Walker Inn, 34 Colerane Street, (902) 485–1433, moderate; and the Braeside Inn, 80 Front Street, (902) 485–5046, with good accommodations and dining, moderate. For dining, the Consulate Restaurant on Water Street, (902) 485–4554, serves European and North American cuisines, and also has attractive rooms. Moderate.

From Pictou you can reach **Caribou,** which has frequent daily ferry service to Prince Edward Island.

If you are heading for Cape Breton Island, continue on the Trans-Canada. **New Glasgow** and **Stellarton,** sister towns, off the Trans-Canada, are industrial centers. Stellarton is the home of Atlantic Canada's largest museum, the Nova Scotia Museum of Industry, at the site of a former coal mine. Interpretive programs and hands-on exhibits show how industrialization changed the way of life. A model railway and Canada's oldest steam locomotives draw rail enthusiasts, and a collection of Trenton glass brings antiques lovers to the museum. Open year-round. Admission charge. At **MacPherson Mills,** via Highway 347, is MacPherson's Mills and Farm Homestead, a water-powered gristmill and restored farm complex. Open June to September. Free.

In New Glasgow, accommodations and/or dining are available at the **Heather Hotel and Convention Centre,** exit 24 off the Trans-Canada in Stellarton, (902) 752–8401, also has a gift shop and dining room. Moderate.

Comfort Inn by Journey's End, 740 Westville Road, (902) 755–6450, has air-conditioned rooms. Moderate.

Country Inn & Suites, 700 Westville Road, (902) 928–1333 or (800) 456–4000, has suites with wet bars, microwave ovens, minibars, TVs, and pull-out couches. Moderate.

Tara Motel, exit 25 off the Trans-Canada, (902) 752–8458, serves breakfast. Moderate.

If you have a few extra hours to spare, take Highways 245 and 337 around Cape George. You will pass through quaint villages clinging to the edge of the sea. The beautiful rolling hills are carpeted with colorful wildflowers, and high cliffs rise from the sea, crowned by a lighthouse at the end of the cape. This is a good route for backpacking and cycling. You'll want to linger a while here.

Antigonish is a Scottish community. It is primarily a university town, the home of Saint Francis Xavier University and the world-famous Coady International Institute, where students from Third World countries learn how to organize cooperatives, credit unions, and adult education programs in their own countries. You are welcome to visit this beautiful campus. Also see Saint Ninian's Cathedral, inscribed in Gaelic: "Tigh Dhe" (House of God). Antigonish's famous Highland Games, in mid-July, are the biggest Scottish bash in eastern Canada. In-town accommodations are difficult to get during the games, but you can stay in surrounding towns and come into Antigonish for all the events.

Accommodations and dining are available at the following places:

Greenway Claymore Inn, Church Street, (902) 863–1050, has a heated swimming pool and dining room. Moderate.

The Coastal Inn, on the Trans-Canada, (902) 863–3730, is a comfortable accommodation. Moderate.

Maritime Inn Antigonish, 158 Main Street, (902) 863–4001 or (888) 662–7484, www.maritimeinns.com, offers fine guest amenities and dining. Moderate.

Lobster Treat, on the Trans-Canada, (902) 863–5465, specializes in lobster and steak. Moderate.

Try **Wong's,** on Main Street, for Chinese food, and the Venice Restaurant, on College Street, for Italian and Greek; inexpensive to moderate. The Goshen Restaurant, on Highway 104, (902) 863–3068, serves seafood and steaks in a Scottish setting. Moderate.

Take the Trans-Canada to **Auld Cove,** where you will cross the Canso Strait on the causeway to Cape Breton Island.

Cape Breton Island

Once you cross the causeway, you enter a very special part of Nova Scotia, considered by countless visitors to be the most dramatically beautiful part of the province. After touring its famous Cabot Trail and the Bras d'Or Lakes region, it is easy to understand why so many visitors make it a must on their itinerary. Cape Breton offers not only inspiring scenery, reminiscent of the Highlands of Scotland, and pretty villages, but also significant historical sites, from John Cabot's landing in 1497 to the strong French presence at Fortress Louisbourg, now resurrected from rubble. It is said that Cape Breton was once the western coast of what is now Scotland and was moved by continental drift. More Gaelic is spoken here than in Scotland.

Port Hastings is the first town on Cape Breton. You can find accommodations at Keddy's Inn, junction of Highways 104 and

105, (902) 625–0460 or (800) 561–7666, which offers a convenient location and a dining room, moderate to expensive; Skye Travelodge, junction of Highways 104 and 105, (902) 625–1300 or (800) 578–7878, also offering a dining room, moderate; or Maritime Inn Port Hawkesbury, off Highway 105, nearby in Port Hawkesbury, (902) 625–0320 or (888) 662–7484, with many conveniences, a dining room, and a lounge, moderate to expensive.

At Port Hastings, the Trans-Canada becomes Highway 105 to Sydney.

On your way to the Cabot Trail, which begins at Baddeck, take a side trip to the Nova Scotia Highland Village Museum at **Iona,** via Highway 223. This unique museum portrays the life of the early Scottish settlers in the province, with a carding mill, forge, country store, school, and settler's home. It's on a beautiful site overlooking the majestic Bras d'Or Lakes. The Highland Heights Inn, on Highway 223, (902) 725–2360 or (800) 660–8122, offers accommodations and dining on the same scenic hillside. Moderate.

In **Wasmatook** on Highway 105 (just west of Baddeck) is the New Wagmatook Culture and Heritage Centre.

The Cabot Trail

It is no exaggeration to call the Cabot Trail one of the most beautiful drives in North America. It is 185 miles (303 km) of dramatic vistas of mountains, cliffs, forests, and the Gulf of Saint Lawrence and the Atlantic Ocean. The trail starts and ends in Baddeck, and the traveler is advised to follow it clockwise for the best views and the security of hugging the sides of the mountains while driving up and down some of the steep and curvy stretches. The road is a good one, but your car should be in good working order to be safe on the steep grades.

The Cabot Trail runs through the beautiful Margaree Valley and meets the Gulf of Saint Lawrence at the fishing village of Margaree Harbour. From Margaree Harbour to the town of Chéticamp, you will pass through French-Acadian fishing settlements: Look for local crafts items such as ship models and hooked rugs.

Baddeck itself is the premier resort town on the Bras d'Or Lakes. Here Alexander Graham Bell lived, and he and his wife are buried at their estate, Beinn Bhreagh (not open to the public). You can visit Baddeck's Alexander Graham Bell National Historic Site, (902) 295–2069, which tells a comprehensive story of the great man's life and exhibits some of his inventions: aircraft, hydrofoil, and, of course, the telephone. Open year-round. Admission charge. Also visit the Victoria County Archives and Museum. Open during the summer. Free. At **South Gut Saint Ann's** is the well-known Gaelic College of Celtic arts and crafts, which has classes in bagpipes, band drumming, and Highland dancing. Its extensive shop sells Celtic music, books on history and culture, and tartan goods. There are beaches for swimming in the Baddeck area.

Accommodations and dining in Baddeck include the following:

Inverary Inn Resort, Shore Road, (902) 295–3500 or (800) 565–5660, one of the very best on Cape Breton, offers a fine dining room featuring Scottish fare (reservations suggested) and a private beach. Moderate to expensive.

Restawyle Bed & Breakfast and Cottage, exit 8, off Route 105 to Shore Road, (902) 295–3253. Inexpensive.

Cabot Trail Motel, on Highway 105, (902) 295–2580, overlooks Bras d'Or Lakes and serves breakfast. Moderate.

Silver Dart Lodge, off Highway 105, near the center of town, (902) 295–2340 or (888) 662–7484, is a renovated mansion overlooking the lake, with a fine dining room, lounge, swimming, biking, and other amenities. Moderate to expensive.

Telegraph House, Chebucto Street, (902) 295–1100, convenient to the Trans-Canada, has a dining room. Moderate to expensive.

Trailsman Motel, off Highway 105, west of Baddeck, (902) 295–2413 or (888) 245–LAKE, offers a swimming pool and dining room. Moderate.

Baddeck Lobster Suppers are held daily at the Canadian Legion Hall, (902) 295–3307. Also try Wong's Restaurant on Chebucto Street.

En route to Margaree Harbour, stop at **North East Margaree** and visit the Salmon Museum, featuring fishing techniques and exhibits devoted to the Atlantic salmon. Open mid-June to mid-October. Admission charge. In **Margaree** see Scottish, Indian, and Acadian handicrafts at the Museum of Cape Breton Heritage. Open mid-June to mid-October. Free.

There are fine accommodations and hearty breakfasts at the Margaree Inn East Bed & Breakfast, Margaree, (902) 235–2524. Moderate. The Duck Cove Inn, Margaree Harbour, (902) 235–2658 or (800) 565–9993, provides guides and equipment for deep-sea and freshwater fishing, a dining room, and lounge. Moderate. Margaree Harbour's Whale Cove Summer Village, (902)

The Highland Games at Antigonish are the Scottish version of the World Series, where cabers are tossed, swords danced over, and bagpipes skirled to the delight of thousands. Nova Scotia is also host for the International Gathering of the Clans. This is the province for you if you have Scottish blood in your veins or if you love the taste of haggis and shortbread.

235–2202, offers housekeeping cottages, fishing, and a sandy beach. Moderate. The Normaway Inn, Margaree Valley, (902) 248–2987 or (800) 565–9463, has been a favorite place with travelers for accommodations and dining since 1928. The inn also offers live entertainment, tennis, and salmon fishing. Moderate.

Chéticamp, an Acadian fishing settlement, makes a good overnight stop before going on through Cape Breton Highlands National Park, which starts just north of town. Chéticamp and the surrounding countryside offer many excellent opportunities for the photographer—sea, islands, and mountains, and the harbor filled with fishing boats, nets, and lobster traps. Visit huge Saint Peter's Church with its ornate interior, and the nearby Acadian Museum with its many interesting exhibits and weaving demonstrations. Open throughout the summer. Free. The Dr. Elizabeth LeFort Gallery and Museum should also be seen. Admission charge. Whale-watching and bird-watching trips operate from town. Accommodations and dining in Chéticamp include the following:

Acadian Motel, on the Cabot Trail (Highway 19), near the church, (902) 224–2640. Moderate.

Fraser Motel Cottages, Main Street, (902) 224–2411. Inexpensive.

Merry's Motel, on the Cabot Trail (Highway 19), in town, (902) 224--2456, is comfortable. Inexpensive.

Ocean View Motel, Main Street, (902) 224–2313 or (877) 743–4404. Moderate.

Park View Motel, on the Cabot Trail (Highway 19), at the entrance to the park, (902) 224–3232, has a dining room and lounge. Moderate.

The Harbour Restaurant, (902) 224–2042, offers seafood and steaks. The dining room at **Laurie's Motor Inn,** (902) 224–2400, and **Restaurant Acadien,** (902) 224–3207, both on Main Street, are also good dining places in town. At the latter you can sample French-Canadian dishes with a maritime province flair.

Cape Breton Highlands National Park, (902) 285–2691, covers 366 sq mi (950 sq km) and lies between the Gulf of Saint Lawrence and the Atlantic Ocean. Drivers must purchase an admission pass to park anywhere in the national park. The Cabot Trail winds along the mountainsides, reaching an elevation of 1,492 feet (455 m) at French Mountain, and descends into valleys in which fishing villages, such as **Pleasant Bay,** are nestled. New in Pleasant Bay is the Whale Interpretive Center, open from June through August. Admission charge. Markland Coastal Resort, 3 miles (4.8 km) off the Cabot Trail in Dingwall, (902) 383–2246 or (800) 872–6084, is an ecologically minded hotel, surrounded by a spectacular landscape of sand dunes, beaches, rivers, and mountains. Moderate to expensive. The views along the Cabot Trail are breathtaking, and there are a number of turnoffs where you can stop. The park offers excellent fishing, camping, hiking, beaches, and, at Ingonish Beach, a great golf course.

At **Cape North** visit the charming North Highlands Community Museum, which portrays the history of this area. Open mid-June to mid-October. Donations welcome. Also in Cape North, swing off the Cabot Trail and follow the road to Bay Saint Lawrence for good views of Nova Scotia's northern end. Try a swim in Aspy Bay and the Cabot Strait.

At **Neil's Harbour,** where the Cabot Trail runs along the Atlantic, is an English-speaking fishing settlement and one of the best places on Cape Breton Island to photograph the maritime way of life—the people, the village, and the sea coming in against the dark cliffs. The drive from Neil's Harbour to **Ingonish** is a very dramatic one of steep grades and magnificent vistas, reminding many people of the Highlands of Scotland. Good beaches and fishing can be found along this route.

Ingonish Beach is part of Cape Breton Highlands National Park and the site of one of the finest eighteen-hole golf courses in all of North America. In addition, there are sand beaches, campgrounds, picnic areas, tennis courts, hiking trails, and many other attractions, including a fine anchorage for even the largest vessels. Cape Smokey has a modern ski facility (tows and a lodge) for winter visitors; the lift also operates for sightseeing in the summer. Because of the popularity of Ingonish Beach, the campgrounds are always full, so plan accordingly. Campsites can be reserved in advance. The world-famous Keltic Lodge, off the Cabot Trail, (902) 285–2880 or (800) 565–0444, operated by the provincial government, offers guests excellent accommodations and some of the finest cuisine on Cape Breton Island, swimming in a heated saltwater pool, entertainment, and many other activities. The setting of the resort, on a headland jutting out to sea, the access to the national park golf course, and the serenity of the environment make the lodge one of the most popular in Atlantic Canada. It is usually booked to capacity several months before the start of the season, but there are always last-minute cancellations and travelers without reservations should give it a try. Expensive. Alternate accommodations on the Cabot Trail are Cape Breton Highlands Bungalows, (902) 285–2000, moderate; and the Glenghorm Beach Resort, (902) 285–2049, moderate.

From Ingonish Beach you can continue on the Cabot Trail back to Baddeck or you can connect with the Trans-Canada and head to the city of Sydney and then to Fortress Louisbourg, the most impressive man-made attraction on Cape Breton.

The Sydney Area

Sydney is Nova Scotia's third largest city, an industrial and steel-making center. It's a convenient base from which to explore the area's many attractions, such as Louisbourg National Historic Site, and to stop in before taking the Newfoundland ferries at North Sydney. Sydney can also be reached by air from Halifax.

In Sydney itself, visit Saint Patrick's Church, the oldest Roman Catholic church on Cape Breton. It has an interesting historical collection. Open June to mid-October. Free. The Cossitt House, built in 1787, is considered the oldest home in the city. Open mid-May to end of October. Free.

Accommodations and dining in Sydney include the following:

Delta Sydney, 300 Esplanade, (902) 562–7500 or (800) 268–1133, offers suites, dining, a lounge, exercise facility, and many other services and amenities. Moderate to expensive.

Cambridge Suites Hotel, 380 Esplanade, (902) 562–6500 or (800) 565–9466, 150 units. Moderate.

Garland Stubbert's Bed and Breakfast, 117 Shore Road, Sydney Mines, (902) 736–8466. Inexpensive.

Days Inn Sydney, 480 Kings Road, (902) 539–6750 or (877) 834–0333, is modern with many conveniences, a dining room and a lounge. Expensive.

Cape Bretoner Motor Inn, 560 King's Road, (902) 539–8101 or (888) 793–9555, has comfortable rooms, swimming pool, and licensed dining room. Moderate.

Rockinghorse Inn, 259 Kings Road, (902) 539–2696 or (888) 664–1010, is a restored heritage inn. Continental breakfast. Dinner by reservation only. Moderate.

Jasper's Restaurant, 1167 Kings Road, (902) 564–6181, pro-

Fortress Louisbourg National Historic site is North America's largest historic reconstruction. When the fortress was built, even King Louis XIV complained of its high cost. Yet for many years the fortified town helped to protect his vast empire in North America. It was destroyed by the British and American colonists in 1760 and reconstructed in our time.

vides a varied family menu and children's specials. Inexpensive to moderate.

Joe's Warehouse, 424 Charlotte Street, (902) 539–6686, is great for beef and steaks. Moderate.

At nearby **Glace Bay,** via Highway 4, tour deep coal mines and visit a miner's village at the Miners Museum. Open during the summer. Admission charge.

Port Morien, near Glace Bay, is the site of the French Mine, one of the earliest coal mines in North America. Here you can see an exposed seam of coal along the rugged shore and fossils of 200-million-year-old trees. For good dining by candlelight, the Miners' Village Restaurant in Glace Bay is recommended.

Fortress Louisbourg National Historic Site, via Highway 22, in **Louisbourg,** is North America's largest historic reconstruction project. In its day Fortress Louisbourg was the French king's bastion against the British in North America. It protected French fishing interests and trade routes in the North Atlantic and the Canadian hinterland via the Gulf of Saint Lawrence. Although it had many conveniences for its civilian and military population, life at Louisbourg was harsh, particularly in the winter. The fortress was subject to repeated attacks and sieges by British and New England forces, until it was destroyed by the British in 1760, not long after General Wolfe took Québec. At any rate, to see the reconstruction from a distance (you leave the visitors' center by park bus—no autos are allowed in the restoration) is to be confronted with an apparition from the past. To step into its confines (and be stopped at the main portal by guards who ask if you are an English spy!) is to enter another age. Fortress Louisbourg is not just a defensive enclosure, like the Halifax Citadel, but a fortified settlement containing ramparts, private homes, barracks, storehouses, barns, a governor's palace, a chapel, streets, taverns, a blacksmith shop, waterfront docks, and so on. Here people dress in the costumes of the eighteenth-century inhabitants: soldiers on patrol, housewives cooking meals and doing various chores, craftsmen making the implements necessary for industry and survival. You can also come in the evening, when the inhabitants pay no attention to you and speak only in French. It's an eerie feeling—almost as if you're intruding on the business of ghosts. Fortress Louisbourg is a marvelous experience for everyone; it's as important to visit as riding the Cabot Trail. The park's visitor center has an audiovisual presentation of the history of the fortress, exhibits of artifacts, and a gift shop. Open May to the end of October. Admission charge.

While in the fortress, dine eighteenth-century style at the L'Epée Royale, where authentic French recipes are served in the style and atmosphere of the period, moderate to expensive. For more affordable fare, try the Hotel-de-la-Marine, also in the fortress.

In the town of Louisbourg, visit the Sydney and Louisbourg Railway Museum. Open June to Labour Day. Free.

North Sydney is the terminal port for those wishing to take the ferries to Newfoundland. The passenger car and freight-carrying ships sail daily for Port-aux-Basques throughout the year and for Argentia during the summer. Accommodations in North Sydney are the Clansman Motel, on Peppett Street, (902) 794–7226 or (800) 565–2668, moderate, and the Best Western North Star Inn, 39 Forest Street, (902) 794–8581 or (800) 561–8585, moderate.

To move on from Cape Breton Island, take the Trans-Canada to Baddeck and Port Hastings. Or take a more scenic way via Highway 4, which runs along the shores of the beautiful Bras d'Or Lakes and next to the East Bay Hills. Just before St. Peter's is **Chapel Island.**

You'll come to **Saint Peter's** on a small spit of land separating the Bras d'Or Lakes and Saint Peter's Bay, which flows out into the Atlantic Ocean. Saint Peter's is a charming historic town, with excellent views of both bodies of water. Visit the Nicholas Denys Museum. Open June to the end of September. Admission charge. Accommodations in this area include Bras d'or Lakes Inn, Saint Peter's, (902) 535–2200 or (800) 818–5885, moderate.

As you drive along Highway 4, consider swinging off onto Highway 320 and then 206 to explore the French Acadian area of **Isle Madame.** Go as far as the village of **Arichat;** the panoramas of the sea and landscape make this side trip well worthwhile. While in Arichat, see the LeNoir Forge, an eighteenth-century blacksmith shop with a working forge. Open during the summer. Admission charge. Continue on Highway 4 to Port Hawkesbury and Port Hastings and then cross the causeway at Canso Strait to mainland Nova Scotia.

CHAPTER 12

Halifax

In many ways, Halifax is the perfect medium-size city: It has nearly everything it needs and far fewer problems than larger cities. A city built on a human scale, it blends urban sophistication and the natural environment. Most people who come to Atlantic Canada do so to shed themselves of their cities. Halifax is one to be savored—allow at least two days for your visit.

Halifax, now with more than 114,000 inhabitants in a metropolitan area of 340,000 people, came into existence as a British military outpost in 1749. Lord Cornwallis founded it, but his interests were more in developing a strategic base to protect British interests against the French than in building a substantial city. His garrison town, the first Canadian community settled primarily by the English, was named in honor of the Earl of Halifax. Cornwallis commenced construction of the Citadel, a star-shaped fortification set on a high hill that continues to dominate the city. During the American Revolution Halifax was a solid, secure British bastion in the North Atlantic and a place of refuge for fleeing Loyalists. Only the quicksilver ships of American privateers, playing cat and mouse with the British, dared to harass Nova Scotia seacoast towns.

The military commanders of Halifax were well prepared for attack from the French and from the Americans, but the Citadel has never yet fired a shot in anger. One of the more illustrious British commanders of Halifax was the Duke of Kent, Queen Victoria's father and a generous benefactor to Halifax. The ornate town clock, which sits on the brow of Citadel Hill and still keeps good time, is one of his gifts to the city.

As a year-round ice-free port, Halifax also plays an important role in Canada's civilian maritime activities, such as scientific

research, which includes the world's third largest oceanographic center, the Bedford Institute; shipping; and the many other businesses associated with the sea. Samuel Cunard, one of the city's leading citizens in the nineteenth century, ran his steamship line from Halifax. Insurance, banking, and international trade have flourished here. Manufacturing also employs many Haligonians. Halifax is also the provincial capital, and most government agencies and departments have their main offices in the city.

Bring comfortable shoes, for Halifax is a walking city. The weather is similar to Boston's, but usually a few degrees cooler in the summer. Haligonians are proud of their city and of their province, and their warm, outgoing nature is pleasantly tempered by a British-style reserve. You will likely experience friendly interest not cold indifference.

How to Get to Halifax

By Car
Route 102 (Bicentennial Drive) will bring you into the city from the north and the airport. From here, you may take Route 102 to the Eastern Shore and Route 111. Route 111 will bring you into downtown Halifax.

By Rail
Passenger trains connecting from major cities in Canada arrive and depart at the VIA Rail station, located off Hollis Street, (800) 561–3952.

By Bus
Acadian Lines provides direct service throughout the province and connecting service to other provinces in the Atlantic region. MacKenzie Bus Lines provides service for the Atlantic route, from Halifax to Yarmouth.

By Air
Halifax International Airport is located off Highway 102, a twenty-minute drive from Halifax center. The airport is situated

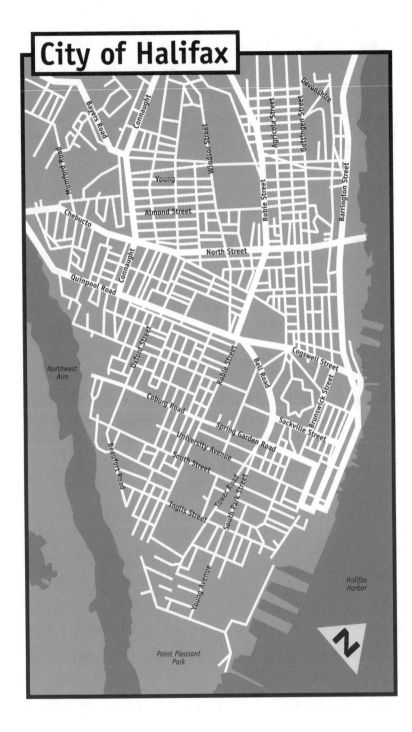

on high ground and not subject to the dense fogs of coastal areas. It is the main air terminus for Atlantic Canada, and there are connections to other parts of the region (Newfoundland, New Brunswick, and Prince Edward Island). The major carriers are Air Canada and its affiliate, Air Nova.

Rental cars—Hertz, Avis, Tilden, Budget—are available at the airport and downtown locations. There is frequent bus service from the airport to downtown Halifax hotels. Taxis are available but expensive.

General Information

Time zone: Atlantic
Telephone area code: 902
Police: dial 911
Medical emergency: dial 911
Help line: (902) 422–7444, a twenty-four-hour service to provide assistance to those in need; also communication services to the deaf

Tourist Information

For brochures, maps, answers to questions, and help with hotel reservations, visit the International Visitors Centre, (902) 421–8736, at the corner of Sackville and Barrington Streets; also the Provincial Information Centre, (902) 424–4248, at the Old Red Store at Historic Properties.

For toll-free telephone information on Halifax, including free brochures and maps (Nova Scotia Information will also help you book reservations for accommodations, ferries, and transportation), call Check-In—the Nova Scotia Reservation and Travel Information System—toll-free (800) 565–0000.

How to Get Around Halifax

The Central Area

Halifax is a peninsula, shaped like a foot sticking into the water. Its toe, at the Halifax harbor, points to the sea. Its heel juts into the Bedford Basin. Its sole forms the narrows, with the community of Dartmouth on the other side. The top of the foot forms one bank of the 3-mile (5 km) North West Arm. Halifax is, therefore, almost completely surrounded by water, and the central city runs

Disaster in the Harbor

On December 6, 1917, during World War I, Halifax was the site of one of the worst explosives disasters of history. The *Mont Blanc,* a French freighter loaded with munitions, collided with the *Imo,* a Norwegian vessel meant to carry relief supplies for war victims in Belgium. The explosion flattened the north end of the city and damaged buildings throughout the city. Some 2,000 people were killed, 9,000 injured; 1,600 buildings in the blast area were totally destroyed, 12,000 others severely damaged. It was a $50 million loss. Today there is very little evidence of this horror, but Haligonians (as the people of Halifax call themselves) remember not only the pain of the event but also the millions of dollars' worth of relief supplies that came from the United States. The people of Boston were especially quick and generous in their outpouring of help. In gratitude, the province to this day presents the city of Boston its giant Christmas tree each year.

along the sole to the toe of this imaginary foot. Barrington, Lower Water, and Hollis are the major streets running through the business and shopping areas in the central city. Perpendicular to these runs Spring Garden Road, the most fashionable shopping street in the central area. Two good landmarks to use are Citadel Hill and Scotia Square (a complex of tall office and hotel buildings). The area from Citadel Hill to Point Pleasant Park (at the toe) is fairly easy to get around, and you should have little trouble on foot or in a car. Some of the outlying neighborhoods can be confusing. Stick to marked routes or stop and ask directions; people want to help and do so by providing accurate directions.

Halifax and the neighboring community of Dartmouth, comprise a metropolitan region of 340,000 people. The two communities are connected at the narrows by the Angus L. Macdonald Bridge and at the Bedford Basin by the A. Murray Mackay Bridge. There is also frequent ferry service, operated by MetroTransit, to Dartmouth from Lower Water Street in Halifax.

Transportation Within the City

Taxicabs are available at hotels, shopping centers, and other high-traffic areas.

MetroTransit buses stop at convenient locations, but drivers accept only correct change. Transfers accepted from ferry; (902) 490–6600.

The Harbour Ferry service to and from Dartmouth is located at the new terminal, off Lower Water Street, and operates every half hour throughout the day and every fifteen minutes at peak times. This is a cheap and pleasant way to ride around the harbor and see Halifax from the water, as sailors have for generations. Dating from 1752, it is the oldest operating saltwater ferry service in North America.

Guided Tours and Cruises

Gray Line, (902) 454–9321, provides a tour of the city, picking up passengers at all major hotels. Also available are Halifax Double Decker Tours, (902) 420–1155, and Cabana Tours, (902) 420–1155. To see Halifax from the water, call Halifax Water Tours, (902) 420–1015. Walking tours are offered by Scuttlebutt 'n Bones, (902) 429–9255, and the Halifax Ghost Walk, (902) 469–6716.

To tour the city by land and sea without changing vehicles, you can take Harbour Hopper, a tour bus that becomes a boat when it hits the harbor. Be sure to book ahead, (902) 490–TOUR or www.harbourhopper.com.

Major Events

Scotia Festival of Music, late May and early June

Greek Summer Fest, early June

Multicultural Festival, mid-June

Nova Scotia International Tattoo, early July: This spectacular event features dancers, singers, bagpipers, military bands, drummers, and gymnasts. It is a memorable experience for the entire family. For ticket information, call (902) 451–1221.

Canada Celebrations, July 1

Metro Scottish Festival and Highland Games, early July

Natal Day, last weekend of July into early August: Halifax and Dartmouth celebrate their birthdays with sports events, shows, fairs, parades, and fireworks.

International Buskers, mid-August: Street performers gather from around the world for nearly two weeks, offering one of North America's most exciting family outdoor events.

Atlantic Winter Fair, mid-October

Attractions

Citadel Hill (Halifax Citadel National Historic Park, 902–426–5080), built in 1828, is on the same site as the bastion built under orders by Lord Cornwallis in 1749. This stone fortress offers the best view of the city and the surrounding country in all directions. By law, no building can be built higher than the Citadel. It has interesting museums on Halifax history, a fifty-minute audiovisual show, guided tours, and military exhibits. Open throughout the year. Free.

Historic Properties, on the waterfront, are refurbished old warehouses containing attractive promenades with boutiques, restaurants, pubs, and offices. Historic Properties gives you a sense of what the waterfront was like in the olden days but with many modern conveniences. It is a perfect place for strolling, browsing, and spending money. Open throughout the year.

Halifax Public Gardens, Spring Garden Road, (902) 422–9407, have pleasant walks among exotic imported flowers, trees, and shrubs. At the entrance is a bust of Sir Walter Scott, and across the street stands a statue of Robert Burns. These are Canada's oldest public gardens, and their design is based on that of St. James's Park in London, England. Open throughout the year. Free.

Pier 21, Canada's Ellis Island, (902) 425–7770, is now designated an official National Historic Site. Between 1928 and 1971, this site was the landing point for more than 1.6 million immigrants, refugees, and citizens returning from war.

Alexander Keith's Nova Scotia Brewery, (902) 422–1077, is open to the public and for private group tours. It offers an atypical brewery tour that includes a lively narration and historical information about the area.

Maritime Museum of the Atlantic, on the waterfront near the ferry terminal, has displays of maritime history, the merchant navy, and the history of wooden sailing ships of the Atlantic. The showpiece of the museum is the *Acadia,* Canada's first hydrographic survey vessel, now a National Historic Site, tied up alongside the building. This fine museum also contains the Halifax Explosion Memorial and a special exhibit on the ill-fated luxury

Halifax Firsts

The first parliament legislature in Canada (1819)

The highest ratio of educational facilities to population in North America

The first postal service in North America (1752, Halifax to New York City)

Britain's first overseas cathedral (St. Paul's, 1750)

The first newspaper in Canada (*Halifax Gazette*)

The first and oldest saltwater ferry service in North America

---

liner *Titanic*. Open daily throughout the year, (902) 424–7490; admission charge.

Nova Scotia Museum of Natural History, 1747 Summer Street, houses extensive natural history and anthropological collections relating to the province. Open throughout the year. Free; (902) 424–7353.

Province House, Granville Street, is Nova Scotia's seat of government and the country's oldest provincial legislative building (1819). It is Canada's finest example of colonial Georgian architecture. Open throughout the year, (902) 424–4661; free.

Saint Paul's Cathedral, Grande Parade, is the city's oldest building (1749), mother church of the Protestant churches of Canada in general and of the Anglican church of Canada in particular. King George II is its royal founder. Known as the Westminster Abbey of Canada, this exquisite wooden church has many memorials relating to famous Canadians, Loyalists, and British.

Dalhousie University, at the end of University Avenue, is one of Canada's premier institutions of higher learning. It was founded in a rather odd way: A British military expedition extracted taxes from the citizens of Castine, Maine, to establish a college in Halifax modeled after Edinburgh University. The impressive campus features a modern library and arts center.

Maritime Command Museum, Admiralty House, C.F.B. Stadacona, Gottingen Street at Almon Street, has a fine exhibition of military and maritime artifacts. Open throughout the year. Free.

Public Archives of Nova Scotia, corner of University Avenue and Robie Street, has historical documents, a genealogical section, and an art gallery, exhibits of coins, stamps, prints, and paintings. Open throughout the year. Free.

Little Dutch (Deutsch) Church, Brunswick Street, built in 1758 for use by German Evangelical Lutherans, is nicknamed the "chicken coop church."

Round Church, Brunswick Street, was built at the instigation of the Duke of Kent, who didn't want the devil to catch him in a corner. Round Church is currently being restored. It was badly damaged by fire in 1994. Visitors, however, can tour the building.

Saint Matthew's Church, Barrington Street, opened in 1859, has a rose window that is a copy of the one at Chartres and a pew for the lieutenant governor. Guided tours are available in the summer.

Fort McNab National Historic Site, on McNab's Island in the harbor—reached by boat, (902) 420–1015—was established in the nineteenth century as one of the most important fortifications protecting the British naval station at Halifax and the city itself. In addition to viewing these old fortifications, visit the beaches, nature trails, and bike paths on the island.

Point Pleasant Park, at the south end of Young Avenue and at the toe of the peninsula, is a safe, wonderful, natural preserve where you can jog, enjoy the tranquillity of the woods and the nearby sea, and visit old fortifications, such as the Prince of Wales Tower, built in 1798 by the Duke of Kent. Cars are not permitted in the park. There are a public beach and a nature trail. Open throughout the year. Free.

Saint Mary's University, Robie Street, founded by the Jesuits, is the oldest English-speaking Roman Catholic university in Canada. Its astronomical observatory is open to the public.

University of King's College, at Coburg Road on the Dalhousie Campus, founded in 1789, is the oldest university in the Commonwealth outside the United Kingdom itself.

Visual Arts Exhibitions

Halifax is Atlantic Canada's thriving center for the visual arts. Some of the places in the city where you can see contemporary painting, sculpture, and crafts follow:

Nova Scotia College of Art and Design, Duke Street

Art Gallery of Mount Saint Vincent University, off the Bedford
   Highway

Art Gallery of Nova Scotia, Old Dominion Building, Hollis Street

Titanic!

In April 1912, Halifax became the base for rescue operations for the *Titanic*, as first the survivors and then bodies of victims were landed in the city. Several sites recall the disaster, including a permanent exhibit at the Maritime Museum of the Atlantic. A special section of Fairview Cemetery was devoted to the burial of 121 known and unknown victims of the disaster; nineteen are buried in Mount Olivet Cemetery and ten more at Baron de Hirsch. Atlantic Tours/Gray Line Trolley offers a Titanic tour to these and several other sites. Waterfront Warehouse offers authentic *Titanic* dinners.

Dalhousie University Art Gallery, Dalhousie Arts Centre
Dresden Gallery, 1539 Birmingham
Manuge Gallery, 1674 Hollis Street
School of Architecture Gallery, Technical University of Nova Scotia, 5410 Spring Garden Road
Zwicker's Gallery, 5415 Doyle Street

Recreational Sports

Cycling and walking are popular with locals, who take to Dartmouth's 4-mile multiuse trail and the 20 miles of woodland trails in Point Pleasant Park. Nearby shores offer scenic road biking routes, although they are often hilly. Herring Cove is a favorite circle route, beginning and ending at the Armdale Rotary. Hemlock Ravine Park has steeper trails through a mature forest.

McNab's Island Ferry, (902) 465–4563 or (800) 326–4563, offers guided nature and birding tours of the island as well as ferry service for those who wish to hike its trails on their own.

Both links and greens courses are plentiful for golfers: Brightwood Country Club in Dartmouth, Briarwood Golf Course on Herring Cove Road, and Glen Arbour Golf Course in Bedford each offers eighteen holes. Northcliffe Indoor Tennis Club, (902) 457–2444, is open to the public October through May. Hatfield Farms, (902) 835-5676, www.hatfieldfarms.com, in Bedford, offers trail rides fifteen minutes from downtown Halifax.

Accommodations

There are plenty of rooms in Halifax, but they are always in great demand by business travelers, politicians, delegates to conventions, and tourists. This cannot be repeated enough: Please reserve ahead. Use Nova Scotia's free Check-In service to help you (see page 268).

Sheraton Halifax, at Historic Properties on Upper Water Street, (902) 421–1700 or (800) 325–3535, is one of the city's finest hotels, offering restaurants, lounges, shops, and a swimming pool. Moderate to expensive.

Airport Hotel, opposite Halifax International Airport, (902) 873–3000, features a restaurant and lounge. Moderate to expensive.

The Delta Barrington Hotel, 1875 Barrington Street, (902) 429–7410 or (800) 268–1133, a Delta Hotel, features a good location and many conveniences, including dining facilities. Expensive.

Delta Halifax, Scotia Square, (902) 425–6700 or (800) 268–1133, is a good convention hotel, with all hotel conveniences and an excellent location. Expensive.

Citadel Halifax Hotel, 1960 Brunswick Street, (902) 422–1391 or (800) 565–7162, offers all hotel conveniences. Moderate to expensive.

Holiday Inn Select Halifax Centre, 1980 Robie Street, (902) 423–1161 or (800) HOLIDAY, has a fine dining room and entertainment. Moderate to expensive.

Westin Nova Scotian, 1181 Hollis Street, (902) 421–1000, next to the VIA Rail station, provides fine accommodations and an excellent main restaurant. Expensive.

Cambridge Suites Halifax, 1583 Brunswick Street, (902) 420–0555, located in expensive downtown, the Cambridge, offers several sizes of suites and many fine amenities at reasonable prices. Ideal for families who want to be in the center of everything. Moderate to expensive.

The Halliburton House Inn, 5184 Morris Street, (902) 420–0658, was built in 1820 and was the home of Sir Benton Halliburton, former Chief Justice of the Supreme Court of Nova Scotia. Halliburton House offers fine accommodations and serves three meals daily. Moderate to expensive.

The Prince George Hotel, 1725 Market Street, (902) 425–1986, offers fine accommodations and dining and a lounge with live entertainment. There is a swimming pool and exercise facility. Moderate to expensive.

Lord Nelson Hotel, South Park Street, across from the Public Gardens, (902) 423–6331 or (800) 565–2020, www.lordnelson-hotel.com, is beautifully refurbished in a fashionable area and carries an establishment aura. It features many conveniences. Moderate.

Keddy's Halifax, St. Margaret's Bay Road, (902) 477–5611 or (800) 561–7666, www.keddys.ca, offers good accommodations, dining, and recreational facilities, overlooking Chocolate Lake. Moderate.

During the summer, local universities offer inexpensive accommodations in their dormitories for families, couples, and singles:

Dalhousie University, (902) 494–8840
Saint Mary's University, (902) 420–5486
Mount Saint Vincent University, (902) 457–6286
Daltech, (902) 422–2495

Dining

Halifax offers some of the best dining in Atlantic Canada and the greatest variety of restaurants, from very elegant affairs to the usual fast-food places:

Salty's, Historic Properties, (902) 423–6818, offers seafood specialties and an eighteenth-century atmosphere overlooking the harbor. Moderate to expensive.

McKelvie's, 1680 Lower Water Street, (902) 421–6161, located in the popular waterfront area, serves tempting seafood dishes. Moderate.

Momotaro Japanese Restaurant, 1576 Argyle Street, (902) 425–7785, is an informal eatery serving sushi, noodles, and other Asian specialties. Moderate.

Five Fishermen, 1744 Argyle Street, (902) 422–4421, features a fresh catch of the day and home-baked rolls, prepared by French and Swiss chefs. Moderate to expensive.

Da Maurizio, 1496 Lower Water Street, (902) 423–0859, is known throughout Maritime Canada for its unfailing attention to detail. Top drawer. Expensive.

The Press Gang, 5218 Prince Street, (902) 423–8816, despite its threatening name, is all about fine dining. Eclectic and sometimes eccentric, its menu is a breath of fresh air. Expensive.

Haliburton House Inn, 5184 Morris Street, (902) 420–0658, has the air of a private club. Wild game may be on the menu, and dishes will be prepared in the French classical tradition, with a Canadian flair. Expensive.

Thackery's, 5407 Spring Garden Road, (902) 423–5995, prepares seafood, chicken, roast beef, and steak. Moderate to expensive.

Alfredo Weinstein & Ho, 1739 Grafton Street, (902) 421–1977. This restaurant's name is no mistake. Under one roof it serves up Italian, Jewish, and Chinese. A fun place. Moderate.

Satisfaction Feast, 1581 Grafton Street, (902) 422–3540, is a restaurant that should easily satisfy vegetarians. Moderate.

Upper Deck Restaurant, 1869 Upper Water Street, (902) 422–1289. One of the most romantic settings in Halifax, this dining room, which has thick stone walls and a wooden beamed ceiling, is on the third floor of Privateers' Warehouse. On the menu are oysters, lobsters, and rack of lamb. Expensive.

Le Bistro, 1333 South Park Street, (902) 423–8428, offers fine French cuisine in a cafe setting. Moderate.

Mother Tucker's, 1668 Lower Water Street, (902) 422–4436, is a relatively inexpensive prime roast beef, baked potato, and salad place. Inexpensive to moderate.

Cafe Amadeus & Gifts, 5675 Spring Garden Road, in the Lord Nelson Hotel, (902) 423–0032, is a European-style cafe and bakery. Inexpensive.

The Green Bean, 5220 Blowers Street, (902) 425–2779, a hangout for trendy, funky types, serves specialty coffees. Inexpensive.

Larkin's Cafe and Bakeshop, 1138 Queen Street, (902) 423–3998. The fragrant smell is enough to entice you inside. Freshly baked bread, mouthwatering cakes, and gourmet coffees and teas. Moderate.

Ryan Duffy's Restaurant Bar and Grill, upstairs in Spring Garden Place, (902) 421–1116, serves superior steaks; cuts and trims U.S. choice grade prime beef at your table. It is cut to your order, and you pay only for the final weight. Moderate to expensive.

Grafton Street Dinner Theatre, 1741 Grafton Street, (902) 425–1961. The days of bebop and speakeasys come to life in an evening of good food and fun. Moderate.

Historic Feast Company, at Simon's Warehouse at Historic Properties, (902) 420–1840, takes you back to the mid-nineteenth century for food, theater, music, and song. Moderate.

Willows Wine Bar and Bistro, 1980 Robie Street, (902) 423–1161. Listen to jazz while sampling wines from around the world. Moderate.

Entertainment

On any given day during the summer, entertainment abounds in Halifax—festivals, theater, music, and more. Hotels provide listings of current events. There is enough going on to make your stay fun and enjoyable.

Theater

The Halifax Metro Centre, 5284 Duke Street, (902) 421–1221, a huge arena, holds many entertainment and sporting events throughout the year. One of the most spectacular of these is the Nova Scotia International Tattoo, which runs for about a week in early July.

Neptune Theatre, 5216 Sackville Street, (902) 429–7070, is the top place to see live drama in Atlantic Canada, and it features leading Canadian, British, and American players.

Grafton Street Dinner Theatre, 1741 Grafton Street, (902) 425–1961. Live theater with comedy, music, and drama; period skits from the Depression era, the 1950s, and the 1960s.

Nightspots

For after-hours relaxation, Halifax has bars, lounges, discos, and nightclubs. Ask your hotel's concierge for suggestions on what's hot in town.

Thirsty Duck, 5472 Spring Garden Road, (902) 422–1548, is the place for traditional pub entertainment and fun.

Wild Hearts Saloon, 3630 Strawberry Hill, (902) 455–5140. This place has the largest dance floor in the city. Bustling bar with live entertainment and karaoke.

J. J. Rosy's, at Historic Properties, (902) 422–4411, is the largest pub in Atlantic Canada.

My Apartment, 1740 Argyle Street, (902) 422–5453, offers glitzy decor and ambience for those who love dancing to rock.

Your Father's Moustache, 5686 Spring Garden Road, (902) 423–6766, is a favorite venue for blues fans. Live music on weekends; open late on Saturday night.

The New Palace, 1721 Brunswick Street, (902) 429–5959. A cavernous and noisy nightclub. Open nightly until 3:30 A.M.

Shopping

Scotia Square and Park Lane are the city's main downtown shopping malls. Each contains more than one hundred shops, restaurants, and services. Halifax's high fashion street is Spring Garden Road. There are many interesting shops and restaurants at the Maritime Mall and Barrington Place on Barrington Street; Historic Properties on the Water Front; Spring Garden Place on Spring Garden Road; and the Courtyard on Dresden Row. All these shopping areas are in downtown Halifax. There are also large shopping malls in West End Halifax.

Side Trips

Dartmouth

You can visit Halifax's neighbor by taking the ferry or going over the Macdonald or the Mackay Bridge. Dartmouth, part of the greater Halifax Regional Municipality, is primarily a bedroom community for Halifax, but it has several interesting attractions. The Dartmouth Heritage Museum, 100 Wyse Road, has historical exhibits and the re-created study of Joseph Howe, one of Nova Scotia's foremost patriots. Open throughout the year. Free. The Quaker House (circa 1785), 57 Ochterloney Street, has items relating to early Nantucket whalers who lived in the city. Open only in the summer. Free. The Bedford Institute of Oceanography, located in the north end of the city, is the country's leading scientific center for marine research. Dartmouth is called the city of lakes: It has twenty-three of them. Seven have public beaches and are stocked with speckled trout.

Cole Harbor, via Highway 207 on the Marine Drive out of Dartmouth, is the site of the Heritage Farm Museum, 471 Poplar Drive, which depicts the area's agricultural traditions. Open late May to early October. Free.

Cape Sambro

Take Highways 253 and 349 for a pleasant drive through small towns and fishing villages. The views of the ocean are lovely, and there are plenty of spots to picnic, hike, photograph, or paint pictures. Near Purcell's Cove is York Redoubt National Historic Park and its fortifications. This is a choice morning or afternoon excursion from Halifax.

Peggy's Cove

Take Highway 333 for one of the most popular side trips from Halifax (or from Yarmouth via the Lighthouse Route). On the way to Peggy's Cove, be sure to take the secondary roads that lead to Terence Bay, Prospect Harbour, and East Dover to see authentic fishing villages where the people still live by old ways and virtues. This journey to a different world is quite a contrast to the sophistication of Halifax and immensely appealing.

Peggy's Cove looks like a nineteenth-century fishing village. Modern structures cannot be built here. It is an ideal place to photograph fishing shacks and boats, lovely little St. John's Anglican church, a majestic lighthouse, and rock cliffs on a thundering ocean. The lighthouse, no longer functioning as a navigational beacon, serves as a post office during the summer. The postmaster sells stamps decorated with a picture of this famous lighthouse.

Also in Peggy's Cove is a carving in the side of a huge granite boulder by the late William E. deGarthe, a Finnish artist who worked in the village for many years. DeGarthe's carving portrays thirty-two Peggy's Cove fishermen, their wives and children, a guardian angel with spread wings, and the mythological "Peggy" for whom the village is named. There are also two deGarthe murals inside St. John's Church.

Candleriggs, in Indian Harbour, (902) 823–2722, offers hearty Scottish breakfasts, lunch, Scottish tea, dinner, and weekend champagne brunch, also fine Nova Scotia handicrafts. Be sure to explore the strange geological terrain around Peggy's Cove, a vestige of the great glaciers.

To Cape Breton Island via Marine Drive

You can reach Cape Breton Island from the Halifax-Dartmouth area by taking Highway 107 from Dartmouth and then Highway 7 along the Atlantic coast, passing through or near such scenic villages as Seaforth, Jeddore, Clam Harbour, Ecum Secum, and Liscomb. Along the way, enjoy the attractions, explore charming fishing villages, take beach walks, and relish the maritime landscape. You can reach Cape Breton in a day from the Halifax area.

At **Musquodoboit Harbor** is the Musquodoboit Railway Museum, with its displays of railroad history in a 1917 Canadian National Railway station. Open June through August. Free.

The Fisherman's Life Museum at **Jeddore Oyster Pond** shows you how inshore fishermen lived and worked. This is one of the most interesting little museums in the province. Open mid-May to mid-October. Admission by donation.

If you want to stay at a special resort, make reservations at Liscombe Lodge in **Liscomb Mills,** (902) 779–2307, a resort operated by the province, with fine accommodations and meals, canoe rentals, hiking trails, swimming, fishing, deep-sea charters, boat tours, and recreational features. Moderate to expensive.

Sherbrooke is the site of the historic Sherbrooke Village, a restored nineteenth-century lumbering, shipbuilding, and gold mining community. There are demonstrations of crafts and trades of the period, a general store, courthouse, school, blacksmith shop, and other buildings. Open mid-May to the end of October. Admission charge.

Highway 7 will take you to the Trans-Canada Highway 104 at Antigonish. Take the Trans-Canada to the causeway at the Canso Strait (Port Hawkesbury) and Cape Breton Island. En route, you might take exit 37 to Highway 16 for a side trip to **Guysborough,** a pretty town with tree-lined streets, elegant homes, a golf course, and the Old Court House Museum, featuring local history. Open June 1 to mid-September. Free. Highway 16 ends at the Cape of Canso. In the town of **Canso** is the Canso Museum, housed in the restored Whitman House. Open during the summer. Free.

An alternate and faster route from Halifax to Cape Breton Island follows Highway 102 and the Trans-Canada. This drive takes about five hours from the Halifax area. Be careful of your speed, as the Royal Canadian Mounted Police strictly enforce speed limits.

CHAPTER 13

Newfoundland Labrador

Newfoundlanders call their homeland "The Rock"—a good name for this craggy stone that juts abruptly from the North Atlantic. And although the people are as tough as their rock, you will find few who are more open, hospitable, warm, and friendly, nor with a better sense of humor.

Where else would you find towns named Jerry's Nose, Blow Me Down, Come by Chance, or Heart's Desire? Unusual place-names aren't Newfoundland's only unique quality. Here you will find rare geological phenomena, icebergs drifting past on a summer day, fjords with walls so steep you'd swear you were in Norway, and a language so different that it has its own dictionary. Where else in North America can you stand on the shore and see France? (The tiny islands of St. Pierre and Miguelon are the last remnant of Franch territory in North America and are officially a department of France.)

A Look at the Past

Human habitation of this huge island began when northern First Nations peoples made their way across the frozen north and landed here. Some of the earliest findings are of the Dorset peoples. The most noted of the pre-European settlers, however, are the Beothuk peoples who were living here when Europeans arrived. Although they lived in small groups and generally avoided

Newfoundland-Labrador

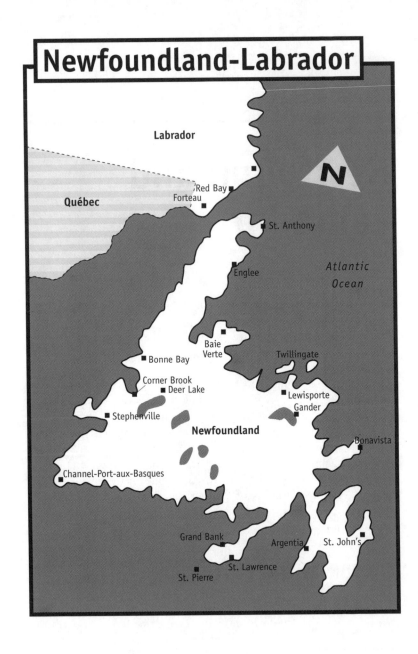

Labrador

Québec

Red Bay
Forteau

St. Anthony

Englee

Atlantic Ocean

Baie Verte

Bonne Bay

Twillingate

Corner Brook
Deer Lake

Lewisporte
Gander

Stephenville

Newfoundland

Bonavista

Channel-Port-aux-Basques

Grand Bank

Argentia

St. John's

St. Pierre

St. Lawrence

contact with the Europeans, they eventually succumbed to conflict and to loss of access to their traditional resource base due to encroachment by Europeans, Inuit, and Mi'Kmaq. The last Beothuk died in 1829.

The first European settlement came in about A.D. 1000 when a group of Norse settlers founded a community at L'Anse aux Meadows. They were driven off by unfriendly natives, who gained an additional 500 years of isolation. In 1497 the Italian seaman-navigator John Cabot, sailing for the English king, came upon the island and claimed it for England. While European fishermen had long known of the great schools of fish in these waters, Cabot's reports led to a great increase in fishing off Newfoundland. The Grand Banks, off the coast, were some of the finest fishing grounds in the world.

George Calvert, 1st Baron Baltimore, obtained a royal grant and between 1621 and 1628 attempted to found a colony he called Avalon, at a place now called Ferryland, south of St. John's. He found the climate too severe and left to try again in Maryland. Extensive excavations of the colony are under way, and you can visit the dig.

Anxious to maintain a monopoly over fishing, England prohibited settlements after 1699, limiting the island to use by its fishermen for processing and shipping fish. Wanting to secure a place in the new world, France contested Newfoundland and established its own settlement at Placentia in 1662. From there French forces attacked all of the English settlements on the island in 1696, 1705, and 1708. From Placentia the French settlers went to Cape Breton and established the community that became Fortress Louisbourg.

During the whole of the seventeenth and eighteenth centuries, Newfoundland remained an English enclave without governmental status. It existed almost exclusively for the fisheries and was essentially the property of the fishing companies and the captains of their vessels. So vast were the fisheries that large numbers of workmen were imported, but it wasn't until 1824 that England finally appointed a full-time governor and council to run the affairs of the island.

The following year, English courts recognized Newfoundland's claim to the strip of mainland across the Strait of Belle Island, but left open the issue of how far inland their rights extended. It wasn't until 1927 that Newfoundland was given control of all land to the headwaters of all streams that flow across Labrador into the Atlantic, a status that Québec province still contests. In 1832 the people were given the right to have their own

The First "Red Men"

The Beothuks painted their bodies with a red soil found on the island. Some historians have suggested that this is the origin of the term "red men" that was applied by early settlers to Native American peoples throughout the continent.

elected legislative assembly and in 1855 they were given full right to govern themselves under the oversight of the crown.

When Canadian Confederation was being discussed in the 1860s Newfoundland participated, but voted not to join and remained a separate colony for almost another century. The island's economy has always been tied to the fisheries; even with the development of some timbering and mining industries, the fisheries have been the key to prosperity. Over the centuries the industry has waxed and waned and the prosperity of the people with it.

Even within the island community, people's status differed widely. By the nineteenth century, the established and wealthier families owned the stores and fish processing plants in the larger communities. The men who fished had considerably less, many of them living in communities on scattered bays and inlets, isolated from other settlements. These small roadless villages were called outports. Rarely with more than a hundred people, they had no land connection to other towns and depended on the sea for communication with the rest of the world.

During World War II, Newfoundland was crucial to the Allied war effort. Its harbors, particularly the protected harbor at St. John's, became staging places for huge convoys and home to their escort vessels. Large airfields were built as refueling and refitting bases for aircraft carrying troops and supplies to England and Europe. The bases also served as home to anti-submarine aircraft that flew protective missions over convoys. With the end of the war, some of these bases, particularly the big airfield at Gander, became stopover places for the aircraft that began the modern era of commercial flight to Europe.

In 1948, Newfoundland narrowly voted to join the Canadian Confederation as a separate province. It wasn't until March 31, 1949, that Newfoundland and Labrador became a part of Canada. The recent history of the province has been one of economic downturn and the virtual end of the fisheries, disaster for most of the island's people. Gross overfishing on the Grand Banks by factory ships from Europe and Asia has all but destroyed fish stocks that only a few decades ago were thought to be inexhaustible.

With severe limitations on allowable catches, and in some instances an outright ban, most fishing boats have been hauled onto shore. Efforts to create new employment have not proven as successful as hoped, and the economy has slowed to a crawl. One bright spot is the steady growth of tourism. The breadth of outdoor activities available, the color of tough villages clinging to rocky coves, and the cultural experience of being a part of this self-reliant outpost make it one of the ultimate destinations for adventurous travelers.

Geography

The land mass of Newfoundland-Labrador is vast. Labrador, the most easterly extension of mainland Canada, occupies 110,000 square miles (286,000 sq km), with its lamb-chop shape bordered by the Province of Québec on the west and south and the Atlantic Ocean on the north and east. Most of the interior of Labrador is a wilderness where few people have set foot.

The island of Newfoundland, where more than 520,000 people live, is 43,000 square miles (112 sq km) in area and shaped like an arrowhead pointing westward into the Gulf of Saint Lawrence. This island is separated from Labrador to the north by the Strait of Belle Isle, with the Atlantic Ocean to its east and south. It is the

Newfoundland Firsts

Newfoundland's position as the easternmost part of North America has made it home to many firsts. The ship *Great Eastern* dropped the end of the first successful transatlantic telegraph cable here in 1866. In 1901, on Signal Hill in St. John's, Marconi received the first transatlantic message on his new invention, the wireless telegraph. Charles Lindbergh flew from here on his historic flight and Amelia Earhart left on her solo fight from a primitive airstrip in Harbour Grace in 1932.

most easterly part of North America—only 1,800 miles (2,880 km) from the coast of Ireland. Most of the people of the island live along its coasts. St. John's is the capital city, with a population of 175,000. Much of Newfoundland's interior is forested.

Speak the Language

Newfoundland even has its own language. Here are a few examples of their tongue twisters and what they mean.

Angishore	Weak, miserable person
Bannock	Round cake of bread
Blather	Nonsensical talk
Calabogus	Rum, molasses, and spruce beer
Crubeens	Pickled pig's feet
Duckish	The time between sunset and dark
Gansey	Woolen sweater
Gommil	Moron
Growler	Small iceberg
Gulvin	Codfish's stomach
Jackabown	Mischievous person
Jinker	Bad-luck person
Kingcorn	Adam's apple
Manus	Mutiny
Mundle	Wooden soup stirrer
Oonshick	Stupid person
Rames	Skeleton
Scutty	Mean, irritable
Sheila's brush	Snow fall after St. Patrick's Day
Squabby	Jelly soft
Titivate	To adorn
Vang	Melted salt pork
Yuck	To vomit

The following is a listing of some old Newfie sayings:

A fisherman is one rogue, a merchant is many.
Fair weather to you and snow to your heels.
Go to law with the devil and hold court in hell.

In a leaky punt with a broken oar, 'tis always best to hug the shore.
Pigs may fly, but they are very unlikely birds.
You can't tell the mind of a squid.
You are as deep as your grave.
Crazy as a loon.
Deaf as a haddock.
Dirty as a duck's puddle.
Hard as the knockers of Newgate.
Like a birch broom in the fits.
Lonesome as a gull on a rock.
Old as Buckley's goat.
Smoky as a Labrador tilt.
Wide as the devil's boots.

How to Get to Newfoundland and Labrador

By Car and Ship

Take the Trans-Canada to the Marine Atlantic terminal at North Sydney, Nova Scotia. Passenger car, trailer, and truck ferry service to Port aux Basques, Newfoundland, operates daily throughout the year. During the summer there is also service to Argentia. The vessels include a cafeteria, a bar, and cabins.

For rates and schedules, contact Marine Atlantic, P.O. Box 250, North Sydney, Nova Scotia B2A 3M3, or call (800) 341–7981 toll-free from the United States; (902) 794–5254 in North Sydney; (709) 227–3755 in Argentia; (709) 695–2124 in Port aux Basques; or (902) 794–8109 for the hearing impaired.

By Air

Air Canada provides service to Newfoundland cities. Connections can be made in St. John's for service to Goose Bay and Churchill Falls, Labrador. Rental cars are available at airports, but advance reservations are important.

General Information

Time zones: Atlantic (Labrador) and Newfoundland (Newfoundland—one-half hour ahead of Atlantic time)
Telephone area code: 709
Emergencies: 911

Climate and Clothing

Summers on the island of Newfoundland are pleasant, but the weather can change fast along the Atlantic coast. The Labrador coast is mild to cool in the summer, depending on how far north you go. Winters range from cold in Newfoundland to arctic in Labrador. Giant floating icebergs can be seen in the late spring and early summer off the Atlantic coast. Dense fogs are not uncommon, especially in the late spring and fall. Generally, good weather and pleasant temperatures prevail from late June to the end of September.

Since much of your visit to Newfoundland will be auto touring, casual, comfortable clothes are sufficient. Bring good shoes for hiking, warm jackets and sweaters, and basic rain gear. There is nothing stuffy about the people of Newfoundland-Labrador, so you don't have to worry about dressing up for dinner, although in the better restaurants of St. John's you may feel more comfortable in moderately dressy clothes.

Tourist Information

For more information write the Newfoundland-Labrador Department of Tourism, Culture, and Recreation, P.O. Box 8730, St. John's, Newfoundland A1B 4K2. Call toll-free (800) 563–6353.

Visitor Information Centres are located in North Sydney (Nova Scotia), Port aux Basques, Deer Lake, Notre Dame Junction, Clarenville, Whitbourne, and Argentia. They are also in St. John's, Marystown, Gander, Twillingate, Grand Falls, Springdale, Corner Brook, Stephenville/St. George's, Hawke's Bay, Happy Valley–Goose Bay, Labrador City, Goobies, St. Anthony, and Port au Port.

How to Get Around Newfoundland and Labrador

The Trans-Canada Highway Route 1, the main transportation route on the island of Newfoundland, is 565 miles (910 km) from Port aux Basques to St. John's, fully paved, and well maintained. Most secondary roads are now paved.

Coastal Newfoundland and Labrador

The coastal vessels that service the otherwise inaccessible fishing outports with supplies and mail are the best way to come close to the traditional way of life along the coasts. For example, you can sail from Lewisporte to Nain, Labrador, 725 miles (1,166 km) one way (you return more quickly by air from Goose Bay). Space on these ships is limited, and the demand for accommodations is great. Meals are provided onboard. For further information, call (800) 563–6353.

Wilderness Tours and Ocean Cruises

One of the best ways to experience the special world of Newfoundland and Labrador is to go out on the ocean or into the wilderness. The following are companies that provide such memorable experiences:

Wildland Tours, (709) 722–3123, explores the island.

Gros Morne Adventure Guides, (709) 686–2241, offers hiking and sea kayaking in Gros Morne National Park.

Whitecap Adventures, (709) 726–9283, offers sea kayaking.

Rockwater Adventures, (888) 512–2227, hosts diving and climbing excursions.

Gander River Tours, (709) 679–2271, runs canoe river expeditions.

Labrador Scenic Ltd., (709) 497–8326, offers boat tours and trips into the wilderness, where participants stay in remote cabins.

Newfoundland and Labrador Ecotours Adventures, (709) 579–8055, leads excursions to marine and bird sanctuaries and to archaeological sites.

Gatherall's Puffin and Whale Watch, (709) 334–2887, takes trips to Witless Bay seabird sanctuary.

Adventure Tours-Scademia, (709) 726–5000, runs tours to "Iceberg Alley," where giant chunks of ice drift southward from the Arctic to the Atlantic Ocean.

Explore Newfoundland, (709) 634–2237, runs coastal sea kayaking tours.

Major Events

June

St. John's Day Celebrations, St. John's
Placentia Landwash Day, Placentia

July

Humber Valley Strawberry Festival, Deer Lake
Burin Peninsula Festival of Folk Song and Dance, Burin
Stephenville Theatre Festival, Stephenville

Trinity Pageant, Trinity
Exploits Valley Salmon Festival, Grand Falls
Fish, Fun and Folk Festival, Twillingate-New World Island

August

Newfoundland and Labrador Folk Festival, St. John's
Une Longue Veillée (Folk Festival), Port au Port
Brigus Blueberry Festival
Regatta Day, Quidi Vidi Lake, St. John's
Labrador Straits Bakeapple Folk Festival, Labrador
Newfoundland Folk Festival, St. John's

Most of these festivals and events involve parades, sporting events, dancing, and singing, plus a lot of eating and drinking—in short, a great time.

Hunting and Fishing

The province offers some 156,000 square miles (406,000 sq km) of almost virgin territory, with more than 13,000 square miles (34,000 sq km) of lakes and rivers—a hunting and fishing paradise. Nonresident hunters must be accompanied by a guide, and you must have a permit from the government to use your own airplane for transportation to hunting areas. Moose, caribou, black bear, duck, geese, snipe, grouse, and rabbit are abundant. Salmon (landlocked and Atlantic), trout (speckled and brown), tuna, pike, and char are some of the species popular with sports fishermen.

For more information on outfitters, guides, and regulations, call tourism information at the telephone numbers given earlier.

Provincial Parks and Campgrounds

Newfoundland is well suited for people bringing their own accommodations (trailers, campers, tents). Provincial parks are located in scenic areas and offer hiking, swimming, fishing, camping conveniences, boating and canoeing areas, historic sites, cultural events, and other features. A listing of government-operated parks follows:

Cheesman Park, on Highway 1, near Cape Ray
Grand Codroy Park, on Highway 406, near Doyles
Barachois Park, on Highway 1, near St. George's

Piccadilly Head Park, on Highway 463, near Piccadilly
Blow Me Down Park, on Highway 450, near Lake Harbour
Pistolet Bay Park, off Highway 437, near Raleigh
Squires Memorial Park, on Highway 422, near Cormack
Notre Dame Park, on Highway 1, near Lewisporte
Dildo Run Park, on Highway 340, near Virgin Arm
Lockston Path Park, on Highway 236, near Port Rexton
Frenchman's Cove Park, on Highway 213, near Frenchman's
Cove
LaManche Park, on Highway 10, near Cape Broyle
The Canadian federal government operates the following as
part of the national park system:
Gros Morne National Park, on Highway 430, north of Deer
Lake. The park has five campgrounds: Barry Hill, Green
Point, Shallow Bay, Lomond, and Trout River.
Terra Nova National Park, on Highway 1
Newman Sound Campground in Terra Nova National Park

Accommodations

Several provincial parks and private campgrounds are near the
main roads, and there are adequate motels, although not as many
as on mainland Canada. Make sure that you have advance reservations. Also consider staying at hospitality homes (known in
other regions as B&Bs), private homes offering inexpensive, good
accommodations and home cooking.

If you find yourself in a town without lodging late in the day,
or if you have car trouble or another problem that prevents you
from traveling farther, ask at a store, post office, or other business—or simply ask someone you meet there—if anyone in town
offers rooms. There will almost always be a room available. Newfoundlanders are among the world's most hospitable people and
they will never leave you without a bed for the night.

Dining

The dishes you will find most often on Newfoundland menus are
fish chowder, cod, and salmon. These fish may be cooked in a variety of ways, but they will nearly always be there. Cod tongues
and cheeks are deep-fried or sautéed, tasting much like scallops.
Cod is often served au gratin. Although you will hear about it a

lot, it is very difficult to find one of the most traditional of Newfoundland specialties on a menu: fish and brewis. Prepared right, it is among the most delectable of dishes, a mélange of cod and softened hard crackers, sprinkled with crisp fried pork rinds. A few places serve it, sometimes as a first course, so watch for it.

You will occasionally find wild game on the menu; the Stone House Restaurant in St. John's is known for its good selection. A rare dish nowadays, although it was once a popular delicacy, is seal flipper pie.

Look for cloudberries, locally called bakeapples. These delicious, earthy orange berries have crunchy seeds and an almost smokey flavor that is unlike any other berry. You can often find bakeapple jam in craft cooperatives. Blueberries are common in pies, and a local vintner produces blueberry wine.

You may often find that the only place to eat in a town is the restaurant at the local Irving gas station. These are plain, clean, and serve a simple menu, but serve it quite well. You might not choose it for a night on the town, but you will be well fed. Remember that what may look like a roadhouse from the outside could have a cozy and creditable dining room inside. The restaurants attached to most motels are also reliable.

Liquor can be purchased at government stores and in licensed dining rooms and lounges. Try Newfoundland Screech, a potent rum and a provincial tradition.

Touring Newfoundland

One of the lures of Newfoundland is the people, especially those living in the little villages and outports along the coasts. Many still pursue a way of life that died long ago in the rest of North America. They are humble, religious, lusty, joyful, and very friendly. There are many similarities between the coastal people of Newfoundland and those of Ireland—their attitudes, thick accents, close-knit families and communities, and strong faith in the will of God. It is the people of Newfoundland and Labrador, plus their magnificent land and powerful ocean, that make this province one of the most unusual places to visit in Atlantic Canada.

The best way to see the island of Newfoundland by car is to get off the ferry at Port aux Basques and get on the Trans-Canada Highway. From Port aux Basques to the capital city of St. John's, use the 565-mile (910 km) Trans-Canada as your primary route, but take frequent side trips to explore the countryside and the seacoast, to swim, fish, camp, and boat. Through these side trips you will discover the essence of Newfoundland, while still having the conveniences (accommodations, restaurants, and the attractions in larger communities) on the Trans-Canada not too far away.

To learn more about the way of life here, do stop in the many local museums. Buy home-baked bread and pies, locally grown produce, and freshly caught fish, and picnic in beautiful natural surroundings. Discover secluded spots along lakes, streams, in the woods, and along the shores for priceless moments of peace and harmony.

Channel-Port aux Basques to L'Anse aux Meadows

Most travelers enter and leave the province at Channel-Port aux Basques, an important fishing community that traces its history back to 1500 and the Basques who fished in its waters. Visit the Community Museum of Maritime History. Open during the summer. Admission charge. At nearby Rose Blanche Point is a lighthouse built in 1873. Accommodations include Hotel Port aux Basques, (709) 695–2171; St. Christopher's Hotel, (709) 695–7034; and the recently refurbished Ocean View Inn, (709) 695–5888. All are off the Trans-Canada, with dining rooms and lounges, moderate.

Highway 1 extends along the Cape Ray shore, an area with many spectacular views of the ocean crashing against the land, and then through the rich agricultural Codroy Valley to Stephenville. The Codroy Valley has a number of excellent salmon-fishing rivers, and the scenery is enhanced by farms.

From mid-July to August **Stephenville** holds a theatre festival, featuring live drama, which has received rave notices from critics. Accommodations include Hotel Stephenville, (709) 643–5176, and White's Hotel-Motel, (709) 643–2101, both off the Trans-Canada, with dining rooms and lounges, moderate.

Take a side trip to **Port-au-Port Peninsula,** which has fine sandy beaches, swimming, and an attractive park. Many of the inhabitants here are of Acadian descent.

Corner Brook, at the mouth of the Humber River, is Newfoundland's second largest city. It is an important transportation and distribution center, and its main industry is the giant Kruger Paper Mill. There are many beautiful drives in the Corner Brook area—along the Humber River to the quaint fishing village of **Bottle Cove** and **Blow Me Down Provincial Park.** Here also is the Captain James Cook Monument, a National Historic Site. Cook charted the Bay of Islands in 1764. Accommodations and dining in the center of town or on the Trans-Canada include Hotel Corner Brook, Main Street, (709) 634–8211, with a dining room and lounge, moderate; Holiday Inn, West Street, (709) 634–5381, with a swimming pool, dining room, and lounge, moderate to expensive; Glynmill Inn, Cobb Lane, (709) 634–5181, with a good restaurant, moderate; Best Western Mamateek Inn, (709) 639–8901, with a dining room overlooking the city, moderate; and Comfort Inn, (709) 639–1980, moderate.

Deer Lake, located on a lake of the same name, is in a dense forested area and at the junction of the Trans-Canada and Highway 430, which goes up the Great Northern Peninsula to Gros Morne National Park and L'Anse aux Meadows. The trip to L'Anse aux Meadows and back will require about three extra days.

Wiltondale, via Highway 430, is at the entrance of Gros Morne National Park. Here starts the drive up the Great Northern Peninsula. A side trip on Highway 431 from Wiltondale takes you to Glenburnie and to Trout River, where you have some fine views of the rugged landscape and the water. You can gather clams and mussels at low tide here. Gros Morne National Park, (709) 458–2417, www.grossmorne.pch.gc.ca, is the visual highlight of Newfoundland, which is quite an accolade for an island with so much spectacular coastal scenery. It has been named a UNESCO World Heritage Site. Here mountains plunge suddenly into fjords, and one entire mountain is made up of a piece of the earth's mantle, which was thrust up when plates collided. Tucked into the coves are tiny fishing towns. Trails bring walkers to an ever changing series of vistas, and boat tours explore the region from several harbors. Two of the best of these explore the park's two landlocked fjords, Western Brook Pond and Trout River Pond.

Towns lie within the park, offering lodging and dining as well as shops where campers can buy supplies. Five campgrounds are within the National Park, along with two private camping areas in Norris Point and one in Rocky Harbour.

Several outfitters in the Corner Brook, Deer Lake, and Gros Morne areas offer guided outdoor adventures in and around the park, both summer and winter. These range from kayaking and sailing to dogsledding and cross-country skiing. Gros Morne Adventure Guides, (709) 458–2722 or (800) 685–4624, www.newcomm.net.gmag, offers a wide variety of mountain and sea trips.

At Port au Choix, about midway on the Great Northern Peninsula, is the Maritime Archaic (Red Paint Culture) burial ground, dating back to 2340 B.C., and artifacts of the Dorset peoples. This national historic park interprets this important archaeological find. Open mid-June to September. Admission charge.

Just above Port au Choix, at the village of **St. Barbe,** you can catch the ferry that crosses the Strait of Belle Isle to Blanc-Sablon, Québec, during ice-free months. The ferry takes cars, trailers, and trucks. From Blanc-Sablon you can drive into Labrador, via Highway 510, which is paved as far as Red Bay. Beyond that a new gravel road goes as far as Mary's Harbour. Accommodations in this part of Labrador include Northern Light Inn, L'Anse au Clair, (709) 931–2332, with a dining room and lounge, moderate, and Barney's bed-and-breakfast, L'Anse-au-Loup, (709) 927–5634, with home-cooked meals, inexpensive.

L'Anse aux Meadows, via Highway 436, off Highway 430, at the northernmost tip of Newfoundland, is the site of the Viking settlement (A.D. 1000) discovered by Helge and Anne Stine Ingstad. At this national historic site, (709) 623–2608, trained guides explain the excavations. There are replicas here of what this ancient Norse settlement might have been like in the days of the Vikings. What is impressive here is not so much the excavations themselves or the moody landscape, but the feeling of the tremendous struggle for survival that must have consumed the inhabitants. Open year-round. Admission charge. In 1978 L'Anse aux Meadows was declared a World Heritage Site by UNESCO, recognized as one of the world's major archaeological properties.

For lodging near L'Anse aux Meadows, treat yourself to The Tickle Inn at Cape Onion, (709) 452–4321. The setting is lovely, with dinners to match. Moderate. Another choice is Valhalla Lodge Bed & Breakfast, (709) 623–2238 or toll-free (877) 623–2018, www.valhalla-lodge.com. Moderate.

St. Anthony, via Highway 430, is the largest town on the Great Northern Peninsula and the place for overnight accommodations after seeing L'Anse aux Meadows. St. Anthony is headquarters for the International Grenfell Association, which provides medical services (hospitals and nursing stations) to isolated communities on the island and on the coast of Labrador. Dr. Wilfred Grenfell devoted his life to the fishing peoples of these northern coasts at a time when they were neglected even by the government. The Grenfell House is open to the public during the summer. Admission charge. While in St. Anthony visit the Grenfell Mission's handicraft center, where you can purchase exquisite hand-embroidered parkas and other beautiful items made by the coastal people. Also visit St. Anthony Museum and Archives at town hall, open during the summer, free. Accommodations include the Haven Inn, (709) 454–9100, with a dining room and lounge, moderate; Vinland Motel, (709) 454–8843, with a dining room and lounge, moderate; and Fishing Point B&B, (709) 454–2009, an original fisherman's dwelling overlooking some of the best iceberg-watching waters; close to all the sights and a good restaurant. Inexpensive.

To return to the Trans-Canada, backtrack on Highway 430 to Deer Lake.

Grand Falls–Windsor to St. John's

Grand Falls, 285 miles (456 km) west of St. John's, on the Trans-Canada, is one of the world's largest producers of newsprint. Perhaps the paper you read this morning was printed on a product made in Grand Falls. The Mary March Museum for the study of the Beothuk Indians is also located here. Open May to October. Admission charge. The area around Grand Falls is popular for moose and caribou hunting and salmon and trout fishing. Recommended accommodations in the town include Highliner Country Inn, (709) 489–5639, with a dining room and lounge; and Mount Peyton Motel, (709) 489–2251, with a dining room and lounge. Both are moderately priced.

Lewisport, on Notre Dame Bay, is known for lobster. Coastal Labrador ferries operate from here to Goose Bay–Happy Valley in Labrador. You can cruise the bay on a pontoon boat to see icebergs, seabirds, eagles, or a British ship that wrecked in the 1800s, (709) 535–3344, www.entnet.nf.ca/kittiwake. Accommodations include the Brittany Inns, (709) 535–2533, with a dining room and lounge, and Northgate Bed and Breakfast, (709) 535–2258. Both are moderate in price.

At **Twillingate,** via Highway 346, in the Long Point area, you can see floating icebergs in the early summer (the *Titanic* was sunk by icebergs off the waters of Newfoundland). This is a rare opportunity to take photos of a natural phenomenon that very few people see. Visit the Twillingate Museum, open during the summer, admission charge. Long Point Lighthouse in this area was built in 1876. Highway 331 runs along Gander Bay and connects with Highway 330, which takes you to the city of Gander on the Trans-Canada.

Gander is famous in aviation history as the last refueling point for transatlantic flights (and for flights coming from Europe to North America). Gander International Airport, known as the "crossroads of the world," was a major military base during World War II, when thousands of Allied flights went through here on their way to Europe. Because modern aircraft have a longer range, Gander's importance as a refueling stop has since diminished, but you can still tour the old military town's streets next to the airport. After the war, the town of Gander moved a short distance away, but remembers its aviation history with a very good museum on Highway 1 near the Tourist Information office, and with restored aircraft displayed in several places in town.

Accommodations are available at the Albatross Motel, Highway 1, (709) 256–3956, with a dining room and lounge, moderate; Comfort Inn, Highway 1, (709) 256–3535, with housekeeping units, moderate; The Irving West Hotel, Highway 1, (709) 256–2406, with a dining room, inexpensive to moderate; and Sinbad's Hotel and Suites, (709) 651–2678, with a very good dining room, moderate.

The Trans-Canada cuts through **Terra Nova National Park,** (709) 533–2801, on Bonavista Bay. This is one of the most popular parks in the province because of its natural beauty, dramatic coastline, and many attractions. You can hike trails in the company of a trained naturalist or go off by yourself. Moose, black bear, and other wildlife move about freely. At the edge of the sea, you can see pods of whales cavorting and many different species of birds wheeling overhead. There are lakes and streams for swimming and fishing, ample areas for camping and picnics, and an eighteen-hole golf course. Terra Nova, like Gros Morne on the west coast, is one of Newfoundland's great natural attractions; it should not be missed. Accommodations in this area are at the Terra Nova Park Lodge and Golf Course in Port Blandford, (709) 543–2525, which has a swimming pool, moderate; Janes Bed and Breakfast, in Traytown, (709) 533–2221, inexpensive; and White Sails Inn and Cabins, (709) 677–3400, in Eastport, moderate.

Eastport, via Highway 310, on the northern edge of the park, is a farming town, where you can purchase fresh vegetables, homebaked bread, and jam. It has a sandy beach for a plunge into the cold Atlantic.

There is an interesting museum of local history at **Salvage,** where you can purchase weaving made to order. Open throughout the summer. Admission charge. Savor the locally smoked salmon while touring or relaxing on the beaches at **Sandy Cove** and **Happy Adventure.**

Cape Bonavista, via Highway 230, is reputed to be the landfall of John Cabot on June 24, 1497. The lighthouse on Cape Bonavista, first used in 1843, is now a provincial historic site. Continue on Highway 230 to **Trinity,** one of the oldest settlements in Newfoundland, discovered by Gasper Corté Real in 1500. Saint Paul's Anglican Church here was built in 1734. Trinity was where the first smallpox vaccination was administered in North America. Visit the Trinity Museum. Open throughout the summer. Admission charge. In town the oldest known fire engine in North America is on display, and the town stages a very popular summer theatre festival; call (888) 464–3377.

At Goobies, the Trans-Canada is joined by Highway 210, which leads down the Burin Peninsula. **Marystown** is a center for the building of ships, and in **Fortune** you can catch the ferry for the French islands of Saint-Pierre and Miquelon. Ferries operate from mid-June to mid-September.

The islands of **Saint-Pierre and Miquelon** are "collectivitée territoriale," a department of France. They are among the last vestiges of the once-great empire France commanded in the New World. Miquelon, the larger of the two islands, is mostly uninhabited, except for a small fishing village of 600 people. Saint-Pierre used to be a thriving fishing and supply center and once served as a quarantine station for cattle shipped to North America from Europe. The islands drew international attention in 1967 when General Charles de Gaulle visited on his way to Montréal.

The architecture in Saint-Pierre is unmistakably French. The buildings that fringe General de Gaulle Square give one the feeling of being in Brittany. Fine wine and expensive French perfumes are sold here at bargain prices, although the bargains are not what they once were. Accommodations are in charming French-style guest houses, and the chefs here conjure up the best cuisine this side of Montréal. Issuing stamps is another key industry, and the products of these islands are highly regarded by philatelists around the world. Visit the post office in the center of town and see its impressive collection of stamps. Free.

The islands have a colorful history, not least during Prohibition, when Al Capone dropped by. Visit the local museum in the center of town. Open year-round. Admission charge. Every July 14 Bastille Day is celebrated with the same joyous passion as in France. This is a grand time for parades, sporting events, fireworks, dancing, eating, and drinking. Another popular celebration is the Basque Festival in August. For more information, contact the Saint-Pierre and Miguelon Tourism Office, (508) 41–22–22.

St. John's

The Trans-Canada, Highway 1 leads into **St. John's** on the Avalon Peninsula, the largest city in the province and its capital. St. John's is the easternmost city of North America and one of the oldest inhabited ports of the continent. The French and the English struggled over it for close to four centuries. The English were victorious, and St. John's and the rest of Newfoundland came under their control in 1762, where they stayed until the province joined Canadian Confederation in the 1940s.

McCarthy's Party Tours and Convention Services offers local city and Marine Drive tours, (709) 781–2244. Cruises from St. John's harbor to Cape Spear, the most easterly point in North America, operate mid-June to mid-September. During this two-hour sail, you may see blue and humpback whales. For information and rates, call J & B Schooner Tours, (709) 753–7245.

Attractions

Signal Hill National Historic Park, on high cliffs, offers some of the best views of the harbor, the city, and the sea. Here is where the last military engagement between the French and the English for the possession of the Atlantic coast took place. The remains of old gun emplacements and fortifications are still evident in the terrain at the Queen's Battery. At Cabot Tower, Guglielmo Marconi received the first transatlantic wireless signal on December 12, 1901. Signal Hill and its tower were the last landmarks for Charles Lindbergh before he crossed the ocean on his historic transatlantic flight. Nearby is Gibbet Hill, where criminals were hanged. The park's visitor center has exhibits on the history of the city and the province. Open throughout the year. Free. The Interpretation Center is open mid-June through Labour Day. Admission charge.

Newfoundland Museum, on Duckworth Street, houses artifacts made by the Beothuks (the original inhabitants of Newfoundland), the Inuit, and the Innu. The museum also documents the regional lifestyles of Newfoundland's pioneers. Other attractions include exhibits highlighting the province's heritage, traveling exhibitions from other parts of Canada, and displays explaining the province's maritime and military past. (St. John's was a major port for North Atlantic convoys during World War II.) Open throughout the year. Admission charge.

Confederation Building, Prince Philip Drive, is the seat of government for the province. Open throughout the year. Free.

Colonial Building, on Military Road, the former seat of government (circa 1850), now serves as the provincial archives and is open to the public. Free.

Government House, on Bannerman Road, a handsome mansion, is the residence of the lieutenant-governor, a native New-foundlander appointed by Queen Elizabeth. Not open to the public, but you may stroll the grounds.

Anglican Cathedral, on Church Hill, is a fine example of ecclesiastical architecture, with a Gothic nave and beautiful stained-glass windows. A small museum tells the story of the various fires the city has suffered. The cathedral also has a tearoom. Tours are available; call (709) 726–5677.

Basilica of Saint John the Baptist, on Military Road, with its familiar towers, dominates the city from its hillside. The interior is very ornate but uplifting. Fishermen from Portugal's White Fleet (no longer in existence) gave the statue of Our Lady of Fatima in appreciation for many years of friendship. A convent and Catholic school buildings are clustered around the basilica.

Saint Thomas Church, on Military Road, dating back to 1836, is a venerable place of worship and was used by the British military.

Commissariat House, on Kings Bridge Road, is an exceptional Georgian-style structure, furnished with period English china, silver, paintings, and Brussels carpets. A major restoration was made possible by the provincial government and the Newfoundland Historical Society. Open throughout the summer. Admission charge.

War Memorial, on Water Street, commemorating Newfoundlanders who gave their lives in the two World Wars and in Korea, is said to be on the spot where Sir Humphrey Gilbert, in 1583, declared Newfoundland a possession of Queen Elizabeth I.

Quidi Vidi Lake and Battery, at Quidi Vidi Village, within St. John's City, via Forest Road, is a provincial historic site overlooking a charming fishing village. Open mid-June to mid-September. Admission charge. At nearby Quidi Vidi Lake, the St. John's Regatta is held every August. The lake and surrounding walking trail are open year-round. Free.

Arts and Culture Centre, at the corner of Allandale Road and Prince Philip Drive, is a modern facility featuring contemporary Canadian painting, sculpture, and crafts. The complex contains a library and a theater, where major dramatic and musical productions are presented. For schedule and ticket information, call (709) 729–3904. Nearby is the campus of Memorial University.

Bowring Park, on Waterford Bridge Road, is the city's most popular place for a stroll and for the kids to let off steam. It has many beautiful statues, including the *Fighting Newfoundlander.*

Memorial University Botanical Garden at Oxen Pond, via Mount Scio Road at Pippy Park, features acres of forest, bog and

Many Newfoundland fishing outports (villages) are built so close to the edge of the sea that homes and work sheds stand on stilts above the high-tide mark. Cod is the prime catch, and it is amazing how many delicious dishes Newfoundlanders can make out of this fish, using even the cod's cheeks and tongue.

fen, heathland, alder thicket, and wild gardens. Open from May to end of November. Admission charge.

Accommodations

Delta St. John's Hotel and Conference Centre, 120 New Gower Street, (709) 739–6404, is the city's best, offering excellent accommodations and dining, a lounge, swimming pool, and fitness center. Expensive.

The Battery Hotel and Suites, Signal Hill Road, (709) 576–0040, offers comfortable rooms in a good location, a dining room, and a lounge. Moderate.

Airport Plaza Hotel, Airport Road, (709) 753–3500, features a beauty salon, dining room, and lounge. Moderate to expensive.

Hotel Newfoundland, Cavendish Square, (709) 726–4980, is the grande dame of city hotels, offering good accommodations and dining and an excellent downtown location. Expensive.

The Guv'nor Inn, 389 Elizabeth Avenue, (709) 726–0092, is a comfortable motel with a dining room that serves pub fare. Lodging moderate, dining room inexpensive.

Holiday Inn St. John's, 180 Portugal Cove Road, (709) 722–0506, has a restaurant and lounge with live entertainment and a swimming pool. Expensive.

Dining

The Stone House Restaurant, 8 Kenna's Hill, (709) 753–2425, is one of the province's best, serving well-prepared seafood and wild game dishes, often quite exotic, in an elegant setting. Expensive.

The Cabot Club, at the Hotel Newfoundland, (709) 726–4980, serves fine food in a congenial room overlooking the harbor. Expensive.

The Cellar Restaurant, Baird's Cove (off Water Street), (709) 579–8900. Fresh pasta, homemade bread, and seafood. Moderate.

Margaritz, 188 Duckworth Street, (709) 726–3885, serves Cajun cuisine. Moderate.

Earhart's Restaurant & Lounge, 106 Airport Road, (709) 753-3500. Buffets are a specialty of this eatery in the Airport Plaza Hotel. Moderate.

Woodstock Colonial Restaurant, on Highway 60, (709) 579-5910, expertly prepares traditional Newfoundland dishes, such as seal flipper pie. Moderate to expensive.

St. John's has several pubs, such as Erins on Water Street for Irish music, in which to relax and enjoy some Newfoundland style. The highest concentration of lively pubs is on George Street.

Your best shopping buys are Newfoundland handicrafts: colorful hooked mats made by outport women, pine furniture, pottery, Labradorite jewelry, hand-knit woolens, Inuit soapstone carvings, Grenfell parkas, painted tiles, crochet work, silk batik, Torbay knitting, and fishermen's mitts. In downtown St. John's visit the Salt Box, Duckworth Street; Livyers, Duckworth Street; the Newfoundland Weavery, Duckworth Street; Nonia, Water Street; and the Cod Jigger, Duckworth Street.

There are crafts cooperatives or shops in most towns and villages throughout the island. For unusual value, be on the lookout for handicrafts being sold at the artisan's own home.

A short but memorable side trip from St. John's is to **Cape Spear National Historic Site**, via Highway 11. Cape Spear is the easternmost spit of land on this continent, a desolate but beautiful place that has been hammered for eons by weather and the sea. A lighthouse and gun emplacements nearby protected Allied military bases on the island during World War II. Stand on the cliffs of Cape Spear. Just the Atlantic separates you from Europe; the entire North American continent lies behind you.

The Avalon Peninsula

From St. John's you can easily tour the Avalon Peninsula. Start with Highway 20 to Torbay, where the English forces, under General Amherst, landed to recapture St. John's from the French. Pouch Cove is a pretty fishing village leading to **Cape St. Francis,** a dramatic headland. Marine Drive leads back to St. John's and goes along a wild coastline through a number of traditional fishing villages.

Highway 1, the Trans-Canada, heading west from St. John's, meets Highway 100, which leads to the west coast of the Avalon Peninsula and the towns of **Argentia** and **Placentia.** Placentia Bay is where Churchill and Roosevelt signed the Atlantic Charter in 1941. Visit Castle Hill National Historic Park to see the seventeenth- and eighteenth-century French and English fortifications. There is ferry service to and from Argentia from North Sydney, Nova Scotia, in the summer (contact Marine Atlantic for details; see page 332).

From St. John's you can also take the Trans-Canada west to Highway 60. In **Topsail** you will have an excellent view of Conception Bay and its islands. The famous American artist Rockwell Kent once lived in **Brigus,** as did Captain Bob Bartlett, who accompanied Commodore Perry on his 1909 Arctic expedition. Even more compelling than its history is its scenic harbor, enclosed in rock. Wander its streets and you'll notice that it looks more like a New England town than a Newfoundland one; that's because it was settled by New Englanders. **Cupids** is where John Guy attempted his ill-fated Sea Forest Plantation in 1610.

Port de Grave Peninsula, via Highway 72, has some of the best coastal scenery and picturesque fishing villages in the province. **Hibb's Cove** has the Fishermen's Museum. **Harbour Grace** was visited by pirate Peter Easton in the seventeenth century. Here are Saint Paul's Anglican Church, the oldest stone church in Newfoundland, and the oldest jail built in Canada. In 1932 Amelia Earhart left Harbour Grace to fly solo over the Atlantic, the first woman to do so. Ask at the information kiosk south of town and they'll give you directions to the lonely airstrip on the hillside above. In **Heart's Content** the first successful transatlantic cable was landed in 1866. Visit the Communications Museum, depicting the role of this community in the development of modern communications. Open throughout the summer. Free.

Another tour from St. John's follows the southern shore, Highway 10, to **Petty Harbour, Bay Bulls,** and **Witless Bay.** During the summer, take a boat tour to view bird colonies (gannets, puffins, kittiwakes, razorbills) on coastal islands. There is a beautiful waterfall at **La Manche Provincial Park,** a delightful setting for picnics and camping. Sir David Kirke ruled Newfoundland from **Ferryland** in the seventeenth century. Sir George Calvert was a Ferryland resident too. An old lighthouse and high cliffs mark this ambitious settlement, which failed because of the cold winters. Visit the fascinating Colony of Avalon Archaeology Dig, where you can watch as artifacts are unearthed, then visit the labs where they are cleaned and identified. A good stopping place here is the warm and hospitable Downs Inn, (709) 432–2808 or toll-free (877) 432–2808, with good breakfasts and a pleasant tearoom overlooking the little harbor. In **Renews,** Roman Catholics secretly celebrated the Mass at a time when it was prohibited by the Protestant rulers of the colony. A grotto commemorates the place where these early settlers kept their faith alive.

Trepassey was another starting point for early transatlantic flights. In 1928 Amelia Earhart flew from here to Southampton, England, as a passenger. Trepassey is now the site of a tower that serves as a long-distance navigational aid for aircraft and ships. Willow ptarmigan is a popular game bird for hunters in this area, and salmon-fishing expeditions go out from Trepassey. West of Trepassey, on the way to **Cape Pine,** you may see caribou grazing in the moss along the roadsides.

CHAPTER 14

Prince Edward Island

Crossing the Northumberland Strait on the new Confederation Bridge isn't as romantic or as scenic as the ferry ride that it replaced, but it seems to cut that psychological tie to the problems and cares on the mainland just as well. Visitors to Prince Edward Island (P.E.I., as it is affectionately and familiarly called) feel a sense of peace and renewal almost as soon as they set foot on its luxurious red shore. Of all the Atlantic Canada provinces, P.E.I. is the most manicured, almost as if an expert English gardener carefully tended its landscape every day. Nearly every town and village seems clipped from a romantic postcard, and even Charlottetown, the province's capital city, is small, intimate, and pretty. P.E.I. is an island gem set off Canada's east coast in the Gulf of Saint Lawrence.

History

Perhaps the most temperate, comfortable, and fertile area in eastern Canada was among the last to be settled. Although Jacques Cartier found it in 1534, he was too intent on the Northwest Passage to stop. Champlain stopped long enough to claim it for France on his way to Montréal in 1603, but didn't leave settlers. The native Mi'kmaq peoples, who came here for hunting and fishing during the summer, had another relatively good century or so. It wasn't until 1720 that the French got around to settling the island, when the Count de St. Pierre and 300 followers established a

Prince Edward Island

Gulf of St. Lawrence

Prince Edward Island National Park

Northumberland Strait

Souris

Georgetown

Murray River

Wood Islands

Montague

Charlottetown

Kensington

Summerside

Borden

Tignish

Alberton

O'Leary

N

fort at Port la Joye, near the entrance to Charlottetown Harbor. Some Acadian French then settled on the southwest coast, but European presence was still light on the land.

About the time of the British victory at Fortress Louisbourg in 1758, the British attacked and captured Port la Joye, establishing their own fort and renaming it Fort Amherst. As in Nova Scotia, they expelled more than 3,500 Acadians, many of whom returned after peace was established in the 1760s.

Aside from this one violent event, the history of the province has been as pacific as its bucolic landscapes. When first annexed as a part of Nova Scotia, it was called the Island of Saint John, but the name was soon changed to Prince Edward's Island in honor of Prince Edward, Duke of Kent. He was Commander in Chief of British Forces in America from 1799 to 1802, and the father of Queen Victoria.

Anxious to secure their presence, the British authorities offered enticements to Scots and Irish, who were eager to escape the bad economic and political situations in their homelands. The lands themselves, however, were granted to absentee British lords to whom settlers had to pay annual land rentals.

Timbering was among the early industries, followed by the usual coastal business of shipbuilding. Both were successful, but as land was cleared, settlers found that the soil could produce fine harvests. Prince Edward Island became a maritime market basket, exporting produce to the other provinces and to New England.

The province prospered and in 1767 became a separate colony, the Province of Prince Edward Island. One hundred years later, in 1867, its capital was the meeting place for discussions on the confederation of Canadian provinces. Until then they were a group of separate and unrelated British colonies.

The delegates to the convention, known to Canadians as the Fathers of Confederation, agreed on general principles and later the same year formed the Dominion of Canada. But the island did not join immediately. It was not until 1873 that Prince Edward Island, after extracting a promise from the Confederation that a continuous connection with the mainland would be maintained, joined the Confederation.

For more than a century, that mainland connection was by two ferries that ran year-round from Cape Tormentine, New Brunswick, and from Caribou, Nova Scotia. An 8-mile-long road connection has now opened via a bridge from Cape Tormentine.

Only two years after confederation, in 1875, the provincial government conducted one of the most successful land reform programs of history by buying the land titles of the absentee British landholders and conveying it to the citizens of the province who were farming it. During the late nineteenth and early twentieth centuries, the area around Summerside became the silver fox capital of the world, famed for the furs raised there. The shipbuilding, timber, and silver fox industries have long since failed, but farming is still a major industry on the island.

Despite P.E.I.'s beautiful beaches and warm swimming waters, it was a fictional character that put it firmly on the world tourism map. Anne of Green Gables, whose adventures were chronicled by Lucy Maud Montgomery, introduced the island and its way of life via books, movies, stage plays, and television. The popularity of a TV show in Japan based on the novels has made the island a mecca for Japanese tourists. This explains why you will see tourist signs in Japanese.

But tourism on the island has always gone beyond this appealing little redhead. The coastline is a beautiful mix of long beaches, red sea bluffs, and sandstone cliffs. The Confederation Trail stretches across the entire island, especially popular with cyclists.

The Landscape

Prince Edward Island, the smallest province at 140 miles long, sits in the Gulf of Saint Lawrence just a few miles north of Nova Scotia and New Brunswick. It is a gentle land of rolling fields and deep red soil, created from the red sandstone that underlies it. In June and early July its roadsides are almost solid blue with lupine, one of the finest floral displays in Canada.

The only major city is the capital, Charlottetown. Across the rest of the island are scattered small towns and villages, often just a few homes where two roads cross in the midst of a sea of fields. If you never thought simple farmland beautiful, take a look at Prince Edward Island's, where each tidy field is a different shade of green or gold, bordered by dark green trees, the red sand, and the deep blue sea.

How to Get to Prince Edward Island

By Car and Ship

The Confederation Bridge now links P.E.I. with the mainland. Reached from the intersection of the Trans-Canada Highway and

Route 955, it stretches from Cape Tormentine in New Brunswick to Borden-Carleton on Prince Edward Island, where the ferries used to dock. Nine miles long, the soaring concrete span, which takes twelve minutes to cross, is quite a feat of engineering. A speed limit of 80 kph (sometimes less if there are high winds) is strictly enforced and the bridge is open twenty-four hours a day. Toll charge.

From Nova Scotia the Trans-Canada takes you to the ferry at Caribou, which sails to Wood Islands, P.E.I., from May to December. There is frequent service from both terminals. The crossing time is seventy-five minutes, and there is a cafeteria on board.

By Air

Air Canada provides connecting service to the Charlottetown airport from major Canadian and U.S. cities. Prince Edward Air also runs services from Moncton, New Brunswick, and Halifax, Nova Scotia.

Rental cars (Tilden, Avis, Budget, and Hertz) are available at the airport, in Charlottetown, and in Summerside. There is taxi service from the airport to Charlottetown.

By Bus and Rail

VIA Rail has bus service to and from P.E.I. VIA Rail buses connect with passenger trains in Amherst, Nova Scotia, and in Moncton, New Brunswick.

General Information

Time zone: Atlantic
Telephone area code: 902
Police and Medical emergencies: dial 911

Climate and Clothing

Prince Edward Island's summer weather is usually perfect for outdoor activities. The natural air-conditioning of sea breezes usually discourages fog and humidity. The winters here are cold, but usually without much snow. Because of the lack of heavy manufacturing or mining, there is little air pollution.

Casual and sporting clothes are appropriate for P.E.I. Business suits and cocktail dresses are appropriate in better restaurants and for the theater, but there is very little fuss over dress codes. You should bring some warm jackets and sweaters for cool days and for evenings.

Inexpensive farm vacations are a holiday treat for city folk on Prince Edward Island.

Tourist Information

Information can be obtained by calling the P.E.I. Visitor Information Service toll-free from anywhere in North America at (800) 463–4734. Reservations may be made by calling (800) 265–6161. Write to Tourism P.E.I, P.O. Box 940, Charlottetown, P.E.I. C1A 7M5. The excellent Web site is www.peiplay.com

For your convenience, the province has tourist information centers at Caribou, Nova Scotia, as well as on P.E.I. at Borden, Brackley Beach, Cavendish, Charlottetown, Pooles Corner, Portage, Souris, Wilmot, and Wood Islands.

Major Events

P.E.I. has many activities and special events throughout the summer. These include country or harvest fairs, special exhibitions of art and handicrafts, concerts, theater, yacht races, and top entertainment from the mainland. There's also harness racing at the Charlottetown Driving Park and at the Summerside Raceway.

June

Summerside Highland Gathering, Summerside
Charlottetown Festival, Charlottetown, June to September

July

Summerside Lobster Carnival, Summerside
Summer Festival, Orwell Corner
National Beach Week, North Shore
Souris Regatta, Souris
Potato Blossom Festival, O'Leary
Charlottetown Race Week, Charlottetown
Rollo Bay Fiddle Festival, Rollo Bay
Canada Day Celebrations, Charlottetown and Orwell

August

Oyster Festival, Tyne Valley
Highland Games and Gathering of the Clans, Eldon
Old Home Week, Charlottetown

Gold Cup Parade, Charlottetown
Festival of the Fathers, Charlottetown
Lucy Maud Montgomery Festival, Cavendish
Harvest Festival, Kensington
Hydroplane Regatta, Georgetown
Annual Green Park Blueberry Social, Port Hill
National Milton Acorn Festival (events around the province)

September
Festival of the Fathers, Charlottetown
Prince Edward Island Festival of the Arts (events around the province)
Festival Acadien and Agricultural Exhibition, Abrams Village
P.E.I. Shellfish Festival

Sports

Hunting and Fishing
While hunting is primarily restricted to shooting birds and small game (goose, black duck, grouse, partridge, and snowshoe hare), fishing (salmon, rainbow trout, and eastern brook trout) is a major sport on the island. Ponds, lakes, rivers, estuaries, and streams offering good opportunities are all over the island. Licenses are required for freshwater fishing and hunting.

Deep-sea fishing for cod, halibut, hake, mackerel, and herring is popular with many visitors. Boats leave from North Rustico Harbor and other north shore towns.

Golf
P.E.I. has some of the most beautiful and challenging courses in Atlantic Canada. Try any of these eighteen-hole, par seventy-two courses:
Belvedere Golf and Winter Club, Charlottetown, (902) 892–7838
Brudenell River Provincial Golf Course, Roseneath, (902) 652–2342
Glen Afton Golf Course, Nine Mile Creek, (902) 675–3000
Green Gables Golf Course, Cavendish, (902) 963–2488
The Links at Crowbush Cove, Lakeside, (902) 961–3100
Mill River Provincial Golf Course, Mill River, (902) 859–3555
Rustico Resort, Rustico, (902) 963–2357
Stanhope Golf and Country Club, Stanhope, (902) 672–2842
Summerside Golf Club, Summerside, (902) 436–2505

Provincial Parks and Campgrounds

Jacques Cartier Park, off Highway 12, near Alberton
Mill River Park, on Highway 162, near O'Leary
Cedar Dunes Park, on Highway 14, near O'Leary
Green Park, on Highway 12, near Tyne Valley
Linkletter Park, on Highway 11, near Summerside
Cabot Beach, on Highway 20, near Kensington
Strathgartney Park, on the Trans-Canada, near Charlottetown
Lord Selkirk Park, off the Trans-Canada, near Eldon
Brudenell River Park, on Highway 3, near Georgetown
Northumberland Park, on Highway 4, near Wood Islands
Campbell's Cove Park, on Highway 16, near Elmira
Red Point Park, on Highway 16, near Souris
Panmure Island, Highway 347, north of Gaspéreaux
In P.E.I. National Park:
Cavendish Campground, on Gulf Shore Road
Rustico Island Campground, on Gulf Shore Road
Stanhope Campground, on Gulf Shore Road

Most government campgrounds provide basic services (water, firewood, tables, toilets, and fireplaces). Some have more extensive services, such as electrical hookups, showers, sewage disposal, and organized activities. They are all situated near woodlands, fishing streams, or saltwater beaches. Some, such as Brudenell River Park, have superior golf courses. Most provincial parks are open from June to Labour Day, and fees are nominal. For more information on these and privately owned campgrounds, contact P.E.I. Visitor Services.

Accommodations

The demand for lodging, especially in the Cavendish area, is heavy during the summer, and reservations are advised.

P.E.I. was one of the originators of the inexpensive farm vacation, where you and your family can share in the daily life of a farm family and their community. The food is wholesome, ample, and well prepared, the accommodations clean, comfortable, and homelike. Discover the true essence of this special island, at a very reasonable price. For more information, call P.E.I. Visitor Services, (800) 463–4734.

Prince Edward Island is home to some of the best harness racing in Eastern Canada. Islanders are proud of their horses, and the results of years of training and driving skills show up in every race.

Dining

To join in a local custom of very long standing, dine at a church or community supper. Here's a chance to fill up on good homemade food without spending a great deal of money. You can have hot or cold lobster (the specialty of the island), ham and beef plates, potato salad, cole slaw—and all the fresh-baked pies, breads, and cakes you can handle.

P.E.I. is famous for its vegetables, oysters, mussels, and lobsters. Islanders are masters in the preparation of chowders. P.E.I. has a number of fine restaurants, including one of the finest in Atlantic Canada, Seasons in Thyme in Summerside. Be sure to check the dining room at your hotel or motel: Many innkeepers pride themselves on their delicious fare.

The following is a listing of popular lobster suppers available around the island throughout the summer season:

Bonnie Brae "All You Can Eat" Lobster Suppers, Cornwall

Fisherman's Wharf Lobster Suppers, North Rustico

New Glasgow Lobster Suppers, New Glasgow

New London Seafood Restaurant, New London

Saint Ann's Church Suppers, Hunter River (probably the most famous of them all)

Liquor is sold by the bottle in government store outlets located in major population centers, open Monday through Saturday. Licensed restaurants and lounges sell liquor by the glass. The legal drinking age in P.E.I. is nineteen.

Touring Prince Edward Island

P.E.I. is small enough that you are never far from warm-water beaches. Charlottetown, on the southern shore of Prince Edward Island, is convenient to all areas of the island. The Trans-Canada Highway 1, the province's main highway, extends from Borden through Charlottetown to Wood Islands. P.E.I. tourism material is organized into three scenic drives: the Kings Byway through King

County, the Blue Heron through Queens County, and the Lady Slipper through Prince County. These drives are further subdivided into six scenic "themed" day trips, sure to keep the family busy and entertained: North by North-West (nature and unusual museums), Ship to Shore (history, culture, and sporting events), Anne's Land (family-oriented activities), Charlotte's Shore (live theater and shopping), Bays and Dunes (quiet walks and beaches), and Hills and Harbours (crafts and fishing villages). Pick up a free copy of the official P.E.I. tour guide at any visitor information center. This publication highlights area attractions, history, and special events. Take time to picnic, swim, hike, and make the effort to get to know the people.

A word of warning: During wet weather, be careful driving on unpaved roads—the red-clay surface gets soft and slippery.

Charlottetown

One of your first destinations will be the island's lovely capital and only city, Charlottetown. This community followed an earlier French settlement known as Port La Joye, across the harbor. After coming under British control in 1763, it was named Amherst. The present location of the island's capital was named in honor of Queen Charlotte, consort to King George III. In 1864 the Fathers of Canadian Confederation met in Province House to formulate the union of the provinces of British North America.

Charlottetown is more like a medium-size town than a city, where you can walk to most places of interest. If you prefer to ride, Abegweit Tours, (902) 894–9966, uses an authentic London double-decker bus for comprehensive tours of Charlottetown and limousine service for the north and south shores. Free one-hour guided walking tours of Old Charlotte Town leave City Hall beginning at 10:00 A.M. Call (902) 629–1864 for more information. Bike rentals are available at MacQueen's Bike Shop at 430 Queen Street, (902) 368–2453.

The most important attraction in the city is the Charlottetown Festival, a series of outstanding theatrical events held at the main stage of the **Confederation Centre of the Arts,** at the corner of Queen and Grafton Streets, during the summer. The most popular show in the festival is *Anne of Green Gables,* a wonderful musical comedy about a red-haired misfit orphan girl who unexpectedly arrives in a small P.E.I. town and turns it head over heels. Millions of people throughout the world have read the story of Anne or seen her on television, and now you have a chance to see Anne on stage. This is delightful entertainment for all ages, with a highly professional cast, orchestra, and settings. *Anne* is the mainstay of the festival, but each year it alternates during the week with new, original productions. The MacKenzie theater, opposite the Confederation Centre, puts on smaller scale productions that are equally entertaining. The theater is fully licensed (drinks are served). These festival productions play to packed houses, so it's important to have reservations; call (902) 566–1267.

In addition to its handsome main theater, the Confederation Centre, a complex of five buildings, has an impressive art gallery and museum, featuring paintings by Robert Harris (a famous island artist) and contemporary Canadian painting and crafts; a restaurant and gift shop; the Provincial Library and Archives; and Memorial Hall. Open throughout the year. Free.

Province House National Historic Site, next to the Confederation Centre, contains the restored Confederation Chamber, where the Fathers of Confederation started the country on its way to self-government. Confederation Chamber is open for public viewing. Province House continues to serve as the seat of P.E.I.'s government. Open throughout the year. Free.

Beaconsfield Historic House, a shipowner's elegant mansion built in 1877, is now the headquarters of the P.E.I. Heritage Foundation. Surrounded by landscaped gardens, it houses historical displays, a bookstore, and a gallery. The handsome house, which overlooks the harbor, was once one of Charlottetown's poshest residences. Owned by James Peake, it was designed by island architect W. C. Harris. Two Kent Street, Charlottetown, P.E.I. C1A 1M6, (902) 368–6608. Open year-round. Admission charge. At this writing, Beaconsfield is under restoration, so it is a good idea to check for current opening information.

Government House (circa 1835), on Pond Road, near Victoria Park, is the official residence of the province's lieutenant-governor, the queen's representative. The house itself is not open to the public, but visitors can wander around the gardens. Open daily from 9:00 A.M. to 5:00 P.M., from 9:00 A.M. to 8:00 P.M. in July and August.

Victoria Park, overlooking the harbor, is a fine place for a walk, offering forty acres of lawns, wooded groves, and playing fields.

Saint Dunstan's Basilica, on Great George Street, the seat of the Roman Catholic diocese, has a marvelously ornate interior.

Saint Paul's Anglican Church (established 1747), 203 Richmond Street, is P.E.I.'s oldest Protestant church.

Saint Peter's Anglican Church, Rochford Square, has murals by famed island artist Robert Harris.

Saint James Kirk (Presbyterian), 35 Fitzroy Street, has relics from Iona, Scotland, and beautiful stained-glass windows.

Peake's Wharf has restored the historic wood and brick buildings along the waterfront and converted them into offices, shops, and restaurants. This is a pleasant place to stroll; harbor cruises dock here.

Harness races are held every Monday, Thursday, and Saturday evening during the summer at the **Charlottetown Driving Park.**

Accommodations include the following:

Dundee Arms Motel, 200 Pownal Street, (902) 892–2496, is an inn, furnished in antiques, whose dining room has been featured in *Gourmet* magazine. Moderate to expensive.

Quality Inn on the Hill, 150 Euston Street, (902) 894–8572. Expensive.

Fairholm National Historic Inn, 230 Prince Street, (902) 892–5060 or (888) 573–5022, www.fairholm.pe.ca, is an elegantly restored mansion close to the waterfront. Breakfasts are excellent. Expensive.

Hillhurst Inn, 181 Fitzroy Street, (902) 894–8004. This heritage home (it belonged to a prominent Charlottetown merchant) is a handsome eight-room hostelry furnished with antiques. Expensive.

The Inns on Great George, 58 Great George Street, (902) 892–0606. This block of historic buildings near St. Dunstan's cathedral has been renovated and turned into an elegant twenty-four-room inn. Some self-catering apartments with fully-equipped kitchens. Moderate to expensive.

Best Western Charlottetown, 238 Grafton Street, (902) 892–2461, has quality rooms and suites, a sauna, hot tub, and a family restaurant. Moderate to expensive.

Rodd Royalty Inn, on the Trans-Canada, west of the city, (902) 894–8566, has excellent accommodations in a new section, a tropical swimming pool, restaurant, and lounge. Moderate to expensive.

Delta Prince Edward Hotel, 18 Queen Street, (902) 566–2222, is the best large hotel on the island, offering all deluxe hotel amenities, including indoor swimming pool, fitness facility, and sauna. Its Lord Selkirk dining room is elegant, with good food and service. There are also facilities for meetings and conventions. Expensive.

Duchess of Kent Inn, 218 Kent Street, (902) 566–5826. An 1875 Heritage inn. Private baths. Moderate to expensive.

Holiday Inn Express Hotel, on the Trans-Canada, northwest of the city center, (902) 892–1201, offers a heated pool, dining room, and lounge. Moderate.

Rodd Confederation Inn, on the Trans-Canada in West Royalty, (902) 892–2481. Moderate to expensive.

For dining, the following places are recommended:

Anchor & Oar House, Peake's Wharf Boardwalk, (902) 566–2222. This eatery, which overlooks the harbor, serves fresh barbecued island seafood and terrific hamburgers. Inexpensive.

Lord Selkirk Dining Room at Prince Edward Hotel, 18 Queen Street, (902) 566–2222, serves gourmet fare in an elegant environment. Expensive.

Papa Joe's, 345 University Avenue, (902) 566–5070. This family-run restaurant is situated in an unprepossessing shopping mall but the food is fresh and good. Daily specials. Moderate.

The Merchantman Pub, Corner of Queen and Water Streets, (902) 892–9150. Pub fare with an exotic touch—Louisiana stir-fry, Thai peanut chicken, Cajun salmon, and the like. Local draft beer on tap. Moderate.

Lobster-on-the-Wharf, Prince Street Wharf, (902) 368–2888. Fresh seafood, water view. Moderate to expensive.

The Inn, 150 Euston Street, (902) 894–8572, daily specials, hip of beef buffet, and homemade desserts. Moderate.

Peakes Quay Restaurant and Lounge, Great George Street, (902) 368–1330. Seafood, steaks, gourmet; waterfront view. Live entertainment on weekends. Moderate to expensive.

Ye Olde Dublin Pub, 131 Sydney Street, (902) 892–6992. Your name does not have to be Murphy to enjoy the pub food and rollicking entertainment served in this historic building. Inexpensive to moderate.

Sirenella, 83 Water Street, (902) 628–2271, serves a good selection of Italian fare—pasta, veal, and chicken. Patio dining. Moderate.

The Dundee Arms Inn, 200 Pownal Street, (902) 892–2496. Its highly regarded dining room has a colonial ambience, and specialties include Malpeque oysters and fresh seafood. Expensive.

Claddagh Room, 131 Sydney Street, (902) 892–9661, is an excellent seafood restaurant. Moderate to expensive.

Shop in Charlottetown at Peake's Wharf, Oak Tree Place, University Avenue, north of the city center, or Charlottetown Mall, on the Trans-Canada, north of the city center. Confederation Court Mall is located on Grafton Street, across from the Confederation Centre of the Arts. At West Royalty Industrial Park is Great Northern Knitters, offering various goods at factory-outlet prices. The downtown area has many interesting little shops selling English china, woolen goods, antiques, and P.E.I. handicrafts.

The Kings Byway Drive

By taking the Trans-Canada Highway 1 east and crossing the Hillsborough Bridge, you enter the scenic Kings Byway Drive in the tourism region known as Hills and Harbors. The area is well named.

From the top of Tea Hill, you'll have a splendid view of Governor's Island and the Northumberland Strait. In this lush farm country, the strawberry is the king crop. Many farms allow you to pick your own baskets of the fruit. The strawberry season on P.E.I. is July.

At **Orwell** you can peek into the island's history. Orwell Corner Historic Village is a collection of restored buildings that conjures up a slice of P.E.I.'s past. The complex includes an 1864 farmhouse (it served as a post office, store, and dressmaker's shop), church, school, barns, a smithy, and a community hall. Ceilidhs (musical evenings) are held every Wednesday during the summer and fall. Admission charge.

A side trip via Highway 207 leads to **Belfast,** founded by Scottish Highlanders under the leadership of the earl of Selkirk. Saint John's Kirk, built in 1823, has a Christoper Wren–style tower and memorials to Selkirk's daughter.

Eldon, back on Highway 1, was also founded by Scots and now holds its annual Highland Games and Gathering of the Clans in early August. Stop and enjoy **Lord Selkirk Provincial Park,** with camping, clam digging, a swimming pool, mini-golf, and a beach.

Wood Islands is the location of ferry service to Caribou, Nova Scotia. Both P.E.I. and Nova Scotia have tourist information offices in the terminal area. The P.E.I. terminal has a gift shop, farmers' market, and seafood outlet, as well as a beach and other diversions while you wait your turn to board the ferry. The Meadow Lodge Motel, 2 miles (3 km) west of the terminal, (902) 962–2022, offers good accommodations in the Wood Islands area, moderate.

The P.E.I. portion of the Trans-Canada Highway ends at Wood Islands. The Kings Byway Drive continues via various highway numbers. Look for the signs bearing the royal crown.

A side trip via Highway 18A takes you to the Log Cabin Museum near **Murray Harbour.** It contains farm and household artifacts going back two centuries. Open July 1 to Labour Day. Admission charge. In nearby **Gladstone** is the Pioneer Cemetery, dating from 1854, and **King's Castle Provincial Park**. King's Castle has large statues of favorite storybook characters, live deer, a miniature log fort, and recreational equipment for the kids. Open late May to mid-September. Free.

The Old General Store and the Free Church of Scotland, built in 1867, are in **Murray River**. Seal and bird-watching expeditions go out from the town's wharf, and there is good canoeing here. Contact Captain Gary's at (902) 745–0014 or (800) 745–0014, or visit www.tamcotec.com/lezek/sealcruisespei.htm.

A long stretch of white sand beach with sweeping dunes graces **Murray Harbour North**. Take Highway 347 to **Panmure Island Provincial Park** for excellent red- and white-sand beaches and a look at the Panmure Head Lighthouse, one of the most photographed in the province.

Take a side trip via Highway 4 to Buffaloland Provincial Park, in **Milltown Cross**, home of a herd of bison and deer that roams freely over its hundred acres. Open throughout the year. Free. Also in Milltown Cross is Harvey Moore Wildlife Management Area, where you may bike or hike natural trails, fish for trout, and see Canada geese and other waterfowl. Open June to mid-September. Admission charge.

One of the province's oldest sandstone cottages is at **Lower Montague**, on Highway 4. At **Montague**, P.E.I.'s third largest town, is the Garden of the Gulf Museum, 6 Main Street, South, featuring artifacts of early pioneer life, an Indian stone collection, and a gun collection. Open late June to mid-September. Admission charge. You can find accommodations and seafood dining at Lobster Shanty Atlantic Resorts, on Highway 17, Main Street, (902) 838–2463, moderate. This town also has a number of curio and antiques shops in which to poke around. In nearby Little Sands, on Highway 4, is Bayberry Cliff Lodge B&B, (902) 962–3395. This comfortable, artist-designed accommodation is set on a high cliff overlooking the Northumberland Strait, moderate.

At **Pooles Corner**, at the junction of Highways 3 and 4, be sure to stop in the King's Byway Visitor Information Centre, which has many interesting displays relating to the past and present of King County and a staff to answer your questions. Open June to mid-October. Accommodations include The Whim Inn, at Highways 3 and 4, (902) 838–3838, moderate.

Brudenell River Provincial Park is one of the best recreational facilities on the island, with an eighteen-hole championship golf course, tennis courts, trail rides, boating, cycling, kayak rentals, a resort, a supervised beach and pool, and many special programs.

Good accommodations and dining are at Rodd Brudenell Resort, Highway 3, 3 miles (5 km) west of Georgetown, (902) 652–2332, moderate to expensive.

In **Georgetown**, reached via Highway 3, the town's many historic buildings create an old-world charm. You can buy fresh lobster at Seafood 2000 Limited. The King's Playhouse is located here, offering repertory theater from July through August, (902) 652–2053. De Roma Cottages, off Highway 3, (902) 652–2330, are comfortable accommodations, moderate.

There are reports of buried treasure at **Abells Cape**, via Highway 310, and a mystery. Charles Flocton, an American actor, bought the cape and wished to be buried there. But through circumstances beyond his control, Flocton was forced to accept San Francisco as his final resting place—that is, until several years after his death, when a casket engraved with the name of Charles Flocton washed up on the Abells Cape shore.

At **Dingwells Mills**, via Highway 2, is Johnny Belinda Pond, named after the character created by writer Elmer Harris. *Johnny Belinda*, the story of a young deaf and mute girl, was set in this area and ran for 320 consecutive performances on Broadway. Harris made his summer home, now the highly rated Inn at Bay Fortune at Fortune Bridge, on Route 310. Airy, bright rooms are well decorated, and the dining room is known for its innovative ways with fresh island produce and seafood. Open mid-May to mid-October, (902) 687–3540, winter number (860) 296–1348, www.innatbayfortune.com.

Farther along Highway 2, in **Rollo Bay**, the Saint Alexis Church has a bell dating from the old French regime, given to the parish in honor of the first white child born on the island. Rollo Bay puts on its annual Fiddler Festival in mid-July.

Souris ("mouse" in French) is the island's fourth largest town. Accommodations in the area include the Matthew House Inn, (902) 687–3461; Hilltop Motel, Main Street, (902) 687–3315, www.peisland.com/hilltopmotel; and Rollo Bay Inn, on Highway 2, 2 miles (4 km) west of Souris, (902) 687–3550. All are in the inexpensive to moderate price range. Matthew House Inn is open only from late June through early September, but is perfectly located for those taking the ferry to Magdalen Islands, right opposite the ferry dock.

Souris is a terminus for the passenger and car ferry service to the **Îles de la Madeleine (Magdalen Islands)**, which operates April 1 to the end of January, depending on weather and ice conditions. The crossing time is five hours. For sailing schedule and fares, call

(902) 687–2181. See Chapter 9 (page 181) for information on the islands.

In the **Kingsboro** area visit the Basin Head Fisheries Museum, with displays and photographs telling the story of fishing and lobstering in P.E.I. waters. Open late May to late September. Admission charge. A side trip to **Elmira,** via Highway 16A, brings you to the old Elmira Railway Station, a museum that depicts early railroading days on the island. Open late May to late September. Admission charge. Elmira is also the starting point of the Confederation Trail, a 140-mile (225 km) recreation path for cyclists and hikers. You can rent bicycles from mid-May through mid-October here or at the Sandpiper Bed and Breakfast, in nearby South Lake, (888) 357-2189.

East Point, via Highway 16, is the last community on this end of the island. From East Point Lighthouse you may be able to see the distant shore of Cape Breton Island on a clear day. Here the waters of the Gulf of Saint Lawrence and the Northumberland Strait converge. From this point the Kings Byway turns west and follows the shore of the Gulf of Saint Lawrence.

North Lake is considered by many sportsmen and -women the tuna-fishing capital of the world. You can charter fishing expeditions from North Lake Harbour from three different captains. Deep-sea fishing is on a "head boat" basis, at a flat fee per person, while tuna fishing requires a charter. For either, contact Bruce's, (902) 357-2638; Coffin's, (902) 357-2030; or MacNeil's, (902) 357-2454. If you'd rather just eat the fish, you can buy it at the wharf.

The town of **Saint Peters** could hardly ask for a prettier setting, gently rising on both sides of the long Saint Peters Bay. Stop for lunch and real espresso at the bright cafe called (with tongue in cheek) Anne of Red Doors, overlooking the bay. You can rent bikes here to travel one of the most scenic stretches of the Confederation Trail, which passes just below the cafe. Opposite, on the road to the new National Park, is the sparkling new Inn at Saint Peters, (902) 961-0135 or (800) 818-0925, www.inatstpeters.pe.ca. The inn has suites in beautiful cottages, each with its own view over the bay. The dining room is outstanding, worth visiting the area just to savor such an experience. Moderate to expensive.

The Highway 6 spur of the Kings Byway takes you to the **Prince Edward Island National Park,** (902) 963-2391, and its **Dalvay** to **Brackley** beaches, one of the the most popular saltwater bathing areas in Atlantic Canada. At the entrance to the park is Dalvay-by-the-Sea mansion, now a well-known resort, built in

1896 by Alexander MacDonald, once the president of Standard Oil. The Dalvay-by-the-Sea Hotel, (902) 672–2048, offers good accommodations and fine dining, plus tennis courts, lawn bowling, and beautiful grounds; expensive. There are many cottage accommodations and small restaurants in the communities along the national park and with easy access to the beaches. Among these is Stanhope-by-the-Sea, (902) 672–2047, moderate to expensive. There is a challenging golf course in **Stanhope.**

In **West Covehead,** on Highway 6, is Saint James United Church (circa 1837), a fine example of early colonial architecture.

After passing through **Parkdale** the Kings Byway ends where it started, in Charlottetown.

The Blue Heron Drive

The Blue Heron Drive also starts and finishes in Charlottetown. It loops around the midsection of the island, through Queens County. Follow Highway 15 from Charlottetown to Brackley Beach (if you have followed the Kings Byway to this area, continue along the coast on Highway 6 instead of going back to Charlottetown). For accommodations, try Shaw's Hotel and Cottages, on Highway 15, (902) 672–2022, moderate.

Take a side trip via Highway 25 to **Marshfield** to visit Jewell's Country Market. More than an emporium of local foods—farm-fresh fruits and preserves to local honey—the market has a restaurant, dairy bar, and a museum of old farming.

A side trip via Highway 243 leads to the Farmers' Bank in **South Rustico,** one of the first "people's banks" in Canada, chartered in 1864. Next to the bank is Saint Augustine's Church, built in 1838, and the old Belcourt Lodge, a former convent. Also in South Rustico is the Barachois Inn, (902) 963–2194, moderate to expensive. Grant's Trail Rides offers horseback treks in the area from mid-June to Labour Day.

In **North Rustico** and **Rusticoville** you have several deep-sea fishing options: Gauthier's, (902) 963–2295; Peter Gauthier's, (902) 963–2129; Aiden's, (902) 963–2442; and Bob's, (902) 963–2666. Accommodations include: North Rustico Motel Cottages & Inn, on Highway 6, (902) 963–2253, moderate; St. Lawrence Motel, on Gulf Shore Road, (800) 387–2053, moderate; Breakers by the Sea Cottages, on Highway 6 in Rusticoville, (902) 963–2555, moderate; Pines Hotel, on Highway 6 in Rusticoville, (902) 963–2029, moderate; Rustico Resort Golf & Country Club, on Highway 242, off Highway 6 in South Rustico, (902) 963–2357, moderate to expensive.

Cavendish has been immortalized by Lucy Maud Montgomery's popular *Anne of Green Gables* books. In the Cavendish area you can visit several "Anne" attractions, including a replica of the fictional Green Gables House, on Highway 6, where the best-known story is set. The site of Lucy Maud Montgomery's home is on Highway 6. Open June to October. Admission charge. Bilingual guides are provided.

Other family attractions in Cavendish include Royal Atlantic Wax Museum, at the junction of Highways 6 and 13, which displays life-size, costumed historical figures. Open late May to the end of September. Admission charge. Rainbow Valley Family Fun Park is an extensive recreational area featuring Anne of Green Gables Land, Children's Farm, boating lakes, and a gift shop. Open early June to mid-September. Admission charge. Cavendish also has an excellent eighteen-hole golf course adjacent to Green Gables. Newer made-for-tourist sites are the Enchanted Castle, housing fairyland scenes; King Tut's Tomb and Treasures; Sandspit, a miniracing car track and roller coasters; and Cranberry Village. Each of these is open from late June until after Labour Day and each charges admission. Great Northern Merchants and Cows, both of which are at the Cavendish Boardwalk, are great places to shop. The former is a factory outlet. Cows is a wildly popular ice-cream store that sells whimsical bovine souvenirs.

Accommodations include Cavendish Beach Cottages, in P.E.I. National Park, (902) 963–2025, moderate; Cavendish Lodge and Cottages, on Highway 6, (902) 963–2553, moderate; Cavendish Motel, at the junction of Highways 6 and 13, (902) 963–2244, moderate to expensive. Also Anne Shirley Motel and Cabins, at Highways 6 and 13, (902) 963–2224, moderate; Bay Vista Motor Inn on Highway 6, (902) 963–2225, moderate; Lakeview Lodge and Cottages, on Highway 6, (902) 963–2436, moderate; Parkview Farm Tourist Home and Cottages, on Highway 6, (902) 963–2027; Silverwood Motel, on Highway 6, (902) 963–2439, moderate; and White Eagle by the Sea, on Gulf Shore Road, (902) 963–2361, moderate to expensive.

Visit the P.E.I. Marine Aquarium in **Stanley Bridge,** via Highway 6. Apart from fish, exhibits include butterflies and more than 750 birds. Kids will enjoy it, along with the Great Island Adventure Park, a theme park with a full-size replica of the space shuttle *Columbia*. Both attractions are open mid-May to mid-September, and there are charges for admission.

New London is the birthplace of author Lucy Maud Montgomery, who wrote *Anne of Green Gables*. On display at her home are her wedding dress and personal scrapbooks. Open mid-May to mid-October. Admission charge. Stop in Memories Gift Shop, across from the author's birthplace. In Park Corner on Highway 20 is Anne of Green Gables Museum at Silver Bush, Lucy Maud Montgomery's home during her adult life. This museum has the largest collection of the author's personal possessions. Open June to October. Admission charge.

Take a side trip via Highway 23 to **Burlington** to see one of P.E.I.'s most unusual and appealing attractions, Woodleigh Replicas. Scaled-down versions of the Tower of London, Anne Hathaway's cottage, Dunvegan Castle, and a number of other English landmarks range from a few feet tall to large enough to walk through. Surrounding these are colorful gardens, complete with a real hedge maze. Open late May to mid-October. Admission charge. Nearby is Burlington Go-Karts. Open late May to September. Admission charge.

In **French River,** back on the Blue Heron Drive, via Highway 20, is the Yankee Hill Cemetery, containing the bodies of American sailors who drowned off the coast in the fierce gale of 1851. Anne's House of Dreams, based on the Montgomery books, depicts the home of Anne and Gilbert as newlyweds. Open early June to early October. Admission charge.

Malpeque Bay is famous for its oysters, which can be bought fresh here or in restaurants all over the island. Include a visit to the Malpeque Gardens, famous for their dahlias and roses. Open late June to mid-October. Admission charge. For great camping facilities, try Cabot Beach Provincial Park, (902) 836–8945.

Saint Mary's in **Indian River** is one of P.E.I.'s most beautiful rural churches, designed by William Harris. The handsome interior was also designed by Harris. Sunday concerts are held here.

The Blue Heron Drive now passes near the communities of Summerside (see The Lady Slipper Drive) and **Borden-Carleton,** jumping-off point for the Confederation Bridge. At the end of the bridge, an entire new community has sprung up, with attractive shops, dining, tourism information, and an excellent exhibition center. Whether you are just arriving, leaving, or passing through, the exhibits on island life, culture, and history here are worth a stop.

At **Cape Traverse,** via Highway 10, a national historic monument tells of the ice-boat service that connected the island to the mainland in the nineteenth and early twentieth centuries.

Victoria is one of P.E.I.'s most picturesque coastal villages. The Victoria Playhouse puts on various theatrical productions—

comedy, drama, romance—call (902) 658–2025. Also here is Island Chocolates, a small chocolate factory with a viewing area, (902) 658–2320, and several restaurants and cafes.

At **De Sable,** the House of International Dolls exhibits its extensive collection, including characters from Charles Dickens books. Open mid-June to Labour Day. Admission charge.

A side trip on the Trans-Canada from De Sable takes you to **Bonshaw** and its Car Life Museum. Open late May to Labour Day. Admission charge. The Bonshaw 500 is an exciting go-cart place for the kids. Open mid-May to late September. Admission charge. **New Haven** is the site of Fairyland Amusement Park, which features miniature golf, a fairy-tale forest, miniature train, and boating pond. Open mid-June to early September. Admission charge. Accommodations are available at Strathgartney Country Inn, on the Trans-Canada, (902) 675–4711. Inexpensive to moderate.

The Blue Heron Drive now leads to **Fort Amherst National Historic Park,** which stands on the site of Port La Joye, the first capital of the island. The Visitor Centre has an audiovisual presentation on the history of the fort and the surrounding area. There are the remains of eighteenth-century earthworks and an excellent view of Charlottetown. The park is a great place to picnic. Open June 1 to mid-October. Free. Nearby is the **Mi'kmaq Indian Village,** a re-creation of life on the island before the arrival of Europeans. A shop sells authentic First Nations crafts. Open June to October. Admission charge.

From Rocky Point, the Blue Heron Drive continues along the scenic coast, passing through **New Dominion, Cornwall,** and **West,** and concludes in Charlottetown.

The Lady Slipper Drive

The Lady Slipper Drive begins and ends in **Summerside,** the second largest community on the island. Its waterfront development area has shops, a marina, a theater (Jubilee), the Canadian College of Piping, and the Eptek National Exhibition Centre. Spinnakers Landing is a complex with nautical exhibits and activities, including displays of traditional boatbuilding, a lighthouse viewing tower, and a historic interpretive center recalling the age of sail. Open throughout the year. Free. Summerside is a charming coastal town with tree-lined streets and many historic buildings. The annual Summerside Lobster Carnival is an eight-day festival of games, entertainment, and good eating held in mid-July. Summerside Raceway has harness races on Wednesday nights during the summer.

Accommodations are available at the following places:

Cairns' Motel, 721 Water Street, (902) 436–5841, is centrally located. Moderate.

Linkletter Inn and Convention Centre, 311 Market Street, (902) 436–2157, serves buffets during the week. Moderate to expensive.

Loyalist Country Inn, 195 Harbour Drive, (902) 436–3333, is an upscale hostelry. Moderate to expensive.

Quality Inn—Garden of the Gulf, 618 Water Street, (902) 436–2295, offers a heated outdoor pool and other recreation. Expensive.

Sunny Isle Motel, 720 Water Street, (902) 436–5665, is centrally located. Inexpensive.

Silver Fox Inn, 61 Granville Street, (902) 436–4033, is a historic house. Moderate.

One of the most memorable dining experiences in all of the Atlantic provinces is in Summerside, at **Seasons in Thyme,** 644 Water Street East, (902) 888–DINE. This chef-owned restaurant is a class act, from the china and the professional service to the sparkling, innovative menu and artistic presentations. A place to savor, Seasons is a destination in itself for those who love fine food.

For informal dining, try **Brothers Two Restaurant,** on Water Street, next to Quality Inn, (902) 436–9654. Downstairs is a lively dinner theater. Performances run late June to September. Advance reservations are a must.

From Summerside the Lady Slipper Drive goes through **St. Eleanors,** a former Canadian Forces base and **Miscouche.** Situated at the junction of Highways 2 and 12, Miscouche has one of the most photographed churches on the island, Saint John the Baptist. The Acadian Museum of P.E.I., via Highway 2, displays its extensive collection of church, household, and agricultural artifacts, including many items of historical and genealogical interest. Open July 1 to September. Admission charge. In 1884 in Miscouche a national French Acadian congress selected the official Acadian flag (tricolor and yellow star) that now flies in many parts of the region.

The small and little-used provincial park at **Union Corner** has a warm-water beach and a picnic area on the bluff above. Within sight is the endearing Union Corner School House Museum, a labor of love for a local family and the community. Open mid-June to Labour Day. Admission charge.

The Église Notre Dame in **Mont Carmel** is noted for its beautiful twin spires and its lavish interior. Mont Carmel's Le Village-des-Pioneers-Acadiens re-creates an early French settlement, including a church, store, house, barns, and blacksmith shop. Bilingual interpreters will show you pioneer skills you won't see in most similar museums, such as making soap from scratch. The Étoile de Mer restaurant serves delicious traditional Acadian food. Open mid-June to mid-September. Admission charge. La Cuisine à Mémé is P.E.I.'s French dinner theater—music, skits, and Acadian food—(902) 854–2227.

The coastline is interesting in the **Cape Egmont** area: Red sandstone cliffs and strange rock formations have been carved by the sea and the weather. At Cape Egmont are The Bottle Houses, via Highway 11, three extraordinary buildings made from more than 25,000 bottles. The folk art is the painstaking work of a retired fisherman, the late Edouard T. Arsenault, who also used his talents to create a wonderful garden. Open mid-June to Labour Day. Admission charge.

Abrams Village is the home of the well-known Acadian singer Angèle Arsenault. Visit Le Centre d'Artisanat for locally made handicrafts. Saturday night dances are held at the Club 50.

There is another handsome church in **Egmont Bay:** Église Saint-Philippe-et-Saint-Jacques.

Farther along the Lady Slipper Drive is the pretty rural community of **Coleman.** Its old Free Church of Scotland was where the Reverend Donald MacDonald preached his fire-and-brimstone sermons. The railway station dates back to the late nineteenth century. Shop for fresh vegetables and flowers at the old School Market.

Take a side trip to **O'Leary,** via Highways 140 and 148, to visit the O'Leary Potato Museum (everything you ever wanted to know about the humble spud and then some). Open June 1 to September. Admission charge. In late July O'Leary holds its annual Potato Blossom Festival (the town is in one of the best potato-producing areas on the island).

Near O'Leary, on Highway 2, 36 miles (57 km) west of Summerside, is Rodd Mill River Resort and Aquaplex, (902) 859–3555, which has a golf course, tennis courts, canoeing, windsurfing, and many other recreational facilities. Moderate.

Back on the Lady Slipper Drive, via Highway 14, there is a fine, sandy beach at **West Point.** The restored century-old lighthouse houses a museum, a licensed dining room, and unusual guest rooms, (902) 859–3605. Moderate.

North of West Point is **Cape Wolfe,** said to be the site of buried treasure belonging to the infamous pirate Captain Kidd. The red-stained boulders here have given rise to other legends.

According to the Mi'kmaqs, an angry god, seeking revenge on an Indian maiden, dashed her against the rocks. Some people also claim to have seen a fully rigged ghost ship in flames, floating off the **Burton-Campbellton** area.

The harvesting and drying of Irish sea moss, used in the manufacture of ice cream, chocolate milk, shampoo, cosmetics, ceramic glazes, and other domestic goods, used to be big business in the **Miminegash** area. The Irish Moss Interpretive Centre explains the manufacturing of this unusual natural resource. Admission charge. Seaweed Pie Cafe serves excellent local dishes. Open the end of June to the end of September. Inexpensive.

The northernmost tip of P.E.I. is at **North Cape**. The sandstone at this point washes away at a disconcerting rate of 3 feet (1 m) a year. Visit the Atlantic Wind Test Site, via Highway 14, where windmills are tested as an alternative energy source. Open throughout the year. Free.

Tignish is one of the world's biggest producers of canned lobster meat. Its fisheries, the canning operation, the credit union, the store, and the gas station are all owned cooperatively by the local people. There are also two blacksmith shops here and a good-natured ghost named Blimphey, whom you are unlikely to see.

Jacques Cartier Provincial Park, in the **Kildare Capes** area, features an excellent sandy beach and a long line of sand dunes.

At the pleasant town of **Alberton** is the Alberton Museum (local history), on Church Street. Open late June to Labour Day. Admission charge. From the harbor in Alberton, you can go deep-sea fishing with Andrew's Mist, (902) 853–2307, or tour the sand hills of the north shore by sailboat with Sandhills and River Tours, (902) 853–2518. For lodging and dining (summer only) look for the historic Hunter House Inn, on Route 152, (902) 853–3936. The congenial owners have created the perfect atmosphere, retaining the look and feel of a distinguished old home while adding the modern luxuries. Expect homegrown vegetables and herbs with your island seafood. Moderate.

A side trip via Highway 173 takes you to **Milligan's Wharf,** where you can buy mackerel and lobsters in season. Another side trip, via Highway 163, goes to the Mi'kmaq reservation on **Lennox Island.** Much of the church interior ornamentation was made by the local Mi'kmaqs. An arts and crafts shop displays and sells local work as well as museum-quality examples from other Native American cultures. Open June to late September.

The Lady Slipper Drive continues to **Port Hill**, via Highway 12, which has a fine provincial park on the former Green Park estate of shipbuilding tycoon James Yeo. An excellent museum depicts nineteenth-century shipbuilding activities on P.E.I. You can wander in a re-created early shipyard. Open mid-June to Labour Day. Admission charge. The park itself offers an excellent beach, picnic area, and nature trail.

In **Grand River,** on Highway 12, is beautiful Saint Patrick's Church, also designed by William Harris.

The Lady Slipper Drive goes through **MacDougall,** via Highway 12, meanders along the Grand River, and comes to an end at Travellers Rest in the Summerside area at Highway 1A.

INDEX

N

O

P